PARCELLS
A Biography

Carlo DeVito

TRIUMPH
BOOKS

This book is dedicated to Dawson Cordell DeVito and Dylan Charles DeVito, the most important football players in my life

Library of Congress Cataloging-in-Publication Data

DeVito, Carlo.
    Parcells : a biography / Carlo DeVito.
        p. cm.
    Includes bibliographical references and index.
    ISBN 978-1-60078-370-8
        1. Parcells, Bill. 2. Football coaches—United States—Biography.
3. New York Giants (Football team) I. Title.

GV939.P35D45 2011
796.332092—dc23
[B]

2011025257

This book is available in quantity at special discounts for your group or organization. For further information, contact:

Triumph Books LLC
542 South Dearborn Street
Suite 750
Chicago, Illinois 60605
(312) 939–3330
Fax (312) 663–3557
www.triumphbooks.com

Printed in U.S.A.
ISBN: 978-1-60078-370-8
Design by Amy Carter

CONTENTS

ACKNOWLEDGMENTS

T
he author must acknowledge and commend Ken Samelson, who offered up my name to Triumph some time ago. I thank him for his advice on this book, his researching assistance, and his diligent fact-checking. Without Ken, this book would not have happened, and I am grateful for his friendship and advice.

Any author of such an effort owes a great debt of gratitude to those who went before him. Several writers' works have proved invaluable, including Bill Parcells' three books, *Parcells: The Autobiography of the Biggest Giant of Them All*, *Finding a Way to Win*, and *The Final Season*; Bill Gutman's *Parcells: A Biography*; and Jerry Izenberg's *No Medals for Trying*. Also included in this group should be David Halberstam's *The Education of a Coach*; Michael Lewis' *The Blind Side*; Dick Schaap's *Simms to McConkey*; Lawrence Taylor's *Over the Edge*; Jim Baker and Bernard Corbett's *The Most Memorable Games in Giants History*; Leonard Marshall and William Bendetson's *When the Cheering Stops*; Michael Holley's *Patriot Reign*, and many, many others.

Many people were interviewed. I would especially like to thank Mickey Corcoran, Jack Giddings, The Honorable Cormac Carney, Steve Nelson, Stephen Baker, and many others who were helpful in giving me insights to Coach Parcells.

Of course, I pored over more than 4,000 original sources, including some 2,000 interviews with players, coaches, owners, and other assorted folks. I also examined newspaper and magazine articles from

Parcells' youth all the way to the present. It is hard to imagine writing this work without the dedicated and hard-working beat writers who covered the team over the years, including Frank Litsky, Gerald Eskenazi, Dave Anderson, Gary Myers, George Thomas, Mike Freeman, Peter King, Will McDonough, Rich Cimini, Paul Needell, Judy Battista, Bill Madden, Richard Sandomir, Steve Politi, Vinny DiTrani, and many others. Without their dedicated coverage and investigative reporting, this book could not have been written. My apologies to anyone whose name was inadvertently left off this list—you can probably be found in the notes at the end of this book.

As ever, I owe a debt of special thanks in all of my professional endeavors to Gilbert King for his ear, opinions, advice, general good cheer, and encouragement.

I would, of course, like to thank Tom Bast and Mitch Rogatz of Triumph Books, who helped make this book a reality. Were it not for their excitement, enthusiasm, and faith in me, I might have given up under the weight of this massive project. I also owe a huge debt of gratitude to editors Adam Motin and Karen O'Brien who helped mold a rather large manuscript into readable shape, and to Scott Rowan.

I would also like to thank my agent and friend Edward Claflin of Edward B. Claflin Literary Agency. I thank him for his encouragement and assistance and for his belief in me. I would also like to thank Marcus Leaver and Jason Prince of Sterling Publishing Company, Inc., for their friend assistance. Without their good will this project would have passed me by. Thank you.

I would like to thank my sons, Dylan and Dawson, whom I have taken too much time away from in order to pursue not only this work but also my other professional aspirations. I have tried to attend as many of their baseball, basketball, and football games as possible, but there is no replacement for a catch or an ice-cream cone, many of which were robbed by my other pursuits. I vow to them to spend more time playing and less time working.

The Making of Bill Parcells

Bill Parcells had seen the abyss. Matter of fact, as the 1984 season approached, the abyss was staring him right in the face. After the debacle of the 1983 season, he had heard boos from the fans, and seen the confidence of his General Manager, George Young, severely shaken. He was there but by the grace of God, with the plan to bring Miami University head coach Howard Schnellenberger having come to naught and with the backing of the benign Wellington Mara, Parcells basically had come to his last chance. The press was already calling for his head. The general consensus was that this year was more of a deathwatch than another chance at life. Another spectacular year of Giants losses lay ahead.

Parcells had made mistakes in 1983. He had benched the oft-injured Phil Simms in favor of the tall, quiet Scott Brunner. The defense was valiant, but the offense had been weak. The running game at times was non-existent, and the passing game was iffy at best. More than that, though, there had been discord. Players had been vocal in their distrust of Parcells. While he had been a favorite coach on the team under Perkins, the crucible of his rookie head coaching season had shown Parcells that there were miles of difference between a coach and a head coach in the NFL.

In his first year as head coach, the Giants had suffered one of their worst campaigns, going 3–12–1. It was a difficult year personally and professionally. A defensive player had opined, "Parcells was distracted last year by illnesses in his family. His mother died toward the end of the season, and his father soon afterward." Not only had Parcells had to endure these huge personal losses, but also the loss of his running backs coach and longtime friend Bob Ledbetter from a stroke in October, and former Giants running back Doug Kotar, who had played for the team from 1974 to 1981, of cancer. The team attended Kotar's funeral in December in Pennsylvania. Optimism was in short supply. The organization's confidence in Parcells was at an all-time low.

"It is only football," immensely popular middle-linebacker Harry Carson had told *The New York Times.* "But to be a Giant is to always feel sad underneath, always a little bit unsteady. Is that okay? Is it okay to feel sad about not winning, about seeing teammates come and go, about seeing other teams that were as bad as you rise out of the ashes, about seeing people you used to play with now playing for these teams, is it okay to feel bad about that? It's only football, but I think it's okay to feel sad because it's my life and I am a football player."

The knock on Parcells was that he was a nice guy. In fact, he picked up the nickname Tuna, after Charlie Tuna, from his players because, like the fictional tuna-fish pitchman, Parcells wanted to be liked. It had happened when he was the linebackers coach for the New England Patriots in 1980.

"Tuna is a nickname I got with the Patriots," Parcells said. "The players pulled a practical joke, and I said, 'Do you think I'm Charlie the Tuna, like a sucker?'

"After that, they called me Tuna and set up a Tuna Award each week. It took me eight weeks to find out what the award was for. It was for the player I had praised the most that week. He got a Charlie the Tuna sticker to wear on his helmet."

"Players from the defensive team, including those whom Parcells coached as an assistant before being promoted to succeed Ray Perkins, say that he felt self-conscious in his new role last year. He had been a confidant to the players as an assistant coach, and for a time he remained such," wrote Craig Wolff in *The New York Times.*

After the 1983 campaign, Parcells met with General Manager George Young. According to Young, Parcells had analyzed the situation perfectly. "He knew exactly what he had to do," Young said. "But you've got to remember other things. In comparison to Perkins, anyone who came in here would not have been tough. But that's how he wanted to be perceived. And Bill is like any other coach in that he thinks of his job in dramatic terms. No one here has made him feel like his back is against the wall, but Bill insists on looking at it that way. Maybe it's good."

"The only fault he may have had—and it was only a fault when he became head coach—was that he was too understanding," star linebacker Harry Carson said. "Guys took advantage of him without even knowing it. They knew it was his nature to help them with problems and let them slide."

"The New York Giants remind me of an old AFL team that had this real nice guy for a coach," wrote Paul Zimmerman in the preseason NFL preview edition of *Sports Illustrated* in 1984. "The younger guys started taking advantage of him; they started letting it slide. The old guard, many of whom had played for some absolute storm troopers in their NFL days, took charge. 'Look,' they said, 'you're never gonna play for a nicer guy. Shape up! We wanna keep him around.'"

"End of parable. Those were the old days, before players got $1.9 million, four-year packages, but the Giants better listen up. Coach Bill Parcells—Coach Tuna, the players used to call him—is one nice guy. He's also hanging by a thread. Joe Paterno, Howard Schnellenberger—those were the names you heard mentioned in the off-season," added Zimmerman. Dr. Z, as he was known, opined that the Giants would finish third in the division. "Everyone's keeping his fingers crossed."

The 1984 season began with as much pain as 1983 ended. Parcells was rushed to Pascack Valley Hospital in Westwood, New Jersey, for treatment of kidney stones. The 1984 preseason would prove to be more painful.

Parcells had been a brilliant defensive coordinator. But he had been a failure as an NFL head coach. Parcells admitted to his team that he knew where he stood. "My back is to the wall," he told his players, "I know I'm on the edge of the cliff." There were some tone-deaf players who thought he was asking them to like him again, but in the crucible of the 1984 training camp, Bill Parcells was telling them. There was a big difference, and they would soon understand that difference.

This year, Parcells realized he had to do something. A shake up was required. There were dissatisfied veterans in the ranks. A few losses would set their tongues wagging again. He would tolerate neither dissent nor players who bred dissent. Anyone who openly questioned him was going to get the message or be gone. Parcells reasoned, if he was going to go down fighting, it might as well be with what he termed "my guys." His guys were men who bought into his system and the game plan. The rest would be gone.

The griping started early. Only minutes after a disastrous loss to the Washington Redskins in December 1983, Harry Carson dejectedly told the press he wanted out of New York. "I doubt that I'll change my mind," Carson said. "Maybe they could do it, but I don't know if I could go to training camp feeling the way I've felt. But if they make a conscientious effort to really improve this team, I'd want to be a part of that. But if it's the same thing year after year." Heartbroken, Carson's voice trailed off. He could not bring himself to finish the sentence. Van Pelt also added that he wanted to sit down with Young and Parcells "and find out a few things." Even star player Lawrence Taylor had been seen lunching with new USFL owner Donald Trump, owner of the New Jersey Generals. While some players were not happy with their contracts, most of the discontent came from the consistent losing. The Giants had gone to the playoffs only once in 20 years, a far cry from when they were in the play-offs consistently in the late 1950s and early 1960s.

In the spring of 1984, more griping came. Parcells had molded one of the best linebacking corps in the NFL with Brad Van Pelt, Harry Carson, Brian Kelley, and Lawrence Taylor. The main corps helped lead a tremendously powerful and vicious defense.

As 1984 began, Phil Simms, the oft-injured golden-haired hurler, was one of the unhappiest players on the team. In 1983, he played behind Brunner and Jeff Rutledge basically as the No. 3 quarterback. He played in two games, injured his thumb throwing, and was out for the rest of the season. Simms, the former starter, fumed openly to the press. The press, who had a field day with the quarterbacking merry-go-round, continued to follow the story through the rest of winter and spring, feeding Simms' discontent.

In 1983, the team had suffered a tremendous number of injuries with 25 players going on injured reserve during the course of the season. This was unacceptable. Parcells hired Johnny Parker, a strength and conditioning coach who had worked for a number of winning collegiate football programs. Parker had come highly recommended by Bobby Knight, who was a close Parcells confidant (the two having worked together during Parcells' college coaching days).

Then came minicamp.

"Pro football's minicamps usually have an air of optimism, but there was none coming today from Brad Van Pelt," wrote William N. Wallace in *The New York Times* toward the end of March. "Van Pelt, the veteran Giant linebacker, reiterated his desire to be traded, saying that he was weary of playing on a losing team and that he saw no particular promise for the coming season."

"The years of so many defeats got to him, though. Late last season, when the Giants finished with a 3–12–1 record, he said that losing 'affects your personality.' He sulked, especially when he was taken out on passing downs for the speedier Andy Headen or Byron Hunt," another sportswriter scribbled.

In what had been an obvious response to Van Pelt's repeated complaints, Young's draft team chose Carl Banks of Michigan as their No. 1 draft choice on May 1, 1984, a seemingly odd choice considering the rich talent pool that the Giants already had in hand. Actually, they drafted several linebackers in the defense-rich draft that year.

When Parcells was asked if Banks had been drafted to make Van Pelt expendable, Parcells fired back, "We have no plans to trade Van Pelt. He has been All-Pro five times, and he still is a solid player."

"It wasn't our intention to trade Brad," Young told the press afterward. "After the draft, when we were successful in getting Carl Banks... we talked to different clubs about Brad. A week before the draft, we didn't think we would be taking Banks. We were more interested in offensive linemen. But when he was still there, we couldn't help but pick him. Then we decided that if we got in trouble at another position, since we had five outside linebackers, Brad had value. What happened was John Tuggle hurt his knee in minicamp...and we needed a backup for Rob Carpenter."

Parcells told the press, "I asked him if he had a pen. Then I told him to take down a number. 'That's the number of the Vikings' general manager,' I told him. 'You ought to call him because you've just been traded to them.'"

"The owner of the nine-hole Club Ten golf course in Owosso, Mich., was called to the telephone yesterday to learn that he had been traded, but not any closer to his clubhouse," Michael Katz wrote in *The New York Times*. "Brad Van Pelt, who, after five years of asking to be dealt away from the Giants, was sent to the Minnesota Vikings in exchange for Tony Galbreath, a badly needed backup fullback."

Van Pelt was so upset by this news that he would not come to the phone. He let his wife, Susan, speak to the press. Van Pelt had been close to the Mara family, owners of the New York Giants. Susan admitted that Brad "may be ducking" questions. "When the call finally comes, it has to sink in," Susan told the press. "Brad may be digesting this. He has a lot of people he loved out there."

A 30-year-old veteran who had experienced eight NFL seasons, Galbreath had intrigued the Giants ever since he left the University of Missouri as the New Orleans Saints' second-round draft choice in 1976, where he spent five seasons before being traded to Minnesota. The 6', 228-pound, sure-handed fullback had five solid seasons with New Orleans before being traded to Minnesota.

The trading of Van Pelt was one of the first significant moves the organization made to start divesting itself of unhappy personnel. Young had grown tired of Van Pelt's whining to the press, and Van Pelt had become a clubhouse lawyer. Young knew that no matter who the coach was, having a player of Van Pelt's stature grousing in the younger, more impressionable players' ears, would be difficult for Parcells or any other coach to deal with. The impact on the other players was immediate. And it was meant to be.

Around the same time, Terry Jackson, the right defensive corner, was traded to the Seattle Seahawks. And Brian Kelley, Van Pelt's best friend on the team and a fellow linebacker, was also traded. Kelley's, Jackson's, and especially Van Pelt's departure were the first of many messages sent to the team. The organization was telegraphing to everyone—we will make the hard choices. No one, especially a five-time All-Pro, is above the team. There was also the impression that new leadership was needed on the team. During the course of camp, they also let go of familiar names like J.T. Turner, John Mistler, Johnny Perkins, and Bill Neill.

Next in line was the quarterback position. Phil Simms, the Giants' top draft choice in 1979 who had missed 28 of the last 30 games with injuries up to that point, acknowledged to the press that he'd spoken to Parcells about his future. In late March, there were rumors that Brunner and/or Rutledge would be traded. When asked if he had been told he would be the starter, Simms snapped, "That's between us. He'll say what he wants to say at his time. I think there's some other things he wants to clear up at the same time."

However, Brunner was traded to the Denver Broncos early in the spring, making the fight for the quarterback's job a two-man race between Simms and Jeff Rutledge. By July, the press had figured out that Simms was the anointed starter, though Parcells would not declare. However, it became obvious that the job was Simms' to lose.

Training camp opened in mid-July, and as Parcells was interviewed on the quiet campus just before the players arrived, he told the press, "I hope we have peaceful days like this all year long." Of course, it would be anything but. It would be among the most tumultuous camps of his career. "This will be a cutthroat time. My back is to the wall."

"I want to see these players because they represent newness," Parcells said. "And this team needs newness. But no one has any assurances of anything. When I say cutthroat I mean competition. I promise that everyone on this team will have to look over his shoulder. I want them to be afraid to come out of the huddle in practice because I want them to be afraid they won't get back in."

Parcells was emphatic about how things were going to be.

"First, starting with me, I'm going back to how I was when I was an assistant," he said. "I think my personality changed last year. I will not just be an overseer. I'm going to be in the thick of things. I'm not going to think about how I should act as a head coach. If I want to get into the trenches and yell, I will.

"Also I will spend only 15 minutes a day with the media, no more. The management has had their turn. Now it's my turn, and everyone else get out of the way."

Peace was short-lived as the Giants, only three days later, cut second-year tight end Malcolm Scott "for inability to adhere to club policies." There was no question among the press that a New Orleans warrant issued for Scott's arrest for illegal drugs was among the "unofficial reasons." Once again, any distractions were being cleared out.

When questioned about Simms, Parcells retorted, "After all our changes, wouldn't it be crazy for me to say to someone who has hardly snapped the ball in three years, 'You have the job?' That's not the way things are going to work this year."

"My fight never ends," he said. "I'm always scrapping for my share," Simms told the press. "It's tiresome. That's why I didn't want to talk about it. This is not a comfortable situation. It doesn't gear you to being a good game player, it gears you to being a good practice player. Because I'm thinking I got to make the yardage. I may go 10-for-10 dumping the balls off to the side on easy plays. But if it were a game, I wouldn't be able to make first down. You think Joe Theismann has to worry about this? He can experiment. He'll have a worse training, but he'll be more prepared. When I play my first game, I'm going to be nauseous."

But Parcells was having none of it and responded hotly to Simms' remarks, telling the press later that day, "It's too bad. That's the way I want it. He has to be able to accomplish all his goals, prepare for the season, and win the job. That's the way a competition is."

The press wasn't completely sympathetic to Simms. Craig Wolff of *The New York Times* wrote, "Simms is fighting for a job that was once his, but because of injuries—two shoulder separations, torn ligaments in his right knee and last year a thumb fracture—he has not played in four consecutive games in three years. In that time, [he] has not played a full game."

But not all the news was glum. Star defensive player Leonard Marshall, who'd come to camp a biscuit shy of 300 pounds in 1983, reported in at a lusty 282 and seemed prime for action. And among Parcells' favorites was a spunky young man, a graduate of the Naval Academy, Phil McConkey. Lieutenant McConkey became a helicopter pilot in the Navy. He selected that route to get away from ships, where he suffered from severe seasickness.

McConkey was 27 years old, 5'10" and 170 pounds. McConkey was a daring kick returner, a great special teams man, and a feisty receiver. "There is something different about Phil," Parcells said. "He plays with such heart that he makes you take notice where you might not have."

McConkey had hoped for an early release from the Navy the previous year, when he had shone brightly in the 1983 preseason, but the Navy thought in the end it would set a bad example. "I was not bitter," McConkey said. "I love the Navy. But I counted the days to when I would have another chance."

McConkey returned to camp in 1984 and his 4.42 in the 40-yard dash was a tenth of a second better than it was the year before. Many remarked that McConkey had remarkably "soft hands."

"That's what everyone thinks," he said, "but look at my hands. They're not the hands of a pro receiver. I do it with good hand-eye coordination that separates me from the average 27-year-old. It's like making a closure with a helicopter toward the ship. I have to clear the blades with just 10 feet. How can you explain doing that?"

The Giants went into August not sure where they stood. They won their first tune-up, a Friday night affair against the New England Patriots. It was a win, a rare commodity in 1983. But even Craig Wolff opined in *The New York Times*, "If the Giants are to break the losers' image that hangs over them like a dark veil, one exhibition victory, no matter how extreme, will not do it."

But a new mind set was being established. And Parcells' new attitude was clearly part of the reason why. He had reiterated his famous declaration, "Everyone should watch out. My back is to the wall, and everything will be different. The things that have changed in me—and it has translated to the field—is that our attitude, mine and the team, and the discipline and concentration of this team, has improved."

And the players could see the difference easily.

"The change has been night and day," running back Joe Morris said. "It's so much harder to satisfy him, and, when you can't satisfy the coach, you don't know exactly what to do. So you try 10 times harder."

"It's very noticeable," punter Dave Jennings said. "He's not letting anything go by the board this year. He sat in and went over each piece of film and personally pointed out every mistake by the veterans and the rookies. In those special meetings, he used to leave it all to the assistant. But now he doesn't. When a head coach makes a point, you feel it more."

Parcells was much more demanding this year, and he was much more open about his demands. It was in this camp that he first displayed what is commonly known as his glare. If a player made a mistake, Parcells openly glared at the player with demonic intensity. He yelled more, screamed more. He was not afraid to embarrass players to motivate them. One particular afternoon he screamed at center Kevin Belcher to run faster during wind sprints. During the fifth sprint, Belcher finally improved his speed, keeping up with the defensive players his own size. Everyone noticed, players and bleacher fans alike.

"He was always coaching, every minute," Harry Carson said. "He was yelling, screaming, chewing out some people, calling them names, making fun of them. Others he would pat on the butt and praise them. He knew exactly what he could do with each player, and what made them tick."

"He was finding ways to get to each player. That often meant doing his homework, due diligence if you will, to learn about the guy," Carson said years later, "both the vets and the new guys coming onto the team. It might be talking to the player's friends or former coaches. [Parcells] was always looking for a hook, something to throw out there.

"For instance, he found out what my nickname was when I was a kid. To this day, I don't know how he did it, but I know he must have worked at it. On day he comes up and whispers it to me, just like that. It was a nickname I didn't want him yelling out to the whole team. But it got my attention and for a while he hung it over my head. But the funny thing was that it told me the guy cared enough to dig into who I was."

Parcells was self-conscious about his image change. "Don't make it like I'm going out of my way to appear this way," he told one reporter. However, this was immediately contradicted with, "But it's no secret this is a crucial year for the Giants. You come off a 3–12–1 year, and you know changes have to happen, beginning with me, or else many of us won't be here next year, including me."

After another preseason game, Parcells named Simms his No. 1 quarterback on August 15. But what should have been the headline was overshadowed by star middle linebacker Harry Carson's bolting camp. Carson left the Pace University grounds on Monday afternoon without speaking to anyone.

Carson did not return the next day and did not speak to reporters. Parcells questioned Carson's leadership on Tuesday to the press.

The New York Times reported: "Parcells called Carson's action 'despicable' and in the most famous quote of the summer, suggested that Carson 'go to the library and look up what leadership means.' And with the summer's most famous retort, Lawrence Taylor said that while Carson was looking up the word leadership, 'management should look up honesty.' Clearly, this was not a pleasant interval."

"I left because of general frustration. I want better things for my team," Carson told the press. But Carson's motives may not have been absolutely altruistic. Rather, it was a personal issue that drove him from the field. Carson, an All-Pro and captain of the defense, earned $300,000 annually, and made much less than Taylor ($750,000) or Banks ($600,000), his fellow younger linebackers.

"Everything comes down to dollars," said Craig Kelly, Carson's agent. "Taylor's contract may be out of line. Banks' may be out of line. I also know Harry plays alongside them, so you can draw your own answers." Taylor's yearly salary was more than $750,000, and Banks' was about $600,000. These salaries enraged many veterans who were not so well remunerated. Indeed, there were wide-spread incidents of walkouts around the league, and the Giants were not immune.

An emotional Lawrence Taylor, upset with Parcells' quote, lashed out in the press saying, "I don't care what Bill says about leadership. Harry's got more respect with all the players around the league than anybody." Carson returned a day later, met with Parcells in the morning, and participated in afternoon workouts.

This was the atmosphere of the camp. With a revamped offensive line, an oft-injured quarterback named its starter (many newspaper writers of the day actually thought Rutledge had won the competition— so both Parcells and Simms had something to prove), with almost 50 percent new faces, including two new receiver returners in Lionel Manuel and Phil McConkey, and a small running back named Joe Morris about to make an impact, Bill Parcells had molded his first team in his own image.

The team won three of its four preseason games. There was some optimism. But preseason wins are cheap once the real season begins.

On September 2, 1984, Parcells approached the tunnel at Giants Stadium with a full crowd on hand. The crowd roared for victory against the hated Philadelphia Eagles. Parcells was no longer the likable, lovable coach. He was now a man determined to shape and mold a team in his own image. Bereft of malcontents and unhappy players, they were now a unit that would take direction—take his direction. And now, the 1984 season was about to begin. Parcells had been saying it all summer, but now it was true—his back really was against the wall.

In 1984, a guy from Hackensack, New Jersey, named Duane Charles Parcells invented a football coach named Bill Parcells. And he and the National Football League would ever be the same.

CHAPTER 1

Jersey Guys

When the Dutch West India Company first arrived in what is now the New York metropolitan area, they also went into what is today northern New Jersey around the 1660s. Chief among the northern inhabitants was the Lenni Lenape nation, who spoke a Munsee dialect of the Algonquian languages. Oratam, "Sagamore of Hacquinsacq," was the Chief representative of this nation. Oratam deeded the land to the Dutch in 1664. The area was taken by the English in 1688 but kept its Dutch name.

European settlers eventually named them the Delaware. Many of these Lenni Lenape lived in a valley called the Achinigeu-hach, or "Ackingsah-sack." The Dutch called the area Bergen, and they eventually settled what they came to call the Hackensack River (a mutation of the Lenape name). The town was originally called New Barbadoes (by a governor who had lived in the Caribbean). It was originally part of Essex County but was annexed to Bergen County by royal decree of Queen Anne of Great Britain in 1710. Hackensack was made the county seat in that year, and it has been the hub of Bergen county ever since.

During the American Revolutionary War, George Washington headquartered in the village of Hackensack in November 1776 and camped on "The Green" across from the First Dutch Reformed Church. This prepared the way for the first American victory of the Revolution the following month at the Battle of Trenton.

On November 21, 1921, based on the results of a public referendum, New Barbadoes Township received its charter to incorporate as a city and officially took on its name "Hackensack." The name was derived from the original inhabitants, the Lenni Lenape, who named it "Ackingsah-sack." Today, Oratam's likeness is part of the Hackensack municipal seal.

In 1869, the Hackensack Water Company was founded to supply water directly from the river to Hudson and eastern Bergen Counties via a network of pipes. By 1882, the company constructed a filtration plant on Van Buskirk Island in Oradell to remove the sediments and other debris that often clouded their product. By the end of World War I, the water company could no longer meet the water demands of the still-growing population. The state of New Jersey began condemnation proceedings against landowners along the upper reaches of the Hackensack River in order to acquire property to establish a reservoir. In 1921, construction of the Oradell Dam was begun, and the Oradell Reservoir was completed two years later.

The most prominent building in all of Hackensack is the Bergen County Courthouse. The current courthouse is the sixth Bergen County courthouse. James Riely Gordon, a civil engineer, born in Winchester, Virginia, won a competition to design the Bergen County courthouse. The style of the courthouse building is known as American Renaissance. Construction began in 1910 and was completed in 1912 at a cost of $1 million. The jail was also completed in 1912, and the style of the jail is medieval revival. The interior dome of the rotunda area of the courthouse is modeled after the Pantheon in Rome. The exterior walls of the courthouse rotunda building were made from Vermont marble. On top of the dome is a copper figure titled "Enlightenment Giving Power." The courthouse was placed on the New Jersey and National Registers of historic places in 1982 and 1983.

The courthouse sits across from The Green, which is the oldest public square in New Jersey. It is located across the street from the courthouse at the corner of Main Street and Court Street. A bronze statue of General Enoch Poor is located at the intersection of Court Street and Washington Place. General Poor, a New Hampshire native, was a hero at the Battle of Saratoga in 1777. General Poor died in 1780 and is buried across the street from The Green at the Dutch Reformed Church. General Washington and the Marquis de Lafayette attended General Poor's funeral.

Woodrow Wilson was the president of the United States. In 1913, the U.S. Congress authorized the federal government to impose and collect income taxes. Camel Cigarettes were introduced. Connie Mack won his third World Series with his Philadelphia Athletics, beating John McGraw's New York Giants for the second time in the Fall Classic. In 1913, the song "Danny Boy" was written by an unknown English barrister. In February, the Mexican Revolution began. In New York City, Grand Central Terminal, "the world's largest train station," was completed and opened, as was the Woolworth Building, New York's tallest skyscraper. And many of the 20th century's most influential painters would first be exhibited at the Armory Show that same year. This was the most celebrated debut of Impressionism, Fauvism, and Cubism art, introducing such well known names as Duchamp, Cezanne, Cassatt, Kandinsky, Picasso, Rodin, Toulouse-Lautrec, Matisse, Renoir, and many others.

It is important to know about Hackensack and Oradell and Bergen County, for the Parcells clan, no matter how far from home, was never anywhere else in mind or spirit. On August 10, 1913, Charles O'Shea was born. He would grow up to be a tall and lanky young man, gifted in sports and very bright. Due to circumstances, he was eventually adopted by his mother's sister, who was married to a man named Parcells. Charles "Chubby" Parcells would go on to be one of the most popular citizens of Hackensack for the rest of his life. He just didn't know it at the time.

Chubby, a moniker hung on him because he was just the opposite— tall, slender, and lanky—was considered one of the greatest high school athletes ever to come out of Hackensack. He was a three-season athlete at Hackensack High School, lettering in football, basketball, and track. Chubby played the same three sports when he eventually made his way to Georgetown University in Washington, D.C. Chubby, who carried his name with him to the nation's capitol, soon established himself as a class athlete at the national collegiate level.

Parcells was one of the stars of the Georgetown Hoyas football team, where he lettered in 1932, 1933, and 1934. In 1934, he was one of the most celebrated running backs of the eastern schools.

Parcells established himself early in the 1934 season, his name appearing in headlines across many newspapers in a season-opening 20–0 win over Mount Saint Mary's. "Parcells and Herron Score in Victory" said *The New York Times* headline. According to newspaper accounts of the time, "Joe Saverine and Chubby Parcells led the Blue and Gray to victory, the latter scoring two touchdowns." What the headline didn't mention was that Parcells also added two point-after kicks to the scoring.

In one of the biggest local games of the year, 15,000 faithful fans came out in the rain to see New York University against undefeated Georgetown at Yankee Stadium. Georgetown had beaten Manhattan and William & Mary in the previous games. The Violet hurled back the Hoya charge, but Parcells made spectacular plays in what turned out to be a tie, and reported on of the best collegiate games of the year.

The Violet kicked from their own 45-yard line. "The ball sailed to the 15-yard line, where it was taken by Charles Parcells, quarterback. Parcells raced through an open field. One by one the Violet tacklers failed, until Joe Mandell remained. A beautiful flying tackle brought to earth the runner after he had covered 55 yards," local sportscribe Lewis B. Funke reported. Parcells made several crucial first-down rushes.

Near the end of the third quarter, Parcells got another chance. NYU's Smith "punted from behind his goal line and Parcells picked up the ball on the NYU 35-yard mark and was off. Machlowitz tackled him, and the ball rested on the 5-yard marker." Four goal-line rushes followed with the last by Parcells, but NYU held strong. The Hoyas could not capitalize.

Despite not winning the game, Parcells established a school record that stands to this day. Charley Parcells racked up 197 yards in punt returns against NYU—still a remarkable achievement.

The Hoyas lost a close game to Richmond, beat Roanoke, and lost to Maryland and Western Maryland to end the season 4–3–1.

Chubby went on to play basketball, lettering in 1933, 1934, and 1935 for the Hoyas. He played in 19 games during the 1934–35 season, wearing

No. 54 his senior year. By this time he had developed. He was now a tall, big man with sculpted muscles, playing power forward.

Parcells also distinguished himself in track while at Georgetown.

More impressive than his athletic achievements, Parcells was an excellent and gifted student. After graduating from Georgetown University, he attended and graduated from Georgetown Law School. Upon his graduation, Parcells accepted a job with the FBI.

It was around this time that Parcells met Ida Naclerio, who grew up in Woodbridge, New Jersey. The two made for an interesting couple. Charles Parcells was by now an imposing man, who eventually grew prematurely gray a trait his son, Duane, would inherit.

"Charles Parcells was a striking, impressive man," said Tom Godfrey, a childhood friend of Duane's who played Babe Ruth League baseball together. "[Chubby] was the type of guy you looked at and said, 'Wow, here's a successful man.' He had rod-straight posture, was tall and slender with a full head of white hair."

Chubby was athletically well built and over 6' tall, while Ida only measured 5'4". He was by turns studious and extremely affable. Ida was well humored and fiery. She was also superstitious, a trait she and her son would share.

"Parcells thinks it's good luck to have an elephant statue with its trunk upturned facing a doorway (he picked up this one from his superstitious Italian mother). Friends and former players still send him elephant statues," sportswriter Carlos Arias reported. Dolphins coach Tony Sparano has one in his office.

"If he crosses a black cat's path, he will walk backward to the point where their paths crossed to undo the jinx. Once, a dark brown cat (it wasn't even a black cat) crossed in front of his car as he pulled into a golf course. Parcells put the car in reverse, backed up to where the cat had crossed his path, and then proceeded," Arias continued. Parcells admitted this was something he also learned from his mother.

And tails-up pennies will never be picked up by Parcells. According to Parcells, "You want to move forward, not backward." One year, while head coach of the New York Giants, there were two tails-up pennies in the Giants locker room that sat there untouched for one full season.

As a running joke and sign of well wishes, the late Giants owner Wellington Mara left a heads-up penny on Parcells' desk before each game.

Chubby and Ida were married, but Ida had misgivings about her husband being an FBI agent. Chubby's being a law enforcement officer worried her. She did not want to raise a family with the worry that he might not come home from work someday. Eventually, Chubby relented and chose a path that led to corporate law. He ended up a senior executive at U.S. Rubber, later renamed Uniroyal.

That day came on August 22, 1941, when his first son, Duane Charles Parcells, was born. Chubby left the FBI and took a corporate law job. Although they would make stops in Pennsylvania and Illinois, the burgeoning Parcells family would eventually settle in Hasbrouck Heights, New Jersey, which was squarely between Hackensack and Woodbridge. The Parcells were now home, near both their families.

In 1943, Donald Parcells was born, followed 12 years later by Doug, the youngest Parcells boy. A sister came along later.

According to sportswriter Carlos Frias, "Ida Parcells, Bill's mother, liked to bring a bit of the old country to her family, spicing up conversations and lectures with Italian. About the oldest of her four children, the former Ida Naclerio would say, '*Le piace mescolare la pentola.*' He likes to stir the pot."

Little Duane was the mischief maker of the Parcells household, and as the eldest son, it made him the center of attention even more.

"There was the time his parents, aunt, and uncle were headed to a dinner and show, and Bill convinced his younger brother, Don, that they should load their pea shooters with blueberries for some target practice," Arias reported. "Bill set his sights on his aunt's crisp, white skirt, hit her in the caboose, and ran off laughing.

"Bill is the one who made mom crazy," Parcells' youngest brother, Doug, said.

Bill was clearly his parents' boy. He was tall and lean and resembled his father greatly. But his personality was that of his mother, prone to laughter but with an absolutely short fuse. Doug said. "She enjoyed a good argument."

Duane was a unique boy among his peers. He was confident and a natural leader. But he would never forget his childhood and his family, and he grew up with a tremendous sentimentality for his parents and his youth.

"When I was a little kid in Hasbrouck Heights, I guess I was 4 or 5," Bill Parcells recalled, "I remember getting little trucks and a red wagon one Christmas morning. I loved that red wagon."

He often quoted his parents to players in later life, and he never forgot where he came from. And he would always have a great regard for family as he grew older, especially his siblings.

If there was one person Duane was especially close to, it was Don. The boys were separated by only two years and remained closely bound by shared experiences, brotherly love, and sibling rivalry. The two were inseparable in youth. And each would excel throughout life and constantly compare and contrast himself with the other, as boys in this instance were bound to do.

"Bill and Don shared a bed in the family's small house in Hasbrouck Heights, New Jersey. After Doug came along 12 years later, Don and Doug shared an upstairs bedroom, the only one with an air conditioner and radio. Bill had his own room, but he'd drag his mattress upstairs, lay it on the floor, and together the Parcells boys would fall asleep listening to doo-wop and rock 'n' roll," Arias wrote.

Don and Duane played all the time as little boys. As was the norm in the 1950s, the two played cowboys and Indians. According to *Newark Star-Ledger* sportswriter Steve Politi, "One afternoon, Bill was the cowboy and Don was the Indian, chasing each other around the front yard. Bill hid behind a shrub with his six-shooter. Don came running up the lawn, one hand holding the tomahawk, the other hand cupping his mouth.

"WOO WOO WOO WOO WOO!"

The tomahawk flew across the lawn, tumbling end over end. Duane ducked, and let the tomahawk pass. However, their small home's large picture window was not so lucky. The two boys went running even before the tomahawk shattered the beautiful living room window. They were scared for their lives. Their mother eventually caught up to them. The two boys quickly blamed one another.

"I thought my mother was going to kill me," Don said with a laugh.

"Don liked to save money. Bill liked to spend it. Don hid his cash around the house, under dresser drawers and mattresses, so he had it when he needed it. Of course, Bill always needed it—and always found the stash," Politi wrote.

"One day Bill asked me if I knew where Don hid his money, and I ratted him out," Doug Parcells said. "He stole it and gave me a quarter as a reward. Don was mad, but he was used to it, too."

"The family always vacationed at the Jersey Shore, usually in Sea Girt, with their parents finding a garage apartment they could rent near the beach," Politi wrote. "Bill framed four black-and-white childhood pictures for Don one year. In one, the two boys are standing near the surf, the pudgy older brother wearing his shorts well above his navel.

"We used to spend a lot of time in the ocean, just swimming and riding waves," Bill said. "We did that a lot. We'd spend day after day after day, riding waves. We were very close. I think we enjoyed growing up together."

"We used to go in the ocean together at 7:30 in the morning and come out at 5:30 at night," Parcells said once. "That's the guy that I was doing all that with when I was a kid. I have another brother [Doug], I love him very much, but by the time he was 6 years old, I was off to college. I didn't quite have the same kind of relationship.... Not the same kind I had with Don."

— —

"My father had very good values as a person—better than me, unfortunately. It's funny, he always used the word 'wrong.' You know, he always used to say things like, 'Well, you don't do that because it's wrong.' He was always involved with right and wrong. Certain things were wrong. You didn't do them and that's all the explanation you needed—or were going to get."

"When I was a kid," Parcells explained, "we had a lot more papers in New York City, and my father would explain to me that a story that appeared in the *American-Journal* wasn't handled in the same way as the story appearing in, say, the *Herald-Tribune*. He explained to me that you had to understand that if you wanted to get to the truth."

"When I was a kid, growing up in Hackensack, my father used to take me out to the river, and we'd sit there and watch the pontoon planes land," Parcells remembered later, as they sat across from Richfield Park.

While Charles never openly pushed his children to play sports, he would offer advice and set the tone with his tough demeanor. One such lesson came when five-year-old Duane came home within minutes after having lost a brief fight with one of his young playmates. Charles told the boy, "You have to go back out there. You always have to go back out there." This would absolutely be the tone both Charles and Ida would set for the boys. Toughness and perseverance were demanded at all times, no matter the situation. The Parcells men, father and sons, were Jersey guys. They didn't back down. They took control of situations. They could be by turns jovial and good natured, studious another minute, and they barked when they had to.

When the boys asked their father questions about his exploits on the sports field, he would offer an immediate and abrupt, "That's ancient history." He rarely opened old scrapbooks or reminisced about his old achievements.

As Parcells got older and became a famous coach, he came back to the words that his father taught him—sayings and quotations that would serve him well all his life.

"Success is never final," his father once told him, "but failure can be."

"You get no medals for trying," Parcells would quote his father to his team about effort and winning. "You're supposed to do that!"

Another Chubby concept was to let your actions speak for you, saying, "Don't talk about it; do it!"

"It's always darkest before it goes pitch black," was another of Chubby's ditties, highlighting his often sarcastic and black sense of humor.

— —

"Anything with a ball was good enough," Don Parcells recalled years later. Duane and Don were especially fond of baseball, football, and basketball. When the professional season was in gear, that's what they played. The boys played sandlot baseball, as many kids did back in those days, constructing a makeshift diamond on some abandon fields between the Curtis Wright and Bendix aviation plants across the street from their home.

Even then Duane was a take-charge character, setting the rules and telling kids what to do. "That was my first ball field. That's where the games were played. And that was the place where I started to love sports," Parcells commented years later.

"He used to tell me what to do, but I could outrun him," Don Parcells recalled. Jokingly, he added, "It was a good thing I could outrun him because otherwise I wouldn't be alive today."

"I grew up a Giants football fan and a Red Sox baseball fan. My father was an obnoxious Yankee fan. And in my growing-up years, he had a lot to be obnoxious about. The only team that could beat them in all those years was the Red Sox," Parcells said. "Baseball was my game growing up."

Duane listened to the Red Sox, Yankees, Giants, and Dodgers games on the family's Bendix radio. He was an obsessive fan of many of the teams from the late 1940s and early 1950s.

However, basketball and football were also important sports in his early life. Parcells was an avowed Giants fan growing up. Duane watched *Marty Glickman's Quarterback Huddle* on television. Glickman had been a U.S./Olympic athlete who had been denied a chance to compete in the 1936 Olympics due to anti-Semitism, but after a brilliant career at Syracuse, he went on to play professional football and basketball briefly. However, he found enduring fame as a New York metropolitan sportscaster.

Glickman's program was on Channel 2. Parcells watched religiously, and in later years recalled watching the Giants football stars of that era such as Charley Conerly, Joe Scott, Arnie Weinmeister, and Em Tunnell.

"I went to my first Giants game at the Polo Grounds in 1954, [and] saw them beat the Steelers. I was thirteen," Parcells recalled. After that he was hooked. He went two or three times a year until he went to college. Whether going with the Little League baseball team, with family, or with neighbors, Duane went when he could.

William Levitt had founded Levittown in Long Island, New York, in 1947, where street upon street of affordable houses were built for returning GIs who wanted to settle down and raise their families. The post–World War II boom saw families moving from the cities out into the newly formed suburbs, and northern New Jersey was one of the great developing suburbs, closer to downtown Manhattan than some of its Long Island competition. With the advent of the automobile and the highway system as well as solid and dependable mass transit, especially in the great metropolitan area, many middle- and upper-middle-class families moved into such towns. Small businesses sprouted up to serve these communities, and trains connecting their sleepy bedroom hamlets to New York City gave the towns a white-collar community that could stabilize it.

"By the time Duane was entering junior high school, the family decided to move. They went from Hasbrouck Heights to Oradell, a small town north through Hackensack and just past the slightly larger town of River Edge. There, they settled into a bi-level ranch-style home on Wildwood Drive," early biographer Bill Gutman reported. "It was in Oradell where Duane Parcells began to be mistaken for the other boy, the look-alike named Bill. Before long, more of his friends and acquaintances were calling him Bill." The name stuck. It was another sign of his independence and outgoing nature.

According to Gutman, "Oradell had fewer than 7,000 people when the Parcells family moved there. As in many other small northern New Jersey towns, a gradual transition had been taking place. What had been a traditional farming community for many years was now turning into a commuter suburb of New York City."

It was during this time that Parcells began to excel at sports in a more meaningful way, and his true personality began to develop. He was a leader. There was no doubt. And he detested losing more than anything.

To increase his chances of success, or extend his control over as much of the game as possible, he gravitated toward those positions that could determine the course of a contest. He was a pitcher in baseball (he also caught), he was the center on the basketball team, and he played quarterback in football.

His physical stature had increased, as well. He was tall, lean, and well muscled, like his dad had been. And he carried himself extremely well.

"He was like a man at fourteen," 1955 Babe Ruth teammate Tom Godfrey remembered. "He was really a leader. He wanted to control everything on the field. At the end of practice he used to say, 'I'll take the catcher's stuff home; you guys just make sure you're here tomorrow.'"

Godfrey later recalled a game from that season in which Parcells was catching with two out in a close game with his team up. The opposing team's best hitter was coming up, Bobby Myslik (who eventually went on to be the athletic director at Princeton), so Parcells called a time out and waved in the left fielder. Parcells took off his catching gear, the left fielder donned the catcher's garb, and Parcells trotted out to left field.

"Myslik hits the ball about four miles," Godfrey said.

Sure enough, the hitter popped a high fly right to left field, and Parcells made the final out.

"That's what set him apart from the average kid. He was always going to win at anything whether it was major sports or something like handball, racquetball, tennis...anything," Godfrey continued.

Walter "Butch" Bartlett met Duane in eighth grade and played competitive sports alongside Parcells until college. "We were a hungry group," he later recalled. "We played everything when we were young...Bill was very demanding, even then, and it is obvious he stayed that way."

"His parents were very friendly with all the kids who came there," Bartlett continued. "Bill's mom was real Italian in that she was always cooking. And she kept the house immaculate. We spent all our time in the kitchen or down in the rec room. I can still remember there was always plenty to eat."

MICKEY CORCORAN

"I met Mickey Corcoran when I was a sophomore in high school," Parcells said. William "Mickey" Corcoran would be one of the most influential people in Parcells' life.

Mickey began his New Jersey teaching and coaching career at River Dell. He coached basketball and taught physical education when River Dell first opened in 1957 until he left in 1965 to become the athletic director at the newly opened Northern Highlands High School. During his tenure at River Dell, he won back-to-back NBIL league championships during the 1962–63 and 1963–64 seasons. His River Dell career coaching record was 82–49.

But more than that, Corcoran had been coached himself by the legendary Vince Lombardi at St. Cecilia. Two decades before he became head coach of the Green Bay Packers and won five NFL titles and two Super Bowls from 1959 to 1967, Vince Lombardi coached football and basketball at St. Cecilia from 1939 to 1947. One of his best basketball players was Mickey Corcoran, a guard who became basketball coach at River Dell High School in Oradell, New Jersey, in the mid-1950s.

Lombardi was the assistant under Handy Andy Palau, who was his fellow teammate at Fordham University. Lombardi was a natural football coach and established his legacy at St. Cecilia's in his first year, as the team went on a run the second half of the season, and beat the powerful cross-town rival Dwight Morrow in Englewood. He stayed at St. Cecilia for eight years, coaching football (head coach five years), basketball, and teaching Latin, physics, and other subjects.

While Lombardi had an aggressive, innovative, and complex football mind, he felt very much out of his element, at least in the beginning, as a basketball coach. Palau, the former Fordham basketball team captain, helped Lombardi through the first five games, and then sent him on his way.

It was in this first season as basketball coach that Mickey Corcoran met Vince Lombardi.

"Corcoran, loose and cocky, with the natural basketball instincts his coach lacked, was Lombardi's pet," Lombardi biographer David Maraniss wrote. As Lombardi's pet, Corcoran saw the wild mood swings and wild outbursts that would become part of Lombardi lore. But first there was discipline.

According to Corcoran, Lombardi's predecessor had been "an easy rider." For Corcoran and the other players, Lombardi's strict style was at first abrasive, with Mickey later commenting, "The change was a bit of a culture shock."

"He had never coached basketball in his life, he never played basketball," Corcoran said. "He wasn't a basketball guy. They gave him $200 to coach the basketball team just to get him to come there and coach.... He and I had a great relationship from jump street. When I was in high school, if we weren't playing a game at night, he'd say, 'Call your mother, we're going out to Sheepshead Bay to have dinner with my mother.' We did that four or five times; it was really tremendous. He wasn't the greatest at Xs and Os; he was just learning the game from other coaches, but he was a great, great coach for me and the basketball team. He really was a great basketball coach."

"He ripped me pretty good in practice one day. He was all over me like white on rice. I came out of the locker room that same day and he saw me going up the steps and says, 'Mick, come in here.... Today is a tough day; tomorrow is going to be a better day.' He was a master psychologist. He took me from the depths right up to the top of the world. His best characteristic was his player-coach relationships. I coached for 40 years, and player-coach relationships [are] the most important thing in the coaching business."

Though not as passionate a basketball mind, Lombardi nevertheless threw himself at the job and kids. "Before practice during the week, Lombardi enjoyed playing H-O-R-S-E with Corcoran" and some of the others players according to Maraniss. "'Match my shot! Make this one!' The outcome was usually the same, the boys outshot him, but Lombardi remembered the one trick he threw in and boasted about it for days."

Lombardi played cards with the boys, and on more than one Friday night, Lombardi would find Corcoran, saying, "Call your Mom, we're going out to Brooklyn for some home cooking."

"All the way out to Lombardi's house, they talked basketball: different defenses, college plays Vince has seen that week at Madison Square Garden," Maraniss wrote.

But being Lombardi's pet meant he was also the most criticized player on the team. Lombardi could yell and scream, shocking the kids. "He made a point of challenging Corcoran the most, as a lesson to the others," Maraniss wrote.

Corcoran learned valuable lessons under Lombardi, who was more than just a coach to the budding basketball star. Once after a bad loss, Lombardi criticized Corcoran, who he felt had taken some bad shots during the game. Infuriated, he insisted Corcoran take physical education for the rest of the semester, even though varsity athletes were not required to do so. After several weeks, Lombardi called Corcoran over, apologized to him, and released him from future gym classes.

"Rip your butt out, then pat you on the butt. Knock you down, then build you back up," Corcoran remembered years later. "He understood human behavior better than any person I've ever met."

"That was the method of Coach Lombardi," Maraniss wrote. "Corcoran learned it from his mentor and used it himself when he became a high school coach years later, and [he] passed it along to his own disciple, a North Jersey boy named Bill Parcells."

"I talk a lot about being a Jersey guy," Parcells recalled. "Mickey is the original: He's got a tough Irish face, seems bigger than he really is, and he's always wearing a hat."

At River Dell, Mickey had a routine summer practice for all incoming student-athletes participating in basketball. Corcoran ran a number of drills, but more than many he noticed the 6'2" center with the piercing blue eyes who stood there after each drill with hands on hips staring at the coach.

"He stood at the back of the line and looked me over good, like, 'Who is this guy?'" Corcoran said. "He wanted to check me out."

Parcells was Corcoran's temperamental star. He was also the coach's pet, and like Mickey had been with Lombardi, so Parcells was with Mickey.

Mickey began pressing his temperamental player. Duane could lose his temper and was thrown out of practice many times for doing so. One time Parcells kicked the ball into the stands, incurring Corcoran's wrath. Mickey would holler at Parcells in front of the other players and eject him from the gym—but every time, Corcoran found the humbled Duane Parcells in his office, "begging to rejoin the team."

"That's when I knew I had him," Corcoran recalled.

"Sometimes," the elder Parcells said, "Duane needs a kick in the ass. Don't be afraid to give it to him."

"Call it youthful exuberance, but Bill was overly competitive and would lose control of his emotions from time to time. He had to learn to handle himself as an athlete. I knew I might have some problems with him, until his father paid me a visit," Corcoran said. "His dad was the best.... His father and I were on the same page. They were just a wonderful family."

"I didn't know it at the time," Parcells said many years later, "but [my father] was in cahoots with Mickey Cochrane.... Anyway, I really didn't know when my father was even at games. Mickey used to sneak him through the field house door, and my father never used to say too much about my games one way or another. So now I'm playing for River Dell High School and I'm leading the state of New Jersey in scoring, and one night my father says to me, 'Are you getting to play much down there?' Now that's a humbling experience."

The most famous exchange between Parcells and Corcoran involved the hot-tempered Parcells losing his cool during a game. Parcells heatedly argued a call with an official and drew a technical foul. It cost the team two points. An infuriated Corcoran ordered Parcells to the bench, where his kept his angry protégé right next to him.

"Mickey Corcoran was the master. Once he got me with just one sentence after a basketball game. Now understand, I'm the high scorer, and he walks over and he says to me, 'Parcells, you weren't worth the two points you cost us on that technical foul you drew, and if you ever get another one, you ain't gonna play another minute.'"

Together Parcells and Corcoran watched the 17-point lead evaporate into a 1-point loss.

"If I put him back in and we win, I don't think he learns the lesson," Corcoran said.

Parcells concurred years later. "See, I was fifteen years old and we were up by 17, and he took me out of the game because I got a technical foul, and we got beat by one. But you see, if he puts me back in I would have had him—forever. He knew that. I thought he'd put me back in at the time, but he didn't. I learned something that day."

Like Corcoran before him, Parcells learned the value of discipline, but he was also an apt pupil. He stayed after school to talk strategy and theory with Corcoran. Corcoran often took Parcells and his teammates to Columbia, Fordham, and West Point games, be it football or basketball, where Parcells peppered the coach with a multitude of questions, points, and counterpoints. "He asked me all kinds of questions," Corcoran remembered.

"It was always defense with Mickey," Parcells remembered. "He said by playing defense you wouldn't win every game, but you would be in every game, with a chance to win."

"Mickey's gift—one of them, anyway—was breaking things down in a hurry, giving you something to rely on, eliminating the surprises, giving you enough information without giving you too much," Parcells explained.

"He worked harder than any other kid I had," Corcoran said. "He was always first one there and last to leave. Same with football and baseball."

Sometime during the first season, River Dell took a tough loss in basketball. "He had played his ass off that night." Parcells, however, was the last to leave the locker room. Corcoran felt bad for his star player. Corcoran told the young and inconsolable Parcells that he had nothing to be ashamed of, and that he should consider the night a kind of moral victory.

"He looked at me very seriously and said, 'Coach, there are no moral victories. You either win or you lose, and we lost,'" Corcoran remembered.

"He's so much like Coach Lombardi," Corcoran said years later. "He wants nothing to interfere with football. You are a football player—that's what you do for a living."

"He was a very unusual kid, unique really," said Corcoran, who lived in Dumont, New Jersey. "He may never have said it, but all the signs were there that he wanted to make coaching his life. He was totally absorbed with athletics but a good student, too. He was the most analytical athlete I've ever been associated with at the secondary-school level. He had an understanding of concepts. The word to describe him was 'commitment.'"

— —

Another coach that Parcells was lucky to encounter was Tom Cahill. Cahill was born in 1919 in Fayetteville, New York, and attended Niagara University in Buffalo, New York. Cahill, years later, would be the head coach at West Point. One of the assistants he took on was a young man named Bill Parcells.

But in those early days, Cahill was a hard-nosed coach. Unlike Corcoran, he played no favorites. However, he was just as confounded about Parcells' high-octane competitiveness and inability to control his temper. Parcells alternated playing quarterback and running back on offense, and he played linebacker on defense.

Parcells called Cahill "a bluff Irishman" who allowed Parcells to call his own plays. "That privilege came with a price, however. Every Sunday at 1:00 I'd meet with the coach at his home to discuss the game we'd just played and the plan for the next one," Parcells recalled. "I'd report what I'd seen on the field, and Cahill...would say what he thought the team was doing well and what we needed to do differently."

Parcells always liked those meetings. Parcells very much wanted to win, but it also gave him a better understanding of what the coach wanted, and Parcells wanted to please his coach. "Today, I consider preparation the most enjoyable part of my work."

On September 28, 1958, Parcells helped to lead River Dell High School to its first-ever football win—in the first game of the season. "The Golden Hawks took a 13–0 first-half lead," reported *The New York Times.* "Lew Frey ran 16 yards for one touchdown, and Ken Tripp took an 11-yard pass from Bill Parcells for another. Parcells ran for the extra point." River Dell held on to beat Ridgefield Park for their first win, taking it 13–12.

Weeks later, on October 19, River Dell Regional defeated Fair Lawn 26–13. "Bill Parcells scored three touchdowns and passed for the other to Bob Mood," reported the *Times*.

Many remembered that football team with Parcells at the controls at quarterback. In one game, the team drove to a first down and goal to go. Cahill ordered two running plays, but the opposing defense still held strong. Parcells called time out and walked over to the sidelines to talk with Cahill.

Parcells walked back to the huddle, and when the team lined up, Parcells was lined up at running back and the running back at quarterback. He took the handoff and burst through the line and scored the touchdown.

"He was the kind of player who was always going to figure out how to get it done, a leader. There was no doubt about it and everybody, all his teammates, knew it," Tom Godfrey recalled.

Parcells was always willing to take on such roles. But every once in a while fate was lurking around the corner with a humbling blow. Such was the case on Thanksgiving Day, when Parcells was at quarterback his senior year. With third-and-goal, Cahill sent in the play, but at the line Parcells audibled and changed the coach's original call. The play failed, and no touchdown was scored. Cahill was furious but kept his composure. He put his arm on his quarterback's shoulders and said quietly, "Parcells, you s.o.b., the next time you make a call like that, your fat ass is going to be sitting on the bench for the rest of your career, which fortunately isn't too much longer."

Nevertheless, an enduring respect remained between the two of them for many years to come.

Despite his exploits on the hard court and on the football field, Corcoran always thought that Parcells' real abilities lay in baseball. "I always thought he was a tremendous baseball prospect. In fact, if he was coming out of high school today, I'm sure he would be offered a nice contract from one of the major league teams."

At 16, Parcells was playing in a semi-pro league, lining up with players 10 years older than him. Parcells was tall, and he could hit and throw. He wasn't the fastest kid on the team, but he was quick and had excellent reflexes. But as with basketball and baseball, Parcells brought along with him toughness, tenacity, and competitiveness that was hard to find in others. And along with those qualities came a belief in himself and a desire to control as much as possible to accomplish only one thing—to win.

Many coaches will tell you that they can teach strategy and techniques, they can improve a player, but they cannot teach talent, and they cannot teach heart—two things Parcells had in spades.

Parcells continued to like baseball, love Mickey, and play football. Parcells also loved his 1956 Ford, a car he bought with his own money, bragging in later years that Chubby never gave him a dime for it. Friends recalled that Parcells was in love with his car, always washing and buffing it. He loved to cruise Hackensack with his friends, sitting proudly at the steering wheel.

As Parcells got older, football captured his attention more and more. And his fascination grew. Parcells even played some playground football with Vince Lombardi Jr., whose father was one of the Giants' assistant coaches at the time. While Lombardi had forged a local reputation as a winner at St. Cecilia, he was not yet the national figure he would become. Parcells' tangential association with Lombardi Jr. made him root for the Giants all the more.

"My father knew Vince Lombardi," Parcells remembered. "The Lombardi family lived in our neighborhood, and I played in the streets with Vince Jr. when we were kids."

"There were friends of mine who knew Vince Jr. a lot better than I did, and they got to go to games with him sometimes, which made me mad," Parcells remembered years later. "I wanted to go to those games."

By then Parcells was a dedicated fan. He even attended the legendary Giants-Browns game in 1958, courtesy of a neighbor who was a season-ticket holder, where Pat Summerall kicked the field goal in blinding snow to win the game.

"I was sitting in right field at Yankee Stadium behind the 344' sign when Pat Summerall kicked the field goal through the snow to beat Cleveland after Jim Brown went 70 yards for a touchdown on the first play," Parcells said.

However, he was not lucky enough to score a ticket to the championship game that pitted the Baltimore Colts against his beloved Giants.

"I listened to it on the radio," Parcells remembered. Parcells and his friends were ice skating at Lake Hoptacong. Parcells could not fathom their interest in skating when Johnny Unitas was about to square off against Sam Huff. "I sat for three hours in the car, listening to the game on the radio." Asked what his thoughts were when Alan Ameche crashed over the right side for the winning touchdown? "Devastation."

By his senior year, Parcells was playing linebacker on defense and tight end on offense. And he had caught the attention of college recruiters. By Parcells' own admission, his best sport was football. But he got offers of all kinds. Both Seton Hall and Fordham both came calling about his joining their basketball programs. Parcells dismissed the offers.

"I think that was Mickey's doing, frankly," Parcells scoffed. "I think he knew somebody at those schools—or knew somebody who knew somebody—and that's where those offers came from."

But the real offers that caught Parcells' interest were football. Auburn and Clemson offered scholarships. But Chubby, along with Mickey's help, had kept Bill's academics in the forefront. When it came time to accept a scholarship, Parcells could afford to be choosy, knowing his academic level could get him into better, more academically challenging schools of the day. Parcells considered some Ivy League schools but ended up going to Colgate.

In the fall of 1959, before leaving for Hamilton, New York, Bill decided to hone his baseball skills. He played semipro baseball with friends Bill and Walter Bartlett. And it was at this time he met Larry Ennis. Ennis was only slightly older than Parcells, but Ennis would go on to be one of the most legendary high school sports coaches in North Jersey.

"Ennis was the player/coach of a couple local semipro teams, the Oradell Raymonds and Clifton Giants. He was a fine pitcher who, like many other young baseball junkies of that era, had professional aspirations," Bill Gutman wrote.

"Semipro baseball flourished here after the war," Ennis said. "We played at twilight and on weekends, occasionally at night if a field had lights. We'd travel locally, also to South Jersey, and made some New York stops. Most of the players were in their late twenties or early thirties. When Bill came to me and said he wanted to play, I took him on right away since I had already seen him in high school."

"I knew he could handle himself behind the plate because I had watched him at River Dell. Plus I also remembered a game he pitched against Teaneck High in a tournament. Teaneck was a county power, but they only beat River Dell by a 1–0 score and had scored that run on a fluke. Bill pitched a tremendous game."

"Most high school players would normally have doubts about stepping up and playing with older guys, but not Bill. He was always wanting to move up, play with older guys," Ennis said. "He had quick hands and called an intelligent game. In fact, he took it personally if you shook him off. He had a quick release and strong throwing arm and was very agile for a man his size."

"The story goes that the team would hit the bars after games and Larry would tell the bartender, 'Just Cokes for this guy,'" sports scribe Ralph Vacchiano related of Ennis and Parcells.

In his freshman year at Colgate, Parcells played baseball and football. In a short period of time, Parcells decided he didn't like the school. His grades suffered. He admitted years later that it was more him than the school. But Parcells remembered at the time that the devotion to sports at Colgate was not at the level he had hoped for. The football team's schedule included the likes of several Ivy League Schools, Army, and Duke. But these were not the football powerhouses he truly dreamed of. The Colgate football team had gone 2–7 in his first year, and that experience had left a bad taste in his mouth. He was obsessed with winning and felt that many of his fellow students were not dedicating themselves to the team's success.

Parcells realized in hindsight that this was not the case. He even admitted that there were probably guys who wanted to win as much or more than he did. Years later Parcells admitted that he was 19 years old and thought he knew better than everyone else.

In the spring, Parcells excelled at baseball and was eventually offered a contract by the Philadelphia Phillies. While Chubby was pleased his son was a prospect, he quickly said, "No." Bill needed to acquire an education first.

Parcells returned to Colgate his sophomore year to attend football camp. After two days, he quit the football team and Colgate. He returned home. It was the fall of 1961.

"What are you going to do now?" an irate Chubby asked.

With typical Parcells wiseguy bravado, Bill responded, "Join the Marines."

Chubby laid down the law. Bill was to find another college immediately, or he would never help Bill out academically ever again. Mickey was also irate with his headstrong pupil.

"He came to me that day after he left Colgate," Mickey said. "He said he was looking for a more competitive atmosphere where there was a greater commitment toward winning. Everything he had done in his early life was geared toward competing. He just didn't find what he wanted there."

Parcells had a friend at Wichita State, which sounded good to Bill. Mickey called the football coach and after a short chat got Bill a temporary scholarship. The school would give him books and free tuition and a football tryout for one semester.

"I got into the car and drove to Wichita. Other than one summer, I wouldn't be back to Jersey for a long time, until 1981."

CHAPTER 2

Traveling Man

WICHITA LINEMAN

The forces of westward expansion and financial rewards attracted the first white settlers to the area that is now Wichita in the 1850s and 1860s. Some men of those times realized great profits from hunting and trapping the wildlife and trading with the native population. Among them were James R. Mead, Jesse Chisholm, William Greiffenstein, and William Mathewson. These men eventually shared a vision for a city on the prairie.

The City of Wichita was incorporated in 1870. In 1917, the first plane, the Cessna Comet, was manufactured in Wichita. Over the course of the inter-war years, this industry grew to establish Wichita as the self-described "air capital." World War II brought thousands of aircraft manufacturing jobs to the city in the early 1940s, resulting in a population explosion. Activation of the Wichita Air Force Base (renamed McConnell in 1954) in 1951 attracted thousands more. The area saw the birth and maturation of such companies as Mentholatum, Boeing, Beech, Lear, Cessna, Coleman, White Castle, Pizza Hut, and Koch Industries.

The trip to Wichita was one of the most fateful moves Parcells ever made and set him on a path he did not realize would one day take him to the pros. It was not quite the path he thought it would be as he started out. He referred to it as a great stroke of luck.

In 1961, the coach of the Wichita Shockers was Hank Foldberg. Henry "Hank" Foldberg had played college football at Army and at

Texas A&M University. From 1960 to 1961, he served as the head football coach at the University of Wichita, where he compiled a 16–5 record. (The school changed its name from the Municipal University of Wichita to Wichita State University in 1964.) In 1961, the team went 8–3 and earned a trip to the 1961 Sun Bowl. He was the Valley's Coach of the Year in both of his seasons at Wichita, and his teams won the conference title twice. He was, in Parcells' eyes, a winner— a competitor.

This was not Colgate in Parcells' eyes. Parcells would play here and play gladly. Parcells was a linebacker at Wichita State. To him, this competitive spirit, this aggressive style of football, was worth playing. They played teams like Louisville, Boston College, Arizona State, and New Mexico State. This was major college football.

"It was a brand of football I wouldn't have seen at Colgate," Parcells remarked years later.

He entered as a sophomore and was a three-year letterman at linebacker on the 1961, '62 and '63 Shocker football teams. Parcells was hooked.

At 6'2" and 225 pounds, Parcells was a big athletic kid. He was not a starter, but he saw considerable action at linebacker. Obviously gifted, he even substituted at tight end, catching two passes for 48 yards, one of them for a touchdown.

Playing alongside Bill was a defensive lineman named Len Clark. A native of Lawrence, Kansas, Leonard Clark lettered in football three times, and in track, baseball, and basketball one season each at Wichita State. In the 1961–62 season, he was named the University's outstanding athlete and earned a B.A. in Education in 1965.

Clark recalled that in the fourth game of the year, against the West Texas State Buffaloes, they faced the prolific star passer "Pistol" Peter Pedro. Pedro hailed from Massachusetts, but they loved him in Texas. Brash and talented, he scared numerous college defenses from 1961–1964. During his career he led his respective college conferences in numerous offensive and passing statistics. As could be expected, Pedro dropped back to pass many times in what turned out to be a shoot-out of a game.

"When we saw another pass play, Bill put the rush on, and I dropped back for a screen [pass]," Clark said. "He beat his man and was almost to Pedro when he tried to throw. Bill batted the pass in the air. I grabbed it and ran 45 yards for a touchdown. I was lucky to be in the right place, but Bill made the play. He had size, and he had pretty darn good speed, as well. He always wanted to win." Wichita won a wild one 41–34.

The 1961 Sun Bowl pitted Wichita against the 7–2 Villanova Wildcats of Philadelphia on December 30 in El Paso, Texas. Wichita State was a 6-point favorite with Coach Hank Foldberg's passing offense featuring Alex Zyskowski and Bill Stangerone. Villanova brought with them one of the stingiest defenses of the entire collegiate season.

The 27th Sun Bowl was televised across the nation on ABC. The series record between the two schools stood at 1–1, with Villanova winning 24–6 in 1957 and Wichita winning 21–6 in 1958.

According to Bowl historian Mark Bolding, "The tone of the game was set early. Villanova's defense bottled Wichita up, and the offense drove 43 yards on two Billy Joe runs. Joe shook off three Shockers on a 19-yard touchdown run."

"Villanova led 7–0 throughout most of the first half. With less than 3:00 to play, with Stangerone at quarterback, the Shockers drove 47 yards to the Wildcat 18-yard line. Bill Seigle kicked a Sun Bowl record 36-yard field goal to bring the Shockers to within four at the half," Bolding recalled. The final score was 17–9.

"The story of the game could be seen in the statistics. Villanova outgained Wichita on the ground, 225 yards to 111. Their defense was simply overpowering. With the pressure on and Zyskowski out of the game in the second half, the Shocks were unable to mount a challenge. They really never found their rhythm on offense."

Change was coming again for Parcells. Foldberg left Wichita right after to be the new head man at Texas A&M.

It was Parcells' first taste of collegiate success, and Foldberg's move was seen as a promotion for his hard-won record at Wichita. In retrospect, these circumstances would not be lost on Parcells. Success bred new opportunities. Opportunities that were due a coach who had a successful run. The reward for a college coach who had a successful run was (and still is) a new job at a bigger and better school that pays more money. This is how coaches get bigger paychecks.

— —

"My roommate was Gene Dempsey," Parcells recalled years later. Dempsey eventually went on to become a DEA agent where he had a long career, eventually living in St. Louis. "He's one of several people who've helped educate me about drugs and drug users and the psychology of that world."

While at Wichita, Parcells met a lovely young girl named Judy Gross, a secretary in the sports information office of the university. They were married and had their first child, Suzy, before Bill even graduated. He wasn't there for her birth. He was playing football.

In 1962, Parcells' second year at Wichita, there was a new coach. Marcelino "Chelo" Huerta Jr. had been a great scholar-athlete in high school. The Hillsborough High School's football and track and field stadium in Tampa, Florida, bears his name to this day. After serving in the army, Huerta attended the University of Florida in Gainesville, Florida, where he played for Coach Bear Wolf's Florida Gators football team from 1947 to 1949. Huerta graduated from Florida with a bachelor's degree in physical education in 1949. Huerta was later inducted into the University of Florida Athletic Hall of Fame as a "Gator Great."

"Chelo Huerta was a born leader," Michael Canning wrote in the *St. Petersburg Times*. "As an offensive linesman for the Hillsborough High football team, he called the plays, a job usually reserved for the quarterback. Not long after high school, he piloted B-24 bomber missions over Germany during World War II. Shot down over Yugoslavia, he evaded the Germans who were occupying the country, hooked up with local partisans, and made it safely back to base.

"The son of Ybor City cigar workers, Huerta, at the young age of 28, was named the youngest university head football coach and athletic director in the country when he succeeded Frank Sinkwich at the University of Tampa. After a highly successful 10-season stint there, followed by shorter ones at Wichita State University and Parsons College, he compiled a 104–53–2 record.

"After retiring from coaching in 1967, Huerta returned to Tampa to serve as executive vice president of the MacDonald Training Center, a facility for the mentally and physically impaired. He developed methods to get them jobs in mainstream society and testified on their behalf before Congress in 1975."

The football stadium at Hillsborough High School was named Chelo Huerta Field in 1986, and a year later, the city dedicated a playground in his name, as well. In 2002, he was posthumously inducted into the College Football Hall of Fame.

Huerta was the 25th head football coach for the University of Wichita when he took over, and he would hold that position for three seasons, from 1962 until 1964.

In Huerta's first season, the Shockers stumbled out of the gate, trading wins and losses until mid-season in October when they stood 2–3. They had two solid wins, two solid losses (Cincinnati and Arizona State), and lost a heartbreaking opener to Louisville. But the Shockers saw their fortunes fade as their record sputtered to a dismal 3–7, ending with three losses. Worse, they were 0–3 versus Missouri Valley Conference teams.

Under Huerta, Parcells played in every game of the 1962 and 1963 seasons. Weighing in at 185 pounds, Len Clark was not the biggest lineman, but he was competitive nonetheless. Clark noticed something different about Parcells in those seasons.

"Bill always had a maturity about him," Clark said, "a drive, an instinct, a knowledge and sense of football that others didn't possess. I guess I could describe it as a kind of awareness of the game that was several steps above his peers. Even during that difficult 1962 season Bill was always focused on winning and never stopped trying to get his teammates focused in the same way. He was the kind of player always willing to turn it up a notch, knew that he could turn it up a notch, and would get others to turn it up a notch or two in order to win. That's why it was such a difficult year for him."

"Bill wasn't the easiest guy to get along with because he wanted to win so badly he was always encouraging other guys to hit someone, then hit them harder." Clark assumed Parcells was just trying to motivate the others, although his fellow players didn't always understand.

— —

The 1963 Wichita Shockers got off to a great start. The team went 3–1, defeating Arizona State, Hardin-Simmons, and Louisville but dropping a 22–16 loss to Boston College. The team would only lose one more time that year on the way to compiling a 7–2 record. In that run, they beat New Mexico State, Dayton, Cincinnati, and Tulsa. The only loss in that run was a heartbreaker, losing 7–3 at North Texas.

The highlight of the season was the final game against Tulsa. It was Bill Parcells' greatest day as a player in his college career. They were going into the game against Tulsa, a team stacked with talent at the skill positions. The Golden Hurricanes sported Jerry Rhome at quarterback and Howard Twilley at receiver. The game promised fireworks. But the fireworks came from Bill Parcells. That day he played like a man possessed. He played the run like a madman, clogging up holes and smothering runners, and he terrorized Rhome all day. When it was all done, Parcells had one of the greatest days in Wichita football history. He had twenty tackles and six sacks. It was easily one of the greatest days any collegiate player had in 1963.

"Bill punished Tulsa that day, he really did," Clark insisted. The Shockers shocked the Golden Hurricanes 26–15.

The 1963 season had been one of real progress for Bill Parcells the football player. He had distinguished himself. He was a standout on the 1963 squad that compiled a 7–2 record and won the Missouri Valley Conference championship. He was named to the All-Missouri Valley Conference team that season. And he was honored after his senior season by being named to play in the Blue-Gray and College All-Star games.

That year, Parcells went to Corpus Christi, Texas, to play in a football All-Star game. Parcells broke his hand on a Tuesday, and it swelled up grotesquely. He went to see a doctor, who told him he had broken four bones in his hand. The doctor put a cast on it and asked Parcells if he was going to play anyway. "Why not," Parcells said. "It's broken anyway."

It was at this game that Parcells met Al Davis. He liked Davis right away. Though he didn't have any real interaction with Davis, Parcells admittedly followed Davis around like a puppy dog. Parcells was "enamored" with and "fascinated" by Davis, who talked in a corkscrew New York accent with a southern twist. He was tall and lean with slicked-back hair. He yelled at the kids a lot.

Davis was from the upstart American Football League. He was the first professional football coach Parcells had ever seen.

"I watched everything he did on the field and listened to everything he said, and one night at the hotel I ended up sitting with him and talking about football for maybe a half an hour, and from then on, I was hooked on him," Parcells remembered.

They had no real contact from that point on until Parcells reached the pros. Parcells reached out to Davis in 1983. Davis would prove to be a real friend and advisor.

That season, Parcells had played with and against a number of men who would go on to play in the pro game, and he proved himself competitive. He played against Charley Taylor (running back, Arizona State) and Brig Owens (quarterback, Cincinnati), both of whom had distinguished careers with the Washington Redskins, Rhome and Twilley, who also went onto NFL careers, as well as a number of others. Parcells proved he belonged to a certain level of football.

He was drafted in the seventh round of the 1964 NFL Draft by the Detroit Lions.

"Four other guys on our team got drafted," Parcells said. "Henry Schichtle, a quarterback, was drafted by the Giants, I was sick. I thought, 'Why couldn't it be me?'"

The Lions were a team stocked with colorful players of the day, with a mixture of young and old, including the brash Alex Karras, Night Train Lane, Earl Morrall, Hugh McElhenny, Yale Lary, Dick LeBeau, and others.

"I was just an in-between size," Parcells once said. "I was about 238, and the best players were a lot bigger, so I became a coach."

"I went to the Lions camp and got cut. I could make the whole experience more dramatic than it was, but the fact is I expected to get cut," Parcells wrote years later of his time in an NFL professional training camp.

During training camp, Dean Pryor, the coach a Division III Hastings, offered Bill a coaching job. Parcells had a baby girl and another on the way, and he needed to make a decision.

"I thought I did real well in camp. So I explained my situation to head coach George Wilson and asked him what were my chances of making the team. He just put me off," Parcells remembered.

He was cut sometime in August 1964. Disappointed? Demoralized? Deflated? Parcells never discussed his failed playing career with anyone, even his lifelong confidant Mickey Corcoran.

"He was a pretty darn good football player," Corcoran once said. "But he never discussed his aborted pro career."

— —

"I decided I wanted to be a football coach somewhere down the road," Parcells explained. Parcells had no idea about how to become a football coach, or if anyone would have someone as young as himself. "I knew it's what I wanted to do. I liked the life.... I used to bitch about coaching, but the truth is, I wouldn't have know what to do with myself without some kind of practice once school let out."

"He didn't want the 9-to-5 world of his father. What he wanted to do was coach," *Newark Star Ledger* sports scribe Jerry Izenberg wrote. "Nobody was killed in the stampede to hire him."

Again, this is where his lucky Wichita connections continued. Dean Pryor, who'd been the backfield coach at Wichita State, was named the head coach at Hastings College. He got the position the year Parcells graduated. He had told Parcells that if things didn't work out in the pros that Parcells was welcomed to join him in the fall at Hastings.

Parcells had no real job prospects, a wife and a child, Suzy, and another baby on the way.

"He told me he couldn't offer me much money—the offer was $1,000 for three months of work," Parcells remembered.

Hastings was a small school that played in the Nebraska College Conference. Parcells liked to joke in later years that the two big events at Hastings were the opening of the football season and the opening of pheasant season. But he was still a coach.

"We lived in a basement apartment underneath a dentist's office," Judy Parcells recalled. "There was a small closet and no window. We didn't have anything and $1,000 seemed like a lot of money. We managed. I don't know how. Obviously we didn't eat steak and shrimp."

The rent was $62.50 a month. The apartment had no windows, just walls of cinder block. It was clean and it was a mile from the University. The biggest man in town was the father of Tom Osborne, the famed ex-Nebraska football coach, and he owned the largest car and tractor dealership in town. He sold almost as many cars as he did farm tractors. And Tom himself had played at Hastings as their star quarterback in the late 1950s. By 1964, Osborne was an assistant at Nebraska.

This was not big-time college football. At Hastings, Parcells not only coached on defense, he also cut the grass, lined the field, helped build the players' lockers, and even helped wash the uniforms. Parcells liked to point out, "I was coaching. I wasn't a graduate assistant, I was one of the coaches at Hastings."

Parcells was a "young man with a whole world to conquer," Coach Pryor said.

"I loved it right away," Parcells remembered. "I couldn't get enough of it."

Parcells learned a lot that year. According to him, the greatest lesson he got harkened back to a bit of coaching wisdom from Mickey—you can't tell the players everything you know. Despite it, Parcells did just that and found out the hard way that it doesn't work.

Parcells would try and tell his players everything he knew. But he could see it wasn't working. "Football players forget things under pressure," Parcells explained. Baseball and basketball players, too.

Parcells like to tell the story about his first real lesson on the sidelines, when he hollered at one of his players coming off the field. Jack Giddings, who played fullback and safety, was one of Parcells' pets. This, too, was a habit he had picked up from Mickey. Parcells described Giddings as a coach's dream. Giddings played hard, did what you told him to do, didn't speak a lot, and just liked to play.

"He was pretty intimidating. But he also had a pretty good sense of humor. He was fun to be around when he wasn't coaching," Giddings said.

"We played Carney State, which is now University of Nebraska at Carney. They were a bigger school. Carney was rotating all these guys in and out, and we played both ways. But Parcells was so intense, and had us so ready, we lost, but the linemen from Carney were crawling by the end of the game," Carney remembered. "If you had a bruise or an injury, it didn't matter. You were going to play. I wouldn't trade those times for anything."

They practiced all week on how to stop the Nebraska Wesleyan College bootleg pass that had been so successful for that school. Nebraska Wesleyan marched down the field. Near the goal line, they ran the play, and Giddings failed to stop the play. As the 20-year-old player approached his 23-year-old coach, Parcells started screaming. Bill was right in the boy's face. Finally, Pryor had had enough.

"I saw him ripping Bledsoe when he was with the Patriots, and I thought to myself, 'I know how that feels,'" Carney said.

"Bill wasn't into apologizing. Today you can't grab someone's face-mask, you can't slap 'em upside the head. You can't do that anymore. But I'm okay," the retired Giddings laughed.

"Leave the guy alone," Pryor said.

"But coach, we worked on the damned play all week," Parcells argued.

"Well, you didn't work on it enough because they scored."

Parcells was flabbergasted. "Lesson? You always better be prepared to honestly take part of the responsibility yourself. The kid was a good kid. He was trying to stop the pass," he said. Parcells learned his lesson. It was up to him to learn how to communicate the best way possible, the simplest way possible. And he was always ready to take the blame.

The team went 7–2. Parcells was thrilled. He'd gotten a season of coaching under his belt. He'd been a real, honest-to-goodness coach complete with his own responsibilities, successes, and failures. And he loved it.

That year the team was invited to the 1964 Mineral Water Bowl, which was played in Excelsior Springs, Missouri. The game was played in 15-degree weather against Fort Hayes State. Currently, the Mineral Water Bowl is an annual American NCAA Division II college football bowl game between teams from the Northern Sun Intercollegiate Conference and Mid-America Intercollegiate Athletic Association hosted in Excelsior Springs, Missouri, at Tiger Stadium.

In 1964 they had a snow fence circling the field. To the 23-year-old rookie assistant coach, this was life and death. The Hastings Broncos defense played with incredible heart, making two field goals stand for a hard-fought 6–0 win.

"At the end of the season we went back to Wichita State to work on his masters," Judy said.

"We packed everything we owned into a 6' x 8' U-Haul trailer and drove back to Wichita, where Judy's family lived. I'm not sure what at that point what my next move should be," Parcells recalled. He was even vaguely thinking about law school and following his father.

If Bill was the erstwhile firstborn son, Don was the dutiful, solid citizen. Like Bill, he was tall, lean, solid, and athletic. "Bill was probably a little better, a better all-around athlete. Don was a great, great football player. Bill was pretty good, too. But Bill played baseball in the summer, and Don, he ran track," Corcoran said. While he was confident and friendly, to a degree he lacked Bill's fiery outbursts. Back on the east coast in 1962, Don was a freshman at West Point, the United States Military Academy. A high school star athlete in his own right, Don was now playing full-back and halfback for the Black Knights.

In May 1962 he had impressed the coaching staff while under the eye of the ever watchful General Douglas MacArthur and Army ex-head coach and legend Colonel Earl "Red" Blaik. *The New York Times* reported, "The best running performances of the day were turned in by Ken Waldrop, Ray Paske, and Paul Stanley from last year's team, and two newcomers, John Seymour and Don Parcells."

"I am honestly impressed," Coach Paul Deitzel said.

In 1962, with President John F. Kennedy in attendance, Don was starting fullback with Army. He scored a touchdown with President Kennedy in the stands for the 34–14 Navy victory.

Unlike Bill, Donald C. Parcells was in the middle of big-time college football. In 1963, Don's team played the likes of Boston University, Minnesota, Penn State, Wake Forest, Washington State, Air Force, Utah, Pittsburgh, and Navy. The team went 7–3.

Don was playing fullback and halfback, wherever he was needed. He also played defensive back. His name was always mentioned in the New York sports pages, especially as Army was still considered a solid football program.

In November 1963, Don's image in a United Press International photo was plastered on the back of the sports pages across the country for breaking up a pass play against Pittsburgh in a stunning defeat.

In the 1963 Army-Navy game, sportswriter Allison Danzig wrote, "The 2,400 cadets in the stands were in a frenzy of joy as Ken Waldrop, a 200-pound tailback, Ray Paske, a 203-pound fullback, and Don Parcells, a 200-pound wing back, and Stichweh [Army quarterback] split the Navy defenses asunder on that second touchdown drive."

By 1964 Don was in his senior year at West Point. What should have been a crowning achievement spiraled into a dismal season. The team that got off to a good start with victories over The Citadel and Boston College but was racked by injuries and slogged through defeats to Texas, Penn State (losing 6–2), Virginia, Duke (6–0), Syracuse, and Pittsburgh. Then they salvaged wins against Iowa State and Navy.

Don scored many touchdowns that year, starting off early with a 9-yard rumble off tackle against a solid Boston College defense.

In a heroic moment in that season, the Army team had made it down to the Penn State 3-yard line with less than 2 minutes to go in the game, when the ball was given to Don. He rammed into the line but was stopped at the 2-yard line by the stout Nittany Lions, who held on for a 6–2 win.

Don even played in the North-South Game on December 25, 1964. "The [North's] second touchdown came less than 2 minutes later. It was set up when Don Parcells, an Army back, recovered the North's short kickoff—it may have been intended as an onside kick—on the South's 39-yard line. Parcells was hurt in hurtling himself on the ball at the sideline and had to leave the field."

In his college career, Don had played against the likes of Roger Staubach, Bullet Bob Hayes, Tucker Frederickson, and many others.

Don graduated from West Point in 1965 with a degree in civil engineering. Then came the Vietnam War. Don served as a Captain in the U.S. Army with the 25th Infantry during the Vietnam War and was a recipient of two Bronze Stars for Valor, the Army Commendation Medal, two Air Medals, and the Purple Heart.

"One night, during an operation in the jungle, his brigade came under heavy mortar attack. He tried to hide in his foxhole, but he still got hit. Both his legs, bleeding badly, needed tourniquets. He knew he would not survive the night, but the rescue helicopters could not get to him. Finally, one made it through. He was taken to an aid station, where he prayed he would make it through triage. His big brother got the news days later and never felt more helpless," Steve Politi of the *Newark Star Ledger* wrote.

"Bill was going crazy," Judy Parcells recalled. "He wanted to sign up and go over there. He felt bad that he never served, that it should have been him and not Don who went to war."

"Don spent four months rehabilitating his injuries in Japan and, when he got healthy, was sent back to Vietnam. The near-death experience gave him a perspective on life," Politi continued.

"You know, I lived longer than I thought I would have anyway," he said. "I could have been dead at 22 or 23."

Through the late 1960s, Don served as an instructor at Fort Sill in Oklahoma where he lived with his wife and their infant son.

CHAPTER 3
You're in the Army Now

B
ill and Judy lived in Wichita for another two years. George Karras took over the coaching responsibilities in 1965. As luck would have it, Karras was urged by many in the town, especially the Shockers boosters, to fill out his staff with the former Shockers star. George was an assistant on the team when Bill played there. Bill was hired to work with the defensive line and linebackers.

Karras coached at Wichita for two seasons, during which the Shockers reached the ignominious record of 4–15. At the end of the 1966 season, the coaching staff was mercifully retired.

Parcells recalled years later that there were mixed blessings about those two years. The good blessings were that he had gone to Wichita, he knew his way around, it had come when he needed employment, and that the competition the Shockers faced was a massive step up from Hastings. On the bad side, he felt he was still close to his college experience, and it made him feel uncomfortable. He had not put enough time between him and the college.

"When he was an assistant coach at Wichita State, he'd work until one or two in the morning sometimes. And then with college ball, there were always the recruiting trips," Judy remembered.

On January 7, 1967, *The New York Times* reported, "Bill Parcells, the defensive coach at Wichita State, was named today to a similar position on the Military Academy's football staff under Tom Cahill, head coach."

In 1966, Tom Cahill took over as the head coach at West Point. Cahill had been Parcells' high school football coach and of course was still friends with Corcoran. Corcoran urged Cahill to take a shot with Parcells. Parcells thought he was blessed.

"See what I mean about luck?" he said years later. "We packed up the U-Haul and drove out to West Point." West Point would be one of those magical places where so many things would go right for a young coach on the move. That's what a young coaching assistant's life was—on the move.

And the Parcells family was growing. Joining Suzy was now a sister, Dallas. "Until the children really started to grow up, it was fun," Judy Parcells said. "I was caught up in all the beauty and patriotism at West Point. And I'm from Wichita. During those years there was always something exciting, and I couldn't wait for the next move."

Parcells admitted later that it was at West Point "That I really began to learn how to coach."

In the previous season, Cahill's team went 8–2, with victories over Penn State, Pittsburgh, California, and Navy. Their only two losses came at the hands of Notre Dame and Tennessee.

Bill was 25 years old, and he was asked to coach the defensive line. Parcells said the first thing he learned from watching Cahill was that he had an excellent staff, and that was one of the first things he filed away for when it was going to be his time. More than that, Parcells said, "West Point was my real basic training as a football coach."

The offensive coordinator was Bill Meek (a former head coach), and other staff members included Dick Lyon and John McCauley. All three of these men were older, more experienced, and happy to share their knowledge with the young, enthusiastic Parcells. He saw it for what it was—a great learning opportunity—and he soaked up their wisdom and advice like a sponge.

Parcells learned that having a first-rate staff was an important building block, and many of the men he met during this era would be with him later in his career, including Al Groh and Ray Handley.

Born in New York City, Groh was a native of Manhasset, New York, on the North Shore of Long Island. He and Bill had their New York metropolitan roots in common. Groh graduated from Long Island's famed Chaminade High School in 1962, and in 1967 he graduated from the University of Virginia. Groh played for the University of Virginia football team from 1963–65, lettering at defensive end in 1965. Groh remained a constant friend of Parcells for many years, and the two worked alongside each other for more than 13 seasons. This was one of the first important football relationships that Parcells would bring with him when he became a head coach.

— —

At West Point, Parcells met another strong influence in his life—Bobby Knight. Parcells liked to say that the reason the two became such fast and intimate friends was that Knight liked football so much, and he liked basketball so much. The two met when Parcells was playing hoops during a lunch break. It turned out Knight knew a lot of the football coaches, and the two were instant friends. Knight admitted that a lot of football coaches were influential on him, including Red Blaik, Vince Lombardi, and Paul Brown.

Eventually, the two started playing basketball together at lunch time. Asked what they were like years later, Parcells responded, "Volatile. No, not just the two of us; we had some other contributors. We had Don DeVoe, who was one of Bob's, went on to coach many years on the collegiate level. Dave Bliss, another assistant for Bob for a long time. Then we had a football player named Bob Mitinger who was a Penn State guy that played with the San Diego Chargers. So we had some athletes who played. Sam Koons played. General Schwarzkopf played with us. Arthur Ashe played. So we had some guys in the game that, from time to time, the competition level was up, and we were young."

The two, as was to be expected, were incredibly competitive, and the pushing and shoving and grabbing turned the games into tough, physical battles. Both admit to elbowing, wrist slapping, grabbing on to jerseys, just about anything to gain a physical advantage. Then the arguments would start.

"What wasn't good was our playing on opposite sides," Knight admitted. "One day, we'd go to lunch, and I think he initiated the conversation, and he said, 'We gotta quit, we gotta figure out how we're going to play together.... All we do is argue with each other. We gotta play on the same team.' So, we kind of made that one of our noontime features that he and I got to choose first. And if he chose, he'd choose me, and if I chose, I'd choose him, and then we went from there."

"He was an impossible adversary. He was tough to defeat mentally. We fought it out quite a bit but enjoyed doing it," Parcells laughed.

"We were the same age, but he was already head basketball coach, and you didn't have to know a hell of a lot about basketball or coaching to see he was going places," Parcells remembered.

Even then, Knight had a pedigree few could match. Knight was born in Massillon, Ohio, and grew up in Orrville, Ohio. Knight began his career at Orrville High School where he played football and basketball with Ron Burns. He then matriculated at Ohio State University, where he toiled under Basketball Hall of Fame coach Fred Taylor in 1958. He was a reserve forward on the Buckeyes' 1960 national championship team. The team featured two future Hall of Fame players—John Havlicek and Jerry Lucas. Knight graduated with a degree in history and government in 1962.

Knight coached junior varsity basketball at Cuyahoga Falls High School in Ohio for one year in 1962. Knight then enlisted in the U.S. Army and accepted an assistant coaching position at Army in 1963. He worked hard as an assistant there for two years before being named the head coach at the relatively young age of 24.

From 1965 to 1971 in six seasons at West Point, Knight won 102 games and made four NIT appearances, where his team reached the semi-finals three times. One of his players was Hall of Fame Duke Blue Devils head coach Mike Krzyzewski, who graduated in 1969. Knight went on to find greater fame at Indiana University, where his teams won three National NCAA championships and one NIT championship. He was later tagged with the nickname, "The General," for his abrasive, dictatorial style and tantrums. But there was no denying his talents and his achievements.

In his 1987 autobiography, Parcells was effusive about Knight. It is hard to fathom two larger personalities together in the same room. "The thing people find it hard to understand about Knight is what great company he is," Parcells said. "He is intelligent, he is quick, he is funny, he is loyal. He is sensitive as hell." Parcells related how Knight, especially after losses, would come over to the Parcells house and hide out, talking until the wee hours of the night with Parcells, discussing each and every play and the strategies he'd employed.

"During the basketball season, I loved just sitting in the gym and watching him taking his team through basketball practice," Parcells said. "It was just so obvious to me that he had greatness in him.... Knight likes to say, 'There's blackboard guys and then there are coaches.'"

Parcells was so enthralled with Knight he even did scouting during the basketball season for Knight, driving down into the city to scout teams like St. Johns, Fordham, and others. But for Parcells the most fun thing was to scout a game with Knight. Knight would compete in the first game of the NIT, and then he would sit and watch the second game for coaching.

Parcells used to tell Mickey, "He's winning 20 with the guys he's getting at Army. Wait until the sides are even."

Of course, while Parcells was obviously charmed by his charismatic new best friend, he also had his feet planted firmly on the ground. "You know, I used to sit down with him, and several times I told him he was nuts," Parcells said.

The two love to tell the story of a 49–47 loss to Rutgers when a fight broke out in the final seconds. Army was looking to get the ball back, and the Army center was instructed to grab the opposing player. When he did that, the Rutgers center turned on him and threw a wild punch. Unfortunately, the Army center retaliated and coldcocked the opposing player. A melee ensued—a real bench-clearing brawl. The Rutgers faithful jeered at the Army hooligans. After the technical fouls were assessed and the Army team was jogging back to the locker room, the arena was loud with angry fans. There were hoots and hollers.

"As we were leaving the floor, somebody made a gesture at Coach Knight and Bill Parcells grabbed the kid and threw him through a door," said Bob Kinney, the sports information director.

"I gotta talk to you," Bill said to an unknowing Knight.

"What is it?" said the irked Knight.

"Come over here," a suddenly sheepish Parcells said.

"When he took that swipe at you, he missed you and I just whacked him back up into the stands.... You know, they might be looking for me." And, in fact, the police were.

"Well just stay here, we'll figure this out," Knight said in the locker room.

Eventually, Knight told his tallest players to surround Parcells (who he told to stoop over), and they walked in a tight-knit group to the bus and were escorted to safety.

"Well, the thing I think I'll always look back upon is just the amount of time we spent together talking about coaching. And what is important in coaching. We're both I think defensive-oriented, but we had a great time," Bob Knight said. "We used to, every Sunday afternoon in our basement, we'd basically watch the Packers play because they were on television, every, every Sunday. We'd talk about what coaches did, and there's nobody that I've known in my background in coaching that I saw become a better coach and that I've had more respect for than Bill and his coaching."

"Well, you know, I was an assistant coach for many years, and Bob at a young age was a head coach. So I think we were both in our formative years in coaching at that time. And we're kind of sounding boards for one another," Parcells recalled. "And that's kind of gone on for many, many years now, that I knew I could always pick up the phone and call Bob and talk to him. Something that related to my football team, that he would identify with because of his coaching experience with basketball."

"Hey, let me tell you. A lot of the conversations were...I'd call him, and he'd say, 'What's going on?'" Knight said. "'We can't guard anybody. I mean, we give up points. We just, we can't guard anybody.' So you know, he'd commiserate with me a little bit. The next call, if he made it to me... 'I got these three defensive backs that can't cover anyone...there's not a receiver in the league they can cover.' I mean, we have more things that we've talked about, more things that have went wrong with our teams than anything that was positive. And I think each of us were kind of good listeners when the other was having problems with something."

"Bob and I would call and tease each other, too," Parcells laughed. "He teased me with the types of offenses and defenses we were using in football. And I would, of course, having more opportunities on a seasonal basis to tease him, the chances were that I was going to [go] one-up on the teasing by the time the season was over since he was playing 30 games, [and] we're only playing 11."

"What are we in that prevent defense for?" Knight chimed in. "Why are we in that prevent defense? It's preventing us from winning. And so, I made the mistake one time of playing zone against Seton Hall. A trap, our half-court trap." And for that reason, Parcells made the same call back to Knight. "What's that defense called?"

The circle of coaching friends has widened to include the great baseball strategist and baseball manager Tony La Russa and the all-time winningest thoroughbred horse trainer D. Wayne Lukas (who was also a former basketball coach). Knight once joked, "I spent half my life trying to keep Parcells and La Russa sane."

— —

Parcells remained at Army for three years. In 1967, Army went 8–2 again. The defense had improved from the year before and averaged giving up only 9.4 points a game. In five games they gave up seven points or less. That year they beat Virginia, Boston College, SMU, Stanford, Air Force, Utah, and Pittsburgh, but they lost to Duke and Navy. The next year they went 7–3, and they beat Navy that year 21–14. In 1969 the team went 4–5–1.

Parcells couldn't get enough football. During the summer of 1967, in the mornings while still an assistant, Parcells would drive across the Hudson River to the Peekskill Military Academy to watch the New York Jets practice.

After that season, Parcells went to Florida State. Again, his move made the newspapers, as reported nationally by United Press International (UPI). Parcells was considered to be an up-and-comer at this point.

Later, when Parcells was comfortably ensconced with the Giants, he and Judy thought a lot about their years at West Point. "I guess it was April or May," Judy remembered, "and he said, 'Why don't we get out and take a ride up to West Point, have lunch at the hotel in Highland Falls, and ride past our old house at the Academy?' We both have a lot of feelings and memories about West Point, so it seemed like a great idea."

As they were driving toward the old house, the road took them near the old stadium. It was spring practice, and Bill suggested they stop in for a second and see what was going on. He wanted to say hello to a few people, like the old bus driver, trainer, and maybe a coach or two.

He chatted for a long while and then came up into the stands and sat and watched practice for a while longer. After an hour-and-a-half, Judy was freezing.

"That's when I tapped him on the shoulder and asked if we were having fun yet," Judy laughed.

But at the time, they were off to explore the unknown. This was the beginning of what Parcells would eventually term "the gypsy years." Parcells was on the merry-go-round of coaching. "I was like everybody else in the business, a transient, looking to hook on with the right coach in the right situation, get noticed, become one of those assistants whose name gets mentioned when a head job opens up," Parcells remembered. "I was getting caught up in the rat race at a young age. I could feel the ambition growing. I felt like I was always looking around."

Parcells was recruited by Florida State head coach Bill Peterson.

Peterson's father had died when he was a young boy, but Peterson persevered. He graduated from Ohio Northern University in 1946 after playing end on the football team. Peterson was team captain. Peterson's brother, Jack Peterson, was the head football coach at Wofford College from 1971 until 1973.

Peterson established himself as a successful high school coach in Ohio before joining Paul Dietzel in 1955 as an assistant at LSU. Peterson was the offensive line coach on the Tigers' 1958 national championship team. He was named the head football coach at Florida State in December 1959.

According to Florida State's 2008 football media guide, "Florida State's arrival on the national map occurred during Peterson's eleven seasons as head coach." It was during his 11 years as head coach that he was recognized for his offensive innovations. Under Peterson, Fred Biletnikoff became the Seminoles' first All-American. Peterson is perhaps best remembered for bringing the Seminoles to the forefront of college football, using pro-style offenses and a much-feared passing game. He led FSU to four bowl games in a five-year span, albeit FSU only triumphed in one.

Peterson became best known within the coaching profession as "the coach of coaches." While at FSU, he mentored such valuable assistants as Joe Gibbs, Bill Parcells, Bobby Bowden, Bobby Ross, Don James, Dan Henning, Ken Meyer, and many others who were highly successful. Coach Pete, as he was known, is also remembered for his colorful reshaping of the English tongue, the most oft quoted of which was, "Pair off in groups of threes, then line up in a circle."

"I liked Peterson," Parcells remembered. At Florida, Bill was not only involved in coaching, but he was responsible for designing defenses and calling defenses in games. He was moving up. He loved this part in it. But like any place, there were things he didn't like. "There were times when this Jersey guy started to feel like one of those screaming, good-ole-boy southern assistant coaches. I didn't like the feeling."

After the first year, Peterson left, winding up as the head coach of the Houston Oilers for a brief stint. The new coach was Larry Jones. In 1971, the team went 8–4 and lost in the Fiesta Bowl. The team followed up with a 7–4 campaign in 1972.

One of the great things that Parcells took with him from his stop in Florida was his relationship with Dan Henning, who would go on to become a head coach in the NFL in his own right. The two became lifelong friends. However, at the time they were just two struggling assistants trying to keep their lives and their families together.

At the end of the 1972 season, Parcells accepted a job at Vanderbilt in Nashville, Tennessee.

Parcells acknowledged that the gypsy life was taking its toll on himself, his wife, and his daughters. By now he had three of them—Suzy, Dallas, and Jill.

"Suzy would get the worst of it, school-wise, and Dallas would get the next worst because they were the oldest," Parcells remembered. "Their lives were inevitably scarred by the travel. Suzy for example had gone to school in upstate New York; Tallahassee, Florida; Nashville, Tennessee; and Lubbock, Texas. She finally ended up graduating from high school in Colorado."

Parcells acknowledged that her grades suffered because Suzy was up-rooted every two to three years and placed in a new situation. That left emotional and scholastic scars. Some of the school systems just weren't very good at the time, and the Parcells weren't in a position to send her to better, private ones. He knew that the stability many children crave during childhood was denied to his girls.

Despite these less-than-positive situations, the Parcells girls excelled as they grew up, and Bill was very proud. Parcells was also quick to point out that the moving may have helped them develop better coping skills early on that would serve them well as they got older, being able to adapt readily to new situations, etc. Parcells was proud to point out, "It's hard to intimidate my girls. They've always been able to walk in and do it."

— —

Steve Sloan was the head coach at Vanderbilt University. Sloan had played football under the legendary Paul "Bear" Bryant at the University of Alabama from 1962–65. Sloan received lots of playing time in the defensive backfield. He was also the backup to quarterback Joe Namath. The 1963 Crimson Tide went 9–2 with a 12–17 victory over Ole Miss in the Sugar Bowl.

With Namath injured, in 1964 Sloan (a junior) was the primary quarterback at Alabama. The 1964 team finished 10–1 and won the Southeastern Conference title. By popular opinion they were considered the consensus national champion. In the 1965 Orange Bowl versus Texas, Sloan was forced out of the game with an injury, enabling Namath to come off the bench. Despite Alabama being on the wrong end of a 21–7 score, Namath took home MVP honors.

In 1965, Sloan was the starter. Namath had left for the upstart American Football League. Alabama repeated as SEC and national champions. The team finished 9–1–1 with a 39–28 victory over Nebraska in the 1966 Orange Bowl. Sloan played two years as a backup for the Atlanta Falcons before accepting a coaching position at FSU and then moved on to the Georgia Tech Yellow Jackets for the same position.

In 1973, Sloan became the head coach of the Vanderbilt Commodores, and Bill Parcells took the job as defensive coach. That year, Vanderbilt finished at 5–6. But in 1974 Vanderbilt went 7–3–1 and earned its place in the Peach Bowl against the Texas Tech Red Raiders. It was only Vanderbilt's second bowl appearance ever. The two teams played to a 6–6 tie.

Then Texas Tech offered Sloan a very lucrative deal, including a $30,000 yearly salary and a television contract for a coach's TV show for another $11,000. Sloan leapt at the chance, taking five coaches with him, including Bill Parcells.

The decision was a hard one for Parcells. When Sloan announced he was going to Texas Tech, Vanderbilt immediately offered Parcells Sloan's old job. As Parcells explained many years later there is a simple dictum— it's easier to turn a program around than to come into a successful program and keep it there. "I was 34 years old at the time," Parcells recalled. "I didn't think Vanderbilt was a good job. I thought Sloan had made the smart play." Parcells argued that Sloan had correctly taken the upgrade, and if Parcells had stayed, then there would have been nowhere to go but down. He argued that what Sloan had achieved was a fluke and that Parcells could not keep it going.

In retrospect, was Parcells correct? Who is to say? Fred Pancoast came over from Memphis where he'd gone 20–12–1 and led Vanderbilt to a 7–4 record the following year, only one loss worse than the previous season. Possibly bearing out Parcells' way of thinking, the 1976 edition of the Commodores went 2–9. But as Parcells was also fast to point out, you're never really sure if the next move is the right one or not.

The Parcells family was on the move again. "The next thing I knew I was in the middle of nowhere—Lubbock, Texas, is the state capital of nowhere," he said.

"I'm from Wichita, so I liked all the flat country around Lubbock," Judy said.

Texas Tech turned in a 6–5 record in 1975, leaving a sour taste in some folks' mouths, considering the only slightly better record of the previous year of 6–4–2. But in 1976, Sloan and his cadre of friends went 10–2 and went to the Bluebonnet Bowl. The next year wasn't as good, turning in a record of 7–5, but it was good enough for a Tangerine Bowl appearance.

During this period, Parcells met Gordon Wood. Wood is one of the great legends of Texas high school football. Through 43 seasons, 26 of them at Brownwood, he won 405 games. During a spring practice at Texas Tech, Parcells met Wood. He saw a "rough looking, leathery kind of guy" wearing a maroon jacket with a "B" on his cap. Each morning the man attended these practices without saying a word.

"We had 20 spring practices," Parcells said. "I know he was there at least 15 times, always down by the linebackers." Parcells finally introduced himself to Wood, who said he coached in "a little town down the road here."

"Outside of Lubbock?" Parcells asked.

"No, a little further," Wood replied.

"How far is it?" Parcells recalled.

"Well it's 2-1/2 hours one way," Wood replied.

After a few minutes conversation, it became apparent that Wood drove the 2-1/2 hours back and forth each day—five hours in the truck—to those practices. "And I know he did it at least 15 times, and at the time he had to be 60 years old," Parcells recalled.

Wood was really 63. Wood complimented Parcells. He said he'd been watching him. And then he asked Parcells questions.

"He asked, 'Why [are] you teaching this? Show me how you do that.' Here's a guy who never lost, he never ever lost. I think of him every season when we start. I think about this guy," Parcells said. "He doesn't even know me. I don't know him. I only crossed paths with him one year, but he was very influential on me. The guy's 58, 60 years old, done 300-something games and is driving five hours a day to find out something."

However, not all was as it seemed. For the first time in his life, Parcells, who by then had developed a map for his defenses and had developed his own personal style, clashed with the young men in his charge.

Parcells was loud and full of energy. And he brought with him "his ever-sharpening tongue, biting wit, and thinly veiled sarcasm," Bill Gutman wrote. "The veteran players on the Texas Tech defense were used to an entirely different style of coaching. For one of the few times in his coaching career, Bill Parcells found players teetering on the brink of open rebellion."

"We didn't understand much about him when he first arrived," said Greg Frazier, a starting safety in 1976 and 1977. "He was very brash, what we would define as a Yankee. He really didn't quite understand how to get the most from the boys from Texas."

Parcells' penchant for goading or trying to embarrass players to motivate them was considered rude and arrogant. But the boys also had a problem. "We felt he had to prove himself to us," Greg said.

"His first year he hated us, and in our view he was a New York asshole," said Richard Arledge, All-Conference defensive end. Arledge summed up the players' perspective the best. They had been recruited by one group of coaches and came expecting one thing. Instead, there was a regime change, and now they had this guy who would grab them by the face mask and start screaming at them and degrading them in their eyes.

Maybe it was just East Coast versus Texas style. During one practice, the player later related, the offense was having a good practice at one end of the field, and the defense was struggling at the other. Suddenly Parcells flew into a rage, screaming and waving his arms.

"You guys make me sick. Just get off the field," he screamed. The players didn't know what to make of it. But hadn't the same thing been done to Parcells when he was a player? Hadn't it worked for Mickey or even Lombardi?

Before one spring game, Parcells went up and down the line roughing players up, asking them if they were ready. He even smacked some players on their pads, shaking them up. Sitting alone, as he always did for a game, psyching himself up was a defensive tackle named Billy Bothwell. When Parcells shoved him in an attempt to motivate the young man, Bothwell, shot up and shoved the coach back, knocking Parcells to the floor.

Without missing a beat, the Texas defensive line coach said, "I think he's ready, coach." Parcells got up without a word and continued to go down the line.

Sloan knew there was a problem. Parcells had not engendered this kind of reaction at Vanderbilt, and as far as Sloan was concerned, Parcells was one of the best defensive coordinators around. "Part of the problem was one of philosophy," Sloan said. "Bill was a lot tougher than they were accustomed to the first year he was there." Sloan knew that Parcells pushed his players harder and made lots of demands. Sloan held several meetings, especially with the seniors. According to Sloan, Bill also realized he needed to get closer to the players before they would understand him.

"Another part of the problem was Bill's feeling of alienation in Lubbock, a sense that he didn't fit and didn't belong. For one of the few times in his life, he found it difficult to assimilate and come to terms with his new surroundings and its people," Bill Gutman wrote.

Sloan had pointed out that during this period Parcells was pretty much a loner, avoiding many staff parties and other get-togethers. Sloan was quick to point out that the Lubbock region was still very much cowboys, and their attitudes and lifestyle were far from Parcells' experience.

But Parcells found a way. He found it the same way he'd met so many other people—by hanging around the gym, playing pick-up games of hoops, and talking strategy with whoever would listen. Parcells played ball with the other assistants and with his own players. He discussed strategy with them and talked football and basketball. Slowly, the players started coming around. Parcells would ask their thoughts and opinions. And soon enough the players started to respect him and even like him.

By the start of the second season, the Red Raiders were ready. Sloan had crafted a solid offense, and Parcells had created a well-schemed punishing defense. Parcells even had a knack for picking up Sloan's castoffs from offense and building a better unit. Sloan complimented Parcells, saying he had a knack for putting people in the right place.

Players noticed Parcells' penchant for halftime adjustments and constant communication with his players. But more than anything it was toughness. He hollered and screamed at players. During one practice, one of his players got clipped on a crack back, and Parcells kicked him in the butt. He told the player, "If anyone ever does that to you again, and I don't see you get up and hit him right there, then you won't ever play for me again." His players learned to love the attitude.

One of the attitudes the students hated was Parcells' motto, "You can't make the club in the tub." The underlying theme was that Parcells did not tolerate injuries.

"He was hard on people who were hurt," Frazier said.

But seniors, especially, learned to like Parcells. For those guys who had gone into battle for him, he could be a nice guy. He could be friendly, and he didn't press them as much to do the grunt drills. They had it a little easier. If you were a senior and starter with Parcells, that meant he probably liked you.

This is where Parcells started to first get the reputation for being a player's coach, something that would be his shield (and almost his downfall). The seniors felt like he would stand up for them.

And thus, as a term of endearment as well as respect, Parcells earned the nickname "Pretty." "We nicknamed him 'Pretty,'" Greg Frazier said. "Sometimes it was 'Coach Pretty' or 'Pretty Person Parcells.' It was the neat way he combed his hair and some of his other mannerisms. But it was also a name out of respect. We weren't making fun of him."

Regardless, the other thing that started to take shape in these years is respect. Many players who feared or even hated him at one point often found years later that Parcells was a man to be reckoned with—a man who would prove to be a life-changer. Many looked back and were grateful that they had the opportunity to play for him and learn from him. There was no doubt he inspired players through whatever means, but that loyalty came back to him in spades. Living inside the crucible that was Bill Parcells, these men found out a lot about themselves. How hard they could push themselves. And what standards they should demand from themselves. Again, like Lombardi, Parcells has inspired others beyond just football.

— —

Parcells' defense, even then, was predicated on big, tough, fast linebackers and hard-hitting safeties. These were the tacklers in the scheme. The linemen were meant mainly for tackling up the gut and on pass plays; after that, the defensive end's job was not to turn plays back inside but to string out sweeps along the line of scrimmage until the linebackers, safeties, or cornerbacks could arrive like vultures. Team speed on defense was everything.

These were all the themes he had been developing during his apprenticeship. And they were theories he would bring with him to the next job and eventually to the New York Giants.

Even back then Sloan wondered if Parcells wouldn't be better off in the pros. Parcells hated recruiting. It was his Achilles heel. He wasn't a big personality like a lot of the successful college coaches. He wasn't comfortable doing that. He was more of a loner. He stayed with the people he knew. And the tough guy stuff might turn some players off. In the college game, Sloan argued, you have to sell yourself and the place. In college, you recruit. In the pros, you acquire.

Parcells fieriness was still with him, whether it was yelling at a player, one of his or one on the offense, there was no exclusion. And he was not above screaming at Sloan in a game if the situation had flared up. Sloan appreciated Parcells' brilliance, but he wasn't sure who would be able to work with him. However, Sloan said there was no mistaking Parcells' ability and knowledge.

Also while at Texas Tech, Parcells met Romeo Crennel, an assistant coach on defense. Crennel attended Western Kentucky. He spent four years as a defensive linesman but was awarded the team MVP trophy his senior year when he was also asked to play offensive line, where he excelled. He never played in the NFL. Instead, Crennel earned a bachelor's degree in physical education as well as a master's degree from the same school.

Crennel coached at Western Kentucky from 1970–74. He then became an assistant for defensive coordinator Bill Parcells and head coach Steve Sloan at Texas Tech from 1975–77. Crennel's was another of the names that came up when Parcells eventually became an NFL coach.

Sloan's record was a solid one. Sloan had gone to three bowls in four years. He was a winning commodity. As such, and being wed to the coach's merry-go-round life, he jumped at the chance to be the head coach at Mississippi. And that's where he and Bill Parcells parted ways.

Bill was now a known commodity himself. In his years with Sloan especially he had turned in some great defenses, and he now had a body of work that university athletic directors could gauge.

That's when the Air Force Academy came knocking.

The Air Force Academy football team had been established in 1955, and Ben Martin had coached it from 1958–77. In his first year with the Academy, Martin took Air Force to a 9–0–2 record, tied TCU in the Cotton Bowl, and the team finished the year ranked No. 6. He had a number of winning seasons and went to two more bowl games (Gator and Sugar) before he decided to step down. However, his last four years as coach were all losing campaigns.

"Ben Martin was the coach before me, and he was a lovely, stylish guy who'd come to the end of his coaching career," Parcells said.

Jimmy Johnson, who was an assistant at Pittsburgh at the time, had also applied for the job. But Parcells had the perfect resume. He'd coached at Army, and he knew what it was like to coach for a military academy. He'd also proven himself at Texas Tech.

"Bill had a fine recommendation from Tom Cahill," former Assistant Athletic Director at Air Force Jim Bowman said. "Coach Cahill told us we couldn't get a better coach. He said Bill was a competitor and a winner, a guy who always plays to win."

Parcells was an up-and-comer, something the Air Force Academy said it wanted.

"I was told they wanted to run a new, energetic kind of program, the kind I'd been used to under Cahill at Army," Parcells said.

Parcells moved his three daughters and wife to Colorado and threw himself into the job while "filled with the proverbial piss and vinegar."

The first and best thing he did was hire a coaching staff. He hired Ken Hatfield, whom he'd coached with at Army and who was then an assistant at Florida. He then hired Al Groh, another former fellow Army assistant, as well as Ray Handley, also from his West Point days.

"It was a great staff, one of the best I've ever been around," Bowman remembered. "Parcells was this very young, very dynamic, very upbeat guy with this great positive attitude. He was aggressive and a disciplinarian. He was just what we needed at the time."

"It took me only three months to know I had made a mistake," Parcells later admitted.

The first problem was that it was a military academy. The higher-ups at the academy had promised Parcells that they would lighten the course work for team players during the season. As the season approached, this promise was reneged on. Academy officials told Parcells this was not possible. As a result, playing football was added stress on student athletes who were also in the midst of military training. It was a difficult position.

According to Parcells, some players just stopped producing or wore down as the season progressed. Some just quit. Parcells was demoralized.

"At that point, I think the academy was content to go 6–5 or 5–6 every year," then assistant Ken Hatfield (and later Air Force Academy head coach) later said. "There was a feeling, I think, that it couldn't be done, that as long as the team didn't embarrass itself, then that was okay. Bill wasn't going to have that. He was too competitive for that. He was too much of a winner."

"It was an amazing year, a year I'll never forget," said Hatfield, who took over the AFA program after Parcells' one season and later coached at Arkansas, Clemson, and Rice University. "Bill made an unbelievable impact at Air Force for only being there one year. I think it's fair to say Air Force wouldn't have had the success it's had over the past 20 years or so if it wasn't for Bill Parcells."

"His goal was to get Air Force up to speed with the things other major programs were doing," Hatfield said. "He wanted to build up the weight-training program, build up the recruiting. A lot of what he did during the year he was there was administrative stuff. I think it was kind of frustrating for him at times because, first and foremost, Bill has always been a football coach."

"That was a very fun time for me and my family," Al Groh said years later. "Every place we've ever been which is, unfortunately, as most coaches' lives go, probably too many places, we've always gone with the intention of staying.... But as Easterners coming out to Colorado, I think we kind of knew that we wouldn't be there forever."

"When we got back to the East Coast, people would ask, 'What was it like living in Colorado?' and we wouldn't have to have a dumb look on our face and say we didn't see too much of it."

Groh stated that his time at the Academy as an assistant helped prepare him for other challenges. "I think that it tied in with a number of other circumstances I was in, in that that can be a challenging circumstance," Groh said. "They've done a very good job with it there, but there are some built-in excuses if you want to take them."

"He loves to win, loves to compete, loves the game of football, and he has a great vision for what it takes to succeed," Hatfield said. "He's a great motivator, and you're going to play it his way or you're not going to be around."

That year the Falcons started off with two wins against Texas–El Paso and Boston College. They experienced a massive five-game slide falling to the likes of Holy Cross, Kansas State, Navy, Colorado State, and Notre Dame. Then came a 26–10 victory over Kent State followed by three consecutive losses to Army, Georgia Tech, and Vanderbilt.

The Georgia Tech was the lowest point of Parcells' coaching career.

"In 1978, the Yellow Jackets didn't care who the new coaches of the Falcons were, or how tough the opposition played, as they drubbed the Falcons. November 11th was a frigid Saturday in Colorado Springs, Colorado containing temperatures as low as 21 degrees. Georgia Tech beat the 'slow' and 'friendly' Air Force Academy for the second-straight year 42–21," Tech sports historian Winfield Featherston wrote. "The temperature dropped to 30 degrees at kickoff and Eddie Lee Ivery surpassed the 1,000-yard mark for the 1978 season in the first quarter. He also set an NCAA single-game rushing record that day against Air Force, amassing 356 yards and three touchdowns."

Tom Saladino of the *Gettysburg Times* wrote of the game, "Neither snow, nor a howling 25-mph wind, not a gnarling stomach ache could deter Georgia Tech's Eddie Lee Ivery from becoming the NCAA's all-time single-game leading rusher. The versatile halfback raced for 356 yards Saturday in Tech's 42–21 victory against Air Force, including touchdown runs of 57, 73, and 80 yards."

Tailback Eddie Lee Ivery, a one-man infantry, finally shot down the

Air Force Saturday afternoon, but it took the most spectacular performance of any rushing back in NCAA history [to do so].... Ivery, who already held virtually all the rushing records in the Tech archives, put on his snow shoes and streaked 356 yards in 26 carries," Jesse Outlar, *The Atlanta Constitution's* sports editor, reported.

Of his rebuilding program, Parcells dejectedly told the press after the game, "This job...is going to take a while."

Ivery was not the only player to have a banner day against the Falcons. Frank Mordica of Vanderbilt ran for 321 yards the following week, still a school record, and he scored five touchdowns, which also remains a school record. Vanderbilt in fact rushed for an average of 9.1 yards per carry, still a team single-game school record.

However, there was a bright spot. His name was Cormac Carney. In 1978 Cormac Carney was a freshman player who Parcells believed in and made a starter. He was a wide receiver, lead the team in receptions, carried the ball on more than a dozen occasions, and returned punts and kickoffs.

"He had a tremendous influence on my life. He gave me an opportunity. I was not highly recruited coming out of high school," said the Honorable Cormac Carney, now a federal judge.

In that one season Cormac Carney became the all-time combined yardage leader, a record that would not be broken until 2005. But more than anything, Cormac Carney symbolized what was wrong with the military academy. After his freshman year, he transferred to UCLA. "Academy life was just not for me."

Parcells had given Carney an opportunity. It enabled Carney to leave. While at UCLA, Carney was named to the GTE/CoSIDA Academic All-America football team and to the All-Pacific 10 Conference teams in 1981 and 1982. He was the Bruins' all-time leading receiver with more than 100 receptions for nearly 2,000 yards when UCLA went 26–7–2. The Bruins were rated as high as No. 5 in the national polls. Carney's highlight at UCLA was when the team beat Michigan in the 1983 Rose Bowl.

To Parcells, Carney's success was the Academy's failure. Parcells envisioned the Carney scenario happening over and over. Parcells said

Carney was one of the best freshmen in the country. "He transferred to UCLA because he just couldn't handle it all. And all I could see was a whole long line of Cormac Carneys, even if I was lucky enough to recruit players of his caliber."

"I looked down the road and knew Air Force was always going to be playing the Notre Dames of the world," Parcells said.

Parcells had a nice home, his kids and wife were happy, and he was making more money than he ever had before. He was miserable. He felt "trapped."

After the season, Parcells licked his wounds and started recruiting. Coming back from a California recruiting trip, there was a phone call from Ray Perkins, head coach of the New York Football Giants. Parcells was ecstatic. He flew out to East Rutherford. Staying in Hasbrouck Heights, it felt like home again. He met with Perkins, who offered him the job. Parcells responded, "When do we start?" Then he flew home to quit and tell his family.

"I just felt like it was something I wanted to try to do, going to pro football," Parcells said Tuesday, explaining his quick farewell. "That's just what happened. I don't know if I could explain it to anybody's satisfaction."

He resigned his head-coaching job, but there was a bump on the road to Nirvana. "That summer Perkins, Bill Parcells, and Bill Belichick stayed at the same hotel near the Giants compound," wrote David Halberstam.

"We were in Colorado and the idea of moving back East really hit the two oldest kids. They had friends and school and it was kind of devastating to them," Judy remembered.

Judy had wearied. Al Groh remembered, "It wasn't sitting well, moving again. He had to say he would come home."

"One day, Parcells asked Belichick to drive him to the airport because, as he said, things weren't working out. He was going back to Colorado," Halberstam wrote. "He had become too much of a football gypsy over the previous fifteen years, had made too many short moves in too short a time, and his wife and daughters were objecting."

"That irritated a lot of the brass at the Academy, who felt Parcells was in a rush to get ahead at their expense. They didn't appreciate the fact he quit shortly before spring practice, either," Colorado sports scribe Randy Holtz wrote. "Parcells' one-year regime also triggered much of Air Force's later success. Ken Hatfield, an assistant hired by Parcells, guided the Falcons to top-10 success in the 1980s."

Holtz also pointed out, "Parcells' complaints about the Academy's institutional barriers also triggered some important changes. At the time, coaches had less access to players, for example. Air Force wasn't a Western Athletic Conference member in 1978, which made everything harder for Parcells, including recruiting."

"But there's no question in my mind he's the one who got the ball rolling there. I learned a lot from him, and in a lot of ways, he made my job easier when I took over," Hatfield said years later.

"Two years after Parcells left, Hatfield brought in a little-known assistant from Appalachian State to install the wishbone offense. The guy's name was Fisher DeBerry," Holtz wrote.

"You can make the argument that without Parcells, there's no Kenny Hatfield, and with no Hatfield, there's no DeBerry," Jim Bowman said. "So who knows where we'd be today if it weren't for Bill Parcells? He's the guy who got it all started. Even though he wasn't here long, he was the catalyst."

"Parcells didn't turn Air Force around. But without him, it might never have happened," Holtz concluded.

Leaving his family behind, Parcells flew East, went to work with the Giants, and worked there for two months. He worked hard every day and phoned home every night. Judy wasn't coming. Parcells had to tell Perkins he had to resign.

Much to his own disappointment, Parcells resigned, saying that his wife and kids needed him more than Ray Perkins did. Parcells had been working 14- and 16-hour days. He left before his girls were up in the morning and returned when they were asleep. And of course, this would get worse after he joined the pro ranks.

"The girls would tiptoe around, careful not to draw their father's ire," Carlos Frias wrote. When he was home, "The tone of the household was different," Suzy Parcells Schwille said. "For most of my life, my dad was there, but not really there," she said. "Unless there was some reason to put down some punishment or discipline.... We were all kind of scared of him, and he wanted it that way."

Suzy was a swimmer and cheerleader. However, Bill never made it to any of her events.

"I don't think he knew what to do with girls," Judy Parcells said.

"When I was young, I was distracted by the challenge of my own ambition to be successful," Parcells says in a video posted on YouTube.com. "It kind of haunts me as a parent that I didn't do, maybe, everything that I could do.... I've been very fortunate. My youngsters are productive citizens of society; a couple of them have families of their own, so I really dodged a bullet in that respect."

Parcells reasoned back in Colorado that his wife and family had been uprooted and moved enough. He now owed Judy a chance to stay some place she liked. He wasn't happy about it, but he understood it and respected her side of it. She had moved whenever he wanted. She had earned the right to veto this move.

It was as if someone had given him his childhood dream and stolen it back.

"So that was the only year since I'd known him that Bill gave up football," Judy said. "He worked for a land development company, and he helped coordinate their recreation centers. But what he really wanted to do was get back into football."

"So, the football coach sold land for Gates Land Co., offered color commentary for high school football games on KRDO-AM, and directed recreation activities at the Country Club of Colorado. Yes, Bill Parcells organized swimming and tennis outings for club members," Colorado sportswriter David Ramsey wrote.

Gates Land was owned by Gates Company, one of the largest multinational companies in America, with sales exceeding $1 billion at the time. Long a manufacturer of tires, the company was a competitor to U.S. Rubber, where Parcells' father worked. Gates acquired 3,000 acres in Colorado Springs, Colorado, and formed the Gates Land Company to oversee development of a planned community called Cheyenne Mountain Ranch. The community included housing developments, industrial and business parks, a conference center and resort, and retail shopping. Parcells had to get a real estate license. He studied for seven weeks and passed easily.

"At the beginning, Bill stated that he and his family needed to settle down and have a home somewhere," David Sunderland, the president of Gates Land, said. "That was one element of why he elected to stop coaching and try something else."

"I was Julie from *The Love Boat*, only bigger," Parcells remembered.

"When I told the Giants I had decided to take a job outside of football, I knew I might not get another chance to coach. It was difficult, but it also put football n perspective for me. I got to see that football is not the only thing on earth."

"I frankly think it took a lot of guts to do what he did. What was he? Thirty-eight years old? A lot of guys talk about doing what he did, but they never do it. He stopped and reassessed what he wanted to do with his life," Bobby Knight said. "He got out for a year and saw just where the hell he was. I've felt in my life like I was at that point, but I never took the step he did. Like I say, not many people have. And his career has gone full speed ahead ever since."

"I was leaving for work at 8:30 in the morning, like a normal person," Parcells remembered. "For my whole adult life, I had been gone for two and a half hours by 8:30 in the morning."

"Bill was an effective salesman," Sunderland remembered. "He was fully committed to the real estate business. He didn't sit around with a long face saying he wished he was back in the football field. He wasn't in a blue funk. He was focused and energetic and committed."

"I think it was a good time," Parcells said of his year away from football. "I had been grinding the wheel there for 15, 16 years in a row on the collegiate level, and it kind of got things on a better perspective for me."

"One Friday night, Parcells sat at a traffic light near downtown Colorado Springs with Jeff Thomas, his KRDO broadcast partner. Thomas, even 26 seasons later, clearly remembers the moment," Ramsey wrote. "As Parcells waited for the light to change, he wondered if he had ruined his chances to coach in the NFL."

"Bill was all right in the spring and he made it through the summer, but as soon as the autumn came I knew he was going to coach again.

He didn't know what to do with himself on the weekends," Judy remembered.

Bill and Judy went to a couple of Air Force games. They bought season tickets to the Broncos. They had end zone seats. "They had a great team, guys like Craig Morton, Haven Moses, Tom Jackson, and Randy Gradishar," Parcells said. Bill and Judy tailgated before games.

After that, "We both knew he ought to be coaching. But it was a scary thing because once you're out of it, you never know if you're going to be able to get back in. I somehow knew that Bill was going to get there," Judy Parcells said.

"I'm going to go back, and someday I'm going to be a head coach in the NFL and I'm going to win a Super Bowl," Bill told her.

"I always believed he would," Judy said.

CHAPTER 4

Searching for a Band of Gold

Ron Erhardt was a native of Mandan, North Dakota. He graduated from Jamestown College in 1953. After serving in the military, he was hired in 1956 as an assistant coach at Williston High School in North Dakota. He had an incredible six-year run as a head coach at two North Dakota Catholic high schools 1957 to 1962 where he compiled a combined 45–9–2 record.

From 1963 to the end of 1966, he was an assistant at North Dakota State University. On February 10, 1966, he took over the program and again put together another impossible run, amassing a record of 61–7–1 in his seven years.

From 1973–76, he moved on to become backfield coach of the New England Patriots, a post he served in for four years before being promoted to offensive coordinator on February 1, 1977. In December 1978, with one game left on the regular-season schedule, head coach Chuck Fairbanks announced he was leaving the team to accept a contract offer from the University of Colorado. The Patriots dropped that contest then lost their opening-round matchup to the Houston Oilers.

Erhardt officially took the reins of the Patriots on April 6, 1979. Noting his .890 winning percentage at North Dakota State upon taking the position, Erhardt said, "I've never been a loser in football, and I don't intend to start now."

He was not the first to call Parcells, but he was the most important.

Parcells had put the word out with Ray Perkins six months after he had told him he was going back to Colorado. He knew he had left Perkins "in the lurch." He did not ask for a job, but he flew to meet Perkins in Kansas City to tell him he wanted to be a coach again.

"I thought you would," Perkins said.

Perkins didn't have anything but said he would make some phone calls and ask around. Parcells also put in a call to Steve Sloan. Parcells' name was out there.

Bill was then asked to go for an interview with Rod Dowhower, who was the head coach over at Stanford. He was offered the job of defensive coordinator and he said yes. The next day, still in his hotel room in Palo Alto, Dowhower told Stanford *adios* and took off for greener pastures as the defensive coordinator with the Denver Broncos. Then Sloan called and asked Bill if he wanted to work for him again and be his defensive coordinator. Parcells promised to think about it. Then Ray Perkins called.

The Giants didn't have a spot for him, but New England might. Erhardt was a friend of Perkins.

"I've got this offer from Steve at Mississippi," Parcells told Perkins.

"Call Erhardt," Perkins insisted. Parcells called Sloan and explained the situation. Sloan, being a friend, told Parcells to investigate New England. If it didn't work out, the job at Mississippi would still be waiting. He flew to Boston and drove to Foxboro.

According to Bill Parcells, the interview went well, but Erhardt told him there were other candidates. Parcells again explained the situation and his commitment to Sloan. Erhardt said he'd get back to him. He called the next day at the hotel.

"The job's yours if you want it," Erhardt said.

The next person Parcells called was Sloan. "Give 'em hell. You've always belonged in pro football anyway," Sloan said. That took from Tuesday to Friday.

"Judy Parcells flew to Boston that Sunday. On Monday they agreed to by a house in Norfolk, Massachusetts. On Tuesday, they got a loan for the Norfolk house. They put the Colorado house on the market," wrote Mike Lupica in *Sports Illustrated*.

And now Bill Parcells was the linebackers coach of the New England Patriots.

Parcells went to work at Foxboro. According to Parcells, Judy and the girls loved New England, and Parcells loved working with Erhardt.

The 1980 New England Patriots were led by Steve Grogan and featured Vagas Ferguson, Horace Ivory, and Don Calhoun in the backfield. The aerial attack included Harold Jackson and Stanley Morgan and tight end Russ Francis. John Hannah anchored the offensive line.

Parcells was thrilled. He had a solid linebacking corps led by Steve Nelson who started for the Patriots since he had come to the team in 1974. Nelson eventually went to three Pro Bowls. Steve's career as a Patriot is legendary and earned him induction into the Patriots Hall of Fame in 1993. He also had his No. 57 jersey retired, one of only seven Patriots to be given that honor. In addition, Steve was named to the 35th Anniversary team in 1994 and the Team of the Century in 2000.

"He was a great influence on me," Steve Nelson said of that time. "It was my seventh or eighth year in the league. I think with that many years in the league I thought I knew everything that could happen on a football field. But he was a tremendous source of information for me."

"The one thing I really learned was, you keep learning. With him I learned to improve my technique by doing lots of little things. He was very particular. There was no wiggle room. Technique was very important," remembered Nelson, who made the Pro Bowl the year Parcells was his position coach. "He was a great motivator. Fritz Shurmur was our defensive coordinator. But you could see Bill's impact on the game planning. He was great on game preparation, and he was great at making game time adjustments. We really hated to see him go."

"I remember he was tough on rookies. He was relentless with Bob Golic," Nelson laughed. "Golic eventually became a down lineman with Cleveland, but he came into the league as a linebacker. He was a first rounder from Notre Dame, with a bonus. He came late to camp. I think Bill wanted to take him down a notch. Parcells was ruthless with him. If Parcells needed three linebackers, Parcells yelled out, 'Gimme two backers and Golic!' He just called him Golic, and he picked on him all the time," Nelson said.

In 1980 the Patriots went 10–6. Things were looking up. They finished second in the AFC East. And then Ray Perkins called.

Did Parcells want the job of defensive coordinator? The answer was yes. Erhardt was disappointed but supportive. Parcells went to East Rutherford. He was going home. For the first time in years, he was going home. "We talked a little bit during his gypsy years. When he was at Air Force we talked. And when he was at Florida State we talked," Mickey Corcoran said. "When he came back to Jersey, that's when we really started talking again. Talking like we do now."

It was yet another move for Judy. "Looking back, all the moving was a kind of cultural shock for me, and when Bill was offered a job as defensive coordinator here, I was really upset," Judy said. "He's from New Jersey, and I'd been back with him for a couple of visits and I didn't like it at all. I thought the people were rude. I couldn't deal with it. I thought, 'I don't want to raise my kids in this.' I'd go shopping and I'd come home and I'd be in tears. You know, people would yell at you, and I'm from the Midwest and I was in cultural shock."

Little did Judy Parcells know that she would be in New Jersey for a long time. Later she would say, "But now I love it. Maybe now I yell like they do. Whatever it is, it's great."

Despite the intervening years, Parcells was not a rock 'n roller. He preferred Big Band radio stations that played oldies.

By 1981 Bill was a defensive coordinator with the New York Giants. "Build me a linebacking corps that I can build a defense around," Perkins told Parcells.

"It won't be easy," Parcells responded. The Giants defense was ranked No. 27 in the NFL in the previous season. The Giants as an organization had suffered through eight losing campaigns, winning just 32 games in that entire period. Perkins had not fared very well, turning in a 6–10 mark his first year and a 4–12 mark his second year.

Despite their horrific performance statistically, there were some quality players on the Giants defense. First and foremost was middle linebacker Harry Carson, who was surrounded on both sides by Brad Van Pelt and Brian Kelley. It was in fact a solid linebacking corps. But the rest of the defense was not well planned. They had two solid linemen— George Martin and Gary Jeter.

"Jeter I was never too crazy about. Just didn't like his work habits.

Just wasn't my kind of player," Parcells said. "George Martin I was crazy about from the start. He is one of the gentlemen of pro football, of pro sports, and certainly of Giants history."

The draft that year yielded two important defensive additions to the team—Byron Hunt, brother of former New England linebacker Sam "Big Backer" Hunt, and Lawrence Taylor.

The important difference between the previous defenses and the one that was going to take the field was the introduction of a rookie sensation—Lawrence Taylor. Taylor had been all world at North Carolina, a school not exactly known to be a football factory. But Taylor was the real deal. He had made one-third of all his tackles behind the line of scrimmage in his senior year. He was a defensive mad man. The New Orleans Saints, the only team worse than the New York Giants in those days, drafted first and chose Heisman Trophy–winner George Rogers. Taylor was picked with the second pick in the draft.

George Young, the Giants General Manager said of drafting Taylor, "I thought they would take George Rogers, the Heisman Trophy running back, but I didn't stop sweating until they did."

As Parcells would jokingly retell it, "[Lawrence and I] came riding in to clean up the town, a couple of guys from an old western."

Harry Carson said of that period that the players hadn't known what to make of Parcells. He'd been with them for three months then disappeared, and the Giants had seen a string of coaches come and go. "We had a group of veteran players, especially the linebackers, and Bill had to deal with guys who were set in their ways. That was the first challenge for him, I think, coaching guys who were good but might have some bad habits."

With talent in hand, Parcells decided he would switch from a 4-3 defense to a 3-4 defense given the talent he had at linebacker. It would make for a faster defense.

As Parcells saw the game evolving, originally linebackers watched the defensive linemen stop the run and kill the quarterbacks. That was the old 5-2 and 4-3 defense. The defensive linemen were the gods of that system. Parcells didn't have those guys. Also, as more college guys came into the pros—as the NFL game was becoming more popular than college football—more of those coaches were preaching the run. The linebackers, who supported run and played pass in the old days, were now dedicated to run and pass evenly, and as Parcells pointed out, they needed to be bigger and faster. They were now assassins. No more read and react. It was now attack.

"Well, the first year, we're in training camp and I made about four or five position changes," Parcells remembered.

According to Parcells, all the Giants had was a new rookie defensive end named Bill Neill. In a big conference room with more than two-dozen football people, Parcells said he was going to move Neill to nose guard. The scouts went crazy; even George Young, the General Manager chimed in, saying he wasn't built like a traditional nose tackle. Perkins said nothing. And Parcells' reasoning was, I don't have a nose tackle, I can only use what I have, Neill is the nose tackle.

"'Unless any of you fuckin' guys has a better idea, I'm gonna move the son of a bitch there tomorrow.' And nobody said a word," Parcells remembered.

And that was that. But that didn't mean everyone liked it.

"When he got here," said George Martin, the defensive end and captain, "he had a team meeting on the first day and told each guy where he stood. There was no deceit. He told the truth."

"He was making major changes that year," George Martin continued. "That was earth-shattering for guys like myself and the other veterans. We were very comfortable playing the 4–3, the traditional four-man front. At first the change wasn't well received by us, and the players put up some resistance."

As at Texas Tech, Bill was seen as someone who was making too many changes. There was too much discussion among the players. But Parcells, having learned his lesson from his Tech days, took the time to explain why he wanted to do this or that. Slowly, the players began to come around.

"He would always tell you the reasons he was doing something different as well as what the cause and effect would be. I would say he was the first educational coach in my career," Martin said.

George Dwight Martin was born February 16, 1953, in Greenville, South Carolina. He played college football at the University of Oregon in the then-Pacific 8 conference. He was drafted by the Giants in the 11th round of the 1975 NFL Draft. He missed only six games his entire career.

"For 14 years George Martin was the emotional soul of the Football Giants locker room," New Jersey sports scribe Jerry Izenberg wrote. "For 10 of those years he was the captain."

"Bill was great at what I called having fireside chatter," Martin said. "He would pull you aside and have these little conversations with you. He didn't have to do it, but for the first time he gave you a little behind-the-scenes look at what he was doing. With those he considered leaders, he did that almost daily." Parcells would ask for help pushing a player, explaining his strategy of a particular defense, let them know how he was approaching the upcoming games or schedule.

"A coach can't be in the locker room all the time, and he can't manage the locker room all the time. And he can't know who's bitching and who's not," Parcells said of Martin. "I don't have to worry about a lot of that because I've got George Martin down there."

It wasn't that Martin was a spy. Martin was like having a player coach. He was one of the older guys, and according to Parcells, Martin told them how to act and what to say and what not to say and what not to do. He told them when to push themselves and where they could skate. He told them what they needed to do to stay on the roster and how to help the team. He helped keep people in line. And if you had a problem with George, you were going to have a problem period.

Parcells wrote, "There's no one I've met in football—hell, in life—I respect more than George Martin. I couldn't have made it without him."

"He had a real good relationship with his players almost from the start," punter Dave Jennings said. "I could see that he really knew how to get players to respond to him in a positive way on the field."

With the veterans coming around, Parcells needed to concentrate on his newest charge. Parcells wrote in his autobiography that his first impressions of Taylor at the Pleasantville training camp were, "Talented. Extremely goddamn talented. Aggressive as hell. Unbelievable quickness. Great natural strength. Hated to lose."

"On the first day of minicamp I was fourth team," Taylor remembered. "By the second day I was second team. I thought I was doing pretty good, but on every damn play, Bill would not let up. Here I was, trying my hardest, and Bill was making me feel like I couldn't do anything right."

"You try to find out what your players are gonna respond to," Parcells explained. "You might even do something that stings him. You're just trying to see what type of competitor he is."

After six days, Perkins, who rarely smiled, approached Parcells with a huge grin.

"I came to camp wondering if he was everything he was cracked up to be," Ray said.

"So?" Parcells asked.

"Well, he's everything he's cracked up to be."

"No shit," Bill laughed.

In the first team scrimmage Taylor had sacked the team quarterback four or five times. As one Redskins offensive lineman eventually put it, "No human being should be 6'4", 245, and run a 4.5 forty."

Parcells wrote of Taylor that he did not know a lot about football. He didn't know about pass coverage or many other nuances. But he was very willing, and he was a fast learner. He was willing to listen. According to Parcells, "He was arrogant as hell on the football field, but not off it."

Parcells also gave credit to Carson, Van Pelt, and Kelley for helping to coach the young talented player. "They all liked the kid because even though he was a thoroughbred, they could see he was a worker, too," Parcells said.

But what neither Parcells, nor Taylor himself, nor the rest of the team realized, was that Parcells would change the way defenses schemed, and Taylor himself, through his play, would forever change the way the game was played. This was a historic moment.

Parcells saw his new toy and decided he could use him like a knife. If Harry Carson was the quarterback of the defense, calling the coverages and defenses, Taylor was its most feared warrior, almost more a weapon than a player. By the mid-1980s, as competing coaching staffs were trying to out-position Parcells and Taylor, Parcells and his coaches were inserting Taylor in numerous places, using him as an offensive weapon. Now offenses were defending against one particular weapon.

"By November 18, 1985, when the Giants went into Robert F. Kennedy

Stadium in Washington D.C., to play the Redskins, opposing teams have been taking to lining up their players in new and creative ways simply to deal with him," Michael Lewis wrote in *The Blind Side*.

"The game of football evolved and here was one cause of its evolution, a new kind of athlete doing a new kind of thing. All by himself, Lawrence Taylor altered the environment and forced opposing coaches and players to adapt," Lewis continued. "Parcells became a connoisseur of the central nervous system of opposing quarterbacks." As Lewis later described it, "Taylor demanded not just a tactical response but an explanation."

Taylor not only earned Rookie of the Year honors in 1981, he was also the defensive player of the year in the NFL. It was the only time one player earned both awards in the same season in the league's history.

Parcells had created, in essence, a new instrument of war. It was a new position in NFL defenses, and a host of teams attempted to copy it, most notably years later at the Kansas City Chiefs with Derrick Thomas and the New England Patriots with Andre Tippett.

"Parcells believed Taylor's greatness was an act of will, a refusal to allow the world to understand him as anything less than great," Lewis wrote.

"That's why I loved him so much," Parcells said. "He responded to anything that threatened his status."

As Lewis astutely pointed out, Taylor and Parcells, especially, were happiest when Taylor rushed from the defense's right side. "The biggest reason I put him over there," Bill Parcells said, "is that the right side is the quarterback's blind side, since most quarterbacks are right-handed. And no one wants to get his ass knocked off from the back side."

As Taylor himself rightly pointed out, it wasn't called the blind side until after Taylor had turned it into the NFL's deadliest corner.

— —

In his first few years, Parcells applied all that he had learned in his previous stops. And he treated some players differently than others. He had a corps of people he relied on with his defense.

One of his all-time favorite people was Harry Carson.

Harold Donald Carson was born November 26, 1953, in Florence, South Carolina. Carson played at two local high schools, graduating from McClenaghan High School. Carson played for Coach Willie Jeffries at South Carolina State University from 1972–75, playing every football game his entire four years attending. He was gifted academically as well as athletically. He became the first Mid-Eastern Athletic Conference player to win defensive player of the year twice, and he helped the Bulldogs to back-to-back conference championships. In 1975, he was a first team All-American and set school records with 117 tackles and 17 sacks. For his university play, Carson was eventually inducted into the College Football Hall of Fame.

Carson was a fourth-round draft choice in the 1976 NFL Draft by the Giants. He spent all of his 13 seasons with the Giants. Carson led the team in tackles in five seasons and was its captain for ten.

A perennial Pro Bowler, Parcells challenged Carson by discussing and questioning his technique. By 1981 Parcells felt that Carson had fallen into a few bad habits. As he said in later years with the Giants, "I don't have to waste my time talking to Harry because he's gotten to the point where he just knows," Parcells said. Parcells considered Carson to be one of the all-time great linebackers—period. Parcells might only say two or three things to him all season—technique things.

Bill Parcells insisted that Carson stand at his side during the singing of the national anthem for good luck.

"Carson did the one thing no defensive player ever gets enough credit for, even though it's the first thing every defensive coach talks about with his team every week: he defended the run," *Sports Illustrated* scribe Peter King wrote.

"He had to walk down that tunnel on a lot of icy Sundays in the Meadowlands when he wasn't feeling pretty good, probably wondering how he was going to get through these games he had to play," Parcells said. "But he was there for all of us, most every Sunday for upwards of 12 years."

Parcells challenged Taylor. Taylor responded to criticism and chiding like no one else. He had an ego, and his ego needed to be satisfied. One of Parcells' favorite stories was that for two games in a row, Taylor was consistently double- and triple-teamed by opposing offenses. He wasn't making sacks and was getting few tackles. The rest of the defense was having an excellent game, and New York won both contests. But the press, not knowing the strategies being employed, kept asking what was wrong with Taylor. Parcells egged Taylor on for an entire week and called him, "What's the matter with Taylor" to his face and in front of the team. Taylor was visibly upset by the taunting by the end of the week. On the third game, the opposing team did not adopt the same tactics, and Taylor had one of his signature games, sacking the quarterback and knocking him out of the game, causing two fumbles, and recovering one himself, making tremendous tackles and creating complete havoc. After the game, Taylor said to Parcells as he practically ran him over, "Tell you what, Coachy. They ain't gonna ask you, 'What's the matter with?!!!'"

— —

Parcells quickly established the Giants as one of the elite linebacking organizations in the NFL. And the players responded to media demands. The linebacking corps was the bright spot of an otherwise anemic football team. The corps, composed of Carson, Brad Van Pelt, Brian Kelley, and Lawrence Taylor is, even today, widely considered one of the best defensive combos in NFL history. Together, they were the Big Blue Wrecking Crew, one of the best group of linebackers ever assembled in the NFL:

Strongside linebacker Brad Van Pelt, 5x Pro Bowl selection
Inside linebacker Harry Carson, 9x Pro Bowl selection, Hall of Fame
Weakside linebacker Lawrence Taylor, 10x Pro Bowl selection, Hall of Fame
Weakside linebacker Brian Kelley, no Pro Bowl selections

The self-described linebackers even incorporated themselves. They created a 16"x20" color poster of the four players on a bulldozer, wearing hard hats and looking mean. According to an article in *The New York Times*, the profits from the $5 poster became "pocket money" for the linebackers.

The four men developed bonds of friendship that lasted long after their football careers ended. They talked on the phone frequently and got together several times each year to play golf, sign autographs, attend charity events, and just talk.

"I feel as comfortable with [Carson, Kelley, and Taylor] as I do with my brothers. Obviously, your brothers are your brothers. But these three are probably the closest thing to them. Brian and I played 11 years together. I played nine with Harry," Brad Van Pelt told *The New York Times* in 2004. "Lawrence being the guy [he is], it didn't take long for him to fit right in and become one of the guys. I can't really explain why but they're the only three I stay close with."

Later, with the addition of Carl Banks, the Giants consolidated their reputation as a team that knew how to draft linebackers and would set an even higher standard for the organization.

— —

With Parcells' new defense and his new toys to play with, the Giants went from allowing 425 points in 1980 to allowing only 257 in 1981. They went from the 27th rated defense in the NFL to the third-ranked defense in the NFL. And with a slightly improved offense they finished 9–7 with an overtime win on December 19, 1981, over the Dallas Cowboys to win a spot in the playoffs for the first time in almost two decades.

The Giants beat the Eagles in a wild card playoff game at Philadelphia the next week only to fall to Joe Montana's 49ers a week later in San Francisco. The Giants had become one of the best defensive teams in the NFL in a year under Parcells.

At the end of the year, Carson and Taylor both went to the Pro Bowl.

The 1982 season started off with two losses and a walk-out by the Player's Union. Games did not resume until November 21, when the Giants lost their third straight. Then they won three in a row.

On December 11, 1982, just after the Giants had beaten the Eagles 23–7, Perkins called a team meeting. Perkins was leaving. He had taken on a new job. He was going back to his alma mater, Alabama, to coach the

Crimson Tide, replacing the legendary coaching icon Paul "Bear" Bryant. Perkins' name had been mentioned as one of the possible successors for some time. The staff was in disbelief. The Giants' hierarchy decided to let Perkins finish out the year. Perkins mentioned to the assistants that one of them might be offered his job.

— —

George Bernard Young was born on September 22, 1930, in Baltimore, Maryland. Young grew up living over a bakery owned by his mother's side of the family. His father had a bar across the street. He grew up in a tough Irish-Catholic neighborhood. In such a setting, he grew up tough and street smart. He was a standout Catholic high school football player just north of Baltimore in Maryland.

He was a starting defensive tackle for three years straight at Bucknell University, including team captain in 1951. He was named to the Little All-America first team and All-East first team in his senior year. Selected to play in the Blue-Gray game, Young was selected by the Dallas Texans in the 1952 NFL Draft.

Young coached briefly at his high school alma mater before becoming the head coach of the Baltimore City College football team. In 15 years his teams won six Maryland Scholastic Association championships. Two of his athletes made it to the NFL, tight end Tom Gatewood and running back John Sykes. Young especially loved teaching; history and political science were his favorites. Young was a brilliant scholar and completed two Master's degrees, one from Johns Hopkins University and one from Loyola College.

Young had accumulated a great number of successes before he came to the Giants. He was a scout, offensive line coach, director of player personnel, and offensive coordinator for the Baltimore Colts from 1968–74. He had been there for Super Bowls III (a loss to Weeb Ewbanks' Jets) and Super Bowl V (a win versus Tom Landry's Cowboys).

From there Young went on to be the director of personnel and pro scouting for the Miami Dolphins (1975–78). The Dolphins were past their three Super Bowl appearances. And following the 1974 season, the

Dolphins lost their three star offensive weapons in Larry Csonka, Jim Kiick, and Paul Warfield to the World Football League.

Miami's fortunes faded in 1976, but they won 10 or more games in four of the next five seasons. With Young at the helm of player personnel, Miami head coach Don Shula built a solid defense around a new set of stars, including linebacker A.J. Duhe and linemen Bob Baumhower and Doug Betters. The Dolphins went to the playoffs in 1978 and 1979.

Young was large in mind, girth, and intellect. And he was not easily intimidated. More often than not, it was the other way around.

Young received his job with the Giants in a most peculiar matter. The Giants remain the only franchise in the entire NFL owned by two families without either holding a majority. In fact, because of the Giants, it is written in the NFL's bylaws that one owner needs to hold some kind of majority. Since its inception, the New York Giants were owned by one family—the Maras. Owner Tim Mara was one of the wealthiest bookmakers on the East Coast when bookmaking was a legal profession. The Mara family imported Irish whiskey, owned interest in a coal company, owned the second-largest bookmaking company on the entire East Coast with betting windows at all the major race tracks in New York state, and controlled all the rights for boxing at the city's three major stadiums: Yankee Stadium, Ebbets Field, and the Polo Grounds.

Tim Mara, before and after he bought the NFL rights to New York City, promoted numerous championship boxing events in New York state. Indeed, his oldest son was married to the daughter of New York state's boxing commissioner. Tim Mara Sr. was also deeply involved in Tammany Hall politics. The Giants were run by a triumvirate of Maras—Tim, and his two sons, Jack and Wellington. After Tim Sr. and his wife's passing, it was just Jack and Wellington. And then after 1965, it was Jack's son, Tim, and his uncle who controlled the team.

While Jack and his brother had run the team incredibly well (six NFL championship appearances in the late 1950s and early 1960s), Tim and his uncle Wellington could not stand to be in the same room with one another. They fought over everything. Their bouts were legendary. In this atmosphere, the team spiraled into disarray, and the Giants lurched into a 17-year losing streak.

In 1976 the new Giants Stadium was opened in the Meadowlands. By 1978, season ticket holders had held bonfires in the parking lot, and one even hired a plane to fly above the stadium with a banner that read, "15 years of lousy football." At one point, the two owners held bizarre dueling press conferences, canceling out the others' statements.

NFL Commissioner Pete Rozelle (whose election had been engineered by the powerful Wellington Mara) then stepped in. The failing of the New York franchise was hurting television revenues (of which it had been the crown jewel 15 years prior). Their failure was, in effect, hurting the league. In private, Rozelle told the Maras that either he would engineer a peace or the NFL would sue the franchise and force a change of ownership. Both agreed to let Rozelle appoint a general manager who would have supreme powers.

That general manager was George Young. Young came in with two things: incredible power and a charge by the commissioner of the league himself to restore the once-proud franchise. Young was a no-nonsense guy and very practical. Once when he was offered a Mercedes-Benz, he passed it up, pointing to legendary Steelers owner Art Rooney. Young stated, "Mr. Rooney drove a Buick all his life. That's good enough for me."

While it rarely came across in the press, Young had a wry sense of humor. Young once said of his new job in 1979 at the Meadowlands, "It's a funny place. Everybody's named either Vinny or Whitey." And on the feud between Tim and Wellington Mara, he said, "I'm just Irish enough to know that you don't take one side or another, or they'll both turn on you."

Young's view on football was something he stated many times, "We are not in the business of well-adjusted human beings."

And the one thing Young could not abide was player's agents. "The three characteristics that I hate most in a person are arrogance, mendacity, and greed. And these guys have all three." Young was also known to refer to certain agents as "cockroaches."

In early December, Perkins had gone to Young and told him that he'd received a phone call from Alabama, and that he wanted permission to talk with Alabama. It was his lifelong dream to be their head coach. The two agreed to keep it quiet in case it didn't work out.

"Bill Parcells walked by my office, and I yelled at him to come in. We talked for two hours," Young said. "I wasn't interviewing him. I was evaluating him. In this job, you're always evaluating people. When I got to a college game or another pro game and I talk to people, I'm evaluating."

"When they had finished their two-hour talk, George Young knew that if Ray Perkins left, Bill Parcells was the man he wanted as Perkin's replacement," veteran New York sportswriter Phil Pepe wrote.

According to Pepe, once Young knew about Perkins' decision he called Parcells and told him he should finish work early and come see him. Parcells generally arrived at Giants Stadium between 5:45 and 6:15 AM every morning during the season, just after Perkins, and tried to return to his rented home in Upper Saddle River, New Jersey, for dinner by 9:00 PM.

Parcells got into work at 6:00 AM on a Tuesday to prepare for the upcoming Redskins game and was in Young's office by 6:00 PM.

"George told me that he wanted to name Bill Parcells the next coach. And he told me he wanted to name him the same day that Ray Perkins made his announcement so there wouldn't be weeks of speculation as to who was going to be the next coach," co-owner Tim Mara said.

"With Ray leaving suddenly like this, I think the most important thing for the organization now is continuity," George said to Parcells. "You must know how impressed we all are around here with the way you got the defense turned around."

Parcells was anxious. Young was a big, bald man with a high-pitched voice who moved at his own glacial pace. Parcells knew why he was in Young's office. So did Young, but Young wanted to press home the points that were important to him. Parcells waited forever for Young to spit out the words.

The two talked for four hours.

"So, do you want the job?"

"Yes," Parcells said. Parcells admitted later, "When the man offers you the one job you always wanted, I don't think you say, 'Can I get back to you later?'"

When Bill Parcells left the building that night, he was the next head coach of the New York Giants. "My first reaction when I got the job was that I was a very lucky guy. I would have done this for free. It's the job I always wanted."

But the real truth was different.

"Parcells was never Young's man," veteran pigskin scribe Bill Verigan reasoned. "Ray Perkins was Young's man and Parcells was thrust upon the GM by the abrupt resignation of Perkins. Parcells was promoted for the sake of continuity."

He drove back to his rented house in Saddle River, New Jersey. Judy was thrilled. And his daughters, Suzy, 20, Dallas, 17, and Jill, 13, were all happy for him. However, not everyone was impressed.

Bill went over his parent's house. His brother Don was also there. By now Don was a successful banker. He'd worked at Chase Manhattan Bank in New York City from 1975–81. And by 1981, he was a senior executive with Marine Midland Bank. He remained with Marine Midland until 1990.

"It wasn't the first time Don had the upper hand," Steve Politi wrote. "There was the conversation at the kitchen table in 1983, when Bill brought good news to his mother about a new job. His mother looked at Bill, then looked at Don, and sighed."

"When are you going to get a real job like your brother?" she asked.

"My main objective was to try and do it as soon in the week as possible to minimize the distraction for the Redskin game as much as possible," Young reasoned.

"The one thing I asked myself is would I make the same decision in January as I would now?" Young said. "The answer was yes, so why wait? Somehow people always think a stranger is a better guy. In Baltimore, we had a guy named Chuck Noll sitting on our staff, and we let him get away," Young said, referring to the four-time Super Bowl–winning Pittsburgh Steelers head coach.

"George Young was not going to make the same mistake the Colts made," Pepe wrote.

On December 15, 1982, it was announced that Parcells would be the next and 12th head coach of the New York Giants.

"Very few people in the world get to do what they hoped to do. I think the New York Giants for Bill Parcells are what the University of Alabama is to Ray Perkins," Parcells told the press. "My first reaction when I got the job was that I was a very lucky guy. I would have done this for free. It's the job I always wanted."

"At age 41, Parcells is like a little boy living out his dreams," *The New York Times* reported.

But the first signs of trouble were already there. Parcells was tough, but he had been a player's coach. With Perkins' ubiquitous frown everywhere, Parcells could afford to sometimes identify with his players. This relationship would eventually backfire on him.

"'He has a good relationship with players," said Harry Carson, an All-Pro linebacker. "It's not like a coach-player relationship but more man-to-man. He shoots from the hip and pulls no punches."

Carson added, "I hope success doesn't spoil him. He's easy-going and well liked. He likes to have fun, but he knows how to be serious. And he'll probably smile more than Ray."

"All right Tuna! Way to move in, Tuna, I mean, Sir Tuna!" Brian Kelley cracked during the press conference. Parcells would be Kelley's fifth head coach. Later he told reporters, "I think he's going to be a personable coach. I think he's the kind you can talk to, and he's going to be very efficient."

"He can get on you when he wants to," Lawrence Taylor added, "But if he does, it's because you're doing something wrong."

Gary Jeter, the defensive lineman, told the press that he had thought the new Giants coach would be Ron Erhardt (who'd come over that year after being fired from New England) or Bill Austin. "They had previous head coaching experience in the pros. But I can't think of a guy I have better rapport with," Jeter said of Parcells. "Most of the guys really really like him. He's a master psychologist. He's done things to get our defense up. He knows what makes Jeter click, what makes Taylor click, what makes Carson click. And it works in a positive manner. I have that much respect for him."

Some reporters questioned the timing of Perkins' announcement, the fact that Perkins wouldn't leave until the end of the year, and the coaching turnover. But many of the players talked about how the coaches that had recruited them weren't there when their time to play came. Regime changes were the norm. Consistency was not common.

The 1982 Giants went 4–5 in the strike-shortened season. The offense was now ranked 17th and the defense was ranked 8th. They were great numbers, but many people could see the Giants were near to turning it around.

It was now all on Parcells' head.

— —

THE LOST SEASON

By mid-January 1983, Parcells was already hard at work. He addressed his players in a team meeting in early January and announced the first rehire from Perkins' staff, Ron Erhardt. "There was never any doubt in my mind about him coming back, but I just wanted to know what his feelings were. I wanted to be sure we were on the same page," Parcells said. "Primarily we talked about his feelings on the offense. There's no question that I plan to give him a lot of leeway."

There was no question Erhardt had made an immediate impact on the team. He had improved the Giants offense from last to 9th in the conference.

At that time, Parcells also confirmed the rehiring of Romeo Crennel as the special team coach and Pat Hodgeson as the receivers coach.

Brad Benson remembered that Austin was not happy about Parcells' appointment. After he was announced as coach, Parcells met with lots of players one-on-one. Benson and several linemen had not been happy with Austin.

"Don't worry what's going on around here," Parcells told Benson. "It's up to me to worry about it. You're staying here. Some people who have affected your situation, they'll be gone soon." When the new season started, there was a new line coach.

"That's when I began to realize that Parcells always meant what he said," Benson recalled.

He also rehired Bill Belichick as the linebackers coach.

—–

William Stephen "Bill" Belichick was born April 16, 1952, in Nashville, Tennessee. Bill was raised in Annapolis, Maryland, where his father, Steve Belichick, was an assistant football coach at the United States Naval Academy. Bill graduated from Annapolis High School and did one year of post-graduate work at Phillips Academy in Andover, Massachusetts. After that he attended Wesleyan University in Middletown, Connecticut. Though smallish for big-time football, Belichick played center and tight end. He also played lacrosse (he was captain his senior year) and squash. He graduated in 1975 with a degree in economics.

Like his father, Belichick knew he wanted to be a coach. Belichick took a $25-per-week job as an assistant to Baltimore Colts head coach Ted Marchibroda in 1975. Marchibroda had been a quarterback for the Steelers and Cardinals, as well as having worked for the legendary George Allen, and 1975 was the first of his many years as a head coach. In 1976 he joined the Detroit Lions as their assistant special teams coach. But there was a change at the top when Rick Forzano was replaced by Tommy Hudspeth after the team started 1–3. When the new regime started in 1977, Hudspeth added tight ends and wide receivers to Belichick's coaching duties.

In 1978 Belichick went to the Denver Broncos, where he was the assistant special teams coach and a defensive assistant. There he worked for Robert "Red" Miller, a well known and successful coach. While there his eyes were wide open. Miller had turned around a laughing stock of the NFL into a powerhouse. In 1977, with their defense nicknamed the Orange Crush publicized by team PR man David Frei, the Broncos went to the Super Bowl. In 1978 the team went 10–6, wining the AFC West, with the No. 2-rated defense in the NFL. They lost in the division round of the playoffs that year, but it was the experience of a lifetime.

So when Belichick was hired by Ray Perkins, he was already a known quantity. He had studied under some very successful coaches before arriving at Newark Airport.

"It was kind of an awkward relationship because in a lot of cases I was younger than the players," Belichick explained. "Each year I was older than a couple more guys. But for a lot of years there were a bunch of players, certainly the high-profile players, who were older than I was."

Belichick was smart enough to know he couldn't gain their confidence hanging out with the players. That would just deteriorate the relationship. He'd been warned about such things by Marchibroda, Miller, and Forzano.

Being young would always be a disadvantage because in the macho world that is the NFL, the players would challenge you. Belichick knew that. His head coaches knew that.

It happened to him after he got to the Giants in 1979. In one of his first full-out team meetings, while he was trying to explain a technique, he noticed two players off to the right having a conversation. One of the players laughed and tried to gain the attention of another player.

"Belichick called the player out, and the player replied with a verbal jab of his own," bestselling sports columnist and television personality Michael Holley wrote. "Perkins was watching the exchange, but he didn't say anything. Belichick took over then."

"Shut the fuck up, all right? If you don't want to sit here then just get the fuck out of here. But this is important. Everybody else is listening."

"No more words were necessary," Holley finished. Belichick had put down the challenge, and Perkins was there to back him up. Perkins told Belichick if the players were late to his meetings then he was to fine them. That was it. Belichick was a coach, no matter how young.

There was no question that Belichick was the boy genius of the staff—young, cocky, aggressive, and a tireless Xs and Os guy. He was a film rat, a blackboard guy.

The linebackers didn't know what to make of Belichick in his first year as linebackers coach under Parcells. According to sportswriter Judy Battista, "They nicknamed him Captain Sominex back then because even when he was first tasting the success that is now the norm for him, Bill Belichick had a monotone that sent Giants linebackers to their slumber in a darkened meeting room."

But those old linebackers had to be persuaded, too. Sometimes, Carson said, "Belichick would draw plays on the board—rushing two defensive linemen and dropping nine, for example—that players thought would never work."

"We were skeptics initially, but he won us over and we bought into the system," Carson said. "As I listen to what the Patriots [today] are saying, I say that's from the playbook of Belichick and Bill Parcells. It's about team. Don't say anything to make people angry. Don't give anybody anything to write about."

When asked about Belichick as a young coach, Carson said, "There were times we didn't know if Belichick knew what he was talking about or not."

"In the beginning Parcells' and Belichick's relationship was a mutually advantageous one, and both men knew it. Each had strengths the other lacked, and they made a formidable combination in that first decade," David Halberstam wrote.

Parcells admitted later that 1983 was his toughest year, even more so than the year he wasn't even in football. It was a "nightmare," according to Parcells

However, there were some good things. Parcells invited Mickey Corcoran to the practices, as well as his father. Parcells quoted his father to the players all the time.

"When I first became coach of the Giants, Vince Jr.'s kids were ball boys for me," Parcells said. Joe Lombardi is currently a coaching member of the New Orleans Saints under Parcells' former assistant and current head coach Sean Payton.

"You're not on scholarship any more," Parcells barked at his new charges in the first minicamp in April. "No one's going to wake you up. But just like any other guy in a production business, I'm interested in production and reliability. I don't want guys who I have to get out of jail or don't know where they are or any of that business."

Bill's father, Charles Parcells, also attended that first day's workout. He stood at his son's side. "The things I told my players, it comes from my father," Bill Parcells said. "He'd grab me by the shirt collar and say, 'Here's what you've got to do.'"

— —

In August, before the season, the team went on a trip after their pre-season game with the Pittsburgh Steelers. "The linebacker Harry Carson led a contingent of 45 Giant players and officials today to visit the ailing Doug Kotar. Kotar, 32 years old, the Giants' fourth-leading career rusher with 3,380 yards, was stricken with an inoperable brain tumor last summer," UPI reported. "Among those who visited Kotar's home 20 miles southwest of Pittsburgh, were the team's owner, Wellington Mara, and General Manager George Young. A bus carrying 45 people, including players, two team chaplains, and several coaches pulled up in front of Kotar's ranch-style home in Canonsburg about 4:30 PM. The players filled up the brick home, where Kotar greeted them sitting up in a hospital bed and wearing a blue Giants jersey." Donna, his wife, offered the visitors ham sandwiches, beer, and coffee.

Kotar's wavering health was a great distraction that year for his teammates.

That year Cormac Carney graduated from UCLA. He had been to and won a Rose Bowl, and he set several school records as a kick returner and a receiver. "Not only did he help begin my career," Carney said, referring to his Air Force days, "but also helped end my career."

"I was at my physical best at UCLA. My body had taken some hard knocks after three years of major college ball," Carney said. "I had a terrible workout at the combines. A horrible performance. It was very humbling, and I was disappointed."

"I was worn down by the time I got to the Giants. The older I got the more I felt I didn't want to go over the middle. I was losing my physical and mental edge."

But Parcells had remembered Carney from his days at Air Force, and Cormac was a free agent coming to the Giants camp. "I guess I didn't make much of an impression because I got cut after two games," Carney said of his preseason pro attempt.

"I'm going to cut you now, that way there's still time to try another team," Parcells told him.

"That was a huge wake-up call. Had I not got cut, I would never have gotten into Harvard, or met my wife, or had my children. It was Bill who started me off when he cut me." Instead of football, Carney went onto a brilliant law career as a presidentially appointed federal judge. "He had a tremendous influence on my life in so many ways. He was tough. He was demanding. He didn't play any favorites when I was with him. If there was a softer side, we never saw it."

〜〜

Parcells was up against several things. If he was enthusiastic about his job, not many members of the team were enthusiastic about theirs. There were a lot of disgruntled players, who, in their time with the Giants, had played for three or four coaches—all of them posting losing records with the Giants.

The Giants also had a major drug problem. "Parcells took over a dirty team in 1983. His methods might have offended some people, but he cleaned the Giants up before the NFL took over the drug program in July 1986," Bill Verigan wrote. It was something even the press did not want to disclose at the time.

"More than a dozen guys were being tested regularly," said a former player who did not want to be identified.

"I think it was my second year coaching there as head coach with the Giants [that] I put myself in a place called Fair Oaks in Summit, New Jersey, as an outpatient," Bill Parcells admitted years later. "I wanted to find out exactly what the problems were and how they were going to be treated. I felt that if I wanted to know as much as I could about drugs and how to help my players, then I better learn everything about it."

Parcells explained that he worked with a woman there named Jane Jones, who also counseled several Giants players. She taught him a lot, but he admitted while he tried to do some things, he wished he could have done a lot more. In the end, he tried as hard as he could to understand how drugs affected people—if he didn't he felt it was going to cost the careers of himself, his players, and his coaches.

One of the most difficult aspects of the upcoming season was that Parcells had yet to divorce himself from the fact that he could no longer be friends with his players. "I think Bill related to his players his first year as head coach much in the way when he was an assistant. That's tough to do. You can't be pals with the players," Dave Jennings said.

"When he was defensive coordinator we talked to him as if he was one of us. Sometimes we would even curse at him," Carson remembered. Carson knew they couldn't continue to talk to Parcells like he was still the defensive coordinator. He knew the young guys would take their cues from watching him and Martin. So Carson and Martin tried to alter the way they communicated with Bill. This added stress to a unit that had seen success and then watched its coach become one step removed.

That was the good part of the season. It quickly unraveled from there. The team was 2–2 after its first four games.

Bob Ledbetter, the offensive backfield coach of the Giants, had been hospitalized since September 24, his 49th birthday, after he suffered a stroke at his home in Northport, Long Island. Mr. Ledbetter, a burly man known for his ability to motivate players, had coached for 24 years. Frank Litsky wrote of Ledbetter, "He joined the Giants this year after six years as offensive backfield coach of the Jets. He helped make Freeman McNeil and Bruce Harper outstanding runners for the Jets."

As if their record wasn't enough of a distraction, Ledbetter's health continued to haunt the team. They would go on to lose three more.

Vexed much they way Perkins was with his quarterback situation, Parcells was in no better a position. Phil Simms, who had come from Morehead State, who had shown absolute flashes of brilliance, had been injury prone his entire five-year career.

Simms had been injured in 1981, missing the last five games and the playoffs in that season, and then he missed the entire 1982 season. Brunner would be the starter in 1983.

When the Giants ran into Philadelphia and were trailing in the sixth game of the season, Parcells pulled Brunner and replaced him with Simms, who immediately lit up the board with some spectacular pass plays. Several series later, Simms' hand hit an opposing player's helmet while he was throwing a pass, resulting in a compound fracture of his thumb. He was gone for the season.

Parcells admitted this gamble was a bad one. Not only had he crushed

Brunner's confidence, but now Simms was gone and he had to put Brunner back out there. Parcells knew he had shaken his offense's confidence in Brunner.

The Giants lost that game to Philadelphia. The awful coda to the Eagles debacle was that Bob Ledbetter had died the Friday night before the game at St. John's Episcopal Hospital in Smithtown, Long Island.

At around the same time, Parcells father, Chubby, needed open heart surgery. In those days, many of the procedures available today were much more invasive surgeries. Chubby's prognosis was not good.

In the meantime, there was an army of injured players going through the training room doors. The disaster was mounting.

They lost to Kansas City the next week, and they tied the St. Louis Cardinals a week later. In the next three weeks they fell to Dallas, Detroit, and Washington.

In November, Ida Parcells was diagnosed with cancer. She was given a month to live and was hospitalized by late November.

On November 20, the Giants beat the Eagles for only their third win and followed that with a loss to the Raiders to end the month. December was no better, as it began with losses to St. Louis and Seattle.

And then the roof caved in.

"General Manager George Young angrily refused to comment on a CBS-TV report that the Giants might dismiss Parcells after his first season as head coach and replace him with Howard Schnellenberger, the University of Miami coach," *The New York Times* reported.

Young angrily protested the report, but the rumors swirling around the Giants were so bad that Schnellenberger (who had turned around the University of Miami program into the No. 1 college football team of 1983) actually called his own press conference for 1:00 PM the next day to quell the various rumors himself.

"The Associated Press...reached his wife, Beverlee. She said she did not know why the conference had been called. The CBS report also said the New Jersey Generals were considering Schnellenberger as head coach, but a spokesman for the Generals last night said the team's owner, Donald J. Trump, denied Schnellenberger was a candidate for the job and said a new coach would be named within two weeks," *The New York*

Times continued. Even Joe Paterno's name had come up in the swirl of rumors surrounding the Giants.

The CBS report was filed by none other than Jimmy the Greek Snyder a sports analyst on the CBS football show, where he said that Schnellenberger had admitted to him that several teams had reached out the Howard.

"I knew the ownership was disgruntled with the way the season turned out. Obviously, Young was disgruntled with me because I trusted the information I was getting," Parcells said.

"It was the talk everywhere that Howard Schnellenberger was going to replace Parcells," Brad Benson remembered. "So, Parcells had a parking place down in the tunnel, and over his name I put white trainer's tape with 'Schnellenberger' written on it."

Schnellenberger eventually left Miami (where he'd turned around the program in the years 1979 to 1983), but not for the Giants. He went to the USFL, but that opportunity fizzled, and two years later Schnellenberger found himself coaching the Louisville Cardinals college football team.

In the meantime, Parcells had reached out to Al Davis. He called Davis for advice. Davis, who according to Parcells always had time for young coaches, told him to just keep coaching your team. Parcells has repeated the mantra Davis taught him, "You got problems? Nobody cares. You just figure out a way to win on Sunday, or then you'll have problems. You just beat those guys." Davis listened carefully and mentored the young Parcells.

Of course, there was no one that Parcells could have picked to gall Giants owner Wellington Mara more than Davis. The two had been bitter enemies in the years before the NFL/AFL merger.

It was at this time Parcells got a phone call from Dan Henning. Henning told Parcells that if he was fired, there would be a job waiting for him in Atlanta. Henning asked Parcells, "What's the worst that could happen?"

Parcells countered, "I could get fired!"

To which Henning replied, "So what?" And they both laughed.

To add to this Zeffirelli-esque atmosphere, the young, tough, hardworking Doug Kotar died the day before the final game of the season with Washington. Kotar, who "had fought an inoperable malignant brain tumor for 16 months, died in his sleep yesterday at Montefiore Hospital in Pittsburgh. He was 32 years old," sportswriter Frank Litsky wrote.

The Giants played with verve at the beginning of the game, but the team did not hold up and lost the final contest 31–22. The Giants finished the season 3–12–1.

Doug Kotar was buried on the 19th. Carson, Kelley, and Van Pelt attended.

Then Ida died before December was over.

By the end of December, the show had gone on long enough even for the sportswriters, whose lives are made so much easier with this kind of circus.

"By keeping the pressure on Parcells, perhaps Young has taken some of the pressure off himself," Bill Verigan wrote in *Sports Illustrated*. "It's time Young started to feel the squeeze. Parcells played with what Young gave him…. Unlike Young, Parcells admits he made mistakes. But Young seems to be turning Parcells into a scapegoat by refusing to reveal the future of the coaching staff."

"It was a big mess," Parcells said. "Don't think it didn't cross my mind to throw up my hands and say, 'Who needs this?'"

The truth was that after a disastrous season Parcells deserved to be on the proverbial hot seat, and he knew it. He would say years later, "It took the threat of losing my job to get me to say, 'I'm doing this my way.'"

— —

"My guys." His way.

"He came away scarred," Young told the press. "But after the season I was most impressed with his evaluation of what had taken place and with his plan to remedy it."

Parcells had seen the abyss and survived. But there might not be any more tree branches to hold onto in the next season. He had to act, and act deliberately.

But before any of that he had to bury his father, who died in February of 1984.

"My father worked for U.S. Rubber for 28 years. And at the end of his career—and he was pretty well up in the company, I'm talking about, say, the top 15 people in the corporation—and just when he could have made it to the top two or three, a new president came in the company. As with those corporate changes, someone else was chosen to do the things that would have put my father into a very big bonus profit-sharing group," Parcells remembered. "He was bitter. So he retired when he was 55 instead of staying with it."

Chubby was a very popular man in his community, and even to this day there is the Chubby Parcells Gin Rummy Tournament held in late December at the Hackensack Golf Club as part of their Christmas week celebrations.

Parcells loved and cherished his father. And for the rest of his coaching career, he would channel Chubby's humorous and wise proverbs. Generations of young men have heard Chubby Parcells' clever bits of advice and admonition. For Parcells, the countless hours spent by his mother's and father's bedsides were now over.

Parcells now returned to his routine. Up by 5:30 AM. At the office around 6:00 or 6:30.

Parcells was facing a near insurrection. VanPelt, Carson, and Kelley all wanted out, and Taylor had been infected by their unhappiness. Simms, since he had been demoted, demanded a trade. There was rampant drug use (one such instance resulted in a botched kickoff return with a ball bouncing off a player's head in a game), and there was outright complaining.

Parcells cut, traded, or retired 22 of the men on his squad that year—a hefty percentage. Healthy or injured, productive or not, popular or not, no matter their relationship with the Mara family themselves, Bill got rid of anyone who wasn't one of, what he termed, "My guys."

He was tired of the injury parade of the previous season, and so the Giants hired Johnny Parker as their conditioning coach. Parcells reasoned that his players wouldn't get so injured if they were in better condition, and they wouldn't fade in the second part of the season.

Parcells also figured that the weight room he insisted on would cost Wellington and Tim Mara about $250,000—a considerable amount, especially in those days. Parcells made his pitch to Young, who made the pitch to the ownership, and the weight room was built. Parcells commended Parker, who turned the weight room into a hybrid of clubhouse, frat house, and engine of hard work. He also credited Parker with building better team relationships, which turned out to be a bonus Parcells hadn't accounted for in his plan. Guys hung out in the weight room and became better friends.

Before the season began, Brunner was traded to Denver, thus stabilizing the quarterback position within the club. Simms would be the starter. Parcells was worried about Simms. Parcells reasoned that Simms had been so oft injured in part because the line play was suspect and in part because the Giants had no ground game. But with the addition of a running game with Joe Morris and the slow building of an offensive line, protection eventually got better. And with Simms embracing the strength and conditioning program, things were about to get a whole lot more stable.

"Simms was great," Parcells wrote in his autobiography. "He never bitched about protection." Parcells was impressed with Simms' ability to take a hit and get right back up.

There were many more personnel moves that season. Leonard Marshall and Jim Burt both joined George Martin on the defensive line. Jeter was gone.

In Burt's rookie year, he was not happy just to make the team. He wanted in the game. But he was not getting a chance to play. "There was one game that I thought I should get in and wasn't," Burt said. "Parcells was the defensive coordinator then. I was walking up and down the sideline, and then, I don't know what got into me. I walked up and gave Bill a forearm in the back and knocked him onto the field."

On an extremely hot day in Washington, Parcells had told the defensive lineman before the game that he would rotate them all through. Burt had less patience than Parcells. "After only the third play, Burt started yelling and then knocked him down," Peter Alfano reported for *The New York Times*.

"This is not a game for well-adjusted people," Parcells explained.

"I thought I was going to get cut. I got into the game on the next series, but Bill didn't talk to me the rest of the year," Burt said.

In the end, Brad Benson and Jim Burt became Parcells' favorite whipping boys. Parcells couldn't beat up the whole team, but he could pound on these two guys, and he knew the rest of the team was watching. He knew the two of them could take it. He knew they responded better when he did.

It got to be so bad with Benson, who was constantly complaining to his peers that Parcells picked on him too much, that Benson claimed one day he would slug Parcells. In his third season with Parcells, Benson walked into the weight room completely upset.

"Fucking Parcells," Benson grumbled.

"What do you mean, Brad. He didn't yell at you today?" someone asked sarcastically.

"Exactly, he's writing me off!"

By this time Parcells had become a master motivator who was good at button-holing players on the field and in the locker room, but he was getting smarter and better at it.

"Honestly, there are times I use the media," Parcells admitted. "Sometimes I will use them to send a message to my team. Rather than bending the players' ears all the time, man-to-man, I might say something to the media early in the week like, 'If we don't throw the ball better this week, we're not going to win.' The quarterback sees that and you can see in his eyes the rest of the week he is pissed and wants to prove something."

"I never use the media if I have a problem with a player. When that happens I bring him into my office and we talk about it directly," Parcells concluded.

— —

The Giants had three solid guys in the defensive back field with Terry Kinard, Perry Williams, and Kenny Hill. Rob Carpenter, Joe Morris, and Butch Woolfolk were still vying for playing time. It was running back by committee. Zeke Mowatt, a solid pass catcher and blocker, became the starting tight end. And with the addition of Chris Godfrey and Karl Nelson, the Giants eventually started to put together a decent offensive line.

And it didn't hurt that there were some new, faster receivers on the team. The receiving corps now had Mowatt, Lionel Manuel, Bobby Johnson, Earnest Grey, Byron Williams, and Phil McConkey, who would all make contributions in the passing game.

Parcells ran out on to the field with his team for that first game of the season. Parcells' placing of faith in Simms was immediately rewarded as the quarterback threw for 409 yards against the hated Philadelphia Eagles. Simms completed four touchdown passes as the Giants survived the Eagles 28–27. The running game produced 109 yards of rushing offense, but no back made any real impact.

It was a sign of things to come. Parcells reasoned that the 1984 season, which was Simms' coming-out party, was a result of Simms' frustration. He was going to let it all hang out in 1984. "He didn't give a shit; he was going to show everybody what they had been missing in those seasons when he'd been hurt."

The Giants were more economical in their next game, as they scored three offensive touchdowns on three Phil Simms passes and linebacker Andy Headen tossed in an 81-yard fumble return for a touchdown as the Giants easily downed the vaunted Dallas Cowboys 28–7.

The Giants struggled to a 4–4 record at the season half, with Philadelphia avenging their loss of the previous year. But by mid-season, the team had not only exceeded the previous year's win total, but the team was beginning to gel. And people were noticing.

By the ninth game of the season, a home win against the Washington Redskins, Joe Morris was getting more carries and he began sharing the load with Rob Carpenter. Tony Galbreath was the third-down back. And for the second half of the season, the Giants finally had a running game.

They swept the Cowboys that year but lost to Tampa Bay, making them 6–5. Then they won their next three and ran their record to 9–5. The Giants were actually winning.

They ended the season with two disappointing losses to the St. Louis Cardinals and the New Orleans Saints.

After the Saints loss, Harry Carson said he was going to church.

"I think everybody should go to church," he said with a weary smile.

"Unless he knew an all-day church somewhere, he found some other way of keeping busy yesterday afternoon to avoid checking whether there was any football season left for him and the Giants. The 31-year-old linebacker, who fears his days are over with the Giants just when they are becoming a winning team, would love to play in the wild-card round of the playoffs next Sunday," Frank Litsky wrote in *The New York Times*.

For the Giants to have a winning record was something to cheer about. But they needed help to get into the playoffs. First, they needed the Redskins to defeat the Cardinals. And that happened. Then they had to wait for *Monday Night Football*, where they needed the Miami Dolphins to put the final knife in the Dallas Cowboys.

"A long weekend of wishful thinking and crossed fingers ended on a stunning note for the Giants tonight when the Miami Dolphins scored two touchdowns in the closing minutes to beat the Dallas Cowboys 28–21, a victory that put the Giants in the playoffs," sportswriter Michael Janofsky wrote in *The New York Times*. "The Dolphins' victory, in the 224th and final game of the regular season, enabled the Giants, whose season ended Saturday in a loss to the New Orleans Saints, to win the last of 10 playoff berths."

"The Giants are in the playoffs. Roll that around your tongue a few times," Bill Verigan wrote in *Sports Illustrated*. "One man deserves the most credit for getting the Giants in the playoffs, for his courage and convictions. The man is Bill Parcells, and he is the single most important factor in the Giants success."

"We played hard and we stuck together, and it all started with what Bill instilled in us in training camp," Simms told the press.

"The biggest reason for our success is the job Bill Parcells did as our coach," punter Dave Jennings added.

"We made some progress," Parcells told the press. "But I'm not under any illusions. Generally, the team was together, and I'm glad they were able to gain a measure of respect. The players deserve a chance to win."

"The Giants' final regular-season record of 9–7 seems just right," sportswriter Frank Litsky opined. "Anything less, such as 8–8, would not reflect the team's vast improvement. Anything more, such as 10–6 or 11–5, might create a false illusion."

Litsky said the team was obviously better than last year's model. They had shown progress. "They have climbed from the lower rungs through the pack." He also pointed out that they had the ability to beat the better teams and rose to that occasion several times. But they lacked the experience to consistently vanquish teams they were better than. "Because of that inconsistency, they do not yet rank with such elite teams as the San Francisco 49ers, the Miami Dolphins, or the Washington Redskins."

Even years later Parcells bristled at the mention that the team had "backed into the playoffs." "We won enough games to make it, and that's all that counts," he countered.

Litsky also opined, "Their turnaround is a result of the single-mindedness of their coach, Bill Parcells. He got rid of players he did not think could win, he took chances on young and inexperienced players, and he made his team believe in itself and its ability to be competitive. Good job by Parcells."

— —

The wild card game was a Sunday game that matched the Giants against the Los Angeles Rams.

"We're not in this for the fun of it. This is serious business. We have a job to do, and we're going to go out there and do that job," Parcells said. "Nobody gives you any medals for trying hard. You're supposed to try hard. Only the results count. The bottom line. If a guy isn't ready to play a game like this, he'd better find another line of work."

The game plan was easy—stop the Rams' raging running back Eric Dickerson. Dickerson and the Rams had bludgeoned the Giants 33–12 in the regular season at Los Angeles. After that beating, the New York defense knew that it was them against the Los Angeles ground attack—that was the whole game. In the fourth quarter, the Giants made a goal-line stand against Dickerson and the Rams, and held on to defeat the Rams 16–13 at Anaheim Stadium, avenging the earlier regular-season loss.

The Giants woke up on Christmas in Fresno, California, preparing for their next game versus the San Francisco 49ers. But Giants employees were working. The coaches had stayed up past midnight on Christmas Eve, working on plans and schemes. Kim Kolbe, Coach Bill Parcells' secretary, had stayed up until 11:30 PM, typing up the game plans and making copies. And Parcells himself had got up early Christmas morning trying to get the scouting report ready.

"It doesn't seem like Christmas to me," Parcells said. "But I would rather be here than home."

The 49ers had come into Giants Stadium and beaten the Giants 31–10. Parcells said of the game that he would have turned it off after the score of 21–0, but he had to watch the whole thing. The 49ers, with Joe Montana, Roger Craig, Dwight Clark, Freddie Solomon, and a slew of other weapons were one of the upper-echelon teams of the NFL that season, finishing with a regular season record of 15–1. The 49ers outscored their opponents 110-to-29 in the first quarter that season. They had scored three times in the first quarter in their first meeting with the Giants.

The 49ers drove the ball on their first possession down the length of the field and scored a touchdown to start the game. On the ensuing drive, the Giants, who were driving the ball well, turned it over when Simms' pass was deflected by the defensive line. Safety Ronnie Lott intercepted the ball and returned it to the Giants' 12-yard line. Russ Francis scored on a pass from Montana. The rest of the game was academic. The real New York highlight was Harry Carson's interception of a Joe Montana pass and return for a touchdown. The San Francisco 49ers took the game 21–10. It was the second time of seven that the Giants would face the 49ers in the playoffs. The 49ers went on to club the Bears 23–0 before defeating the Miami Dolphins 38–16 in the Super Bowl.

"'We had our chances," Parcells said. "We were down there three or four times, but we couldn't get the ball in the end zone."

Parcells had accomplished what few before him had done. He'd waded mid-way into the playoffs. The Giants had a great season.

— —

"On the eve of the National Football League draft, the Giants announced yesterday they had negotiated a multiyear extension of the contract of

Bill Parcells, their head coach. This will be the last year of Parcells' original three-year contract," *The New York Times* reported on April 30, 1985. "Neither Parcells nor the Giants would discuss the terms of the extension, though Robert Fraley, Parcells' lawyer, told The Associated Press, 'It will guarantee him security for more than two years and less than a lifetime.'"

The training camp was less eventful than the previous year's edition. The biggest thing of note was Phil Simms holding out for a contract extension.

"I was a hold out when training camp started. Actually [David] Fishof was a hold out," Simms admitted later, referring to his agent. "Parcells called me at home the first night."

"How close are you?"

"We're getting pretty close, Bill."

"How much have they offered you?" Parcells asked.

"I was embarrassed talking about money with him," Simms said.

"Well, it's a lot," Simms told Parcells.

"Well, how much is it?" Parcells insisted. Simms finally told him.

"My God, Simms! How much money do you want?!"

Simms admitted that Parcells had made him feel guilty, and he was itching to get to camp. His agent told him he was a terrible client. Simms said he was driving his agent and his wife crazy. Simms reported two days late after signing a $3.8 million, five-year contract. He was not the highest-paid quarterback in the league, but it was a solid contract.

The Giants brought in Bart Oates from the USFL to the Giants. He would be the new center. And Parcells cut long-time favorite punter Dave Jennings for Sean Landeta another USFL player. Parcells was obviously choked up by the decision in front of the press. Jennings immediately caught on with the neighboring Jets.

Parcells said of his decision, "The toughest cut I've ever made with the Giants." Parcells admitted he was happy when Jennings was picked up by the Jets.

The Giants went 5–0 in preseason. Parcells pushed his team harder.

The Giants beat the Eagles twice in four weeks and raced out to a 3–1 start. Then they dropped two, one to the Dallas Cowboys and one to the

Cincinnati Bengals, before going on a four-game winning streak in late October and early November.

By now Phil Simms was a on his way to a Pro Bowl season, and Joe Morris was on his way to a 1,300-yard season. By the end of the year, five Giants were selected to the Pro Bowl.

"We were very close to being an outstanding team," Parcells thought.

The Washington Redskins remained one of their toughest opponents. Before the first game against the Redskins, in late October, Parcells needled the affable prankster and nose tackle Jim Burt.

"Parcells came into the locker room and sought out Burt. He started giving him the needle," Harry Carson remembered.

"That Jeff Bostic [Redskin offensive guard] is really playing well," Parcells said to Burt. "If you don't do the right stuff, he's gonna hand your ass to you."

"He would make little comments away from Burt, but always so Burt could hear them," Carson continued. "For example, he would come over to me and say, 'You better be ready. I think Bostic is going to eat Burt for lunch.'"

Burt had a great game. And at the end of the game, he approached team captain Carson.

"That cocksucker, I really want to get him," Burt said to Carson.

"So Carson and Burt both got a bucket of Gatorade, and when Parcells took his headset off at the end of the game, they dumped it on him. With Carson involved, it was more of a prank than payback. This was the first time they dumped Gatorade on Parcells. No one even wrote about it when it first happened. But in 1986, it would become a whole new thing.

On November 18, 1985, the Giants played the Washington Redskins, one of their toughest opponents. Every time they played the Redskins, Parcells would harangue Taylor all week. He would say that coach Joe Gibbs was telling his players that Taylor was all washed up. Or that they would block him with three men again and he wouldn't do anything. Parcells knew how to push Taylor's buttons.

Down in Washington, though, Gibbs was diagramming every play, always taking into account where No. 56 was. "If you looked at our overhead projector or our chalkboard," Joe Theismann said, "all the other Giants players were Xs and Os. Lawrence was the only one who had a number: 56."

This was the night Lawrence Taylor broke free and raced to the quarterback—nothing new there. This was the infamous Monday night game. When he sacked Joe Theismann, there was a loud noise. Taylor had snapped Theismann's leg in two. The compound fracture was spurting blood onto the field. The irony was that Jay Schroeder, the back-up quarterback, came in and won the game for the Redskins. Even Parcells commended Schroeder for his play.

The Giants finished the season 10–6 in 1985. They finished second on the NFC East behind the Dallas Cowboys. They had the fifth best defense and the sixth-rated offense in the NFL and were not considered a team to be reckoned with.

Throughout 1985 Parcells talked with Mickey Corcoran often. He called Al Davis occasionally, as well. Parcells' relationship with Young was professional. Young would not allow anything else. As Parcells was always happy to tell anyone who asked, Young and he were never going to go out to dinner and have a few laughs. Their relationship was strictly professional.

"I think the main thing that I can say that worked well for George and myself was that philosophically—and the personnel acquisition— we never really had any strong difference of opinion about what to try to do," Parcells said. "Now obviously there's an individual thing here or there that we discussed and maybe one of us thought one thing and the other thought another. But overall the philosophy of what we were trying to do and how we were trying to build a team and the critical factors for the players that were going to be on the team, we were very, very much on the same page on that, along with the personnel department, which obviously he was in charge of."

Parcells also acknowledged the work of the scouting department as being a major factor in his success in that period.

"The scouts and the front office people were bringing me the type of players that they knew I would like. They knew I wanted to work with a certain style of player, and we tried to fit that into the philosophy that we were using. And when you're there for awhile, they get used to knowing what you're looking for and they're able to get it for you," Parcells continued.

In that year, John Madden, Super Bowl winning coach and television analyst, said, "I've always felt this was a game of people, not charts and figures, and that's how Bill coaches."

On a personal level, Parcells was very honest. "I don't have anything concerning football at my house. My wife does not understand a lot about football, but I know she feels the pressure of winning when it's on this visible level. I know I am a very subdued individual when we've lost, and it affects her and I am sad that it does. My youngsters in school are from time to time the recipients of verbal abuse because of the way the team is playing, and that's not fair."

One of Parcells' most famous comments about his wife was that she didn't know if the football itself was pumped up with feathers or air. The season was at an end, and Christmas was coming.

In 1985, it was the Giants who opened their presents at home on Christmas day. The 49ers were the traveling Wild Card team that year.

"The Giants played a magnificent game on defense today, and their offense, especially the line, did almost everything it had to do. The result was a 17–3 thrashing of the San Francisco 49ers in the National Conference wild-card playoff game," Frank Litsky wrote in *The New York Times*. "This was the Giants' first playoff game at home since 1962. The victory on this chilly afternoon put them into the conference semifinals next Sunday against the mighty Bears in Chicago."

The build-up to the Giants vs. Bears divisional playoff was intense. It pitted two of the best defenses in the NFL against one another. The Bears were having an incredible season with a 15–1 record, having only been beaten by Dan Marino and the Dolphins in a Monday night game.

The game itself was anticlimactic. The Giants took their opening drive and were producing very well when Rob Carpenter fumbled the ball. Later, the winds whipped through Soldier Field and pushed the ball while Landeta was kicking. Instead of shanking the ball, Landeta whiffed completely, the Bears picked up the fumbled ball and raced in for a touchdown.

"The wind just blew it," the Giants' punter said. "I did everything normal, but when I dropped the ball, I saw it moving. I tried to swing my leg into it. I missed it, or maybe I grazed it with my foot."

When the punter returned to the sideline, an angry Parcells asked him what happened.

"I missed it," Sean Landetta said.

"You what?!" an astounded Parcells said.

"I don't know about that. That's hard to do, what happened there," Parcells said after, still angry.

Later, the Giants drove the ball only to drop a touchdown pass in the end zone. From there the game was essentially over. Once the Bears had the lead, Mike Ditka, the Chicago coach, and Buddy Ryan, his defensive coordinator, unleashed the physical Bears defense on the Giants offense with a mass of blitzes, especially targeting quarterback Simms. It was a brutal loss.

In the locker room Parcells promised Carson and Martin they would get another shot, and then he literally said nothing until halfway back to Newark. He was fuming. He had spoken to Carson and Martin because they were team leaders and because they been with the Giants through all the losing years and he felt they deserved better.

Parcells said that other than his press conference and accepting the handshakes of a few people, he spoke little. During the press conference, one writer asked, "Shouldn't you have used more three-step drops?"

"You wouldn't know a three-step drop if it grew teeth, jumped up, and bit you on the ass!" Parcells responded.

Parcells cut the conference short and left for the coaches' locker room and then the bus to the airport. On the plane home, Parcells sat next to Mickey Corcoran. He brought Mickey to almost all of his playoff games since he had become a professional football coach. Parcells had a couple of beers, trying to ease the tension he felt in his body. Parcells was angry because while any team can beat another on any given Sunday, Parcells thought that the 1985 Bears would have beaten his 1985 Giants eight out of ten times. He believes that today.

"He must have been about sixty-five then," Parcells said. "So now we're flying over Pittsburgh and Mickey's sitting next to me and I still hadn't said a word to him. He tapped me on the shoulder.... He didn't say, 'Nice goin.' He didn't say, 'Good season.' He didn't say, 'Your franchise is makin' progress.' All he did was tap me on the shoulder and say, 'You gotta figure out a way to beat those fuckin' guys.'"

That was it. Before the plane landed, Parcells was already thinking what had to be done to beat the Bears the next year. That was the value of Mickey.

"Bill Parcells was asked yesterday if he felt some sense of satisfaction at what the Giants had done, he stared hard at his questioner," sportswriter Dave Anderson wrote.

"No," he said quickly.

"Why not?" he was asked.

"Wild-card games and all that, I don't care about that. I just want to get in the championship game, and that's all there is to it. I'm not interested in doing the job just good enough to keep it. It's too hard on me," Parcells responded after the season was done.

Anderson pointed out, "Another coach might have been satisfied. His team had an 11–7 record over all. It had advanced to the Super Bowl divisional playoffs for the second consecutive season. And it had lost to the team with the National Football League's best record for the second consecutive season. Quite an accomplishment, especially for a franchise with a recent history of not even challenging to qualify for the playoffs." But that was Anderson's point. Parcells was not happy.

―—

The Parcells family was firmly ensconced in New Jersey by 1986. Don was working at Midland Marine. Doug was living in Oradell, where he taught school. And Bill's sister Debbie worked as a secretary in Montvale, New Jersey.

In May 1986 Suzy Parcells married a sports trainer from Temple and moved to Philadelphia. She was Bill and Judy's oldest daughter. Suzy was from the class of 1980 USAF Academy High School and graduated from Idaho State University. Dallas was matriculated at East Carolina, and Jill, the youngest, went to Gettysburg.

Parcells tried to stick to his routines.

Back then he was a smoker—Marlboros. He drank Miller Lite. He drove a Lincoln Continental. He got up at 5:30 AM, was gone by 6:00 AM when milkmen and longshoremen get up, and drove in the darkness to Elmer's Country Store on Upper Saddle River Road, a true old-time general store, more than 100 years old. That's where he got his first coffee of the day. Probably a few of the papers. Maybe a pack of cigarettes. He was a local. Most people in town knew who he was, but they rarely said anything more than, "Good luck on Sunday."

And of course there was Manny's in Moonachie. "About a mile from Giants Stadium, down several potholed roads running through an industrial area," sportswriter Juliet Macur wrote. It was a place Parcells "once called home."

Manny's is a friendly Italian restaurant. On game days Manny's serves a large buffet. It is a local hangout, a neighborhood place. Many guests "greet Jerry the bartender and John the general manager with a stout, 'How ya doin'?' as if they'd been friends since grade school."

Near the bar are photos of Phil Simms, Lawrence Taylor, and other famous Giants including Bill Parcells himself. The dining room walls of Manny's are festooned with large paintings of famed New York Giants past and present tackling, scoring, and winning.

"He came here to have beers and kick back and relax," said general manager John Cimiluca, owner Manny Cimiluca's son, before pointing to one end of the bar. "That was Bill's spot."

"Parcells used to go to Manny's after Giants practices or games or simply on Saturday afternoons. He'd sit on one side of the U-shaped bar in his reserved seat, drinking his Miller Lites, smoking his Marlboros, talking football," Macur said.

Manny's also played an important role in the Parcells' family dynamic.

Every once in a while, the girls would come home for a home game. They would have dinner around 8:30 PM on a Friday night. "They talk some about the game but not very much," Jerry Izenberg explained. "They have been through nights like this too many times in too many places not to know the rules of the game. They make the most of dinner."

Parcells would leave on Saturday morning at his usual time. They will not see him Saturday. He may not even call from the nearby hotel the Giants used as their headquarters before the game.

"If the Giants win, Judy Parcells will leave the Stadium and drive directly to nearby Manny's Restaurant to wait for him. Whenever they win, she will meet him there."

"If they lose, she will return to an empty house to wait. He will come straight home, eat a sandwich, fall into the big easy chair in the family room, and stare at the television screen." After half an hour or so, he would go to bed and start all over again.

— —

The most interesting moment of the early part of the 1986 season was when a furious Jim Burt came flying into Parcells' office. "You guys have got to be the dumbest sons of bitches in the whole world. Get rid of me. I don't want to play here anymore! You're getting rid of Simms, you get rid of me, too!" the big nose tackle shouted at Parcells.

"What the hell are you talking about, Burt?" an astonished Parcells thundered back.

Burt and McConkey and Simms all shared the same agent. When Burt called up to talk to David Fishof, Simms and Fishof decided to play a practical joke and insisted that the Giants had just made a huge trade, sending Simms to the Rams for a number of players and draft picks. Fishof insisted that the story remain quiet for several days. But Burt could not contain himself.

It took Parcells five minutes to cool off the distraught Burt.

During training camp, Parcells cut McConkey. McConkey had been a Parcells pet. Coach liked the fiery, wiry former Naval Academy wide receiver and punt returner.

"I think I should have made your team...I think I'm better than the next guy," McConkey told Parcells. But he also thanked Parcells for taking a chance on him in the first place "You gave me a chance when other team would never even have looked at me. For that, I'll be forever grateful. You helped make a dream come true." Parcells got choked up. The receivers coach Pat Hodgson said, "I am not gonna say good-bye, 'cause I'm gonna see you again. You know, you're going to be back." But McConkey wasn't sure.

The 1986 season started off ominously with a 31–28 loss the Herschel Walker–led Cowboys on *Monday Night Football* at Dallas.

"They were believing what they read about themselves," Parcells said. "But if we didn't have one penalty, we would have won that game. Everybody was telling them they're going to do this and do that, and going into the season they believed that was going to happen." Parcells used the loss to motivate the team.

One of the things Parcells liked to say was, "You are what your record says you are." But this was not the time for that kind of speech.

"When they lost, I told them it was a long season and we were not going to die because we lost one game. I said maybe my expectation for some of them was higher than theirs. I told them if some of them didn't start doing a better job, we wouldn't have a chance."

— —

They then won the next five games.

A portion through the season, Forrest Gregg, Packer immortal and then Green Bay head coach, called Phil McConkey into this office. He had a big smile. McConkey had been playing for Green Bay while Eddie Lee Ivery was injured. Gregg told McConkey he'd been traded back to the Giants.

"When you get back here, you're going to play your ass off," Parcells told McConkey. McConkey vowed to be there the next day. Parcells told him no one would be there; it was a day off. "The grass is greener— my ass!" McConkey told Parcells. Ending phrases with "my ass" was a Parcells favorite. Parcells chuckled.

Parcells told McConkey that Gregg had driven a hard bargain. "We had to give up a blocking dummy and a couple of brand new clipboards for you."

On October 19 the Giants lost to the Seahawks at Seattle before running the table and finishing with nine consecutive wins for a 14–2 record.

Parcells remained an avid sports fan and a loyal Red Sox fan. In his office he kept a white golf shirt with a Red Sox emblem on it and a Red Sox trivia book. That year the Boston Red Sox played the New York Mets in the World Series. On October 27, 1986, after the game against Washington, Parcells recalled, "The first thing I found out when we got back into the locker room was the final score of the seventh game of the World Series. Mets 8, Red Sox 5. It was a result I understood perfectly from my youth."

What was fascinating was that in the middle of their winning streak, the running game was carrying the team. Simms admittedly went through a dry spell. He was uncomfortable throwing. Even when he had a decent game, he was never able to settle in. After he turned 32 in early November, Parcells called Simms into his office.

"I don't know what you're thinking, but here's what I think: I think you're a great quarterback, and you got that way by being daring and fearless," Parcells said. "Be the sort of quarterback that has the other guy worrying on Saturday night."

Simms said Parcells' meeting "pumped me up." Simms went out in the next game, threw one of the best games of his life, and beat the Minnesota Vikings late in the fourth quarter, bringing the team down to the Vikings' 15-yard line for a game-winning field goal by Giants place kicker Raul Allegre.

Simms followed up with another stunning performance the following week in a game against the Denver Broncos.

The Giants were losing, and Parcells approached Ron Erhardt. All the plays were run through Parcells by Erhardt, but now Parcells was desperate. "Ron, I don't give a shit what you call. Get me some goddamned points," Parcells bellowed.

The Giants scored a bunch and won the game. Simms made some spectacular passes. The most telling victory was against the vaunted 49ers in San Francisco. Montana put two touchdowns on the board, and the team tacked on a field goal to take a 17–0 lead in the first half against the Giants on a *Monday Night Football* broadcast. The Giants came back and won 21–17. They followed that effort with a victory at Washington.

"It is now permissible and altogether proper to talk about what a marvelous team the Giants have," Peter King wrote in *New York Newsday.*

The offense finished eighth in the NFL, and the defense finished second. The Giants were now a championship-caliber team. They would have home-field advantage throughout the playoffs.

The Associated Press named Taylor the NFL's Most Valuable Player, the first time a defensive star had won the award in fifteen years. And AP named Bill Parcells the NFL's Coach of the Year. In typical fashion, Parcells went right back to work.

"Parcells began abusing the offensive line as soon as he knew we were playing San Francisco," Simms remembered. "He started calling them 'Club Thirteen' because Joe Morris ran thirteen times against the 49ers the last time we played them and gained only 14 yards."

This was not the first nickname Parcells had given them. The first one he gave that stuck was the Suburbanites because they were all so mundane and business-like. In the off-season, Billy Ard was a stockbroker, Brad Benson owned a Jaguar dealership, Chris Godfrey was a banker, and Karl Nelson was an engineer. "We don't have any tough linemen from Detroit. Our guys are from Watchung," Parcells chortled. "They sound like a law firm Benson, Ard, Oates, Godfrey & Nelson." Of course, the sarcasm had a point. He was challenging them, and they knew it.

Benson and Bart Oates were practical jokers. Oates could be confounding, hot wiring people's cars, etc. "Bill tended to get real nervous before games that weren't big games," Oates said. "Before a Phoenix game or something, I had a football and we were changing drills."

"I need a ball, Oates, give me that ball," Parcells ordered.

"No," Oates to Parcells. "Guys are looking at me like, 'What did he say?'"

"Oates, give me that ball!" Parcells insisted.

"No," Oates repeated. "He turned red as a beet."

"Oates! Oates! I'm going to get you!" Parcells hollered.

Parcells also told them to be careful how they talk to the media. "He was always telling us to be careful with the media," Simms said. "He'd like us never to say one bad word about our opponents and never say one good word about ourselves."

The 49ers divisional playoff game got a lot of hype. The games between the two teams had started to take on more and more vibrancy, and lead-ups to the game were intensely scrutinized by the press. This one was no different—except for the result.

The 49ers turned over the ball four times, and the Giants made them pay each time with a touchdown. Simms completed only nine passes that day but threw TD passes to Zeke Mowatt, Mark Bavaro, Bobby Johnson, and Phil McConkey. Morris ran for 159 yards. The Giants won 49–3, and Harry Carson dumped Gatorade on Parcells at the end.

Next was the NFC Championship Game against the Washington Redskins. The Wednesday walk became a zoo when hundreds of reporters flooded the locker room for interviews. "There must have been 9 million reporters in the locker room. I never saw so many," Phil McConkey said.

In those days, Parcells' office was studded with the elephants his mother had told him about—the ones with the trunks pointed upward. He picked up pennies only if they were head's up. At that point Wellington Mara, the long time Giants' patriarch, used to leave a shiny, heads-up penny on Parcells' desk before each game.

In those days, Simms thought he saw another superstitious move by Parcells. "He always comes out to practice wearing gray sweats with the initials B.P. on them, and sneakers and socks, and he always has the right pant leg rolled up."

"Aside from his very public bathing habits, consisting of a Gatorade shower at the end of his team's victorious efforts, the country doesn't know all that much about Giants coach Bill Parcells," Dave Sell wrote in the *Chicago Sun-Times*. Parcells liked it that way.

"That's okay," Parcells said with a smile. "I'm not interested in being known around the country. I'll just hang around Hackensack."

The Redskins came into Giants Stadium on the windiest day in many people's memories. The Giants had beaten the Redskins twice that year, though the Washington club under Coach Joe Gibbs was very formidable.

"Parcells had me find the direct line to the tower at Newark Airport. He called down there at 10:00 in the morning."

"This is coach Parcells," Bill said. "Here's what I want to know. At 1:00 this afternoon, which way will the wind be coming from and what degree is it gonna come from?" With that information, Parcells knew which end of the field to pick so that the wind would be at their backs in the fourth quarter.

The Giants won 17–0 in a swirling 32-mph wind, making their two combined wins a 66–3 outcome.

By this time the players were over the whole Gatorade thing, but the television viewing audience was hot on it. CBS's John Madden even diagramed it for those watching it at home. Parcells was ready this time. After Carson dumped the cold bath on him, Parcells turned around and shot back at Carson with a water pistol.

"Parcells, a player's coach and a Jersey guy, may be closer to his players than any head coach in the league," *New York Magazine* reported. "Some coaches think he's too close." The article reasoned that Mike Ditka of the Bears ruled through intimidation and Tom Landry through calculation. "Parcells rules through something dangerously close to affection. The players call him Bill, and they play practical jokes on him, many having to do with his superstitions."

Burt, whose troubled relationship with Parcells ran the gamut of hate to real affection (Parcells once said Burt was like a son to him), once hid Parcells' lucky sweatsuit. The coach had half the staff scouring the stadium complex.

"They know where the line is, and they don't cross it," Parcells said.

The Giants were going to Pasadena. There they would face the Denver Broncos, who had just won in a late, dramatic fashion over the Cleveland Browns. The Giants were favored and had beaten the Broncos 19–16 when they played one another in the regular season. It was a close game. This one would be, as well—at least until the third quarter.

"When the Giants left for Pasadena, California," sportswriter Peter Alfano reported, "Corcoran was in the traveling party as Parcells' guest. Over the years, the relationship between a coach and athlete evolved into one between friends and confidantes. Corcoran is the old coach now, 64 years of age and retired. Parcells, 45, is the coach, putting some of those concepts he learned into practice."

"We talk every week and usually the conversation starts off with him saying, 'This is a tough game coming up,'" Corcoran said. "I don't understand too much about football, but I can see that Bill is a player's coach. He's low-key. Knows how to motivate. But on the field, he's a good disciplinarian, too."

In some respects, Parcells still had a bit of the student athlete within.

"After the national anthem, Bill Parcells looked back and I was standing right behind him and he had the look of a kid. And you could tell he got a real shiver up his spine. You could tell he was as giddy about it as anyone," Corcoran said.

The Giants went into halftime losing 10–9.

Parcells had a favorite line for halftime speeches, "Maybe it's time to sew up our skirts, girls." In some speeches he'd been loud, angry, and used rough language. This time he did not. "I don't mind losing the game, but let's not give the damn thing away," he said to his team.

"I just don't think we played very goddamn well out there. We're not playing well as a team," Parcells continued. He exhorted the defense to play with more discipline. The Broncos were purposely spreading the field, and the Giants were not playing under control. There was effort, but too many people were freelancing. As Parcells pointed out, "You can't do it alone. It's got to be a damned collective effort."

Belichick carried the same message to the defense. "I always said he was one of my all-time favorite coaches," Perry Williams remembered. "He made some little adjustments at half time. 'Everything is working. We just missed a couple of little plays here. Don't panic. We've got them right where we want them.'"

Then the third quarter started and the Giants rattled off 24 unanswered points before the Broncos responded with a Rich Karlis field goal. During that stretch Parcells called for a fake punt on fourth-and-1 and made it, and he threw in a flea flicker, as well. The teams traded touchdowns in the fourth quarter, but by then it was all over and the Giants won 39–20.

During the fourth quarter, some defensive players were laughing and celebrating, and Parcells blew a gasket, "Don't you guys start the god-damned victory party until the goddamn game is over!"

To Parcells, the last five minutes seemed like five hours or five years. Later Parcells said, as he tried to keep himself busy on the sidelines, he thought of Chubby and Ida, Mickey, Judy, and the girls. He thought about Al Davis watching. Bobby Knight. And he said he thought a lot about Hastings and how far he had come.

Of course, he received a Gatorade bath. His famous retort about the Gatorade bath? "I'd rather get doused with Gatorade than bust my ass selling it." Parcells said he didn't clamp down on the Gatorade showers, and they weren't staged or planned. They were just fun. "I went along with it because I am one of them."

Parcells had brought Mickey with him. Mickey and he had found each other in the locker room. "This one going home from here should be a lit-tle more pleasant than the one from Chicago last year, don't you think?"

"It's pretty difficult for me to describe how I felt yesterday," Parcells said after the Super Bowl. "I think I know what real euphoria is. It's ab-solutely wonderful. I don't know if you can ever duplicate this feeling. I sure hope so; it was terrific."

"With a minute to go, really, honest, I don't want this to sound dra-matic or anything, but I thought back to the first game I ever coached, at Hastings College in 1964," Parcells said. Hastings beat Colorado School of Mines, 24–0. "It's all relative. It's just as important to you at the time."

Judy Parcells was in the stands with her parents, her three sisters, her three daughters, and her mother-in-law. With them were some team-mates from Bill's days at Wichita State. Judy remembered it saying, "It was such an emotional experience for both of us. I remember that day when they came running out of the tunnel for the start of the game." Judy could see him and tried to understand what he must be experiencing.

"When it ended, they played that song, 'New York, New York,' and it just filled the stadium. And you just had to stand there and listen to it. I got goosebumps."

When the team finally left the Rose Bowl on the team bus, there was Parcells sitting right next to Mickey Corcoran. "If it wasn't for you," the

Giants coach said, patting his high school basketball coach on the knee, "I wouldn't be here."

However, three days later, the euphoria had passed. The Atlanta Falcons were searching for a coach after dismissing Dan Henning. They had been rebuffed by Dick Vermeil and Terry Donahue. The Falcons sought permission to talk with Parcells, according to reports from *The Atlanta Constitution* and *The Boston Globe*.

"The Giants denied Atlanta permission, though the Falcons have been in contact with Parcells' attorney, one report said. The Falcons are willing to offer Parcells $900,000 a year to become coach and general manager, another report said, and the Falcons are ready to offer Parcells a five-year contract. Parcells, contacted by *The Constitution*, said there was no truth to the reports," *The New York Times* reported.

NFL Commissioner Pete Rozelle confirmed that Robert Fraley, Parcells' agent, had called him after Young denied Fraley permission to talk to the Falcons about a joint coach and general manager's job. Fraley had urged the Commissioner to allow the talks.

Rozelle said of the Giants' refusal, "That ended it."

Parcells had two years remaining on a four-year contract that paid him a reported $300,000 a year. "Atlanta was reportedly willing to pay $4.5 million over five years for a combined coach–general manager post. If nothing else, any offer might have given Parcells a wedge for reopening his Giants' contract," *The New York Times* said.

Rozelle had talked to Falcon's president Rankin Smith Jr., who had said Parcells was not on his list of prospective coaches. Rozelle stated that both Smith and Giants president Wellington Mara were satisfied with the situation.

"It seems it was a case of the agent more or less pushing the situation on his own," Rozelle said. "I told the agent, 'Nope, that's it.'"

"I've learned not to say never in this business," Parcells wrote in his auto-biography. "Hell, it might have gone down to the wire with the Falcons."

This situation would not be the last of such instances in Parcells' professional coaching career. Again, like the college coaching merry-go-round, success bred other offers, other opportunities. Wasn't that the coach's reward for a job well done?

With winning came egos. Parcells and Young were both being hailed, but the friction between the two of them was beginning to grow. The incident with the Falcons pissed off George. Young had a contract with Parcells and felt Parcells was being disloyal. Parcells, and especially his agent, felt it was his opportunity to explore. However, even Parcells knew that he had taken some of the fun out of the Super Bowl celebrations with the ill-timed fiasco.

CHAPTER 5

Do It Again

T he 1986 Giants went 14–2 and won the Super Bowl. By December 1987, the Giants finished this season with a 6–9 record. Only seven of the National Football League's 27 other teams did worse.

Some of it was Super Bowl hangover.

"Don't get me wrong, it was a great thrill, it's what we play for, and I'll never forget it. I only hope we get back someday," Parcells told the press. But he admitted, "I was dead. I just felt like I didn't have time to do anything in the off-season. Until the Super Bowl was over, I had to be concerned with Denver. And I had to be concerned with hotels and security and a lot more, too."

Also, the league grinds on. Parcells went from the Super Bowl to the combines only two days later.

Sports scribe Frank Litsky wrote of the Giants, "In the season opener, they were routed by the Chicago Bears 34–19. Six days later, they lost to the Dallas Cowboys 16–14, when Raul Allegre missed a last-minute field-goal attempt. Then came the National Football League players' strike, and the Giants' woeful replacement team lost its three games."

"I think the strike put Bill in a bad position," Brad Benson remembered. "In a way, I think he took it personally and held it against us somewhat." Benson said he was torn between his loyalty to the coach who had turned the team around and his loyalty to his fellow players.

"Bill felt as if we did it to him," McConkey agreed.

"I don't think we ever recovered from that 0–5 start," Parcells said.

"That's difficult psychologically. That leaves so little margin for error. There were opportunities, but we weren't able to put together enough wins. We were still 6–6 with the regular team, and 50 percent football doesn't get you in the playoffs. You need to get to 75 percent or 70 percent."

"Losing is frustrating to everybody," Parcells said. You're supposed to win. You're paid to win. When you don't it's frustrating to the players, coaches, and organization."

The Giants were not a consistent football team in any area. After the strike, they were good on defense but still didn't make some plays in the fourth quarter that they needed to make. Offensively, they were not as consistent scoring, turnovers went up, penalties went up, and sacks went up. On special teams, they were not very good at all.

There were also injuries. Karl Nelson was lost for the season due to being diagnosed with Hodgkin's disease. Chris Godfrey had strained knee ligaments half the season. Since they played side by side on the offensive line, their absences led to inconsistent blocking and poor play up front.

Parcells also pointed out that the strike hurt Joe Morris, who usually ran better as a season progressed. The offensive linemen who replaced Nelson and Godfrey didn't have enough time to train up to their potential and thus were not reliable substitutes for the two.

"I don't think our team is so far down in every area that you can't see an opportunity to improve," Parcells said. "But what will happen, I don't know."

TAYLOR AND DRUGS

On October 20, 1985, when the Giants beat the Washington Redskins 17–3, Taylor snapped out of a half-season slumber with a spectacular game that included two sacks and 11 tackles. After the game, in an impromptu news conference in the middle of the locker room, he talked of personal problems.

"I prepared this week," he said during the season in 1986. "I got some sleep. I didn't go to bars much. I decided to go back to my old self. My wife and my best friend told me I wasn't playing like the old Lawrence

Taylor, and that bothered me. Maybe football wasn't as important to me as it should have been. Last year, it lasted eight games. This year, I have to catch it before it starts. I have to catch it now."

In March 1986, Parcells indicated that he knew what rehab facility Taylor was in "and that he had been instrumental in arranging his treatment. Both Parcells and the newly appointed Buddy Ryan of the Philadelphia Eagles were the only head coaches absent from the NFL's annual meetings in Palm Springs, California. Parcells was reportedly visiting college players eligible for the April 29 draft. However, one source said he might have visited Taylor during that period," Frank Litsky reported.

"I assume he's working out on his own," Parcells said.

"Parcells had encouraged Taylor to get treatment and helped arrange for it," Litsky continued.

"Bill has taken so much pressure off me," Taylor said in an interview after resurfacing in 1986. "He was ridiculed. I think he was the big reason I had a good year this year, not having to deal with the press.... The things I went through served as motivation for me. I'm competing not only with myself but with the people who said I couldn't do it. Bill Parcells said he had confidence and pride in me. I had pride in that. I appreciated that."

Parcells said that from 1983–86, he knew of 20 to 30 players on the team who had used drugs. Some, he said, were still with the team in 1987.

Taylor claimed he got caught using crack cocaine in the Giants 1985 minicamp when his urine test turned up dirty. Taylor said that Parcells' response after Taylor tested positive "was to try to help me," Taylor said. "He got someone in New York to help me. I went for a short while, but that didn't work. I didn't want the Giants or the NFL to have anything to do with this."

Taylor revealed that in February 1986 that he, "stayed in a Houston rehabilitation facility only a few days." Then he moved to another part of Houston, though for a time he continued daily talks with the therapists.... "The Giants did a lot for me in six years. Bill Parcells is one of my best friends on the team."

"When you find a player with a drug problem," Parcells wrote in his autobiography, "the best thing you can do, one counselor told me, was, 'Bust their chops.'" And he did. Parcells once called a Giant player into his office and then phoned that player's mother. Parcells told her that her son was involved with cocaine with the player standing right there. "Sometimes, they're more scared about mamma finding out than they are about losing their jobs," Parcells wrote.

Parcells disclosed in his book that the Giants' front office "spent nearly $60,000 trying to help one guy, and we failed." The Giants spent $25,000 trying to save another guy. That failed. Even after one Giants player had been released, Parcells persuaded the Giants to pay for his rehab care.

There was no question that the Giants organization had attempted to help Taylor and that Parcells attempted to help Taylor. And Taylor was grateful for both but admitted he knew that as long as he kept playing well, no one could stop him. A double standard?

Parcells said that the concept of a double standard was naive, since there was no set standard in place in the NFL or in society. What he advocated was drug testing and lots of it.

To that end, Taylor was tested twice a week throughout the 1986 and 1987 seasons. On August 29, 1988, Taylor was suspended by the NFL for 30 days after he tested positive on his NFL drug test.

BELICHICK

By 1985 Bill Belichick was the defensive coordinator of the New York Giants. His knowledge and confidence were growing. And confidence in him was growing.

"When Belichick came in, he just wanted to learn," Jim Burt remembered. "He would sit right next to Parcells in the meetings."

Burt loved Belichick's penchant for preparation. Burt said the defense could go into a game confident because Belichick had dissected the other team so well. "Bill [Parcells] wasn't a people manager, but he was a great evaluator of talent. I loved Belichick because he gave me the opportunity to succeed. He and Parcells were interesting people to play for."

In his autobiography, Parcells had nothing but good things to say about his young protégé Belichick. Calling him "bright" and "creative," Parcells lavished infinite praise on the young defensive guru.

Parcells said that Belichick was never afraid to speak his mind or make his point. Parcells said what he admired in Belichick was his aggressiveness. "In his job, you can't be afraid to attempt aggressiveness," Parcells wrote. Parcells admitted that Belichick was a lot more aggressive than himself. Parcells said he was the conservative one.

"Bill has been terrific for me and for the Giants."

Of course, with Parcells, not all was roses.

"What the hell is this?" Parcells thundered during a defensive game plan meeting.

"Well, we're up against a run-and-shoot, and we need as much speed in there as we can get," Belichick said.

"Don't you think we need to be more physical?" Parcells asked. Belichick shook his head no. Parcells pounded the table.

"Why the hell don't you just put Stephen Baker in there—he'll give you the speed," Parcells said as he shook his head with aggravation.

From there on in, occasionally, when game planning a similar defense, Belichick would say to Parcells, "And we're going to put Stephen Baker in on this particular defense."

"One of the things I really appreciated from Bill was the opportunity he gave me to coach the way I wanted to coach," Belichick said. "He never asked me to coach the way he coached, and I probably wouldn't have been very good at it anyway. He gave me a lot of latitude. He gave me the flexibility to do what I thought was best in the areas that I had responsibility for. In a lot of respects, the things I did were pretty independent of him."

In tough games, where the teams were decidedly even, Parcells was a firm believer in just being physically tougher than the other guy. These were the times when disguising formations was all frills to him.

"All the film guys in the world aren't worth shit. I remember a couple of years back," he said in 1989, "when we'd stop 'em on three plays and out and the next sequence, we're doing something entirely different."

"Are you watching the game?" Parcells screamed at Belichick. "What the hell are you doing?"

"I just wanted to give them a different look," Belichick said.

"What the hell for? We're stoppin' 'em, ain't we?!"

Parcells point was simple. If you're a baseball pitcher and you're getting by on your fast ball, then just keep throwing it until there's 27 gone or until they've figured it out.

"If you're getting away from that in a game like this, it's only because you want to show everybody how smart you are as a coach. That's like carnival football," Parcells said.

Belichick could drive the players (and especially Taylor) crazy with his long meetings. Belichick would drone on in his monotone. The entire defense would be there, but Taylor used the time in the dark during film sessions to sleep. Taylor became irritable when Belichick would wake him up or have another player wake him up.

Once Taylor exploded with a loud angry tirade to which Belichick bellowed back. Taylor stormed out of the room. Later, Banks found Taylor asleep on a couch in the player's lounge.

"I'm so fucking tired. Belichick was keeping me awake with all that crap I had to get out of there," Taylor told Banks. Taylor had staged the whole thing just so he could go sleep.

Belichick was not without his own sense of humor. Once during an evening meeting in Dallas, Lawrence Taylor came late to a team meeting. He had his sweater on, but his arms were underneath the sweater, not in the arms. And he jingled. Taylor had been with a woman before the meetings, and she had handcuffed him and either lost or took the key. By the time the news worked its way up to the front of the room, Belichick asked Taylor to come up to the front to diagram the next play. The team broke out in laughter. Taylor was saved when the hotel security finally found a key that would unlock the cuffs.

MOVING FORWARD

In February, Bill Parcells got a sizable and deserved contract extension. He was now making $325,000 in the last year of his contract. The Giants had agreed to a new three-year deal, tying him up through 1991. He would earn $750,000 per year and received a $400,000 signing bonus. However, the press treated the event with suspicion.

"Shortly after the aborted talks with the Falcons, the Giants and Parcells supposedly reached agreement on a lucrative contract extension. Mysteriously, that deal wasn't signed until yesterday," *Daily News* sports scribe Paul Needell wrote. According to Needell, the delay had further fueled rumors that Parcells was in fact destined for an exit, perhaps to join Al Davis with the Raiders. Another report had put forth the idea that Parcells would take over the New England Patriots, replacing Raymond Berry after the franchise was sold.

"Ever since Parcells had his much publicized flirtation with the Atlanta Falcons," Needel continued, "rumors have run rampant regarding his dissatisfaction with his overall role with the Giants. He and General Manager George Young don't have the best working relationship." In short, Parcells wanted more power in personnel decisions.

The relationship between Young and Parcells wasn't always acrimonious. Young loved to tell the story of Art Donovan, a legendary Colts defensive lineman and a prodigious eater and drinker.

"A few months ago I went over to the Downtown Athletic Club where Artie was to be honored at a dinner. He never touched the prime rib. When the dinner ended, he went out for a big box of hot dogs and went upstairs to his room with that box of hot dogs under one arm and the plaque he got at the dinner under the other. He had some beer sent up to wash down the hot dogs."

The story went that Donovan had set down the plaque to open the door to his hotel room. He went in and ate the dogs and washed them down with the beer. He'd completely forgotten about the plaque. "When he looked out in the hall the next morning, no plaque. But he didn't forget to eat the hot dogs," Young laughed.

Sometime later, Parcells was going down to Atlantic City and he was going to see Donovan. Parcells asked Young if he had anything to tell Artie. "Ask him how many hot dogs he ate that night at the Downtown Athletic Club the night he left the plaque outside his room," Young said. Parcells smiled.

The next time Parcells saw Young, he was driving into the stadium parking lot. Parcells rolled down his window. "Twenty-two," was all Parcells said. The two laughed.

The draft was a positive one that year. The Giants were all in agreement that in the 1987 season, their offensive line, due to age and injury, had been a weak link.

The Giants would have William Roberts and Doug Riesenberg at tackle; Billy Ard, Chris Godfrey, and Damian Johnson at guard; and Bart Oates and Brian Johnston at center. Brad Benson retired, and Brian Johnston was not offered a new contract. But the Giants had also drafted two new tackles, Eric Moore and John "Jumbo" Elliott. They would be great additions to the line.

These men were great additions since the size of the two tackles were both near 300 pounds. Moore was just under and Elliott just over. The sizes of these two men were huge upgrades and they significantly increased the bulk of the Giants' line.

However, the season started with a 30-day suspension of Taylor for testing positive for drug use, and the preseason was marred by a contract dispute with Banks.

Every training camp, with the draft still fresh in his head, Parcells always remembered what Tom Landry had told him, "If they don't make it by their third year, get rid of them."

The season confirmed what many thought. The Giants finished 10–6, and Parcells had righted the ship again. They had beaten the Cowboys and the Redskins twice each but dropped a pair to Buddy Ryan's Philadelphia Eagles. That was the difference in the final standings. Philadelphia went to the playoffs, and the Giants went home. The wild-card teams that year were the Vikings, who finished 11–5 behind the 12–4 Bears, and the Los Angeles Rams, who got the second wildcard spot with a 10–6 record due to tie breakers.

"I didn't like my '88 Giants team even though we won ten games," Parcells said years later. "When clutch time came, that team just didn't have it. I knew when that season was over we had to change if we were going to get better."

Parcells knew the price of professional sports and recalled Chubby's words, "I sometimes think about what we're doing here, and how hard some people work at it, and then when it isn't happening, some player will say to me, 'I'm sorry coach, but I am trying,' and I tell him exactly what my father told me: you don't get any medals for trying."

"One day at practice—I think it was '88—the defense is bouncing me around," Simms recalled. "The line's playing sloppy, and it's causing me to take some shots. Bill explodes."

"You %$@#&^$ linemen stink!" Parcells yelled. Then he turned to Simms.

"Simms, it's your damn fault. If you weren't so chummy with those guys, they'd have more respect for you, and they'd fear you, and they'd never let you get hit. You're an idiot!"

"I think Bill's full of it. Then I'm driving home, and I start to think, *God, he's right.* My linemen aren't scared that I'll get ticked at them. I needed to be more of a jackass to them. It sounds cold, but it's true."

The toughest part of the 1988 season may not have been the toughest part for Bill Parcells. The thing more difficult for him to deal with was the loss of George Martin and Harry Carson after the season. These were two of Parcells guys. He could go to them and say, "Fix it." and it happened. These were men who had helped him take control and run the team. These were leaders. And they were gone.

Another loss was Jim Burt. Parcells told Burt that he thought he was finished. Burt was upset, saying he was still very valuable, but the Giants had the younger, cheaper Erik Howard. The separation was bitter. Afterward, Burt played for the San Francisco 49ers from 1989 to 1991. He won his second Super Bowl ring when the 49ers beat the Broncos in January 1990.

The 1989 team was absolutely better. The team finished 12–4 and took the division. They beat the Cowboys, the Cardinals, and the Redskins all twice for six divisional wins. But they dropped another pair to the Eagles, who finished 11–5 that year—only good enough for second place.

But Buddy Ryan would be a thorn in Parcells' side as long as he was with the Giants.

James David "Buddy" Ryan was born on February 17, 1934, just outside of Frederick, Oklahoma. Ryan played college football for Oklahoma A&M University (which is now Oklahoma State) and played all four years as a guard, graduating in 1955.

He was a sergeant in the U.S. Army during the Korean War. Ryan coached Texas high school football for a few years before graduating to college football. He was an assistant at Pacific, Vanderbilt, and Buffalo. He then made the jump to professional football, starting with the American Football League's New York Jets in the 1960s.

Ryan and Walt Michaels created the defensive game plan that helped the Jets win Super Bowl III. In the mid-1970s Ryan was the defensive coordinator of the Minnesota Vikings' famed defense the Purple People Eaters. He went to another four Super Bowls with the Vikings, though they never won one.

In 1978, George Halas brought in Ryan as defensive coordinator. With the Bears, Ryan created the 46 Defense, which took him years to perfect. In 1982 Halas brought in Mike Ditka. Ryan had felt passed over, and Ryan and Ditka warred openly. Ditka basically let Ryan run the defense without much interference, but Ryan was irascible, and Ditka was fiery.

At one point Ditka challenged Ryan to a fight during halftime of the Bears' only loss, a 1985 matchup versus the Miami Dolphins. The Bears went in 12–0 but lost to the quick passing of Dan Marino.

"The guys on the team had to separate them—the offense getting Ditka away from Ryan and defensive guys holding Buddy."

The Bears defensive unit carried Ryan off the field after the Bears won the 1986 Super Bowl, right behind Mike Ditka, who was also being carried off the field.

In 1986, Ryan took over the Philadelphia Eagles. "You got a winner in town," Ryan boldly declared at his press conference. "We plan on winning the Eastern Division." Parcells, Gibbs, and Landry were formally put on notice.

Ryan was controversial. In one game against the Cowboys he ran up the score when the final outcome was no longer in doubt. This was payback for Tom Landry's using real Cowboys players who had crossed the picket line to pound Ryan's pathetic replacements during the strike-shortened season the year before.

Another calamity was the Bounty Bowl, played on Thanksgiving Day, November 23, 1989, at Texas Stadium in Dallas. Jimmy Johnson, the new Dallas Cowboys coach, accused Ryan of taking out a bounty on two Cowboys players—quarterback Troy Aikman and kicker Luis Zendejas.

While Ryan never achieved postseason success, he was quite successful in wreaking havoc within the division. With his brutal defenses and Randall Cunningham guiding the offense at quarterback, the Eagles gave the Giants and their fans ulcers.

At one point, Parcells' secretary, Kim Kolbe, (who has been with the Giants from Perkins to Coughlin) said to Parcells while he was watching Eagles tapes, "I want these guys. The Eagles. I want them humbled."

Parcells was obsessed, "I've seen them so often and know their personnel so well, I could probably coach them."

"Buddy Ryan is a Neanderthal and he attracts Neanderthal players. Neanderthals can win certain kinds of wars, but they lose some they should win if you find a way to make them make enough choices," Parcells said. He also commented, "Buddy Ryan is a very dangerous opponent because he has no regard for anything but to put the best team he can on the field. He doesn't care about anything except what he deems to be his job."

"Personally I like him. He's caustic and unpretentious. I wouldn't say we're close friends, but yes, I like him," Parcells added.

"What [tees] me off is that they talk about [Randall] Cunningham being a great athlete and that seems to supersede the development of him as a quarterback. In other words, I think he's paid his dues. He's learned," Parcells said. "But I don't think you can term anybody great until he puts pelts on his pony, and right now he don't have any. When he does that, I think you can put him in a different category."

In a season where the Giants were one of the best teams in the NFL, they could not seem to beat the Eagles, who beat them 21–19 in Philadelphia and 24–17 at Giants Stadium two months later.

One of Parcells' favorite moments in coaching came that season versus his other nemesis—the Washington Redskins.

"Judy Parcells wasn't on the sideline at RFK Stadium in 1989, with the game tied, one play left, and Giants kicker Raul Allegre lining up for a 52-yard field goal amid a barbaric yawp from 56,000 Washington Redskins fans," sports scribe John Powers wrote.

"It's so vivid, even now," Parcells said. "It was a Monday night game early in September, and it was about midnight, and the fog was coming in right on top of the stadium. And when Allegre's kick went through, the whole place went silent as a morgue. Running onto the field, I could hear a muffled sound behind me. I looked around, and my players were rolling around on the grass, howling. 'Listen to this place,' I told them. But unless you're there and it happened to you, it's tough to describe."

In 1989, the Giants had home-field advantage and eventually wound up facing the Los Angeles Rams at Giants Stadium on January 7, 1990.

"Giants linebacker Lawrence Taylor struggled against Rams tackle Irv Pankey, so before the teams' 1989 playoff game Parcells handed Taylor an airline ticket and told him to fly to New Orleans and give the return ticket to Saints linebacker Pat Swilling," Peter King wrote in *Sports Illustrated*.

"He's the only guy who can handle Pankey. You can't," Parcells said. Taylor was angry and played that way. He beat Pankey for two sacks that game.

By the fourth quarter, the Giants were leading 13–6. Their offense had driven the field brilliantly but stalled and had to settle for field goals instead of touchdowns. This was the difference.

The Rams tied the game with a 22-yard Mike Lansford field goal, and the teams were headed for overtime. Momentum had shifted in the second half from the Giants to the Rams. In overtime, Rams quarterback Jim Everett threw a 30-yard strike to wide received Flipper Anderson, who raced unchallenged down the length of the field, through the end zone, and never stopped. He kept on running into the Rams locker room. A promising season had just come to a disappointing end with the Giants' hopes carried away by Flipper Anderson.

"The game was lost in the kicking area," Parcells said. "We missed two field goals. We dropped a punt, something we've done two times in six or seven years. We gave up a long kickoff return near the end."

"One of the toughest losses I've ever had," Parcells said. The coach went home and went to bed. He awoke at 3:19 AM that morning. "Then I was up and I couldn't get back to sleep." Parcells was in his office by 6:15 the next morning. "It's going to take a lot of work to get in that same position, but those are the games I want to coach in," he said.

— —

The 1990 campaign was an altogether different story.

On the plus side, the Giants signed safety Dave Duerson from the Chicago Bears. "The thing that hit me first when I got here was this team is hungry and it is loose. Those are two things you have to have."

He also had guys who'd been with him two and three years. He had grizzled veterans like Ottis Anderson, who they'd picked up from the Cardinals at the end of his career there. Parcells referred to him sometimes as Old Red, or his hunting dog. It was meant as a compliment. Someone who could be counted on. Someone who was reliable. A war horse.

"I want my players to be smart, disciplined, confident, have strong will and come up with a kill shot when they can. If you don't have those things you can throw talent out the window," Parcells said. "I got some guys I can talk to now and can get messages to the right people if we have to."

To fill the leadership roles, Parcells counted on Everson Walls, Banks, and Duerson on defense, and Simms on the offense.

"It's not just veterans. It's getting the right veterans. A lot of veterans you can put 'em all in rockers and let them sit on the front porch. Old players are not necessarily good players. The guys we've brought in here, though, have been the right players. They fit in," Parcells concluded.

The Giants raced out to 10 consecutive wins.

During the seventh victory, against divisional foe Washington, Taylor ambled up to Parcells in the waning minutes of the game.

"You think this team has the ability to go all the way, huh, coach?"

"Yeah," Parcells said without elaborating.

"Um-hmm," said Taylor before walking away. A "yeah" from Parcells in the middle of a game talking about postseason spoke volumes.

That season the team practiced outside in late November and

early December. Wide receiver Stephen Baker, coming from Texas via California, hated the cold weather. In one practice he dropped seven balls. He was trying to catch them with his hands, the way the coaches were telling him to, especially receivers assistant coach Tom Coughlin. But Baker kept dropping the balls.

"Then at the end of practice, they'd throw you a lob, so everyone goes in feeling good. I dropped that one, too. Parcells was screaming at me. The next day, I caught everything with my body. Let them holler at me for bad technique. Not for dropping the ball."

One day Parcells said to Baker, "You're too small, you're from California, you eat tofu, and you have an earring in one ear; I don't even know why we drafted you."

"He didn't even smile or smirk, you know, to let you know he was just having fun. Just said it with a straight face. That was it. Nothing else. After he said that to me, I worked my ass off," Baker said.

Tight end Howard Cross once told the story of how Parcells told his team that he was going to put a rock in his shoe and walk around with a sore foot so he wouldn't back down on his guys. And sure enough he didn't let up on the players all day long. Cross thought it was the dumbest thing he'd ever heard of.

"After practice he came over and sat on a stool right beside me, and took off his shoe and dropped a little rock out of it, and put his shoe back on and walked away," Cross said.

"Parcells was very good at picking on guys," defensive back Greg Jackson said. "He would pick a certain person out during that week of practice and stay on him all week long—if he had to motivate you or make you concentrate or whatever it might be. He did the same thing with me."

"Parcells had an unusual way of doing things, and I didn't particularly care for that. I didn't like some of his tactics and how he handled people," Perry Williams said. "Hey, that's him, that's how he wanted to do things."

That season Parcells again suffered from kidney stone problems. He was hospitalized on a Saturday night at Morristown Memorial Hospital. He showed up in pain to coach the Giants through an ugly 23–15 victory over the Minnesota Vikings, and then he went back to the hospital. The win clinched the NFC East title and put the Giants at 11–2.

Many of his own players were unaware of his situation. Walls didn't know, but he sensed something was wrong. "You mess up, he'll let you know. But I messed up once, and he just said, 'Everson, did you revolve on the play the way you're supposed to?'"

Parcells' kidney stone was disintegrated the next day at Robert Wood Johnson Stone Center in New Brunswick using a new procedure that included the use of shock waves. One of Parcells' favorite sayings was, "Don't tell me about the pain. Show me the baby." He had shown them the baby that night.

During the fourteenth game of the season, against the Buffalo Bills, Simms's foot was broken, and he was lost for the rest of the season. Backup Jeff Hostetler finished out the season and postseason.

"I have nothing but great things to say about the man as a coach," Hostetler said, "But I didn't enjoy one minute of my time with him. I know that sounds strange, but that's how it is when you're around Bill Parcells."

When the season ended the Giants were 13–3. They were the No. 2 seed in the playoffs—"The Tournament," as Parcells liked to call it.

"His team has won only two of its last five games. He doesn't have his No. 1 quarterback. His short-yardage game is yards away from where he wants it. The defense isn't as dependable as it was. And, look, he can still smile," *Sports Illustrated* columnist Vic Ziegel wrote. When asked if he would play his starters in the last game of the season, Parcells shot back sarcastically, "They'd look at me as if I were nuts. I make them play in the preseason. Why wouldn't I play them in the regular season?"

"Hard not to like Parcells," Ziegel continued. "If you're a fan, his team usually wins for you. If you're a player, especially an older player, he lets you know where you stand. If you're a rookie, you don't stand. You sit."

The first game of the playoffs pitted the Giants against the Chicago Bears. While there had been much anticipation of this matchup of defensive titans, the game was lopsided. The Giants limited Chicago to 27 rushing yards and one field goal, taking the game 31–3. The next two games would be much closer.

The next game was against the San Francisco 49ers at Candlestick Park. It pitted the explosive 49ers offense against the vaunted Giants defense. That year, the Super Bowl season was truncated, and there would only be a week between the conference championships and the Super Bowl. It made travel a concern. Parcells used it to his advantage.

In one of the last meetings at Giants Stadium before the Giants left for the west coast, Stephen Baker remembered that Parcells walked into the Giants locker room with two suitcases—a little one and a big one. And he said to the gathered team, "I don't know about you guys, but I'm bringing my big suitcase, 'cause I'm not just going to San Francisco, I'm going to Tampa Bay." Baker said it was the simplest pep talk he'd ever heard—and the most effective. "All the guys started talking about bringing their big suitcases. It became the running theme for the whole week. We were all pumped. All of us were just so excited."

"They are so over-confident they're going to beat us that they already have their staff down at the Super Bowl. They've moved in. That's how confident they are," Parcells told his team.

"But he didn't tell them that the Giants had their people in Tampa, too!" San Francisco linebacker Bill Romanowski recalled. "It was the only way you were going to be able to pull something like this off without having the two weeks to prepare for it."

The 1990–91 playoff season was marred by the impending war with Iraq. Saddam Hussein had invaded Kuwait, and during the NFC Championship Game, America sat perched at the precipice of war. Patriotism was at an all-time high.

This would be one of the toughest and closest NFC Championship Games in memory. In the first half, the Giants missed out on a golden opportunity when Dave Meggett rolled out on a halfback pass. He threw a strike to Maurice Carthon in the end zone, who dropped the ball. Although the Giants out-rushed the 49ers—152 yards to 49—the game was tied 6–6 at halftime.

In the end, this contest was the defensive struggle many expected, as it pitted the No. 2 defense (the Giants) against the No. 2 offense (the 49ers). The Giants went into the fourth quarter trailing 13–9. In the fourth quarter, defensive end Leonard Marshall knocked 49ers quarterback

Joe Montana out of the game. Shortly thereafter, the Giants successfully completed a fake punt when Gary Reasons ran 30 yards. That set up a Matt Bahr field goal that cut the lead to one point, 13–12. As time wound down and the 49ers had possession, Roger Craig fumbled the ball while crashing through the line with 2:36 left in the game. Erik Howard's tackle dislodged the ball. Lawrence Taylor recovered the fumble. The Giants made five offensive plays, as the clock ticked on. Matt Bahr came out and kicked a 42-yard field goal to give the Giants a 15–13 victory as time expired.

The Giants were going to the Super Bowl again.

One of "the happiest days I ever had as a Giant was when Matt Bahr kicked the field goal in San Francisco to win the NFC Championship Game 15–13 because that was a game that many people didn't think that we had a chance. We had our backup quarterbacks. San Francisco was going for a three-peat. We were on the road. It was pretty gratifying there," Parcells said two decades later. "I would say that NFC championship in San Francisco was one of the best times, and certainly the plane ride to Tampa, which was about five hours, was one of the happiest times of my whole life and is certainly vivid in my recollection. And I think to anybody who was on that plane, it's pretty vivid."

"Everybody was congratulating everybody," Sean Landetta said. "I haven't seen Bill Parcells smile like that in years."

As if he could describe the plane ride, Parcells responded, "Well, I wouldn't say it was a party atmosphere, but it was euphoric. I'm not saying we didn't have a couple of drinks because we did. It was just a kind of a euphoric time for all of us, and I think everybody who was on that plane felt a great sense of accomplishment. Then of course the trip ends, and my secretary, Kim Kolbe, is waiting for us in Tampa and she's got our keys. That plane ride ends, and we go right to work."

THE GAME PLAN

It is without a doubt the most incredible game plan ever devised in the history of the Super Bowl. Bill Parcells created the broad strokes, and his coordinators fleshed out the most important parts of it. But the Giants needed a brilliant plan—they were about to face a brilliant offense.

The Buffalo Bills had tinkered with and perfected a no-huddle offense that they used throughout the season. The no-huddle offense kept the opposing defense from having time to send in personnel packages, and it kept those defenses confused and on their heels. It worked. The Bills were the No. 1 ranked offense in the NFL.

Parcells had game plans for both Buffalo and the Los Angeles Raiders (in case they had some how beaten the Bills in the AFC Championship Game). He had assigned advance scout Tim Rooney to create a detailed file of the game the Bills had played with the Raiders. It was waiting for Parcells when he arrived in Tampa.

"It allowed us to jump right into the game plan," Parcells said. "So we didn't feel bad for ourselves about not having the week off."

Parcells' broad-stroke game plan was simple in concept. The Giants would create a defense designed to give up yardage but would try to take away the passing game and make the Bills work harder than they had in the regular season. Parcells brilliance was that he would use his offense to his advantage. The Giants offense was a slow, churning, smashmouth running game. It was jokingly referred to as "three yards and a cloud of dust." Parcells concept was to "shorten" the game.

With the offense taking up huge chunks of time, using the entire play clock on each play, running the game clock down by executing as many running plays as they could afford to run, the Giants effectively shrunk the amount of time the Bills offense would be on the field.

"Parcells couldn't have designed his offense any better," *Sports Illustrated*'s Paul Zimmerman pointed out. "The grinding attack, much of the time operating out of the three-tight-end set, ate up the clock and not so much kept the Bills' no-huddle offense off the field—you never keep an offense off the field—but delayed its entry and gave it a sense of urgency, a feeling that it had to score right away."

"Two drives, that's all it takes, two of those long, time-consuming drives," Simms had said two days before the game. "That's all it takes to screw up the other team's offense, to foul up the tempo of their game. You see them on the sidelines, getting all antsy: 'God, we've got to get something going.' It's all part of Coach Parcells' master plan, and it's taken me a while to understand that."

As Zimmerman pointed out then, "The defense that Parcells, an old linebacker coach, teaches is linebacker-oriented. While other teams go into a nickel or dime defense and remove all but one linebacker, Parcells keeps at least three linebackers on the field at all times. He feels comfortable with them. He collects them. That was the heart of the defensive scheme New York threw at Buffalo. Parcells was in charge of the overall concept, but the implementation was left to Bill Belichick, the brilliant, 38-year-old defensive coordinator."

Parcells had nicknamed Belichick "Doom" because of his constantly sour demeanor. Parcells once said, "His glass was usually half-empty."

Making things even tougher, Bills quarterback Jim Kelly was having a career season. "There comes a time when things just open up for you as a quarterback, when you just see things," Simms said before the Super Bowl. "You see all the soft parts of a defense, the things you can attack, instead of the bad things. It happened for me in '85, and right now it's happening for Kelly."

Instead of creating elaborate blitzing schemes that would tire out his aging defense, Belichick created a defense that would slow the Bills down and blunt Kelly's lethal attack. Belichick chose a coverage defense that would "rush three or four people, drop the rest of the defenders back and give up the underneath stuff, though making sure the receivers got jolted," Zimmerman explained. "He went with two down linemen, usually nosetackle Erik Howard and end Leonard Marshall, all day, but one of two linebackers, Johnson or Lawrence Taylor, would line up in a rush position, sometimes coming, sometimes dropping back." That was the initial package, but there were variations. Safeties would drop back or blitz, or they might trade places with a linebacker.

"Belichick used all these wrinkles, and the result was a Buffalo offense that didn't convert a third-down play until less than two minutes remained, that was hammered and often frustrated but that remained game to the end," Zimmerman concluded.

When Parcells and the Giants arrived in Pasadena, there were still banners up in some places welcoming the San Francisco 49ers. Parcells used this fact to his advantage in motivating his players. And he used other things as well. He told them that the Bills fully expected to win. He told them about the Bills' arrogance.

"He told them that Thurman Thomas fit himself for a Super Bowl ring four days before the game. Players also witnessed first hand the Bills violating curfew by partying throughout the week," Super Bowl historian William Bendetson wrote.

"The thing about Thomas was a complete ploy by Parcells," Bills linebacker Cornelius Bennett said. "We all had to get measured for Super Bowl rings that week because it was the only time the team was together. But I give Parcells a lot of credit because it was a great motivational technique for his team."

"You guys get me to the Super Bowl, and I'll show you how to win the Super Bowl," Parcells had told his players before the playoffs began.

Now, as Parcells entered the room for the first team meeting in Tampa, Lawrence Taylor stood up.

"Well?!!"

"Well, what?" Parcells asked.

"Well, we got you here. Now what the hell are you going to do to help us win this game against these Buffalo Bills?"

"I always hold up my end of the bargain," Parcells laughed. "You guys are going to read a lot of things from my mouth this week in the press. Don't believe a word. I'm going to blow so much smoke up Buffalo's skirts all week. Let 'em start believing how good they are."

Toward the end of the week, Parcells told Taylor to pick a fight with Jumbo Elliott.

"Off the field, Jumbo was our mild-mannered offensive left tackle. But he was mean on the field and had a short fuse," Taylor remembered.

"The thing about Jumbo was, if you beat him on a pass rush in practice you better watch your eyes, your throat, your head, and your ankles or else he'll get you," Michael Strahan once said of Elliott. "Jumbo was just plain vindictive. He made you want to spit in his face damn near every practice. He's always sliding his fingers under my facemask, into my eyes, or punching my throat."

Taylor beat Elliott the first time, and Elliott mumbled something at him.

"I started talking a little smack and gave him extra smacks," Taylor remembered.

The second time, the short-fused Elliott screamed at Taylor, "Yeah, well you're nothing but a fucking crackhead."

"It was on. The fight was a doozy, too!" Taylor remembered.

The two mixed up pretty ferociously from there and had to be separated by teammates. Parcells explained to Elliott that he had asked Taylor to instigate the fight but that Elliott was facing one of the game's best pass rushers in Bruce Smith, and Elliott had to play his best game ever in this Super Bowl. Elliott forgave Taylor after Parcells' explanation.

"But it fired the team up," Taylor added.

"LT's relationship with Bill was the way I wanted to be with my head coach," Dave Meggett remembered. "They were like brothers and friends, and Bill was also a mentor and a father figure. That was a beautiful relationship those guys had. They would talk all the time."

Parcells remembered once before a Redskins game when Taylor was pacing the sidelines during the National Anthem. While Parcells had been on a number of players that week, he hadn't really been on Taylor's case much. As the music ended, Parcells turned to Taylor.

"Are you gonna play today?" Parcells hollered at Taylor.

"You just worry about those other SOBs you coach!" Taylor screamed back.

"Bill was my number-one motivator. When shit wasn't goin' right, and I wasn't playing right, he always had a way to get me excited about playing the game," Taylor said.

Four days before the Super Bowl, Parcells was asked what he would do at the end of this football year. "The year isn't over yet, so I'm not thinking about that. When the year is over, I'll answer what you're thinking about asking now," Parcells answered.

Speculation was circling in the press that this would be Parcells' last hurrah with the Giants. There was even speculation he would leave to coach the Tampa Bay Buccaneers.

"They haven't talked to us to get permission to talk to him," Wellington Mara said. "It's another story. He's under contract to us. As far as I know, he has no intention of not fulfilling his contract."

"He's under contract to the Giants. So if he's going to coach, he will coach for the Giants," co-owner Tim Mara said.

"It's total speculation, an old story they're beating to death. Tampa Bay has said they're not interested in people under contract," General Manager George Young told the press.

"The last time we won one of these," Parcells told the press, "there was a little controversy about me and it didn't allow my owners and general manager to enjoy this very much. They're going to enjoy this one, I promise you. There's not going to be any controversy."

— —

Finally it was game day.

"I hate waiting," Parcells has often said. "Every game should start at 1:00 in the afternoon."

"As a creature of habit and superstition, Parcells had been in the lobby of the Hyatt Regency Westshore in the darkness before dawn, drinking coffee with his now backup quarterback Matt Cavanaugh and his one-time high school basketball coach, Mickey Corcoran," Dave Anderson reported.

"Mickey's like my second father, he influenced me toward the profession," Parcells has often said. "He's had a tremendous effect on my life. You're seeing a reflection in me now of what he was as a coach. How things should be done. Things you don't do. Things you do do. He's almost 70 years old, and all he talks about is winning games. I hope I have something like that to keep me going when I'm 70."

The Buffalo Bills were heavily favored to win Super Bowl XXV. The Bills had scored 95 points in two playoff games. Many thought the New York offense was suspect since it had failed to score a touchdown against the 49ers the previous week.

The Giants' game plan was in evidence the first time they touched the ball. After forcing a punt, the Giants offense marched slowly and methodically down the field, taking 6:15 off the clock, and took a three-point lead on a Matt Bahr field goal. The Bills answered back, marching the field in 1:23 and scoring their own field goal. But the Bills gained momentum after another offensive drive yielded a touchdown, and Bruce Smith sacked Hostetler in the end zone for a safety. By then the Bills led 12–3. Smith had attempted to strip the ball, but Hostetler held on valiantly, which may have been a game-saving play by the quaterback. The Giants made a solid drive before the end of the half, closing the gap 12–10.

"I was at a Super Bowl five years ago and some of you guys were with me and we were in the exact same situation as we are now," Parcells said at halftime in the locker room. "I told them the first drive of the third quarter was the most important of the game. We had to do something with it."

In the beginning of the third quarter, the Giants went on a brutal, grinding 9:29 offensive drive that was capped by an Ottis Anderson 1-yard touchdown plunge. The offense was holding up its side of the game plan. The Giants led 17–12.

True to form, and by Belichick's design, Thurman Thomas ate up huge chunks of real estate running the ball, but the Bills had been stymied. However, Buffalo did put together a 63-yard, four-play drive, and on the first play of the fourth quarter, Buffalo scored on a 31-yard run by Thomas to take a 19–17 lead.

Unfortunately for Buffalo's defense, while the score was useful, the offense hadn't held onto the ball very long at all. The Giants ran another time-consuming drive, 74 yards and 14 plays, eating up 7:32 from the clock. The drive stalled, but the Giants scored on a Matt Bahr field goal.

After trading punts, the Bills started their last desperate drive, coming down to the Giants 29-yard line, setting up a 47-yard field goal with time nearly running out. Scott Norwood, the Bills' kicker, took the field and pushed the ball wide right on his subsequent kick. The Giants won 20–19.

The Giants were world champions, and Bill Parcells was hailed as a hero and a genius. Tim Mara called Parcells the greatest coach the Giants ever had.

"Power football wins games," Parcells proudly stated to the press. "It's not always the fanciest way, but it can win games."

He was also modest, saying, "I realized a long time ago that God was playing in some of these games. He was on our side today. We played as well as we could. If we played tomorrow, they would probably win 20–19."

"Bill ended up having a private party after the game for about a hundred people," then rookie NFL coach Charlie Weis said. "At about 3:30 in the morning, I went up to him, I slapped him on the back and said, 'I thought you said this was tough.' It was probably the only time that you could ever get away with saying something like that to him."

"I'll see you next year," Parcells said. "I've got to talk to my assistant coaches, I've got to get Plan B [free agency system] straightened out. I've got to go to the scouting combines."

"Whenever Parcells talked about Sunday's victory, he thanked the general manager, George Young, and the Mara co-owners, Wellington and Tim, for their support in supplying players," Dave Anderson of *The New York Times* wrote.

"Everything written about me is a fabrication," Parcells said firmly. "I've talked to no one in any field."

— —

On the Monday morning after the Super Bowl, Parcells held his last press conference of the Super Bowl weekend. After answering the last question, he requested a photo of him and his wife, Judy, standing next to the Lombardi Trophy. Bill Pennington of the *Bergen Record* wrote, "And what a picture it made. They were supposed to be posing behind the sterling silver Super Bowl trophy that sat on a low table before them, awash in spotlights. But Mr. and Mrs. Parcells stole the scene. You couldn't focus on anything else." According to Pennington, "No man-made object could match those smiles. You can hardly describe a twinkle in someone's eyes, let alone duplicate it. This was a lifetime of work, struggle, and union captured in a moment."

"I'd like a copy of that picture, guys," Parcells said, and repeated it several times. "Can I get a copy?"

Parcells said that after the Super Bowl, he celebrated quietly. "Got my family together. We had a few beers, talked, and ate some hors d'oeuvres. I had to get my wife away from that shrimp plate. She ate two to three pounds of that." Judy gave him a dirty look, and they both laughed.

"I always felt like that it would have been a shame had we lost that game, and we could have. But I always felt like it would have been a shame because I really think that we did a better job in that game and our players did a better job than the opponent did. And it would have been sad for us to lose that one, fortunately we didn't," Parcells said of the accomplishment.

CHAPTER 6
Movin' Out

"**B**ill left the Giants four months after Super Bowl XXV. He'd told me a week or two before the game that this was it. I just listened. It was sad. I always thought we would go out together," Taylor wrote. "I couldn't see how George Young and the organization could allow him to go. But I could see the power struggle."

"The silence at Giants Stadium is deafening. And in the silence, Bill Parcells' return as the coach of the Super Bowl XXV champions is suddenly uncertain," Dave Anderson wrote in *The New York Times* in March 1991.

"I don't really know what I want to do," Parcells answered when pressed. "I'm thinking it over."

As Anderson explained it, "Less than four weeks after the Super Bowl triumph, 50 percent of the Giants stock as held by Tim Mara, his sister Maura Mara Concannon, and their mother, Helen Mara, was sold to Preston Robert Tisch, the billionaire president of Loews Corporation, for an estimated $70 million. And for Parcells, Tim Mara's departure was significant." Parcells liked Wellington, but he was closer to Tim. They talked regularly. Now Tim was gone, and with him yet another attachment for Parcells was severed.

According to Anderson, Tisch didn't seem disturbed. "Bill is at the age where he's wondering what he's going to do with the rest of his life."

"I expect Bill to be back with us. It's strictly in George's hands," Wellington Mara said.

143

Young thought such posturing was part ploy, as Parcells was up for a contract renegotiation. Parcells' contract was stalled. From the outside many thought it was Young's doing (he was attending the annual NFL meetings and the competition committee meetings) but the truth that few knew was that it was in fact Parcells who was stalling.

In early May, Richard Sandomir of *The New York Times* reported that Parcells had auditioned with NBC Sports. "In what could be termed a serious flirtation with television or a tactic aimed at raising the ante in his contract negotiations with George Young, the Giants' general manager, the person seeing the audition said that Parcells and Don Criqui teamed up several weeks ago. They were reported to have provided analysis and play-by-play of a tape of a 1991 American Conference playoff game as if the contest were live."

"Is that what I did?" Parcells commented with his customary touch of sarcasm when asked for a comment.

Young expressed surprise at Parcells' television foray. "I'm being most frank I've never heard of it. He never mentioned it to me. But I don't think it's a negotiating ploy. I put a lot of things in the category of ploy, and I don't think this is one. I don't know if he did it just to see if he'd like it. But he's been saying he's uncertain, so that's all I can go by."

By now, the "brilliant" defensive coordinator, Bill Belichick, had left to be the head coach at Cleveland.

When asked about Erhardt, Parcells said ominously, "Ron will always be with me. Either here or wherever I am."

Bill Parcells announced his retirement from the New York Giants on May 15, 1991. Parcells, who would turn 50 that August, had recently complained of chest pains. He had also re-gained almost 30 pounds he had lost during the previous season when he was on an Ultra Slimfast diet promotion. Parcells was alarmed; he was shocked when Chicago Bears head coach Mike Ditka was hospitalized after a heart attack the previous season.

"Any of us in this business can identify with it," Parcells said the day the news about Ditka was released. "I drink coffee. I smoke regularly. I'm 30 pounds overweight. Real smart."

Also, there was the ultimate challenge—rebuilding the Giants. Its main stars—Simms and Taylor—were getting older. And a down year following a second Super Bowl would surely draw ire from the fans. Parcells had always repeated what he'd learned in the college ranks—it's easier to turn around a bad program than it was to keep a good one afloat.

"I feel like it's time," Parcells said regarding his resignation. "I don't have a crystal ball. I don't know what's going to happen. About coaching again, I don't know. Not this year."

"There's a big difference between trying to maintain something and trying to achieve something. I've always found that I function a lot better in achieving."

"Players come and go, coaches come and go, and recently, owners come and go," he added, referring to Tim Mara's recent sale to the Tisch family.

Asked if he had any criticism of the Giants, Parcells said, "Yeah, I think they ought to throw a little more on first down."

Asked how he would fill that competitive void in his life, Parcells answered, "That's a good question. I really don't know. I'm hoping I can find something that challenges me. Being a coach is what I've been, so I'm not going to say I won't miss it. That's going to be hard, but I'm not going to be detached completely."

"A coach couldn't have had a better general manager to work for and with," Parcells said of Young.

"I'm not ruling anything out, but I'm not looking for a job."

The Giants announced that Ray Handley would be the new coach the same day.

"We kinda got this feeling that [if] Bill Parcells stayed, we would win forever," Mark Bavaro admitted. "We had a really young team, a young offensive line, good running backs, and two really good quarterbacks. When Parcells retired, it came as a shock to so many."

"I heard 'em from time to time, but I never believed 'em," Phil Simms said of the rumors of Parcells' departure. "When he told me, in all honesty, I was shocked. I didn't think it would ever happen."

"I always thought if Bill had stayed we could have won one more Super Bowl," Taylor agreed. "You just get the feeling we could have done more."

TALKING HEADS

In June 1991, NBC Sports announced that Bill Parcells would join their team as a studio analyst for their *The NFL Live* show. Parcells would be paid $250,000 for the first two years and $400,000 for the last in a three-year deal. Parcells would also be paired with Will McDonough to preview NFL games after six Notre Dame games.

"This is a chance to stay close to the game and hopefully provide some expertise that may not be available," Parcells said.

"Parcells said one of the deciding factors in his becoming a studio analyst rather than a game analyst in the booth was his friendship with McDonough, one of the *NFL Live* mainstays," wrote *The New York Times'* media reporter, Richard Sandomir. "'When you're doing something that's a new career endeavor, you want to talk to somebody you have confidence in, who'll give it to you straight. Will convinced me that this would be a real good opportunity.'"

One important aspect of Parcells' contract with NBC was an escape clause that allowed Parcells to leave in his first year for a job as a coach or general manager.

Almost one week later, Parcells added a second television gig to his resume, signing on to co-host an NFL preview show on the Madison Square Garden Network. The hour-long weekly program provided analysis of upcoming games and featured sports radio WFAN's Mike Francesa on a show called *Around the NFL*.

Parcells and Francesa had built a friendship over the last three years as Francesa's reputation had grown on WFAN radio and on CBS television, according to Sandomir. The two were both known to go to Manny's in Moonachi, and both dabbled in race horses.

"Over time, we'd talked about if Bill decided he didn't want to coach that we might put together an NFL show that we'd have a lot of control over," Francesa said. "Then we put it aside until he made his decision."

In mid-July Parcells attended what NBCers called Camp O'Neill, "a two-day conclave of NBC Sports' football announcers, producers, and directors summoned annually by executive producer Terry O'Neil to prepare for the coming season, which will combine NFL and University of Notre Dame football," according to Sandomir.

Parcells was welcomed by the team in a unique way.

"They had put together a few outtakes of some of my more, uh, raucous conduct on the sidelines"—in reality a fast-paced, endless barrage of profanity-laden clips—"and showed them to the group yesterday as a welcome for me. I had forgotten I'd said some of those things. I was quick to get my hands on the only copy of it."

Parcells was asked to speak on certain topics, and former 49ers coach Bill Walsh spoke on others. Mostly, he listened to others speak. "I'm learning about the technical aspects, which is where I'm lacking," Parcells said. "I knew nothing, so I learned something, but I'm well below 1 on a scale of 10 in that area."

In his NFL debut, Bob Raissman of *Sports Illustrated* wrote of Parcells, "The Parcells humor—very Maddenesque at times—was apparent," referring to making up a name for versatile running backs who could be used at other receiving positions, excitedly calling them "satellite players." The regular guy in Parcells came out, too. It wasn't forced or contrived. He seemed a bit harried at times. Chalk that up to excitement."

Richard Sandomir opined of Parcells, "He defined mediocrity at NBC in the studio and on games in 1991 and 1992; the Parcells that television may never get is the one who saves his best stuff for off the air, or in off-the-record conversations."

Parcells proved both entertaining and insightful, as well as earning listener and viewer respect for his brutal honesty. His chatter with Francesa was fun and loose.

In a run-through of the show a few days before the debut, Parcells started in and selected the Bears to finish ahead of the Vikings in the NFC Central.

Parcells: "I'll bury you on this."

Francesa: "How many winning teams did Chicago beat last year?"

Parcells: "I don't care." (They were both wrong, the Lions went 12–4.)

There was also some discussion about the transition to the separate console where Parcells would diagram plays.

"This is a crisis? For three weeks, we've been talking about this. What can happen while I'm walking there? Do I need a cab? I don't have to take my clothes off, do I?"

At one point Parcells was asked about Vestee Jackson, a Dolphins defensive back.

"He's an icewhacker," Parcells said.

"He's what?"

"Slow. Very slow," an irked Parcells said.

"Parcells is the dominating personality on the show, but he knows relatively little about television. Francesa is a radio guy whose past work on CBS as a college football and basketball analyst hasn't required him to carry the show," Sandomir wrote.

"I don't want Bill just to say a team can do this or can't do this," Francesa said. "I want him to say, 'People don't know he's the most underrated player in the league,' or 'You know why this team does this?' or 'People see this team one way, here's how I see them.'"

"I don't think Mike will have to get under my skin," Parcells said. "If there's good interaction, I'll respond honestly. Mike isn't going to make me mad. What do I have to be mad about?"

"Getting under his skin won't be a problem. And I don't mind if he gives me a hard time," Francesa responded.

Around the NFL, the MSG Network show, was not renewed for a second year.

"I'm disappointed, I wanted to do a second year, but it's a very expensive show to produce," Francesa said.

Francesca and Parcells also owned thoroughbred race horses together. In 1999, their horse, Alpine Mickey, won for his owners on a Sunday race in August in Saratoga. Parcells loved horse racing. "My dad was interested in horses, and I used to go with him once in a while to Monmouth Park," Parcells said. "I was 17 or 18. I always liked it. I liked being with him. I'm not a horse fanatic; I like it," he said. Parcells estimates he took part in owning 15 horses over the years.

"The best was a little filly called Personal Girl," Parcells said. "John Hertler trained her." From 1993 to 1996, Personal Girl won 11-of-63 races with 11 seconds, six thirds, and earnings of $366,945. The pair also owned a horse named Nickel Defense. He also partnered with John

Perrotta, who owns and operates Star Stable. Parcells' involvement with thoroughbred racing has included meeting numerous famous horse trainers, including Hall of Famer Shug McGaughey.

"Shug is one of my best friends," Parcells said. "He's the guy I know best. I love him. He's a great guy. Shug has helped me eye horses, and maybe I've helped his eye with football. We talk a lot about athletes, people, and horses. I don't think there's a great difference. You have characteristics in football players and you see the same characteristics in horses. Some are lazy. Some work hard. Some get hurt. You see horses that want to go to the track and run. You see some similarities."

Parcells likes to spend time around the back stretch, as well. "I go to the barns in the morning," he said. "I've known Nick Zito. I have a high regard for him, too. I've played golf with Stanley Hough and Kiaran McLaughlin. I've known Wayne Lukas for quite a while."

TOTAL ECLIPSE OF THE HEART

Parcells knew his health had not been good and that he was under tremendous stress, some of it placed there by himself. It turned out after many doctor's visits, tests revealed that Parcells had a heart arrhythmia. Heart problems would hamper Parcells until the middle of 1992.

"He used to smoke, he didn't sleep enough, and he wasn't eating right," remembered Johnny Parker, who was Parcells' strength and conditioning coach with the Giants. "Bill would have these big ol' bowls of peanut butter, and he'd just eat it by the barrel. He never could relax."

Parcells was not exactly eating the breakfast of champions. He had a large appetite, and when not eating peanut butter, he was known to gobble donuts, cookies, candy bars, and lots of other foods. He was known to eat an entire sleeve of Fig Newtons in less than 10 minutes.

"We were having problems finding out exactly what was wrong with me," Parcells said. "For eight or 10 months, the doctors weren't able to tell me. Well, we think it's adrenaline, they'd say. Or we think it's anxiety. But nobody knew, and that was exasperating to me."

"It was tough to admit that I really couldn't coach, and the doctors told me that. I wanted to coach, but I had a host of physical problems with my heart and everything. It was a sad day for me because of how good the Maras were to me and how much I enjoyed the experience," Parcells said.

Parcells' first heart procedure was in December 1991. He underwent an angioplasty procedure to clear his left anterior descending artery, which had a blockage of 95 percent to 99 percent.

"Mr. Parcells tolerated the procedure well and is now listed as stable," said Dr. Michael Kesselbrenner, attending cardiologist at Valley Hospital in Ridgewood, New Jersey. Angioplasty is a nonsurgical procedure to improve blood flow, generally in patients with milder blockages. He was released the following day.

Two months later, in February 1992, Parcells was back for a second angioplasty procedure. "No matter what you do, one-quarter to one-third of these recur," Dr. Kesselbrenner said. The doctor explained that the artery was now 80 percent blocked as compared to 99 percent blocked from the previous procedure. Parcells also underwent stress tests.

"If he were 20 years old," Kesselbrenner said, "he'd be in the top 5 percent of conditioning. Among 50-year-olds, he's in the top 1 percent."

However, Parcells' health did not improve, and by April he was scheduled for surgery. This time he was scheduled with Dr. Patrick Whitlow, a cardiologist at the Cleveland Clinic. Whitlow performed an atherectomy. "In this procedure, the plaque is scraped from the artery walls or destroyed by laser. Dan Reeves, the head coach of the Denver Broncos, underwent an atherectomy in August 1990," the *Times* reported.

"I feel fine," Parcells told sportswriter Bill Madden. "I'm just unlucky. At least that's what the doctors tell me. The problem is that the scar tissue from the scraping they did has caused a blockage. That happens with certain people no matter how well they follow their diet."

However, this surgery was not successful either, and by June 1992, Parcells was scheduled for major heart surgery at Temple University. "I went to Temple University to have the bypass. And I was on the stretcher being wheeled down to the pre-op room, going in for my surgery. And there was this young black intern that had played football at Temple that was wheeling me down there," Parcells recalled.

"He said to me, 'Coach, could you sign this? Could you sign this for me?' So I looked at him and I said, 'You know, you're just going to sell this for a lot if I don't come out of here, aren't you?'" Parcells said. "You know, he said to me, 'I'll be there when you get out.' And you know, the very next day he was there."

Parcells had bypass surgery, wherein a bypass artery was inserted on either side of the blockage to create a free flow of blood to the heart. "This could have been managed with medication, but he still would have had chest pains. He wanted to be active. He's in excellent shape. He runs every day. He got some pain on Friday when he was running and didn't like it. So I recommended the surgery," Dr. Kesselbrenner said. He was released six to eight days after his surgery.

OF PIRATES AND MEATPACKERS

There was no question that at the end of 1991 and the beginning of 1992, Parcells missed coaching. But was he ready to return? He was still having health problems, but, as the coaching merry-go-round began to swirl, Parcells was an obvious candidate.

In December 1991, the team that made the most serious effort to engage Parcells' attention was the Tampa Bay Buccaneers. The Associated Press reported, "Hugh Culverhouse, the owner of the Tampa Bay Buccaneers, has flown to the New York area and, according to a published report, hopes to persuade Bill Parcells to take his team's coaching job."

"He's gone off in the hope of bringing home the big trophy," the *Orlando Sentinel* quoted an unidentified person familiar with the situation, alluding to Parcells. "Culverhouse had reportedly told Buccaneers officials to prepare financial information to take with him," the *Sentinel* said.

But that was not the only job Parcells was considered for. Parcells was good friends with Ron Wolf, the general manager of the Green Bay Packers, who had just fired his most recent head coach, Lindy Infante.

Two days later, Culverhouse's camp leaked information that Culverhouse and Parcells had come to an accord, with the *Orlando Sentinel* reporting that the two sides "have successfully negotiated most of the key components of a long-term contract agreement."

"Most of the key points are in place," the source said. "There is one key point remaining. I think it would be fair to say that if there were 60 points to the deal, they are in total agreement on 59 of them."

According to Richard Sandomir, Greg Gumbel of CBS's *The NFL Today* reported that Parcells had met "within the past few weeks" with Hugh Culverhouse, the Tampa Bay Buccaneers owner, at Teterboro Airport in New Jersey.

"Before his next round of denials," Gumbel asked his studiomates, Terry Bradshaw, Mike Francesa, and John Czarnecki, "where do you see Bill Parcells going?"

However, Parcells balked in public. "There's no truth to anything you've heard," he said from his office in Lyndhurst, New Jersey. "Nothing has changed. Write it."

Reports put the Tampa Bay Buccaneers offer at $1.5 million a year to become their head coach. The Bucs wanted to sign Parcells by the weekend; however, the Packers were taking their time.

At a news conference, Wolf was asked if Parcells was one of his candidates. "I won't touch that with a 10-foot pole," Wolf said, though he said he would at least contact Parcells.

"Bill likes the idea that the Packers have five draft choices in the first three rounds this year, four in the first three rounds next year. They're only a couple of drafts away from being a competitive team. They're not a horrible 4–12 team. They lack mental discipline, but they were competitive in every game this year," an unidentified source in Green Bay told the press. "They're the only show in town. They have a lot of money in the bank, and they're willing to spend it. He could rebuild in three years in Green Bay where it might take seven years at Tampa Bay."

Culverhouse told the media that Parcells had agreed Thursday on a five-year, $6.5 million contract to coach and also run the entire football operation. And then on December 30, Culverhouse said that Parcells backed out.

"In the end, I thought it may be too big a job, too many hats to wear at this time in professional football. It was just something about it in the end that didn't feel right," Parcells said.

"I was to hear from him Saturday afternoon to determine if we would do it Tuesday or announce it sooner," Culverhouse told the press. "I called him at 10:00 PM Saturday night at home. He said he had a change of heart and was not coming to Tampa Bay.... He would be director of football operations with complete control."

Culverhouse continued, "We agreed last Monday night, person to person, somewhere in New York or New Jersey, I forget where. Then he wrote down the points we agreed on and put it in a letter, which I received Thursday. We talked and went over it point by point."

During the conversations Parcells decided he wanted an experienced NFL executive to run the front office and handle contracts. Culverhouse agreed.

"He said we were all set; we will execute the contract," Culverhouse said. "It was executed by Tampa Bay. We now feel we have been jilted at the altar. I regret it for the team's sake and the fans and the community because I thought we had reached a milestone."

"Are you sure Tampa Bay is where you want to go?" Culverhouse reportedly asked Parcells.

"Your contract will not be used to negotiate with someone else," Parcells said.

"He said he had one other team to talk to, but he was coming to Tampa Bay and we had an agreement," Culverhouse remembered. "I respect Bill Parcells' decision. I don't like it. I'm not angry, but I'm disappointed."

Parcells had seen their conversations differently, saying, "We had not agreed. I agreed to consider the job on the basis of a number of things that we enumerated in writing. I never said I would take the job."

Regardless, there was no question that Parcells' conversation with Ray Perkins, who had also coached at Tampa Bay, played some role in Parcells' decision making.

"Bill Parcells pulled off what many in pro football thought was impossible: He made Tampa Bay Buccaneers owner Hugh Culverhouse a sympathetic figure by rejecting a written deal he had negotiated for a week," Vito Stellino at the *Baltimore Sun* wrote.

According to Stellino, Culverhouse "made a giant attempt to gain credibility for his downtrodden franchise last week by giving Parcells what he said even Parcells called a 'fabulous offer.' Culverhouse offered the former New York Giants coach everything he wanted—total control of the franchise spelled out in 38 points in writing."

Parcells and Wolf did meet to discuss the Packers' job. The meeting took place on a Wednesday in New Jersey.

Wolf issued a statement, saying, "We had a preliminary discussion. A contract was not offered."

"I met with him. No job was offered. We discussed the parameters of the job, and I have an understanding of what the job is," Parcells told the press.

On January 5, 1992, Parcells said on *The NFL Live*, "I had spoken to Ron Wolf on Wednesday and we agreed to talk later in the week, if necessary. I think we mutually agreed that it wasn't necessary and that was the end of that."

Parcells elaborated, "It's not a change of heart. It just never progressed to where a lot of people in the media thought it did."

Having turned away from both Tampa Bay and Green Bay, Parcells said, "I don't think there will be any other interest" from teams seeking coaches.

Several days later Parcells wavered and contacted Culverhouse, who agreed to meet Parcells in Washington D.C. The two met for 2-1/2 hours, but no agreement was reached. The next day Culverhouse issued a statement that verbally spanked Parcells, saying, "Mr. Culverhouse stated that today's meeting did not provide him with the comfort level to pursue further discussions. There was no discussion of any modification of the monetary terms or other conditions of the original offer."

"Bill was disappointed," said Stephen Story, a Bucs attorney who attended the meeting. "He had looked forward to the possibility of being coach. He had his opportunity, and it just didn't happen this time."

— —

"Explain why you continue to do this?" Judy had once asked her husband in one of the two seasons after the first Super Bowl. "The times that you do it are so much fewer than the rest of the other stuff. What kind of ego do you have that you have to keep proving it to yourself?

What else do you have to do? Is it that you have to prove you can get to the top of the profession, that you can sustain yourself at the top of your profession? Why do you do it? You're not happy, so why do you keep doing it?"

"I told her she didn't understand," Parcells said. "I told her it's just about competition because my whole life, since I was seven years old, you went to the gym or you went to the playground. It was always, 'Who are we playing and where?' I'm still doing it. Nothing has changed. Who are we playing today?"

In October 1992, it was clear Parcells was missing the action. He arrived at Giants Stadium to do announcing for a Giants-Seahawks game with Marv Albert. Parcells was sentimental, saying, "There's a lot of my blood in this place."

Amid the chant of the stadium faithful, "Ray must go! Ray must go!" Parcells talked like a man with something on his mind. Asked if he would return to coaching, or even the Giants, Parcells said, "After having seen some of the things here today, I'm not sure. But you never know. I miss the big-game thrill as much as anybody."

"Standing in the Super Bowl tunnel, that doesn't happen up here in the booth," he said after the game. "Once you've experienced that, it's a little like a narcotic. You do chase it. You don't do something for 28 years without some of that."

"I'm not into nostalgia," Parcells told sportswriter Gary Myers. "But I'm not without memories."

Ray Handley's days were numbered, and the press was abuzz about Parcells' imminent return. And it was revealed years later that Parcells had called Wellington, asking about the team's plans for the job after Handley was gone.

"If the Giants wanted me 100 percent, I'd think about it hard," he confided during that time to Dave Anderson. "You could blow your whistle six times and find out who wanted to be part of it," Parcells said, referring to his players.

— —

The entire NFL world waited for the return of the Giants' favorite son.

But George Young never picked up the phone. Young felt betrayed by Parcells' desertion in early 1991 and refused to discuss the possibility of his return. Behind closed doors, Young vehemently denounced Parcells, reminding the owners of Parcells' and Fraley's threats after each Super Bowl. The owners stood by Young. He had been associated with Super Bowl winners his entire career, and he had been responsible for resurrecting the franchise and remained loyal to it.

Young was intent on signing Dave Wannstedt, the Dallas Cowboys defensive coordinator, but was out hustled by Ed McCaskey of the Chicago Bears. Dave Anderson of *The New York Times* admonished Young, writing, "By waiting instead of acting, Young committed pro football's deadliest sin, on or off the field: he got out-hustled."

If it was true that Young never called Parcells, it was also true Parcells never called Young. By mid-January, the Giants had been spurned by former Parcells assistant Tom Coughlin, who instead chose Boston College, and were in discussion with Dan Reeves, the former Broncos coach.

One of the jobs still open was with the New England Patriots.

The Patriots were talking to everyone, including Mike Ditka, Buddy Ryan—both of whom were no longer employed—and Ray Rhodes, the defensive coordinator of the Green Bay Packers. Bill Parcells auditioned just as the others had.

"I think Bill felt it was time to move on from the Giants, even though he has roots there," said Will McDonough writer for the *Boston Globe* and an NBC and CBS commentator who had befriended Bill on his first time around with the Patriots. "He had lived in New England in 1980 and liked it there. His wife liked it, too. So I think it became a matter of if he had the opportunity to come here, he would. That message was passed along to James Orthwein."

Orthwein was a St. Louis business executive. He had bought the Patriots from Victor Kiam. There was a movement in St. Louis at the time to find another football team. There was also some conjecture that

Orthwein would try to move the team at one point. The team did not own the stadium; that was owned by paper tycoon Robert Kraft.

"He also liked the situation with Orthwein. He was a hands-off owner who planned to live in St. Louis and wouldn't even be around the team."

"This is it, carry the ball. You're the boss," Orthwein reportedly told Parcells.

On January 22, 1993, at the Westin Copley Hotel, Bill Parcells was announced as the new head coach of the New England Patriots and had reportedly signed a five-year, $5 million contract. Owner James Orthwein was ecstatic.

As Judy and Bill were driving through Connecticut on their way to his first Patriots press conference, Judy turned to Bill and said, "This is the first day I've seen you excited in two years."

And he was. But it was more about the competition than it was about the money. "I could get the same feeling at Smithfield [Rhode Island] High School. The magnitude of where it is or what's on the line doesn't matter."

For Parcells it was the challenge—to rebuild an NFL franchise from the ground up. "I wish it wasn't ground zero, and I don't know that it is. But whether it's ground zero or it's halfway done made no difference to me."

But the first few questions were all about the Giants. In their first meeting, Orthwein told Parcells he wanted a "competitive team."

"I told him I wasn't interested in a competitive team, but if he was interested in attempting to bring a championship team to New England, then I was his man," Parcells said.

"It's something I've missed very much," Parcells said of coaching. "It's like the schoolyard when you're kid. You have to grow up sometime, but fortunately, I haven't had to. But this is my last coaching job, without question...this is my last deal. I'm John Wayne after this one."

"The Maras are the two men responsible for what Bill Parcells has," Parcells told the press. "There'll always be a warm place in my heart for them."

"Did George Young think you didn't have commitment anymore?" one reporter asked after the conference.

"I don't know what he thought," he said. "You're telling me what he thought. I don't know what he thought. All I can tell you is what Bill Parcells is thinking."

"Why didn't George even call you?"

"You'll have to ask him. Don't ask me," Parcells said.

"Did you think of calling him?"

"No, I never thought about it."

When asked for a comment on Parcells' signing, Young told the press, "Bill had a great career here. He was a great asset to the club and a great help to my career. If he feels he wants to continue to coach, I wish him a great deal of luck. I've always felt that way and nothing has changed."

Bill Parcells as head coach of the Air Force Falcons in 1978 at Falcons
Stadium in Colorado Springs, Colorado. Parcells coached the team for one
year before leaving to be an assistant with the New York Giants in 1979.
(AP Photo/NFL Photos)

Bill Parcells (center) in a discussion with Giants quarterback Phil Simms. At the right is offensive co-coordinator Ron Erhardt. They were in Fresno, California, on Saturday, December 26, 1984, for the second day of workouts in preparation for a game against the 49ers. (AP Photo)

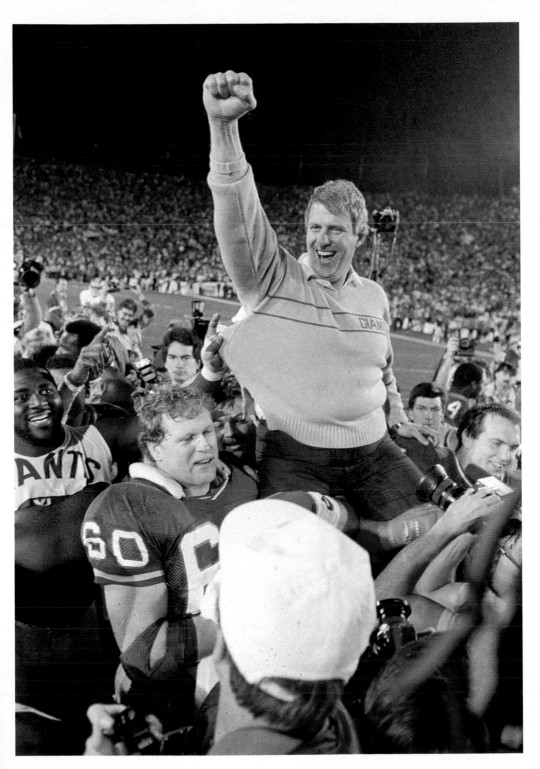

Bill Parcells is carried off the field after the Giants defeated the Denver Broncos 39–20 in Super Bowl XXI in Pasadena, California, on January 25, 1987. (AP Photo/Eric Risberg)

Bill Parcells receives a cooler full of Gatorade over his head courtesy of Giants players Everson Walls (28) and Carl Banks (58) as time runs out in the Giants' 31–3 victory over the Chicago Bears at Giants Stadium in East Rutherford, New Jersey, on Sunday, January 13, 1991. To the right of Parcells are Giants Pepper Johnson (52) and Lawrence Taylor (56). (AP Photo/Mark Lennihan)

Head coach Bill Parcells calls out during the game between his New England Patriots and the Pittsburgh Steelers on December 16, 1995, at Heinz Field in Pittsburgh, Pennsylvania. (AP Photo/Paul Spinelli)

Head coach Bill Parcells of the Dallas Cowboys looks on during a game against the New York Giants at Texas Stadium in Irving, Texas, on December 21, 2003. Dallas won 19–3. (AP Photo/G. Newman Lowrance)

Seattle Seahawks coach Mike Holmgren (right) and Dallas Cowboys coach Bill Parcells chat in the stands during the NFL Combine in Indianapolis on Saturday, February 25, 2006. (AP Photo/Michael Conroy)

In December 2007, Bill Parcells signed a four-year contract to become the executive vice president of football operations for the Miami Dolphins. This image was taken in 2009. (AP Photo)

CHAPTER 7

Please Come to Boston

"**I**n 1990 my brother, Don, was part of a new management team that took the reins at First Fidelity Bank in New Jersey. At the time the bank was in a tenuous position; it was in imminent risk of a takeover, either by the government or by some other group," Parcells wrote.

"The bank is on a death march," Don told Bill. "We're going to concentrate on three or four things here, and we're going to get these things done."

The management team came up with a philosophy, and no matter its popularity with insiders or outsiders, they remained true to their core principals. They dissolved unprofitable or less productive groups, they consolidated operations, they installed new computer systems and made 30 high-revenue acquisitions. The stock value increased sharply.

In 1991 Donald C. Parcells was made the northern regional president of First Fidelity, later known as First Union Bank. And he would keep that job for the next eight years.

"One day in 1993, Don Parcells was sitting behind his desk at First Fidelity," Steve Politi wrote. "He was a man on top of his profession, a successful businessman who climbed the corporate ladder to become a wealthy bank president. He was feeling pretty good about his life."

Then his phone rang. It was his brother.

"You know, it's just not right," Bill said.

"What?" Don replied.

"You were always the good kid," Bill continued. "You did the right thing. You went to West Point. You fought in Vietnam. You worked hard all these years to get into a position to do well in your career."

"Yeah, so?"

"I was the P.E. major from Wichita State, the guy who bounced around from job to job all those years, and I just signed a $5 million contract to coach the New England Patriots," Bill said. "It just doesn't seem right."

The law of averages says a bank president would make a lot of money. And First Fidelity was one of the largest banks on the East Coast. In 1995, Don was elected to the board of First Fidelity. Between 1995 and 1996 Don would exercise options for 127,695 shares of common stock that he then cashed out for more than $6 million. This sum did not include his annual salary.

Boston Globe columnist Jim McCabe had some fun at Don's expense when he wrote a column of fictitious answering machine options listed on Don's work phone. A few prime examples included:

"Good afternoon. You've reached the office of Don Parcells, the banking brother of Patriots coach Bill Parcells. As you know, I'm a source close to Bill. If you'd like to discuss mortgage rates, please press 1.

"If you'd like information on mutual funds, investment opportunities, IRAs or other retirement plans, please press 2.

"If you'd like to talk about why my brother's team suddenly can't score touchdowns, please press 3.

"If you'd like to know more about the problems with New England's offensive line, please press 4."

And so on.

"In 1996, he was appointed president of First Union North after a merger with First Fidelity. The merger sent him home with a huge paycheck—and bragging rights," Steve Politi wrote in the *Newark Star-Ledger*.

"Don made about $5 million on that deal," Doug Parcells said. "I called Bill that night and told him, 'Well, it looks like you may have been knocked out of the top spot. I think maybe Don has more cash than you.'"

— —

Doug had played at Virginia, where he was a varsity tackle. In 1972, Al Groh was head coach of Virginia's freshman team recruited and landed, on Parcells' recommendation, Parcells' brother, Douglas, for the Cavaliers.

"Very intense guy," recalled Doug. Douglas Parcells had a daughter at U.Va. in 2002, and he still followed the football program closely.

Douglas Parcells lettered for the Virginia Cavaliers in 1973, 1974, and 1975. In those seasons, Virginia's record was 4–7, 4–7, and 1–10, respectively.

Doug married Helen Joanne Thompson, who was from Lexington, Virginia, on August 20, 1977, in the U.Va. chapel at Charlottesville, Virginia. They both became teachers. Doug taught physical education. They had two daughters, Laura Elizabeth Parcells (born in 1982) and Keri Susanne Parcells (born in 1985).

Doug taught in elementary schools and ran the summer recreational program in Oradell.

"One of the most important men in town was a guy named Doug Parcells. He was in charge of Oradell's recreation department, which pretty much meant he was a God to us kids," wrote Robert McGovern, a U.S. Army captain who grew up in Oradell. "I got to know Doug, or Dougie, really well when I was growing up. If there was a game being played anywhere in Oradell, Dougie Parcells was there, either as an umpire or a referee or just an interested spectator. Dougie was an incredibly funny and warm man who devoted his life to children."

Like his brother Bill had in his early career, Doug maintained all the ballfields and made sure the Oradell sports train ran on time. In 1987, Coach Doug Parcells took a physical education teaching position at Ramsey Elementary School. He has remained in the Ramsey school district ever since. He also coached the offensive and defensive line for the Ramsey High School football team.

"Every kid who grew up in Oradell in the 1970s and 1980s knew and loved Doug. If they built statues for people who made kids laugh and enjoy their childhood, there should be a huge one of Dougie Parcells right smack-dab in the middle of Memorial Field," Captain McGovern concluded.

~ ~

It took Bill Parcells four days to raid the Giants coaching staff and bring five of his assistants to New England, including Romeo Crennel (defensive line), Fred Hoaglin (offensive line), Johnny Parker (strength and conditioning); Mike Sweatman (special teams), and Charlie Weis (tight ends). Ray Perkins was tapped to be offensive coordinator, and Al Groh was tapped to be defensive coordinator.

Weis knew how tough Parcells could be. In his first few weeks on the job with the Giants, he spoke up at a meeting only to have Parcells bark at him, "You've been in the league five minutes. Shut the hell up." According to Peter King, Weis didn't talk again for eight weeks.

For Parcells, it was a chance to gather his old coaches for one "last round-up…. When I hang it up next time, that'll be it," Parcells vowed. "I'm gone. I'm history."

"He knows the downside of the job by heart—the crazy hours, the knotted stomach on game days, the sleepless nights after losses. And he has no illusions about professional immortality," John Powers wrote in the *Boston Globe*.

"Ten years from now, nobody will know if I coached or not," Parcells said. "I'll be like a grain of sand on the beach. I understand that probably better now than I did before."

"You really want to do this thing?" Parker asked when Parcells called him.

"As bad as I ever did," Parcells told him.

The running gag before too long was that the coffee shop waitress, Gretchen, was the only person who put in more hours than the coaches. "I've been eating twice a day at the hotel, early in the morning and then at night, but no matter when I am there, Gretchen's on duty," Parcells said. The other consistent entity in their life beyond game film and player profiles was Donut World.

"This job is like being a full-time resident of the Lincoln Tunnel. I haven't been off these little roads and the Foxboro circle since I got here," said Parcells, who drove back and forth to Foxboro in his black Cadillac. "There's some nice restaurants in town, but I've never been to them. Just Donut World. This isn't what I would call a cultural experience."

While it sounded like the old Parcells, he'd made a couple of lifestyle choices. Pushing himself like he had done with his last job had nearly killed him. He now drank decaf coffee. He quit smoking. He'd lost weight.

The Patriots were at their lowest point, and their stadium was one of the most illustrative examples. "The stadium was a dump. The locker rooms were small. You never knew if you were going to have hot water or not," then Patriots assistant Charlie Weis recalled. "You never knew if a pipe was going to break, and if one did, you didn't know who was going to fix it. Just trying to keep the place serviceable was a struggle. It was a significant step down from what [we] had been around with the Giants."

"Coach Bill Parcells emerged from his self-described bunker today, brandishing the top pick in the National Football League draft and, as usual, playing it coy," Gerald Eskenazi wrote in *The New York Times*.

It was rumored that the Patriots received several offers for their No. 1 pick in the 1993 NFL Draft. "The offers could be a competitive thing and in the Patriots' best interests," he said. "What I'm trying to do is to get better as quickly as possible."

The two top picks in the draft were possible franchise quarterbacks, Drew Bledsoe of Washington State and Rick Mirer of Notre Dame.

"I don't know if the Patriots are improved," Parcells said. "We made some changes we think will be helpful. I look at this as long range, and I don't think we can do anything overnight."

The Patriots had waded into the unrestricted free agent market with four pick-ups.

"Parcells defended his isolation from the news media since he became coach. He has avoided news conferences and has seldom spoken to the reporters covering the team," Eskenazi continued.

"We're trying to get things done," Parcells said. After staying longer than he had planned, Parcells asked, "Any other questions? I want to make sure I answer them all. I'm going back in the bunker."

The Patriots picked Drew Bledsoe. Typical of Parcells, he started haranguing Bledsoe before he even donned a Patriots jersey. Reporters were calling Bledsoe a "franchise quarterback." Parcells said to the press, "I detest the word. I think it's a term that has to be earned on the field by performance. When he is ready, I will use him and not before."

Bledsoe told the press that he heard Phil Simms was once asked, "What do you need to have to play for Bill Parcells?" and Simms answered, "Thick skin."

By training camp the media had created a whirlwind of excitement as to who would be the starting quarterback. "Parcells would not name a front-runner for the starting quarterback position among No. 1 pick Drew Bledsoe, Tommy Hodson, Scott Secules, and Scott Zolak," the *Boston Globe* reported.

"Everyone thinks it is a normal progression before [Bledsoe] starts at quarterback," Parcells said. "But if he is not and someone is better, that guy will play. It is unfair to the players for politics to infiltrate the team. I wouldn't let it. I go by what I see on the field."

"I don't know what happened here before," Parcells said. "I'm not into that. My main objective in camp is getting ready to play the Buffalo Bills. I'm not here to send messages or establish anything. I'm here to get a good design, get the team in condition to play well, and get ready to play Buffalo.

"This is not some dog training school. I'm not into rewarding and penalizing. I told the players I wanted them in condition and working hard and to behave in a manner that reflected discipline on and off the field. That still doesn't ensure winning, but if we don't, I guarantee that we wouldn't win."

"I promise you that we will try to win every game here and establish winning as much as we can," he said. "Exhibition games don't count, but there is a degree of importance on them. There are other priorities that are important in the preseason, and I will try to mix these together. That is what I have always done. The objective is to try to play for championships, that's why we're in it, at least why I am. I don't have anything to prove to myself."

Even while training camp ground on, Parcells' personal life intervened. They still did not have a house in New England. "Judy Parcells over the weekend finally dragged her husband, Bill, out to see the house they are having built in Foxboro, but she discovered he was a bit distracted," Terry Price of the *Hartford Courant* reported.

First she asked the Patriots coach how he liked the Corian sink tops in the bathroom. "If they can block for the quarterback, I like them," was Parcells' answer.

She then moved onto landscaping, and she inquired as to Bill's preference, mulch or wood chips? "I don't know," Parcells replied. "If they can run with the ball, I'll take the wood chips."

Parcells was preoccupied that day. He had signed one free agent, traded one player, waived eight players, and terminated the contracts of eight others. And he was looking to add 13 more if possible. The Patriots had first claim in the league on any players waived with less than four years of experience.

"We will look and see what's available there," Parcells said. "Then we'll have some further announcements [today]."

Parcells was hoping to bring back a few of the terminated players. "We'll see. Any time you put a player out there, there's no guarantee you'll get him back. There's a couple we're interested in bringing back."

When Reggie Redding, the previous year's starting left guard, showed up at training Camp at Bryant College in Smithfield, Rhode Island, he was overweight, and Parcells cut him instantly.

In another instance of Parcells' toughness, there was a player whose workouts had not impressed Parcells. During a physical conditioning test, the player passed out from exhaustion. Parcells yelled to the trainers, "When he wakes up, tell him I just cut him."

When asked, "Why did you throw [quarterback Tommy] Hodson out of the huddle?" referring to an incident in the fifth day of camp, Parcells answered, "Because he didn't know what he was doing. I threw [quarterback Scott] Zolak and [quarterback Scott] Secules out, too."

When several players high-fived each other during a practice, he screamed out, "You guys high-five every fucking thing. Wait until you beat somebody!"

On August 20, 1993, Drew Bledsoe did play plenty and well. He passed for 245 yards and two touchdowns in a 21–17 exhibition victory against Green Bay in Foxboro, Massachusetts.

"A lot of people are going to draw some conclusions, but it could be erroneous to do that," Parcells said. Bledsoe played the entire game. He completed 19-of-29 passes with no interceptions.

"He helped his chances tonight, but I think he's going to have to play a couple of more games before we put him in Canton, okay," Parcells told the press. "We knew we were going to take him into the second half, but I thought once he got going, it was a chance to maybe build something."

In 1992, en route to a 2–14 record, the Patriots started four men at quarterback, including Hugh Millen (seven games), Scott Zolak (four games), Tommy Hodson (three games), and Jeff Carlson (two games). Only Zolak remained. Secules made the team, and Bledsoe was named the starter at the end of August.

"When you're happy with a kid's progress, that's all you can ask from him. He's still going to make mistakes," Parcells said. In the preseason, Bledsoe completed 43-of-72 passes for 549 yards, five touchdowns, one interception, eight sacks, and a 106.0 quarterback rating. He led six of the Patriots' seven scoring drives.

"You can't compare him to veterans yet," Parcells said. "He hasn't had a game with four interceptions or six sacks. He hasn't hit his head on the turf. You don't know how he will come through that. But he's definitely improving, and that's all I can ask from a kid like that."

It was a one of the most anticipated first games of the season. Before the game, Bledsoe said that Parcells told him, "Hey, this isn't that hard. You can do this. Otherwise, I wouldn't put you in this."

The Patriots laid an egg. "Bill Parcells returned to pro football today. He also returned to reality," Frank Litsky wrote in *The New York Times*. "Midway through the third quarter, the Patriots closed to within 17–14. Then, in the first six and a half minutes of the last quarter, they made three big mistakes and the Bills pounced on them for three touchdowns and a 38–14 victory," Litsky wrote.

"Quite obviously," Parcells said, "we lost our poise in the fourth quarter. A lot of bad things happened to us. We had a chance to win the game.

At the end, they played well and we didn't...I'm not pleased with the outcome or what happened late in the game."

When asked what he would do next, Parcells shot back, "I go on vacation in the Bahamas."

"At least the old sarcasm is still there," Litsky wrote.

In late September, the winless Patriots arrived in the Meadowlands to play the New York Jets, and Parcells was asked about how he felt about coming home. "A stadium is just a stadium. I have no feelings. I'm just going. That's just the way I am. I have never been too nostalgic," Parcells told the press impatiently. "Most of the reactions that I term important come from the people that are involved. It's from people. That's the only thing that ever made Giants Stadium personal to me was the people."

It was a homecoming of sorts. That is, the hometown team won 45–7.

When asked again about any special feelings, Parcells snapped, "There was no strange feeling. Not at all. You want a history lesson? What's that got to do with this game? Let's just talk about this game."

Reporters also asked about Bledsoe, to which Parcells countered, "I didn't think he played well at all, did you?" Almost to himself he said, "I know what the process is, and it's going to be a long one.... We've played four games and haven't won any."

After that, the Patriots began to play better. But by November 25 the Patriots were 1–9. At that time the Patriots had lost two overtime games and lost six games by four points or less.

"My team is hanging in there. We're not playing sloppy football and we're pretty determined and we don't have anything to show for it, and as long as it stays that way, I think eventually things'll work out," Parcells said. "When you're in as many close games as we've been in, you would like to think you can do one thing that would help your team get over."

The coach was despondent with losing. "I think it does create a little bit of anxiety on the part of the coach. Certainly we're competitive, but you're on the threshold of winning but you don't win. You have a tendency to look at yourself and say, 'What's the one or two things I could have done that allows us to win instead of lose?'"

New York Post sports columnist Steve Serby asked Parcells how he kept his players playing so hard.

"Like I tell 'em, I'm not worried about their morale. They better worry about mine."

They lost to the Jets in Foxboro 6–0.

"I feel sorry for my players. They're playing their tails off," Parcells said.

"Five games in a row like this, it's something you can't explain," Patriots nose tackle Tim Goad said. "It's like something out of *The Twilight Zone*."

The Patriots ran their record to 1–11, and then things started to change. They won two close games, beating the Cincinnati Bengals 7–2 and the Cleveland Browns 20–17, and then they wholloped the Indianapolis Colts 38–0.

In the final game of the season against the Miami Dolphins, the Patriots found themselves in their third overtime game. The Dolphins had beaten them 17–13 down in Miami, and now in Foxboro, the Patriots hoped to return the favor.

Miami trailed the entire game and only led for the first time with 4:30 minutes to go. Then Bledsoe took his team on a 75-yard touchdown drive. Miami scored on a field goal, tying the game 27–27. In overtime, Bledsoe connected on a 36-yard pass play to Michael Timpson for the winning score, 33–27. The Patriots had not won four in a row since 1988. They finished 5–11, an improvement over the year before.

"How do you like that quarterback? Is he something?" Parcells asked the press happily. Bledsoe had completed 27-of-43 passes for 329 yards. He completed four touchdowns and was intercepted once.

And then Parcells wondered about the Giants, who were playing Dallas with the division title at stake.

"How did they do?" he asked. He was told they had been behind, tied it, and lost to the Cowboys on a field goal.

"Oh, no," he said, grimacing.

NO REST FOR THE WEARY

On January 21, 1994, Robert Kraft, the owner of Foxboro Stadium for six years, won a bidding war for the New England Patriots that included a nominally higher bid from a group that hoped to move the team to St. Louis. The *Boston Globe* reported the bid at around $160 million, which made it the most anyone had paid for a NFL franchise—$20 million more than Jerry Jones had paid for the Dallas Cowboys.

Robert Kraft was born in Brookline, Massachusetts, on June 5, 1941. Kraft graduated from Brookline High School in 1959. He graduated from Columbia University in 1963, and he received an MBA from Harvard Business School in 1965. He married Myra Hiatt, a 1964 graduate of Brandeis University.

Kraft began his professional career working at Rand-Whitney Group, a Worcester-based packaging company owned by Jacob Hiatt. Kraft still serves as this company's chairman. In 1972, he founded International Forest Products, a trader of physical paper commodities. The two combined companies make up the largest privately held paper and packaging concern in the United States.

In 1986, Kraft was a minority investor in WNEV-TV, now NBC affiliate WHDH-TV, and over the years he acquired several Boston radio stations.

Kraft grew up a New York Giants fan. This was not uncommon in the days before the AFL. The Giants were the most popular single team in New England before the establishment of the AFL. Kraft was Patriots fan since their founding, and he was a season ticket holder since 1971, when the team moved to Schaefer Stadium.

Kraft once owned a tennis team known as the Boston Lobsters and made passes to buy the Red Sox and the Celtics. He had tried to buy the Patriots twice before. It took Kraft 10 years to slowly assemble the parts necessary to purchase the Patriots. In 1985, Kraft bought an option on the parcel adjacent to the stadium. In 1988, Kraft outbid several competitors to buy the stadium from the bankrupt Billy Sullivan for $25 million. The purchase included the stadium's lease to the Patriots—which would later provide Kraft leverage in purchasing the team.

In 1994, James Orthwein offered Kraft $75 million to buy out the remainder of the team's lease at the Foxboro Stadium. If Kraft bit, Orthwein would then be free to move the team to St. Louis. Kraft brilliantly counter-offered. He offered $175 million for the team, and Orthwein had no alternative but to accept.

The day after the NFL approved the sale in January 1994, Patriots fans showed their appreciation by purchasing almost 6,000 season tickets en route to selling out every game for the first time in the team's 34-year history. Every home game has been sold out since.

"I made the best bid with the least headaches," Kraft said. "People have offered me all sorts of money for the lease, but I let it be known that I wouldn't sell at any price."

"I'm not going to be the most popular man" in St. Louis, Orthwein said. "I'm going to still do the best I can for my hometown to help them get a team. As far as owning a team, I'm done with that."

"I'm taking my wife and four sons to a Celtics game. We're all sports nuts," Kraft laughed.

This new ownership guaranteed that Parcells would remain with the Patriots organization since there was serious speculation in the media that Parcells would not move to St. Louis. "Bill Parcells has created tremendous expectations in New England after a red-hot finish in his first year with the Patriots. And Parcells' history with the Giants indicates a drastic improvement in the second year," Gary Myers opined in *Sports Illustrated*.

"My expectations are higher, too. I frankly don't pay too much attention to prognostications," Parcells told the press at the beginning of training camp. "But I told the players at the end of minicamp that the expectation would be greater this year as individuals and as a team. All I know is that we'll be better than last year. Whether that translates into more wins remains to be seen."

＿＿

For his second season Parcells raided the Giants once again, bringing over offensive guard Bob Kratch for a four-year contract and safety Myron Guyton. He also brought in Maurice Carthon as his rookie assistant coach. He also signed former Giants linebacker, Steve DeOssie, who'd been cut by the Giants but picked up by the Jets the previous season.

During the first two years, Parcells had reassembled a number of Giants coaches or players. "I guess some of the funniest things I've heard about this," said Romeo Crennel, who was one of the re-assembled family, "is that this is the new Boston Giants. Or the New England Giants."

The next thing he did was draft linebacker Willie McGinest.

Parcells puts a lot of emphasis on interviewing his prospective draft choices. "A half hour of candid conversation tells more about people than a mountain of statistics. For starters, I might ask them to name three or four of the most important things in their life," Parcells said. "Family or religion often top the list, which is fine; football doesn't have to be number one. But football better be in there somewhere, or I'll deduce that this guy isn't all that interested in the job."

"Sometimes I'll sting the player a little, just to see how he'll respond," Parcells said.

"Will I be getting the Willie McGinest who played against Penn State, or the Willie McGinest who played against UCLA?" Parcells asked of the talented USC linebacker the coach made his No. 1 draft pick in 1994. "I don't want the guy who played UCLA because he isn't very good. But the guy who played Penn State has a chance to be great."

"McGinest assured me that we'd be getting the Penn State version. More important, he didn't try to alibi or blame his college coach for his off day against UCLA," Parcells said.

"I didn't play well," McGinest admitted. "I got too emotionally involved, just couldn't cut loose."

"There is only one Dallas Cowboys, only one defending champion, and only one team that can boast that they have the league's superior personnel," McGinest told the press.

The Patriots now boasted their own pool of talented players, including Willie McGinest, Drew Bledsoe, Marion Butts, and Vincent Brown. A change was being experienced within the organization.

"We've been through so many changes and there has been so much optimism before," said Bruce Armstrong, the perennial All-Pro offensive tackle in his eighth year with the Patriots. "But a lot of that was just like applying a fresh coat of paint. We never touched the core. I look at it this way—this organization suffered from severe structural damage."

"I looked around the league the last few years at the winners—the 49ers and the Cowboys and the others—and saw that it started with ownership and management and coaching and the medical staff," Armstrong continued. "Then you get to players. Now we've got the structure in place. We're sound on the inside."

"Few things have changed with Parcells," sportswriter Thomas George wrote. "He still runs from the media's scrutiny. He is as irascible as ever and still full of one-liners and button-pushing with his players."

"I try to get the team to reach its potential. What other people think about the ability that I have or what the prognosticators think of the ability I have is irrelevant. Because I know better than anybody what it is," Parcells said to his men at the beginning of training camp. "When you ask the question about expectations and whether I am going to get the most out of them, I will know whether I do or not. I will know."

During May mini-camp, Parcells spoke of watching NBA coaches, including Mike Fratello of the Cleveland Cavaliers and the Chicago Bulls' Phil Jackson.

"I'm even watching [the New York Rangers'] Mike Keenan and I don't even know what the hell is going on in that sport," Parcells said. "I just watch what they do with their teams. Right now the guy I'm watching the hardest is [A's manager] Tony La Russa. His teams were great and now he's fighting to win a game here and there. I respect this guy. He's one of the great baseball managers."

"The process is going to go quicker. Beating the drums does not do it. Confidence, efficiency [are] only born of demonstrated ability. You do it or you do not do it," Parcells continued. "There is really no gray area. There are no quarterly earnings that can go up just a little bit. We do not have that in this business."

"Just remember one thing," Parcells told Bledsoe at training camp, "I don't want a celebrity quarterback on my team. I hate celebrity quarterbacks. You understand?"

~ ~

"It only takes a minute to see that the New England players believe in Parcells. In turn, they appear to believe more in themselves," George wrote.

The season itself started out poorly. They lost two shoot-outs.

Drew Bledsoe and Dan Marino combined for 894 passing yards and nine touchdowns. The Dolphins won 39–35 after the Patriots failed to convert a touchdown in the Dolphins' red zone in the final minute. Against the Buffalo Bills, the Patriots rallied from down 35–21 to tie the game, but Steve Christie's 32-yard field goal won the game for Buffalo 38–35.

The team went on a three-game run, beating the Bengals, Lions, and Packers, to establish themselves at 3–2. Then they lost four in a row. While they lost to Miami by 23–3, they lost each of the other three games by a touchdown or less. Things were not looking good, as the team was a disappointing 3–6.

"Bill was a power football guy when he coached the Giants. He designed that team to specifically beat the Washington Redskins," Will McDonough said. "He simply went out and got bigger and stronger players than they had. When he came to New England, he didn't have those kinds of guys. He knew he couldn't play power football, even if he wanted to."

In October, Phil Simms came to visit the Patriots. He had been cut by the Giants in a salary cap squeeze. "Has he talked to you about cabin fever yet?" Simms asked Bledsoe.

Bledsoe laughed. Just a few days before Parcells had reminded him to "plant your feet in quicksand against the rush, don't get cabin fever back there."

"The more experienced quarterbacks, you don't fool 'em," Parcells said. "They know when their secondary receivers are open. They're patient. A bad play doesn't affect them. Simms was like that. Isn't it great how much Simms is appreciated now?"

Then they had a breakout game against Minnesota. Drew Bledsoe set NFL records in passes (70) and completions (45) as he rallied New England from a 20–0 deficit to a 26–20 victory against Minnesota. A week later the team beat San Diego 23–17.

"He turned Drew Bledsoe loose and [he] began throwing the ball all over the field. With no running game whatsoever, he got the team on a terrific run the second half of the year," McDonough wrote. "Throwing the ball and playing finesse defense did the trick. And he showed for the first time that he was capable of changing his coaching style to adapt to whatever he had, doing whatever it took to win."

The Patriots won their last seven games and finished 10–6, good enough to take the AFC East Division crown. The press and the fans were effusive.

"Ten years from now, you will tell people that you watched the entire Patriots operation steadily upgrade itself from pitiful to powerful," *Boston Globe* sportswriter Michael Holley wrote. "You will not be exaggerating. You will also remember late 1994 as the time when the Dallas Cowboys began to share the America's Team stage with the New England Patriots."

"No matter where I go and no matter what I do, everybody's talking about the Patriots," defensive back Corwin Brown said. "All my neighbors and that sort of thing. Everybody is talking about how exciting this is. I know it's exciting for the fans and it's exciting for us. I guess that's all good."

According to Holley, the day after the team beat Buffalo 41–17, Patriots fans spent $15,000 on merchandise in the team's pro shop.

"They're like Dracula," Parcells said. "You've got to put a stake in their heart, and then you still wonder if it's in there. They were ready to go, and they shook us."

"The same day, Bledsoe was involved in a true black-tie affair, reading *'Twas the Night Before Christmas* with a symphony behind him," Holley continued.

"Did he do that?" Parcells asked with subtle sarcasm. "That must have been nice."

"I'm quite sure people think more of the Patriots than they did seven weeks ago," safety Myron Guyton said.

On New Year's Day 1995, Bill Parcells' Patriots played Bill Belichick's Cleveland Browns in an AFC playoff game at Municipal Stadium. Belichick's defenses the first three years in Cleveland were good, but the 1994 edition was ranked the No. 1 defense in the NFL, having yielded a league-low 204 points for an average of just 12.8 per contest. While Belichick obviously had a hand in the defensive decisions, his defensive coordinator was Nick Saban. The Patriots had lost to the Browns in the first week of November, before their big run. Cleveland also had veteran quarterback Vinny Testaverde.

The Browns jumped out to a three-point lead, but the teams went into the locker room tied 10–10. Belichick had started his rebuilding program one year ahead of Parcells, and the effort showed. The Browns were an excellent team on defense, and they prevailed in a tough game 20–13.

"I didn't want to play Bill, and he didn't want to play me," Belichick said after the game. "One of us had to lose. I wouldn't be here if it wasn't for Bill. I have a real debt of gratitude to him. I think he's done a heckuva job with that football team. They left here 3–6. When they came back they were 10–6."

There was a virtual reunion at midfield. There were Parcells and Belichick, but also all of the other Giants that were now on the Patriots, as well as Pepper Johnson and Carl Banks, who were now on the Browns. It was an emotional conclusion.

"I think our team made progress. I think we're a better team than we were last year at this time. We don't get to go on. We don't play this to progress; we play this to try and be champions," Parcells said.

On March 3, 1995, the New England Patriots signed Giants star Dave Meggett to a major contract.

"My wife said, 'You paid $9 million to a player who's shorter than you. Bill always says bigger is better. Have you gone crazy again?'" Kraft said. It was a five-year, $9 million contract.

"When Dave Meggett touches the ball, he makes things happen," Parcells said. "The first time we threw a pass to him, he went 62 yards for a touchdown."

"The joke going around the Giants late last week was that Bill Parcells was so desperate to get a former New York player he had agreed to terms with Y. A. Tittle," sportswriter Mike Freeman wrote. "Humor is sometimes a way to deal with frustration, and the Giants are still somewhat rattled about losing running back David Meggett to the New England

Patriots.... It was one of the biggest free-agent losses for the Giants in years, and there is no question it will hurt."

"Some people fall by the wayside, whether it is mentally or physically," Parcells said as he and his staff were re-tooling the Patriots for another season. "Whatever it is, they can't compete. My experience in this business has always been, and I do not think it is an archaic thing, that football players usually find a way to surface. Some are capable of finding a way. Others are not. I don't want those others on my team. I don't mean any disrespect."

Parcells continued, saying, "I am just saying when it's all said and done in the final analysis, when you put your roster together, you got to put it together with people you believe are dedicated, committed, effort-giving, and hopefully, talented enough players."

As successful as Parcells had made the Patriots, they also suffered some losses, the reward of moving up, is that you get pilfered. The 1995 Patriots lost several key players to free agency that year, losing Kevin Turner, Michael Timpson, Harlon Barnett, linemen Tim Goad and Ray Agnew, and running back Leroy Thompson.

Parcells was working hard to dispel the pressure. The New England Patriots were the popular pick of the 1995 to win the AFC. "I don't care about expectation. The criteria I use are my own, if I can get my team to play to its potential, whatever I perceive it to be, then I feel like I did a good job. I don't care what anybody else thinks," Parcells said.

That year the Patriots drafted running back Curtis Martin.

The season began with a win over the Cleveland Browns at home in Foxboro. But then the team lost five in a row. During the season, the Pats swept the Bills and Jets, split with the Dolphins, and were beaten twice by the Colts. They finished 23rd in offense and 25th in defense. The team finished fourth in their own division. Parcells was not happy. Owner Robert Kraft was even more unhappy. The 1995 season set the stage for one of the most remarkable years any professional football team has ever experienced.

For the entirety of his professional career, Bill Parcells was for all intents and purposes spoiled. As a head coach, he never had a meddlesome owner. The Maras were not absentee owners, but they were hands-off owners. Parcells always gave credit to George Young that any unhappiness or desires to meddle were stopped at Young's door and were never visited upon Parcells' door step. Actually, that structure had been insisted upon by Rozelle when the Mara family was going through its own crisis. And when Parcells had taken over New England, Orthwein, who only bought the team so he could move it to St. Louis, was as benign and absentee an owner as the NFL had ever seen. This was not Robert Kraft.

The NFL had seen a new rash of owners who came in and wanted to be seen as movers and shakers, the most notable being Jerry Jones. But there were others.

Kraft was an interested party. He was a 24-year season-ticket holder. He'd been watching the team his whole adult life. Not only was he a huge fan, but he loved to listen to the coaches talk about football. For a man as accomplished and successful as he was, he had a bright new shiny toy, and he intended to make the Patriots the best team in the league. He wanted to work with Parcells.

The only problem for Kraft was that Parcells was arrogant where owners were concerned. Owners didn't know anything about football. They know how to make money. In Parcells' mind, the coaches would worry about football, and the suits would worry about the money. In his mind, this was the division of labor. But Kraft wanted to run a business and make the Patriots a first-class organization. And he was going to be involved. This set the stage for a train wreck because neither man was going to blink.

"Look, we're going to pay attention. I think fans want owners who pay attention. I think fans should want owners who are going to pay attention," Kraft said. "It's our financial net worth on the line."

Parcells was wary of Kraft and their new relationship. Kraft kept telling Parcells and the media that he wanted to help build a solid support structure for Parcells, but in reality he was slowly taking power out of Parcells' hands and learning all the parts of the business.

"I had become aware through conversations with Kraft and Parcells of a growing, mutual dislike between them," Will McDonough of the *Boston Globe* wrote. "Parcells considered Kraft a meddler and double-talker. Kraft regarded Parcells as an ingrate and someone who had no respect for him."

"Soon after the 1995 season, Parcells asked Kraft to void the final year of his contract [1997]," Felger wrote. "Kraft readily agreed. That made Parcells a one-year-and-out prospect heading into the '96 season. Not many owners would give total control in that situation—and Kraft didn't."

"The next-to-last game of '95 he came to me and said he wanted to cut a year off the contract," Kraft said. "This guy's a legend. One of the greatest coaches in the history of this game. Am I going to keep him in prison?"

"In Parcells, we had a guy who was coaching year to year. And the issue of his contract was supposed to be irrelevant to us?" Kraft added. "That's preposterous."

What many fans did not know was that Parcells had made some interesting deals while running the organization that Kraft was not happy about. As usual, Kraft was smart.

"In addition, a marketing deal with Apex One, a clothing outfit, that gave Parcells rights to the clothing worn on the sideline by Patriot personnel, was bought out by Kraft in 1995 for $800,000, paid out over three years," Will McDonough wrote in the *Boston Globe*. "The first payment, according to the June 1995 agreement, was for $400,000 in September of that year. The next payment was to be $300,000 on September 16, 1996, and if Parcells was still the Patriots coach on that date, he would be paid an additional $100,000 in September 1997."

According to McDonough, "Parcells thought he was buying out that last year of his contract for $300,000. But there were two separate amendments, and the one in which Parcells gave up the $300,000 for his clothing deal contained no language about his coaching agreement."

"I told Kraft he could use the money to help bring [Bill] Belichick here," Parcells said. "Bill was still in Cleveland, but everyone knew he was going to be fired, and I told Kraft we should get him."

"Robert is careful and diplomatic when talking about Parcells today," sportswriter Michael Holley wrote. "But you can sense that there is a vast network of emotions lingering beneath each safe sentence."

"He is someone who tried to make my father look bad. He tried to make him look foolish," said Jonathan Kraft, the team's vice chairman. "And as a son, I hated him for that."

In mid-February, Art Modell of the Cleveland Browns dismissed Bill Belichick after a disappointing 1995 campaign.

"We've had some success with Bill, including an 11–5 playoff team in 1994," Modell said in a statement. "However, I believe to get to the next level, a change at head coach is necessary. I've said this before, I have great respect for the effort Bill puts into his coaching and preparation."

"The Browns got off to a fast 3–1 start in 1995, but things turned sour after Modell announced his intentions to move the team out of Cleveland," Timothy W. Smith wrote in *The New York Times*. "Belichick benched quarterback Vinny Testaverde for three games during the middle of the season in favor of the rookie Eric Zeier in an effort to spark the team. It didn't work. The Browns, 4–4 at the time of the announcement, dropped seven of their last eight games and finished 5–11."

Many in the coaching community thought that Modell had thrown Belichick under the bus when he made the announcement, sending the organization into a tailspin and turning the fans against the franchise.

Belichick was hired by Parcells two days later. Parcells and many other people knew what the Patriots needed to get to a championship game—a great defense. With Belichick in place, all Parcells needed were a few more studs for his defense.

"He did so with certain misgivings," Halberstam write about Belichick. "He knew better than anyone what it was like to work for Bill Parcells, and he knew there was a roller coaster quality to it. Good days were followed by bad days, when he was very tough on you; his tongue could sting in front of others, even if it was followed by some form of muted apology."

And Belichick could also feel something wasn't quite right in the Patriot offices.

"Obviously a lot of things had happened before I had gotten there. My sense of it was there wasn't a lot of communication," Belichick said.

While Parcells and Kraft were often uncomfortable with each other in the room, Kraft and Belichick enjoyed one another. "There was the brainy Wesleyan graduate, with credentials in economics and Super Bowl defenses, talking with the multimillionaire Columbia University and Harvard Business School grad," *Boston Globe* sportswriter Michael Holley wrote.

When Parcells had first arrived with the Patriots, he insisted that the director of football operations, Patrick Forte, be fired. It was a shrewd move, which then allowed Parcells to operate unencumbered. But the truth was that Parcells' contract did not give him absolute written authority of personnel decisions. He was never guaranteed final say. Orthwein was a benign owner and granted Parcells control. But the 1995 season results and Parcells' attitude had turned a corner for Kraft.

"The scales of power had shifted that off-season, as Kraft asserted the authority of head scout Bobby Grier, who had been promoted to director of player personnel the year before," Patriots historian Michael Felger wrote. "Starting in the '96 off-season, Kraft determined that Grier would have the final say."

Grier had been hired by Ron Erhardt as an offensive backfield coach in 1981. Grier moved back and forth between college scouting and backfield coaching between then and 1992. In 1993, Parcells moved Grier back to the personnel department as the Patriots' director of pro scouting. In 1995, Kraft promoted Grier to director of player personnel.

"Parcells' record of choosing players the previous three years was good but not great. He did well cleaning house early on, but his dips into free agency were mixed," Felger pointed out.

"Any time before the draft, Bill and I would talk five or six times a day," Grier said. "We would have lunch together. We would talk at football practice. Bill is a great storyteller, and I would enjoy those talks."

On NFL Draft day in 1996, the New England Patriots were set with the No. 7th pick in the first round. In the days before the 1996 draft, Will McDonough was trying to get a fix on who the Patriots were going to draft. On the eve of the draft, about 5:00 PM, Will called Robert Kraft and asked him who the pick was going to be.

"Well, it all depends on who is there, but my boys [meaning Parcells and Grier] tell me we're going to take a defensive lineman. There's three guys we're interested in. Cedric Jones. Duane Clemons. Tony Brackens. We'll have a shot at one of those three."

"Within 30 minutes of that conversation, I called Parcells and told him what Kraft said," McDonough wrote.

"That's right," Parcells answered. "One of those defensive linemen. That's where we need the help. We stink on defense." McDonough asked specifically about Terry Glenn, the spectacular Ohio State wide receiver.

"We're not taking a receiver there," Parcells said. "We're going to get the defensive lineman and then get the receiver at the top of the second round. There still will be some good ones left around."

"Just before the selection, the Patriots' owner, Robert K. Kraft, called a meeting in a small room near the Patriots' large draft room here at the team's offices at Foxboro Stadium. Present were Bill Parcells, then the head coach, and Bobby Grier, then the director of player personnel," *The New York Times* sportswriter Thomas George described. George imagined the war room conversation:

"Okay, Bill, who do you want?" Kraft asked.

"Duane Clemons or Cedric Jones. I want defense," Parcells said.

"Okay, Bobby, who do you want?" Kraft asked.

"I want Terry Glenn. I want offense," Grier responded.

"Okay. Let's go with Glenn," Kraft said.

Parcells was shocked. He implored Kraft to listen to him, to understand what he was trying to do, what he needed, but Kraft was having none of it. After all his hollering and pleading, Parcells was said to have kicked either a trash can or a door and stomped out.

"I didn't know what was happening," Parcells said later. "Then they said that Glenn was going to be the pick. I said we had agreed it was going to be a defensive player and that was it. I was mad as hell. I said, 'Okay, if that's the way you want it, you got it.'"

Kraft and Grier took over the rest of the draft. When asked afterward by McDonough if either had said anything to him before the draft, Parcells responded, "They never said a word."

Reportedly, Kraft came out of the war room and said, "Well, there's a new sheriff in town." In the time Kraft had owned the Patriots, he and Parcells had been sizing up each other. But he always gave way to Parcells. In the war room that day Kraft knew exactly what was going to happen even before he went in there. His choosing Glenn was a statement that it was now his team—and that Parcells answered to him. Kraft was willing to live without Parcells. It was about Kraft taking control of his organization.

"I almost fired him right after the draft. I had it up to here with that guy. It just isn't any fun to go down there," Kraft told McDonough. "I'm not having any fun. You keep telling me he won't come back. I'm telling you, it's not his decision. It's my decision. I own this team. He works for me. With me, it's a matter of respect. We give him everything he wants, and still he shows no respect for me."

"My father—I think people have always, throughout his life, have underestimated him," said his son, Jonathan Kraft.

"When the draft was all over," Groh said, "Bill called us all together and told us that this was done to publicly humiliate him and that he would never forget it."

McDonough had also ended up with egg on his face, since the story he filed, based on information Kraft had given, was hideously wrong. Kraft had in fact double-crossed him. McDonough and Kraft had known each other 20 years, and McDonough had even helped Kraft through some of his thorniest moments when Kraft was trying to buy the Patriots. But McDonough sided with the coach, a betrayal in Kraft's eyes, and in teaching Parcells a lesson in humility, Kraft was obviously teaching the same lesson to McDonough, who had the misfortune of being friends with both men.

"That was the beginning of the end with Parcells and the Patriots. Probably, as far as Parcells was concerned, it was over right there. Parcells would not be back with the Patriots for the 1997 National Football League season. And the Patriots' way of doing business, on and off the field, would never be the same," Thomas George wrote.

"Then, after the draft, we might have talked a couple of times a day and most of it on the phone. It was never like it was before," Grier said. "I had to deal with some things, some attitude from him. Let's just leave it at that."

It was a mixed draft. Grier drafted Terry Glenn with the first selection, and that turned out to be a brilliant pick. He also drafted Lawyer Milloy and Tedy Bruschi in that 1996 class, both of whom would become Patriots stalwarts.

On the down side, the Patriots took a shot at drafting Christian Peter in the fifth round. Peter had been an incredible talent at the University of Nebraska, but Peter's off-the-field problems including sexually assaulting women, alcohol abuse, and being prone to violence made him almost untouchable. The Patriots took a shellacking from the press and dropped Peter three days later.

"For about 24 hours I made up my mind I was finished here," Parcells told McDonough, "I didn't want any more to do with this guy. But now here's what I am going to do. I am going to get in the greatest shape of my life. I've already started to lose weight. I'm not leaving here 6–10. I'm going to come back here and prove I'm better than that. I did a lousy job in 1995. I know that. But next year we've got a chance to be pretty good. I'm just going to have as little to do with this guy as I can and just focus on coaching the team. Then when it's over, I'm outta here. This will be my last year coaching."

— —

When camp opened, Parcells was trimmer, leaner, and in a fantastic mood. He openly discussed his trimmer contract, brushing it off, saying, "I coach year to year, anyway." There were no contract disputes, and everyone was on time to camp.

The only thing that proved to be a wrinkle, still, was Terry Glenn. Parcells openly told the story about how he hadn't wanted Glenn and still didn't.

Glenn was suffering from what Parcells referred to as a "mild" stress to his hamstring and wasn't practicing with the team. Parcells said that if Glenn didn't get back on the field soon, he would miss the season opener.

"He has missed an awful lot of practice," Parcells said. "For someone to expect him to be ready—to say, 'Okay, he's healthy now so he's ready to play the first game'—if that's one week before the season, I mean, do you think that's realistic?"

When asked about Glenn's progress at one point, Parcells responded, "She's making progress."

"That's not the standard we want to set," Kraft admonished Parcells in the press. "That's not the way we do things. It's just like there was a player last year that gave the finger to the crowd. He's not here anymore."

"One of Terry's biggest adjustments was learning how to deal with Parcells' button-pushing," said Charlie Weis, then the receivers coach for the Patriots. "Terry wasn't a great practice player, which didn't fit well with Bill's mentality. But he always showed up on Sundays. He caught 90 balls for us as a rookie."

"No one in the history of the modern NFL excels at mind games like Parcells," *The New York Times* columnist Mike Freeman wrote. "Parcells can be funny, nasty, and cruel—all requirements to be a distinguished head coach in the NFL. His tactics, both gentle and abrasive, are infamous."

One of the projects Parcells took on personally that year was to turn Willie McGinest into Lawrence Taylor—sort of. The Patriots switched to a 4-3 defense, and McGinest came up to the line like a stand-up linebacker on a blitz. Parcells saw early that McGinest was playing his new position reacting to what the offensive tackle was doing instead of making the first move.

"McGinest," Parcells said, "has to learn that he is the aggressor now and that the tackle had to react to him—not vice versa."

"I'm learning," McGinest said time and again. "I've got a way to go."

"Parcells has taken the McGinest project to the personal tutor level, talking and talking with him, telling the new lineman that he not only has to have one move, but a 'package' of moves, that McGinest should think of how he used one move on a third-and-8 in the first quarter, and how the tackle opposite him might be looking for the same move now that there is a third-and-11 in the fourth quarter. Then, of course, McGinest should come with another move from his 'package,'" Michael Madden from the *Boston Globe* explained.

"From week to week, he has played better," Parcells said. "I've spent a lot of time with him, talking about his techniques and talking about the mental side of them—how to vary them. What he needed was to have a plan of attack, not just one move."

"What Willie really needs is that plan," Parcells said. "He's got some moves, and by that I mean he's got some individual moves, but he's got to be able to put those individual moves together into a package. He's not really been able to create indecision on part of the offensive linemen."

"If you beat a guy on one move," McGinest said of the plan, "I can promise you that he'll be looking for that move the next time. You've got to be thinking of something else. Football looks physical, but it's all a mind game."

— —

The Patriots spent the first two weeks on the road, dropping their first two games, one in Miami and the next in Buffalo. But they bounced back for three wins in a row before falling to the Washington Redskins at home to level out their record to 3–3.

Then they won two more.

On October 30, Kraft called McDonough. "Your boy wants to coach again. Asked me about it today," Kraft said. "See how this guy changes? He does it all the time. Now he wants to coach again." McDonough was astonished.

"He was talking to me about all the stuff in the media about us not getting along and how it was hurting the franchise," Parcells said. "I told him, 'Okay, let's do something about it right now. We can end all of that stuff with a new contract. Let's talk right now.' He told me that I really didn't know what I wanted to do, and he didn't want to talk about it until the year is over."

Parcells was not happy. Neither was Kraft. Fraley, Parcells' agent, contacted Kraft one more time, in mid-December. But Kraft told him they would chat at the end of the season.

"That was twice he had the chance to sign Bill and decided not to do it," Fraley said. "We got the message. He didn't want Bill to coach the Patriots again, no matter what happened."

Then they won two more, including a win over the New York Jets, bringing their record to 7–3. The Patriots had been behind the Jets 21–7 at halftime. "There's still time to win the game. You need to decide if you want to be champions," Parcells exhorted his team in the bowels of Giants Stadium. The Patriots rebounded to win 31–27. Bledsoe completed 24-for-34 passing, including three touchdowns.

"We've been showing some maturity," Parcells said. "That [comeback] wasn't about maturity. That's about getting your butt kicked and having enough guts to get back up."

The Patriots lost their second-to-last game against the Cowboys at Texas Stadium.

On December 21, 1996, a small article appeared in *Sports Illustrated* titled, "Tuna Makes Splash With Players." In it, Rich Cimini speculated on Parcells coming to the Jets in 1997 and quoted a number of Jets players speculating on how much they would want him in the Jets locker room. Surely it had to be a slap in the face for Kraft, who was in town to hopefully watch his Patriots clinch a first-round bye in the AFC playoffs.

The team won its last game against the woeful Giants to finish first in the AFC East with an 11–5 record. "When it was over yesterday, Parcells turned to the crowd behind the Pats bench and raised his fist where he thought his two daughters were sitting," Gary Myers wrote in *Sports Illustrated*. "He ran onto the field and jumped into Bledsoe's arms. He was emotional with his team and hugged and clenched hands with owner Robert Kraft. The Pats had already clinched the AFC East, but this clinched the first-round bye and a home game in two weeks at Foxboro."

— —

"Everybody knows how I feel," Parcells said about New York. "I grew up just down the street. This is not my home away from home. This will always be my home. Right now, I'm just not living here."

The Patriots had finished second in offense and 14th in defense in the NFL. Two weeks later the Pittsburgh Steelers came in, and the Patriots got them right from the start. Parcells predicted Rod Woodson would, on the very first play, come up on Terry Glenn.

"Even with a chai, the Hebrew symbol for life carried in his pocket as a good-luck charm, Bill Parcells was nervous in the moments before the Patriots' first snap of today's playoff game against the Steelers. For in Saturday night's meeting, the coach had reluctantly given Drew Bledsoe a chance to challenge the great Steeler cornerback Rod Woodson with a deep pass," Gerald Eskenazi wrote.

"I was choking a little bit," Parcells admitted. "But it was a planned play."

Woodson bit. The Patriots had planned for this. Glenn ran an up-and-go, left Woodson in the dust, and caught a 53-yard pass.

"They press you," Parcells said after the game. "You press them."

The Patriots put up two scores in the first quarter and one score in the second and took a 21–0 lead into halftime. By the time it was over, Curtis Martin had run for 166 yards, and the Patriots won 28–3. While the press was effusive, almost every article discussed his being a free agent once the season was over.

Up next were the Jacksonville Jaguars coached by Tom Coughlin, who'd been with Parcells at the Giants.

"I don't enjoy it," Parcells said of meeting Coughlin in the playoffs. "It's not pleasant for either of us. But that's the way the business is. He is one of my favorite guys I ever coached with. It's simple really; I like him. Of all the things that are very important in a coach, he is all of those things. And he is not afraid. That's the main thing. He's got conviction."

One the favorite stories of Coughlin was of the days back in the 1980s when he was the receivers coach. "On Christmas Day Parcells called the Giants Stadium office to leave a message on Coughlin's voice mail. The phone rang. No one would be working on Christmas Day," sports scribe Mike Freeman wrote. "The phone rang again. Coughlin answered. He was the only coach at the office that day—had been for hours."

"I don't know if I should be proud of that story or not," Coughlin said years later. It was the kind of effort Parcells never forgot.

"He's someone who I have a great deal of respect for," Coughlin said. "When we were together, I just gave him everything I had, which was in return for what he gave me. I've always tried to instill in my staff that your reputation is based on your work ethic, and you have to prove yourself every day. The other thing that I learned from him is that it's necessary to have a chain of command."

Asked about their social relationship, Coughlin responded, "There's no social with Bill. You just work your butt off."

Throughout their careers, Bill Parcells occasionally sent Coughlin a pair of gray socks. "That's it. Just a pair of gray socks in the mail. When Coughlin played football at Syracuse in the 1960s, the field was so muddy white socks couldn't be cleaned properly and cost too much to replace," *Sports Illustrated*'s Dave Hyde reported. "So players wore gray socks."

"I smile when I get them," Coughlin says. "What he's saying is, 'Don't forget your roots, who you are.'"

On January 12, the morning of the AFC Championship Game, McDonough was on assignment for NBC-TV. He was there to tape an interview with Parcells that would air during their pregame show. It was 9:00 AM.

"Parcells was ripping mad. He had seen a story in that morning's *Boston Herald* by Kevin Mannix, who wrote that he had learned an agreement between Parcells and Kraft gave the Patriots the right to deny Parcells permission to sign with another team unless New England received satisfactory compensation," McDonough wrote.

Mannix also wrote that the agreement "includes a provision that the Patriots would get compensation in the event Parcells signs with another team after the current season."

"Parcells was furious," McDonough wrote.

"Imagine, we're here today playing for the Super Bowl, and Kraft is planting this garbage in the paper. This is unbelievable. This never stops," Parcells said.

First, they did the interview.

"Listen, I'll grab Kraft when he gets here, bring him into your office, and straighten this thing out. He told me all along he wants to take the high road. Let's see what the deal is," McDonough tried to reassure Parcells.

Parcells waited for Kraft to show for three hours. In the meantime, Kraft told McDonough, before he got to Parcells, "I closed the door and began the meeting by recounting the conversations about 'taking the high road.' Now, in front of each other, they agreed that this was the way to go. Then Parcells extended his hand across his desk," McDonough wrote.

"Bob, this is what I'm going to do. When the season is over, I say that it is time for me to move on. That I've enjoyed my time here. The fans were great. You treated me well," Parcells said. "I wish you the best, and I even give you a plug for a new stadium. And the next day, you notify Tagliabue that I am free and clear with no further obligations to the New England Patriots."

"Kraft withdrew his hand like a piston. I was stunned. He started talking in fast-forward," McDonough wrote.

"We shouldn't even be having this conversation," Kraft told Parcells. "Our agreement is to talk when the year is over."

Parcells looked up and said to McDonough, "I want to talk with Bob alone."

The AFC conference championship proved to be a defensive struggle. The game started off well for the Patriots when the Jaguars were forced to punt on their first possession. A high snap enabled Patriot Larry Whigham to tackle punter Bryan Barker at the Jacksonville 4-yard line. Curtis Martin scored a 1-yard touchdown moments later, and the Patriots took the lead.

The Jaguars broke back with a field goal, but later Jacksonville punt returner Chris Hudson's fumble set up a 29-yard Patriot field goal. The Patriots added another 20-yard field goal before the half, making the score 13–3.

In the third quarter the Jaguars added another field goal, making the game 13–6. With less than 4:00 left, the Jaguars drove down to the red zone where a Mark Brunell pass was picked off in the end zone. But the game was finally sealed with 2:27 left when Patriots cornerback Otis Smith picked up Jaguars running back James Stewart's fumble and returned it 47 yards for a touchdown, putting the game virtually out of reach at 20–6.

The Patriots were going to the Super Bowl.

— —

"Talk about his deteriorating relationship with Kraft has become spicier than the Cajun food down here," Gary Myers wrote in *Sports Illustrated*. He wasn't the only writer using that gag.

But Parcells and Kraft were doing their best at damage control down in New Orleans. "Fellas, whenever we see each other, we talk," Parcells said at one of his pre Super Bowl press conferences. "It's not like we're from some foreign countries or something and we don't talk. It's funny. I get a kick out of this. It's so ludicrous."

"I'm saying right on the record—I do not dislike him. I like him. He's fun to be with most of the time," Kraft said afterward. "The bottom line is that we are in this game. If everyone wasn't pulling together, we wouldn't be here. And I'm going to enjoy it." When asked if Parcells was coming back, Kraft answered, "He's mercurial. What he feels at this moment, he might feel something different in a day or two."

While putting on a good show publicly, Kraft was bitter privately. According to *The New York Times*, during the week of the Super Bowl, a business friend of Kraft said that the owner complained about Parcells, saying, "This should be a great week for us, but he's sticking the knife in my back and twisting it."

"Next week divorce is apparently on the agenda," Myers wrote. "This morning, they will be at a podium together. What's in store? A vaudeville act, perhaps?"

"Yeah, I'd say it was a little bit of a distraction all the way around," Belichick said. "I can tell you firsthand, there was a lot of stuff going on prior to the game. I mean him talking to other teams He was trying to make up his mind about what he wanted to do. Which, honestly, I felt [was] totally inappropriate. How many chances do you get to play in a Super Bowl?"

According to the Patriots, Parcells' phone records were filled with phone calls to Hempstead, New York, the home of the New York Jets home offices. It was either brazen or foolish on Parcells' part.

"We were still new to the business," Jonathan Kraft said of the time. "Big Bill had kept us in the dark on a lot of things. He probably misled us on some things. And we didn't know how to go about questioning it."

— —

The Patriots were installed as 14-point underdogs to Brett Favre and the Green Bay Packers. Getting back to the Super Bowl was magical for the big Jersey guy.

"'I have a greater appreciation for how hard it is to get here and all the work it takes to get here. When you're first starting out, you really don't know how hard it is," Parcells said. "I've always done it the same way. I believe you have to have a team that's battle-hardened, competition-hardened. That's the way I like to get them ready."

Parcells admitted to the press that their underdog status made his team pay special attention. "I think it makes a team fully aware that they're going to be challenged, or that the majority of people think that they're going to be challenged on a very high level," he said. "If the under-dog role serves you well, it's in the ability of the coach to really just point out what the public perception is and what the experts think. You want them to feel challenged."

Green Bay began the scoring with Brett Favre's 54-yard touchdown pass to Andre Rison on their second offensive play of the game. The Packers then got an interception at the New England 28-yard line. On the next play, the first play after the turnover, New England lineman Ferric Collons sacked Favre for a 10-yard loss. A running play and a pass completion later, the Packers kicked a field goal and to make the score 10–0.

The Patriots powered back, scoring touchdowns on both of their next two possessions. By the end of the first quarter, the Patriots were winning 14–10.

In the second quarter, Favre completed a Super Bowl–record 81-yard touchdown pass to receiver Antonio Freeman followed by another short scoring drive with the Packers settling for a field goal, making the score 20–14.

After taking the ensuing kickoff and moving the ball, the Patriots turned the ball over on an interception. The Packers took the ball over at their own 26-yard line and drive it all the way for a touchdown, taking 5:59 minutes off the clock and making the score 27–14 Packers going into halftime.

In the second half, at one point, New England's defense forced the Packers to punt, and the Patriots got the ball back with great field position after Meggett returned Craig Hentrich's 48-yard punt six yards to the New England 47-yard line. The Patriots drove 53 yards in seven plays and scored on an 18-yard touchdown run by Martin to cut the Packers' lead to 27–21. However, Desmond Howard returned the following kickoff for a 99-yard touchdown, and the Packers made it hurt even more by making a two-point conversion stick, giving the Packers a 35–21 lead.

That was the last score of the game. The Packers won. Dave Meggett had amassed 155 combined yards, and Bledsoe, though he had 25 completions, tied for a Super Bowl record four interceptions. The Patriots' leading receiver was Ben Coates with six catches for 67 yards and a touchdown.

"Bill Parcells went over to Bill Belichick in the Patriots locker room, they said a few things to each other, then Parcells embraced his long-time assistant and friend," sportswriter Gary Myers wrote. "He walked through the New England locker room and down a hallway. A Super Bowl loser for the first time."

"Anytime you get to this game, there's a measure of satisfaction," Parcells said, "but when you lose it, you're disappointed. No one could be more disappointed than I am because I thought we had a good opportunity to win when we got it to 27–21," Parcells said. "We had a lot of momentum on that drive because our defense was playing better. But that kickoff return by Desmond Howard was the big play, and I credit him for it. That was a huge play. We failed to concentrate on one play and it cost us, but the Packers played better than we did."

"I talked to my players about the game, and what happened in the game, and some of the reasons why you lose a game like this," Parcells said. "Then I thanked them for what they've given me this year in terms of effort because they've given me a tremendous amount. They fought hard. We just cracked a little bit under the pressure."

"In winning two Super Bowls as the Giants' coach, Parcells outcoached and outpsyched the Buffalo Bills and the Denver Broncos," Dave Anderson wrote. "But in last night's 35–21 shootout loss, the Patriots couldn't outscore the Green Bay Packers after their coach had outlasted all the questions regarding his expected departure from New England in order to join the Jets."

"I'll know more very soon," he said. "I would think in the next couple of days."

Parcells was coy with the press about his plans. But he did not get on the team's chartered jet back to Boston.

"I've got my family here," he said, "so I don't know exactly what I'm going to do, but I'll be back in New England by Tuesday at the latest."

"Not flying back after the Super Bowl kind of—it sent the message to the team that probably wasn't a good one," Belichick said.

In the locker room after the game was the last time Parcells saw his players. He never addressed the team again.

"You'd like to think that you go through some things with a guy, he can at least say goodbye; but that's the way Bill is," said Bledsoe, who played four years for the coach. "Bill, from the get-go, has been about Bill."

CHAPTER 8

Once You're a Jet

"In Boston, three things matter—sports, politics, and revenge," Kraft told the press. The drama of Parcells' departure started with the final gun of the Super Bowl. From then on in the stage was set. Kraft wanted revenge. And Leon Hess wanted Bill Parcells.

Leon Hess had built the Hess Oil Corporation with his bare hands. He was the son of Russian immigrants. His father was a kosher butcher in Asbury Park, New Jersey. Leon's father had a one-truck oil delivery business during the Great Depression in the 1930s.

"Everybody was broke in those days," Hess recalled. "I had to pay for the truck before I could deliver the oil."

Leon married New Jersey attorney general David T. Wilentz's daughter, Norma, and they had two daughters, Marlene and Connie, and a son, John B. Hess.

As a petroleum supply officer in World War II, Hess supplied oil to General George Patton's 3rd Army. After he continued to build up Hess Corporation, he acquired Amerada in 1969 after an ownership battle with Phillips Petroleum. The combined company became known as Amerada Hess. He stepped down as chairman and chief executive officer in 1995, and his son, John, succeeded him as CEO. At one point in the 1990s, *Forbes* magazine listed his net worth at $720 million.

As a businessman, Hess excelled. He founded the company in 1933 with one truck. By 1937 he had five trucks. In 1947 the company expanded its storage capabilities and purchased its first tanker. By 1957 the company first acquired the First Reserve terminal in Perth Amboy, New Jersey, and built its first refinery in Port Reading, New Jersey.

He was a partner in the original group that bought the New York Titans and remaned them the Jets in 1963. By the mid-to-late 1970s he'd bought out all his partners and owned the team outright. He moved it from Shea Stadium to Giants Stadium in 1984. While he had been a quiet and benevolent owner who was proud to create a 'family' atmosphere, the team had only small bursts of glory. The team was mostly shrouded in disappointment and failure.

"As an oil baron, Hess once sat with the Libyan leader Colonel Muammar al-Qaddafi's negotiator, who put a revolver on the table. Another time he went to see the Shah of Iran in a car with soldiers' guns sticking out its windows," Dave Anderson wrote. "Each time, he got the oil contract he wanted. So the negotiations with Kraft weren't about to intimidate him."

Kraft was not playing against a football coach now. He was going up against a businessman who was infinitely more experienced than himself. But Kraft had always been able to hold his own.

Right after the Super Bowl, NFL commissioner Paul Tagliabue announced that he would mediate the ongoing battle. Kraft had requested Tagliabue's intervention. He did not want to make it easy on Parcells. "In what has escalated into a distinct battle of ego and will, as well as legal niceties, Kraft believes he is entitled to compensation if Parcells departs. Parcells believes none is necessary," sports scribe Gerald Eskenazi wrote.

In the meantime, reports were already surfacing that Pete Carroll, the San Francisco 49ers defensive coordinator and former Jets head coach, would be the new head coach of the Patriots. Commissioner Paul Tagliabue said that Parcells' assertion that he was free to leave New England and coach wherever he wanted next season ran "contrary to common sense." Parcells "may pursue other NFL coaching opportunities for the 1997 season only with the Patriots' consent," Tagliabue said. The commissioner ruled that Kraft still had the rights to Parcells for one more year.

"You tell me what someone with three Super Bowls is worth on the open market," an ecstatic Kraft told associates when learning of Tagliabue's ruling. Kraft added, "I didn't break."

Now it was between Kraft and Hess to make a deal. The negotiations between Steve Gutman, the president of the Jets, and Robert K. Kraft started the next day. Kraft started playing to the press immediately. He went public for his demand—he wanted compensation—he wanted the Jets' No. 1 draft pick for 1997.

"I've been through hell because of this," Kraft said in a television interview. "I'm just supposed to hand Bill Parcells to a team in my division? I don't think so."

Parcells fired back saying famously on January 30, 1997, "It's just like a friend of mine told me," Parcells said. "'If they want you to cook the dinner, at least they ought to let you shop for some of the groceries.'"

While the public was having fun watching the fireworks, the contracts of the Patriot assistants were not being addressed. According to one assistant coach, Parcells told them, "Give me your phone numbers, and I'll be in touch."

Said one coach, "We're in a tough situation. We're getting hung out to dry."

There were only two similar events in NFL history. In 1970 Don Shula left the Baltimore Colts to coach the Miami Dolphins. Colts owner Carroll Rosenbloom then petitioned Commissioner Pete Rozelle, complaining he had not personally let Shula go. Rozelle sided with Rosenbloom and awarded the Colts Miami's No. 1 pick in 1970. In 1995, the Carolina Panthers wanted Pittsburgh Steelers' defensive coordinator Dom Capers and had to forfeit second- and sixth-round picks along with $150,000 to the Steelers for their man.

Kraft wanted a No. 1 pick. In a surprise move, the Jets announced in early February that they would sign Bill Belichick as a temporary head coach instead to run the team for one year while they waited for Parcells' contract to run out, in essence calling Kraft's bluff. They also threatened to hire Parcells as a consultant. The Patriots objected.

And indeed, the Jets did hire Belichick, and it made a difference right away.

"When I became the Jets' head coach, there were a lot of things to be done and that had to be started," Belichick said. "I knew it was going to switch at some time. We did a lot that week—bringing people on the staff, starting talks with players, arranging to hire the three holdover coaches."

"I was the head coach," Belichick said. "I hired Scott Pioli and Eric Mangini. I spoke to Mike Tannenbaum, I spoke to John Lott, I hired Linda. Pioli became the club's pro personnel director, Mangini became a defensive assistant. Tannenbaum became the contract director, Lott the strength coach, and Linda Leoni was hired as Parcells' secretary. Wrote Gerald Eskenazi in *The New York Times*, "In that week's work, Belichick helped alter the direction of the front office and the way it operated."

Kraft was flummoxed. "They haven't made a formal offer. I said, 'Make me an offer with players or picks,' but [Gutman] has made no offer. I don't know what they're doing.... Gutman suggested to me that perhaps they'll talk to Bill without talking to us. I told them make me an offer we can agree to, and then you can talk to him."

Eventually, Tagliabue inserted himself into the process. A week later, it was done.

"A penthouse conference room at a midtown law firm became the scene of the Jets' greatest triumph since Super Bowl III in 1969," Rich Cimini wrote. "It took 6½ hours of emotionally charged negotiations with Patriots owner Bob Kraft and NFL commissioner Paul Tagliabue, but Jets owner Leon Hess and president Steve Gutman pulled off the coup of a lifetime."

"They broke for lunch," Hess recalled, "but I didn't want to break. I've learned over the years, in negotiations, don't break. If there's air-conditioning on, shut it off. If there's heat on, shut it off. That's the way I've always been. Stay there until you get it done." Tagliabue eventually requested that Hess and Kraft discuss the situation privately.

"Kraft showed some give; we showed some give," Hess remembered. "He put his offer down one side of a piece of paper, we put our offer down the other side, then I suggested that we give the offers to the commissioner and accept his decision. The commissioner took 10 minutes to go over the offers, and then gave his decision. Kraft and I shook hands. He got more out of us than we wanted to give, but he got less than he wanted. We were both disappointed, but we agreed to live with it."

"We're very happy, and the commissioner did a hell of a job," said the usually reclusive owner, Hess. "This ought to be the turn around of the Jets."

Tagliabue made the final call after both parties went to arbitration at 4:30 in the afternoon. The commissioner awarded the Patriots four draft picks—No. 3 and No. 4 picks in the 1997 draft, a No. 2 pick in 1998, and a No. 1 in 1999. The Jets also had to pay a charitable contribution of $300,000 to a Patriots foundation.

"Hardly a steep price for a three-time Super Bowl coach," Rich Cimini wrote in *Sports Illustrated.*

"Sure, the Jets got their man, but at a great cost," Timothy W. Smith wrote in *The New York Times.* "Wonder what Bill Parcells, the Jets' consultant, would have advised the Jets to do if the deal involved a coach other than Bill Parcells?"

"When I told him the price...was too steep, he said he didn't care," Parcells wrote. "He wanted to win. And he didn't want to wait."

Perhaps the most astute observation was made by Robert Lipsyte of *The New York Times* when he wrote, "Personally, I don't much like Bill Parcells, smirky bully that he is. Not a nice guy. But I am delighted that he is coming back to town. It's been awhile since we've had the kind of coach we deserve—a winner with a mean streak who wants to be here."

Lipsyte continued, writing, "New York is a rough stage for people of the athletic persuasion, be they players or directors, but the rewards are as great as the punishment is severe." Parcells knew both sides of the coin Lipsyte was referring to.

——

"Leon Hess was greeted by a small group of Jets fans Tuesday as he left Weeb Ewbank Hall following the news conference to officially announce Bill Parcells will coach his beleaguered franchise this year," Vinny DiTriani wrote in *The Record.*

"Hey, Leon, way to go!" yelled a happy fan as a small group applauded the venerable owner as he left the press conference.

"Bill talked about going shopping and buying some of the groceries to do the cooking," said Hess, referring to Parcells' comments. "All I want to be is the little boy who goes along with him and pushes the cart in the supermarket and let him fill it up."

"Lookit, I don't have a crystal ball for anything. What I've got is a plan," Parcells said. "My goal is to get my team to play at the level of potential as I perceive it. Not someone else's judgment."

About the players Parcells said, "I'll tell them what we want to do and that the complaint department is on the fourth floor."

Parcells declared to the press, "This is my last job. After this, I'll ride off into the sunset."

"What's the highest rating on the Richter scale?" Parcells said when asked what kind of commitment for winning he received from Hess during their meetings. "Whatever the top number is, that's it."

Parcells and Belichick, who had inherited a 1–15 football team, went to work immediately, evaluating players, office personnel, etc. The Jets staffers, to differentiate between the two, called them Big Bill and Little Bill. Many thought of Belichick as Parcells' quieter, more cerebral alter ego. It was obvious Parcells valued Belichick. Belichick was the highest-paid assistant in the NFL, making $750,000 per year. It was always known that it would be Bill Belichick's job to refuse when Parcells finally decided to call it quits.

"I think he likes it here," Parcells said of Belichick. "He's had his share of overtures. He knows what I'm thinking. But a lot can happen."

"Here's the relationship," Parcells explained. "It's a kind of water-cooler deal—you know, at the office when you meet at the water cooler to discuss business. It only lasted two minutes today, but we'll both think about it." Parcells admitted that he and Belichick did not interact socially outside of the office. "But when I look back on my coaching career, I'll think of him," Parcells said.

During the draft, Parcells traded several picks, sliding down the ladder each time but always getting back two for one. The Jets traded the No. 1 pick to St. Louis for the No. 6 pick in the first round as well as the Rams' third-, fourth-, and seventh-round selections.

"Today's deal gives us some ability to acquire young, fixed-cost players," Parcells said. "I watched what Jimmy Johnson is doing. We started this up in New England. The salary constraints on our team are so great, we have to get our costs fixed. I just felt that one player is not going to help us as much as multiple players—and also we're able to recoup the players we lost. It would have been a very long wait from the second round to the fifth round."

Parcells wasn't done, and by the time the draft was finished, he'd traded picks again and finally drafted 11 college players. And he had traded one pick for Ronnie Dixon, a veteran defensive lineman from Philadelphia. It was clear from the draft that Parcells was going to be making wholesale changes to the roster. It was also clear that he was taking dead aim at the defense and special teams. Of the 11 players drafted, seven played defense.

"We improved the size of our defensive front quite a bit," Parcells said after drafting a pair of 300-pound defensive linemen. "I would have liked to get even more special teams players. When you have a poor defense, as the Jets had, then normally your special teams are lousy, too."

Dixon weighed more than 300 pounds, as did the Jets' final pick of the draft, Georgia's Jason Ferguson. On Saturday, the Jets drafted another 300-pounder, Rick Terry of North Carolina, with their second pick. That made three 300-pounders for the middle of the defensive front. The previous week, the Jets had none.

As for kick returning, it was another woeful area last season, with the Jets ranking 30 out of 30 teams in punt returns and 29 in kickoffs. Thus for the third-round pick, the Jets sought out Dedric Ward, a receiver-returner from Northern Iowa who was 5'9" but had David Meggett–type moves.

In the middle of May, Parcells was finally seen on the practice field with his new team.

He talked to the press. He referred to running back Adrian Murrell as "my kind of guy." Linebacker Marvin Jones "has been working pretty hard, and he's starting to get in pretty good condition.... I'll tell you something: the kid can run and hit and that's all you need." When asked his thoughts on veteran signal caller Neil O'Donnell, Parcells responded, "If he gets his team in the end zone, I'll like him. If not, I won't like him. That's how I judge quarterbacks."

Most fascinating were Parcells interactions with linebacker Mo Lewis. "It was one of the most interesting conversations I had," Parcells said. "He said, 'I'm sick of people running up points on us. I'd like to know coming out of the huddle that we'll stop them.'"

"It's time for me to win," Lewis said. Lewis had recently admitted that, "losing took its toll on me. This is what we need. A change. You've got to be angry about losing."

By now, Parcells and his guys were making more improvements everyday. By May, 99 percent of the season-ticket holders had renewed their seats. Sales were up. Along with his usual group of coaches, Parcells brought in former Giants tight end Mark Bavaro to work with the tight ends and Carl Banks to help the younger players especially acclimate to the metropolitan area.

"It was one of the most flattering calls I ever got when he asked me to join his staff," Jeff Hostetler said, "because he had never given the slightest indication I had earned his respect when I was with the Giants. But I honestly don't know if I could work with him. He makes a lot of demands, and I don't know whether I could make that commitment."

"Everybody knows it's going to be a tough camp," O'Donnell said before taking the field. "We need it. We deserve it. It's not like we're a veteran, winning group. Guys who have been around here for a while are fed up with losing. I was around here for one year, and I was miserable. I feel 10 times better."

Parcells opened the year with a team meeting. In it he stated that those who did not participate in the off-season conditioning program would not be there in the fall. Parcells said there were too many injuries on this team last year.

"On my teams," Parcells told the Jets, "not many players get hurt."

He spoke very clearly. His Jets team would not tire in the fourth quarter. He said his Jets team would be bigger, stronger, and faster. The players, even outrageous ones like Keyshawn Johnson, got the message. As several players said, it was time to stop renting a room in the metropolitan area and buy a house.

Parcells gave basically what was his signature speech. He didn't care about your problems. He didn't want the guys with troublesome girlfriends, bad habits, drug problems, nightclub partiers, or sticky relatives. He wanted football players who were willing to commit. He wanted football players who could focus.

Everyone started working out.

"Even the coaches were working out," Jumbo Elliott said. "Our coaches will whip the other teams' coaches."

At the minicamp, Parcells was back to being a coach. He yelled a lot.

"Brady, get off the field," Parcells screamed during a line-up shift when tight end Kyle Brady was supposed to shuttle to the sideline. He verbally throttled another tight end, Fred Baxter, yelling, "Where are you lining up? Don't you know where you're supposed to be?"

To a player who was throwing up from exhaustion at one point, Parcells barked, "Throw up on your own time."

Parcells was loud and his whistle louder. He stopped three offensive plays at one point as players were not lined up properly. When asked about their first workout, he responded that it was, "A little bit sloppy...It was a little hard to be impressed with that," he said.

"He had a few choice words for me," defensive end Hugh Douglas said. "But not screaming. He told me not to jump offside. They were very big on fundamentals. When you go through the fundamentals, it makes a big difference in the way you practice."

"When the coach screams, I know he's only doing it to make me a better player," wide receiver Keyshawn Johnson said.

Perhaps no other player drew the negative attention of the public more than Keyshawn Johnson, whose autobiography, *Just Throw Me the Damn Ball*, ridiculed the former coaching staff and criticized his fellow players. He called Neil O'Donnell "a stiff puppet" and fellow receiver Wayne Chrebet a "team mascot."

Fans and veteran media members expected fireworks between the Johnson and Parcells. But almost the opposite happened. Keyshawn had wanted to be on a winner, and head coach Rich Kotite's teams weren't anywhere close. He was frustrated and depressed. In Parcells, Johnson found a leader he wanted to follow—someone who had been to the mountain top and through whose personal demeanor and magnetism Johnson believed would help the team achieve great things.

"If I didn't have Bill as a head coach right now, I don't know where the hell I'd be in terms of football," Keyshawn told the press. On Parcells' side, Bill never talked about Keyshawn's literary efforts. Johnson became the possession receiver he was expected to become, a real gamer, and Parcells appreciated Johnson's efforts. In time, Johnson would be one of Parcells' "guys." Parcells was asked if Keyshawn would show up in a parking lot to play.

"He'd show up," smiled Parcells. "But he'd like people to be there watching."

More than anything else, Parcells admired toughness. And more than any other analogy Parcells could draw on was boxing, even more than football, to help someone understand his code of toughness.

"Parcells loves boxing; his idea of a perfect day in the off-season is to spend it inside some ratty boxing gym in North Jersey," bestselling sports author Michael Lewis wrote.

"It's a laboratory," Parcells said. "You get a real feel for human behavior under the strongest duress—under the threat of physical harm."

The story dated back to a middleweight fight Parcells never saw between Vito Antuofermo and Cyclone Hart in the 1970s. Regardless of the veracity of the story boxing manager Teddy Atlas told Parcells, the story Parcells illustrates his idea of mental and physical toughness.

Hart was the big puncher, and Antuofermo was a wiry fighter with more heart than talent. Hart hurt Antuofermo in the first, second, and third rounds of the story, breaking Antuofermo's ribs. Antuofermo just kept taking the punishment, and bleeding profusely, but he kept answering the bell. By the fifth round, Hart was tired, more mentally than physically. He had brutalized and beaten Antuofermo yet Antuofermo would not go down. In the fifth round, seeing his opening, Antuofermo turned the tables and blazed away at Hart, knocking him down and taking the fight.

"When the fighters went back to their makeshift locker rooms, only a thin curtain was between them. Hart's room was quiet, but on the other side he could hear Antuofermo's cornermen talking about who would take the fighter to the hospital," Lewis wrote, quoting Parcells.

"'Every time he hit me with that left hook to the body, I was sure I was going to quit,' Hart heard Antuofermo say to his trainers. 'After the second round, I thought if he hit me there again, I'd quit. I thought the same thing after the fourth round. Then he didn't hit me no more.'

"At that moment, Hart began to weep. It was really soft at first. Then harder. He was crying because for the first time he understood that Antuofermo had felt the same way he had and worse. The only thing that separated the guy talking from the guy crying was what they had done. The coward and the hero feel the same emotions. They're both human," Parcells said, finishing the story.

The inaccuracies of the story are multitudinous. Hart never broke Antuofermo's ribs, they didn't share a locker room, and neither of the fighters went to the hospital. Antuofermo was a New York City Golden Gloves champion in 1970 and was a well-known fighter in the city. However, Antuofermo was an easy bleeder, and it became a problem for him much later in championship fights against Marvin Hagler.

But the basic tenants of the story are important. On March 11, 1977, Hart did beat Antuofermo brutally that day for five solid rounds before he finally quit, unable to beat down the smaller opponent. And indeed, Antuofermo went on to be the middleweight champion in 1979.

But Parcells' perception of what makes a true champion is clear. What a Bill Parcells "guy" is cannot be mistaken. Bill Parcells wanted his teams to be a small army of Antuofermos. His worst fear, what kept him awake at night, as Lewis so insightfully pointed out, was that Parcells' teams might turn out to be an army of Harts.

By now Parcells was back to his old, irascible, cranky self.

"It's tough. He kinda shuts everyone out. Not on purpose," Judy Parcells said. "But I understand that his mind is always on football and I just, I try to leave him alone and not put any pressures on him during the season." Judy told Mike Wallace of *60 Minutes* that Parcells is "miserable, anxious, exasperated, and depressed" during the entire season.

According to Wallace, one former player said, "If Parcells were named King of the World on Sunday, he'd be miserable by Tuesday."

"Well, I don't think he's happy unless he's mad, you know," Keyshawn Johnson said.

"Have you ever met people that like to be miserable? He's one of those people," Bryan Cox said. "He likes to be miserable."

There was reason to celebrate by August 16, 1997, when the New York Jets played the New York Giants at the Meadowlands. While it was only an exhibition game, one couldn't tell that from the fans—more than 57,000 came out to see their old/new coach.

"Before the game, there was an edge to the normal goings-on. In the stadium's tunnel, the Giants massed too early as they got ready to run on the field," Gerald Eskenazi reported. The Jets had not yet come down the tunnel. "So they stood in a blue wall, [Dave] Brown clapping madly, players bouncing on their toes. Suddenly, the Giants spotted Parcells, lips drawn tight, leading the Jets toward the tunnel. He was accompanied as always by Steve Yarnell, his security chief, a former FBI agent whom Parcells coached back at West Point in the late 1960s."

The blue wall of Giants stiffened as Parcells headed toward them and then past them. There were boos and cheers as Parcells entered the stadium floor. Parcells approached sports radio personality Suzyn Waldman and kissed her cheek. Parcells also greeted Billy Taylor and O.J. Anderson, both ex-Giants and radio personalities, and he then turned his attention to one of the Giants' longtime equipment aides.

"I can't get rid of you,'" Parcells told him.

Another visitor was ex-Giant Ottis "O.J." Anderson, another radio personality, and the second running back Parcells had greeted this unusual evening. Earlier, Rodney Hampton had come over to say hello.

"As the Jets went through their pregame routines, Parcells found himself alone at the goal line for a few minutes. He rubbed his chin and looked around as if thinking," Eskenazi wrote.

The fans responded with both boos and cheers as the Jets took the local bragging rights in a 27–17 Jets victory.

"I told them good teams will come back," Parcells said. "Probably the most positive thing for me was we were down by 10 and came back." It was their third victory of the preseason. The next week the Jets needed overtime to beat the Tampa Bay Buccaneers to run their preseason record to 4–0.

By the end of August, Charlie Weis was the new play caller on offense, and Wayne Chrebet was the hot new receiver. Chrebet led American Conference receivers during the preseason with 18 catches. "This guy's going to play a lot. It's not going to make any difference who starts," Parcells said.

By then people started to realize half of what made Parcells effective were the people he surrounded himself with. Belichick had certainly resurrected his reputation during his short stay in New England. Parcells was honest about his coaching staff, saying, "I'd be nothing without these guys."

"Ninety percent of it here is the way it was with the Giants," said Belichick, known here as Little Bill. "There [are] plenty of jobs to do. There are some things Bill asked me to do because of my experience. He's working 24 hours a day. I'm working 24 hours a day."

"The whole thing is building a mentality and commitment, not only to the program but to each other," Belichick said. "It's thinking, 'I don't want to let anyone down.'"

"We both like football," Parcells said about himself and Belichick. "We don't have much in common. Different backgrounds. But we've got one thing in common."

"I had plans to talk to Bill Belichick about coaching," Kraft said at the time. "But Parcells' departure had created such a whirlwind, a storm, and I couldn't talk to his people. We were just left in such turmoil and uncertainty, and I knew that Parcells would be taking the staff with him. We thought it was better to start fresh."

"Bill Belichick stole my heart a long time ago," said Pepper Johnson, once a Giants inside linebacker under Parcells and now a Jets middle linebacker. "You have to be a student. You don't want to be embarrassed by not knowing the answer to his question."

But there were coaches other than Belichick.

"We get written tests in meetings," running backs coach Adrian Murrell said of running backs coach Maurice Carthon. "And during the game he's always asking me, 'What did you see?' right there on the sideline when I come off."

"They really complement each other," Johnson said, alluding to Belichick, Groh, and Crennel, known as Rac. "Bill is all Xs and Os. Al is a philosopher; he talks about day-to-day things that help guys relate. We linebackers were the last guys out of our Saturday night meeting because he was telling every guy what he expects of him. And Rac is rah-rah—just knock everybody down. If you listen to all three, you'll be a complete player."

— —

Perhaps one of the most impressive things about Parcells during this period was his star power. In the early 1990s, he and good friend (sports TV and radio talk show host) Mike Francesa also did a television spot for their favorite New Jersey restaurant, Manny's in Moonachie.

In New England Parcells had made a series of commercials for an electronic appliance store, Lechmere's. It was a sizable New England brand, and they ran a series of commercials starring the charismatic coach. But when he came back to the New York metropolitan area, he was an advertising legend. His image was everywhere. Magazine and newspaper ads. Television ads. He became the face of the Tri-State Cadillac dealers. He may not have wanted to bust his ass selling Gatorade, but he didn't mind endorsing a few products and businesses along the way, including Apex One, Backyard Drills, Bumble Bee Tuna, Casual Male, CBS Corporation, Dunkin' Donuts, Frito-Lay, General Motors, LCI International, Lechmere, MCI, Mforma, NBC Sports, New York Stock Exchange, Ocean Spray, Reality Games, Shell Oil, Slim-Fast, and The Wiz.

The final football team that hit the field did not look anything like the team from the year before. As promised, the defense was completely recast and featured a linebacking corps of Mo Lewis, James Farrior, Marvin Jones, and Dwayne Gordon. Ernie Logan anchored the defensive line at nose tackle and included Hugh Douglas and Rick Lyle at defensive ends. Aaron Glenn and Victor Green anchored a defensive backfield that also included Jerome Henderson and Otis Smith.

The New York Jets welcomed in the Parcells era with a 41–3 blowout of the Seattle Seahawks. The press and fans went crazy. They had already tied the number of wins they had all the previous year in the first week. They lost a tough one in Buffalo 28–22 in what was a closer game than the score indicates.

The next game was the game everyone in the northeast and a lot of the rest of the country was waiting for—the Jets at New England. This had all the hype and atmosphere of a playoff game. And the game itself delivered.

More than 60,000 people showed up to watch Parcells' new Jets face the team he'd taken to the Super Bowl less than a year ago. The Jets shocked the football world by hanging tough with the Patriots through the whole game, especially when the Jets tied the game in the final minute of the fourth quarter only to lose to an Adam Vinatieri field goal in overtime that sealed the game 27–24.

"I'm disappointed because we had the opportunities to win," Parcells said. "We should have scored more points in the first half."

"No one cares when you lose. You've got to win ugly, and you've got to win pretty," Jets quarterback Neil O'Donnell said.

The headline in *The New York Times* the next day? "Patriots 27, Parcells 24"

After the Jets beat the Oakland Raiders the following weekend at the Meadowlands, the Jets never had a losing record again throughout the rest of the season. The shocker came when the Jets returned the favor to the Patriots, beating the vaunted New England team 24–19 in the Meadowlands.

Pepper Johnson, however, who had been with Parcells for six years, was lost for the season.

"Their relationship was almost like that of a father and son," *The New York Times'* Mike Freeman remembered. "With the injured Johnson sitting on the table in the training room, Parcells crowded the team around the linebacker and proceeded to say how important Johnson was to him, not just as a player but as a person. Those present say Parcells had tears in his eyes as he spoke, and the moment proved to be a truly unifying one for the team, sort of [a] rallying point."

By October 29, 1997, the Jets had a record of 5–3 and were tied with the Patriots for first place. Going into the last game of the season, the Jets were 9–6 with a chance to go 10–6 and make the playoffs. But the Cinderella story was still one more year in the making. The Jets pulled out to a first-quarter 10-point lead and then blew several chances throughout the game and watched as Barry Sanders finally started to work his magic. The Lions scored two field goals and a fourth-quarter touchdown as well as an interception of a Jets pass late in the game to seal the final victory of the season. The game was marred by a paralyzing hit to Lions player Reggie Brown that shook Parcells.

Still, by all accounts, 1997's 9–7 finish was a miraculous turnaround. But Parcells would do one better in 1998.

- -

The changes for the 1998 season started happening quickly. In January 1998, Ron Erhardt retired. He had been in a diminished role for the previous season, sitting next to Charlie Weis as Charlie called the plays, and he had decided at 67 years of age that it was time to go. Next, Parcells promoted Weis to offensive coordinator and then brought in Dan Henning to be his quarterback coach. They had been friends since they had worked at Florida State. In Henning, Parcells was bringing in someone who had head coaching experience.

The next thing was the uniforms. The Jets had changed their uniforms five times since 1977. As a sign of their new direction, Parcells decided it was time to go old school. With Joe Namath on hand, the organization unveiled a new uniform. Mo Lewis, Adrian Murrell, and Wayne Chrebet modeled the modernized version of the old uniforms from their Super Bowl III years. The new logo had reverted to the old logo.

"I always identified the Jets with those uniforms," Parcells said.

In the meantime Parcells wasted no time in upgrading his offensive line. The Jets signed the Chicago Bears' 300-pound offensive guard Todd Burger, who played alongside the $3 million center Kevin Mawae from the Seattle Seahawks. They also acquired backup lineman Mike Gisler from the New England Patriots. With Jumbo Elliott anchoring one tackle slot, the Jets needed one more tackle.

Parcells also brought in 12-year veteran fullback/tight end Keith Byars, who was a hard-hitting and versatile player.

Mawae became the highest-paid center in National Football League history with a five-year contract worth $17 million. "When I met Bill Parcells, he said to me, 'I'm 56, I'm getting old. I've won two Super Bowls. I want to win one more.' I wanted to jump on the boat with him," Mawae said. "What can you say about a coach that takes a 1–15 team to one play from the playoffs?" Mawae said of Parcells and the Jets. "What put it over for me is that Bill Parcells runs everything. No controversy between the general manager and coach."

In March one of the most controversial signings was when the Jets announced that they had offered New England Patriots running back Curtis Martin a 6-year, $36 million contract. The offer was multi-layered and purposely designed by Jets management to make it hard for the Patriots to counter. Parcells had developed a penchant of poaching players from teams he'd previously coached. But this was also a shot at Kraft, which doubled the excitement.

"This was an opportunity that we felt was difficult to pass up," Parcells said in a statement. "Curtis has always displayed character and passion for his job, and I expect he will bring that energy, character, and passion to this team."

"Parcells told me he believed in me, and at the right time he would show me how much he believed in me," Martin told newyorkjets.com. "And when I came to the New York Jets, the way Leon Hess and Parcells made it so easy, the negotiations and everything, they laid out the red carpet for me and they just made me really feel like I was important to them and they were willing to do anything to get me there."

The move had massive impact. It weakened the AFC East's most powerful team. It also increased the Jets' level of attack, and it changed the balance of power within the division. It was a masterstroke.

"Bill Parcells is a great coach," said Indianapolis Colts coach Jim Mora. "It may be that he thinks now is the time to make a run at the Super Bowl, and Curtis Martin is the final piece."

Yes, maybe Parcells was thinking they could make a Super Bowl run. But one general manager at the winter meetings said, "When I first heard about him signing Martin to the offer sheet, I said, 'Uh-oh, Bill's gone. Two years max.'"

Both opinions were right. It was a calculated and costly acquisition. And there was a definite sense of urgency with the Jets swirled up by both Leon Hess and Parcells. Both men wanted an NFL title, and both were willing to do almost anything. In Martin, they paid an incredible price. He would drastically limit their cap spending, and bringing him in would cost the Jets a No. 1 and No. 3 pick in that year's draft. In the 1998 draft, the Patriots would have three of the Jets' draft choices.

The Jets on the other hand wouldn't get to pick until the 56th overall selection. But the Jets had addressed the issue of those lost draft choices when they traded away several players in return for draft picks, so the Jets had restocked several spots.

Behind closed doors, Kraft was furious. So was Pete Carroll. Martin would not even return calls to Carroll when the offer was first made to Martin in an attempt to persuade him to stay. Kraft and the Patriots petitioned the commissioner, saying that the contract was invalid due to side clauses that were contradictory or maybe even outside of the NFL contract laws. But after lots of controversy, the NFL held that the contract was allowable.

The only problem the Jets faced now was at quarterback. Neil O'Donnell, the team's original starting quarterback who had previously led the Steelers to a Super Bowl berth, was on the outs with Parcells. Since coming to the Jets, he'd suffered two difficult injuries that had placed him on the sideline. His comeback from both injuries was spotty. Playing poorly at mid-season, Parcells had benched O'Donnell. For the remainder of the season, O'Donnell played but saw the two backup quarterbacks, Glenn Foley and Ray Lucas, increasingly rotated into games and pressure situations. He didn't like it.

The other problem between O'Donnell and Parcells was O'Donnell's contract. It was a hefty contract that made maneuvering the Jets' cap that much more difficult. Parcells tried to convince O'Donnell to renegotiate it, but O'Donnell and his agent resisted.

During the Jets' minicamp, O'Donnell and Parcells met and had a closed-door meeting. After the meeting, O'Donnell and the coach played nice in front of the cameras. But O'Donnell's contract continued to pose a problem. Parcells told the media that O'Donnell would be their quarterback, and indeed, O'Donnell took all the first-string snaps in minicamp that year.

But on June 24, Parcells called Leigh Steinberg, O'Donnell's agent, and told Steinberg that the Jets would indeed begin talking with other quarterbacks. Steinberg said publicly that for all intents and purposes, O'Donnell would not be playing for the Jets in the 1998 season.

On the other hand, Vinny Testaverde was thrilled. "Certainly if I had a chance to play for Bill Parcells, that would be a great opportunity for me, knowing his past in taking teams to the Super Bowl," Testaverde said. In his career, Testaverde had completed 55.1 percent of his passes, thrown for 29,223 yards, and tossed 175 touchdowns to 183 interceptions.

"I played well when I was under Bill Belichick in Cleveland," Testaverde said. Vinny, who had grown up in Elmont, New York, and starred at Sewanhaka High School added, "Me being from Long Island, I'd be coming home."

By the end of June, Testaverde was the Jets' new quarterback with a $1.5 million deal and a second-year option of $4 million.

At the end of July, Marvin Jones, the team's leading tackler, suffered a freak accident in training camp and was lost for the season. In typical Parcells fashion, a veteran replacement was found in less than a week.

The controversial Bryan Cox, formerly of the Miami Dolphins and the Chicago Bears, was available, having been cut by Chicago earlier in the year. Cox had been a problem child throughout his career, garnering fines from the NFL. He was once called for two flagrant personal fouls in a row during his career and had paid more than $100,000 in fines to the NFL. He was also a three-time Pro Bowler and a tremendously aggressive defensive whirlwind.

"I've been lucky with veterans. O. J. Anderson, Everson Walls. They just want to know what you want," Parcells said. "I know he's a good kid."

Parcells admitted that he and Cox shared a special bond—both were horse racing enthusiasts. Both Parcells and Cox had owned and raced thoroughbreds. "I used to see him in the winter at Gulfstream," Parcells said.

It had been one of the busiest and most daring off-seasons.

While everyone was amazed by all the goings on in Hempstead, reality came crashing down in the second game of the preseason when the Jets were thoroughly crushed by the Baltimore Ravens 33–0. Neither Glenn Foley nor Vinny Testaverde had played well at quarterback, but Foley's numbers were noticeably off.

"I didn't quite expect this, but sometimes you need this to put you back to reality," Parcells said. "You've got to be able to take this for what it is—a preseason game." But people knew Parcells wasn't happy.

Throughout the season, Parcells and his staff would have to tinker with their lineup, dodging obstacles like injuries and poor performances.

— —

The first two weeks of the season were ominous. With Glenn Foley at the controls, the Jets lost first at San Francisco 36–30 and then lost to the Baltimore Ravens 24–10 at the Meadowlands. In the Ravens game Foley was injured, and Testaverde was called upon. In Testaverde's first game as a starter for the Jets, he lobbed four touchdowns, and the Jets won 44–6 against the Indianapolis Colts.

"I feel good about what Vinny did," Parcells said. "That's what I was hoping for.... He made good decisions. He didn't do anything to hurt us. I was very pleased with him. I'm glad I've got the guy."

In the next game, the Jets won 20–9 against division rivals the Dolphins.

However, Foley was reinserted in time for a game against the St. Louis Rams in which the Rams humbled the stumbling Jets 30–10 and sent Foley back to the bench.

"We had 45 guys dressed for this game, 12 guys coaching," Parcells said. "Everybody stunk."

The Jets were at 2–3, and the season seemed to be sitting on the brink. Curtis Martin, who had been injured, was ready to return. And Parcells decided to make Testaverde the No. 1 quarterback in an effort to energize his team.

"We've shortened the season to six games," Parcells said. "If we don't win five of those games, we won't be playing for anything. We have to put ourselves in position if we want to compete for the division. The next six weeks are critical to me to have the opportunity in the last month to compete. If we're not successful in the next six weeks, the ability to do what the objectives were would probably be gone."

At one point that week, on October 16, Parcells was desperate.

"With his team facing a crucial game that could dictate the course of the Jets' season, Coach Bill Parcells pulled one of the most extraordinary motivational stunts in his career," Rich Cimini wrote in *Sports Illustrated*. "Disturbed by the team's lethargic attitude in Friday's practice, Parcells walked off the field with his assistant coaches, according to team members."

Defensive co-captain linebacker Pepper Johnson, who'd been with Parcells on the Giants and Belichick at Cleveland, ran the practice for the last hour. The players were stunned. Parcells got their attention.

The Jets stepped up. They won the next four, lost a squeaker at Indianapolis, giving that game away 24–23, and then they ran the rest of the table, making their final record for the 1998 season 12–4.

During the course of his time with the Jets, Parcells did a television show with Phil Simms. They recorded the show in a television studio near the New York Jets' training complex. The two were having a good time.

"You've been riding on my back for so long, Simms," Parcells said, "they should call me ol' Paint." After that remark, Parcells suggested they tape their final Thanksgiving holiday well wishes.

"Well, we have another show to tape before Thanksgiving, right?" Simms asked.

"No, we don't, Simms," Parcells said. "This is the night we'd have to do it, Simms. Unless there's a different calendar for you than for everybody else." Parcells was right. They did the Thanksgiving ending, and it was nice, an acknowledgment that they have much to be thankful for. The moment the cameras are off, Parcells turned to the small group of technicians and the fans in the studio audience and, with a wide smile, delivered the final zinger

"I almost said, 'And the thing I have to be most thankful for is that you're not playing quarterback for the New York Jets.'" He got a big laugh.

On December 13 the Jets played the Miami Dolphins. In the days leading up to the game, Parcells gave the gift of a gas can half-filled with water to Bryan Cox. On it was a note that read: "To: Bryan Cox. From: Bill Parcells. Merry Christmas." Cox said the question was loud and clear—was he running out of gas?

"I'm going to keep that forever," Cox said. "I knew who it was from right away. It's getting late in the season, and he wanted to know how my gas can was doing."

The Jets beat the Miami Dolphins 21–16. Then they beat the Buffalo Bills 17–10 to take the AFC East crown.

"You hear same old Jets, same old Jets," said Parcells to his team, choking up. He was emotional and had to take deep breaths even to finish phrases, words. "Well, now you're the champs and nobody can take that away from you. You have a responsibility to keep playing that way." To the press, Parcells said, "Our guys, they just try hard for me all the time. They're not the greatest team. But mentally, they're really tough right now. I'm proud and happy. It's pretty emotional for me today. I can't even recount much of the game."

In the last game of the season, the Jets beat the New England Patriots 31–10 at the Meadowlands. They were now the No. 2 seeded team in the playoffs.

On January 10, 1999, the Jets hosted the Jacksonville Jaguars. It was Coughlin versus Parcells in the playoffs again. Neither man was happy about it. Coughlin had a great deal of respect for Parcells, and Parcells also had a lot of admiration for Coughlin. They were both tough task-masters. Demanding. Difficult. Detail oriented. And successful.

All week, Parcells rode Jets left tackle Jumbo Elliott. He needed Elliott to have a big day. But coming into the game, the press had written feature stories on Tony Boselli, the Jaguar's All-Pro left tackle. "Who's this left tackle I'm reading about this week?" Parcells needled Elliott.

The game was an exciting one. But it was Keyshawn Johnson, he of *Just Throw Me the Damn Ball* fame, who stole the show. "He ran for one touchdown on a reverse, scored a second touchdown on a 21-yard pass from Vinny Testaverde, recovered a fumble at a pivotal moment by racing 60 yards in pursuit of a Jaguars player, and put the finishing touches on the game by moving to defense and intercepting a desperation pass from the Jaguars' Mark Brunell," Gerald Eskenazi reported in *The New York Times*.

The Jets won 34–24. They were headed to the AFC Championship game against the Denver Broncos, with the possibility of playing the Super Bowl in Miami, the scene of the franchise's historic championship in 1969.

The Jets took a slim 3–0 lead into halftime in what was to be John Elway's last game in Denver. It was a tough, hard-fought half. In the early part of the third quarter, Jets tight end Blake Spence blocked a punt, recovering it on the Broncos 1-yard line. Curtis Martin made a 1-yard touchdown plunge to run the score to 10–0.

But then the wheels came off. The Broncos scored 20 unanswered points in the third quarter and another three in the fourth quarter to give Denver a 23–10 victory. Elway completed only 13-of-34 passes, and running back Terrell Davis ran for 167 yards and a touchdown. In the meantime, the Jets had turned over the ball six times (two interceptions and four fumbles). Curtis Martin was held to just 14 rushing yards, and although Vinny Testaverde threw for 356 yards, he threw no touchdowns.

"This wasn't baby steps," Parcells pointed out about his team. "You can compare that with any team in history over a two-year period. I am not saying that from an egotistical standpoint but from an accomplishment standpoint on the players' part."

— —

"Oh, yeah, my intention is to coach this year. I want to try and do this. I like the players. I like this team. I like coaching this team. I do. It's not an easy job, but I like it," Parcells said a week after the championship game. "I told the players I won't rest. My whole idea is to try to improve this team each year. We'll see what we can do to do that."

And the coaches seemed committed, as well. Whether by hook or by crook, the 12 assistants showed remarkable loyalty. Belichick turned down two inquiries from Chicago and Kansas City for head coaching jobs. Parcells had recommended Chris Palmer for the Cleveland head coaching position. But Palmer, though he wanted Romeo Crennel for his defensive coordinator, never offered Crennel the job because he didn't want to raid his friend and former boss' staff. And when George Seifert offered Al Groh a defensive coordinator job with the 49ers, Parcells slapped a "supervisor" tag on Groh, preventing the move. There was no doubt that the Jets thought they were going to make a Super Bowl run.

On May 7, 1999, the organization was dealt a massive blow when owner Leon Hess died. "We buried Mr. Hess, and I miss him already," Parcells wrote. "I loved the guy, and I had a tremendous amount of respect for him. To me he was what an owner should be—he was in it to win."

Parcells said Hess called him "a couple of times a week about eight in the morning to discuss the team, see how things were going, and to make sure things were okay. We also talked about Jersey."

This was now the third time Parcells was involved in an NFL team where there would be some kind of transition from old to new ownership. While the press was excited to see the newest edition of the Jets on the field, the intrigue of selling a team and acquiring a new owner would be deleterious in its effect on the organization.

All summer, the Jets were constantly splashed across the sports pages. The opening of Jets camp was one of the most anticipated sporting events of the season. Articles were filled with Super Bowl expectations. The Jets in the off-season had brought in safety Steve Atwater, an eight-time Pro Bowler with the Denver Broncos. Parcells had also traded Glenn Foley to Seattle for Rick Mirer.

"The most eagerly awaited season in Jets history starts today with Tuna Bowl V. If it lives up to the hype, the season will end four months from now with another Roman-numeraled game," Rich Cimini wrote in *Sports Illustrated*. Bill Parcells was 58 years old, and this was his 15th season as a head coach. And probably his last with the organization.

The Jets' season pretty much ended with 7:12 left in the second quarter when Vinny Testaverde dropped back to pass and—completely untouched—fell to the ground. He had ruptured his left Achilles tendon. All-purpose running back Leon Johnson, a special teams star, was also lost for the season. Their seasons were finished. So were the Jets.

Curtis Martin looked up to the sky and asked, "Why?"

Keyshawn Johnson was so angry he pounded the podium with his fists in the press room and just walked out.

"God is playing sometimes," Parcells said. "That's life in the big city. That's the way it goes. It's a humbling game, a game that can turn very quickly. We've got 15 games to go, and we've got to figure out a way to approach those."

In an unsuspected move, Parcells named punter and former Cardinals signal-caller Tom Tupa to replace Testaverde but later replaced him with Mirer. Mirer quarterbacked the next six games, and the Jets ran their record to 1–6, beating only the Denver Broncos. The Jets beat the Arizona Cardinals in Week 9 by the score of 12–7. But the anemic Jets offense could not muster enough touchdowns. Mirer was benched, and Parcells promoted Ray Lucas, a special teams player who had quarterbacked in college.

Arguably, Parcells may have never coached as well in his career as he did in the second half of that season. With Lucas at the helm, they won two games, lost the next two games, and then ran the table with four wins.

Of course, the loss that put the stake in their heart was their eighth and final loss, which eliminated them from the playoffs—a 41–28 loss in the Meadowlands to the New York Giants. "We were outplayed, outprepared, outcoached, out-everything, and I am ashamed," said a grieved Parcells. "It's the first time in three years I am ashamed."

They had only lost two of their last nine games and finished their record at a remarkable 8–8. The last three wins were against playoff-bound teams. In the last home game, the stadium reverberated with the chant, "One more year! One more year! One more year!"

— —

On January 4, 2000, Parcells announced his retirement. "There won't be any coaching rumors about Bill Parcells because I coached my last game. This is the end of my coaching career," Parcells told the press.

Parcells had told his coaches, the staff, and the players. He read aloud to them a poem called, "The Man in the Glass" by Dale Wimbrow.

The final stanza was powerful:

> *You may fool the whole world down the pathway of Life*
> *And get pats on the back as you pass*
> *But your final reward will be heartaches and tears*
> *If you've cheated the man in the glass.*

"He dropped the mic and left teary-eyed," linebacker Dwayne Gordon said. Parcells told his men there was no shame in crying.

This of course was all carefully orchestrated. A year later Parcells admitted that he pretty much knew he was going to retire that year, and he even told Belichick before their last game that he was officially retiring.

A week earlier, Commissioner Tagliabue had told the Jets brass and Parcells that they could not stop the Patriots from talking with Belichick or any other team, despite the clause in his contract that he was heir apparent. If he was still an assistant, then he was able to interview. Parcells knew what he was doing.

"The reason [Parcells] is going to make a rapid decision is that he thinks the Patriots are offering the job to Belichick," an anonymous source said. Surely Parcells would do anything to thwart Kraft, the source reasoned.

"By contract, you're the next head coach," Parcells said to Belichick.

"I've been waiting a year for this," Belichick said. Parcells told Belichick that he would inform Jets president Steve Gutman right after the game.

"As soon as I do that, you're the head coach, and I plan to do it right after the game," Parcells told Belichick.

"During that last season, I had a lot of meetings with him, sort of preparing him to take over this season, things I would not have shared with him in the past. Even before the season started, I had heard rumors that New England was interested in Belichick."

At 9:00 AM the morning the next morning of Parcells' official resignation, the New England Patriots faxed the New York Jets requesting permission to interview Bill Belichick for their head coaching position. Parcells and Gutman refused the request because as far as the Jets were concerned, Belichick had been on the clock since 5:00 PM the night before as the new head coach of the New York Jets.

Parcells then announced his retirement and met with the coaches to discuss injuries, and according to Parcells, Belichick set up meetings with all the staffers for the following week as the new head coach. What was Machiavellian about Parcells' "retirement" was that he would in effect still be running the show as "the head of football operations."

Around 6:00 PM, Belichick approached Parcells in the coach's locker room. He had heard about the fax inquiry from New England and said he wanted permission to speak with them. Belichick felt that after 18 years of service, Parcells owed him that.

Parcells refused. The conversation was less than friendly. Belichick went home. After taping his weekly television show with Phil Simms, Parcells returned to the office the next day, Tuesday, to see a visibly upset Belichick. He had a news conference scheduled that day as the new head coach.

Belichick told Parcells that he was going to resign. Parcells was surprised but not shocked and told Belichick that he could do whatever he wanted, but that he, Parcells, would not give him permission to speak with any club regarding a head coaching position.

"I don't know what my role will be," Parcells told Belichick. "If you feel that undecided, maybe you shouldn't take this job."

Belichick wrote a hasty resignation note, scribbling HC of the NYJ, and then he took the podium.

"I took Bill's words to heart," Belichick told the press. A visibly nervous and upset Belichick looked out of sorts and preoccupied. He told the press he was stepping down as the head coach of the New York Jets.

"Due to various uncertainties surrounding my position as it relates to the team of new ownership, I've decided to resign as the head coach of the New York Jets. I've given this resignation very careful consideration. I would like to wish the entire Jets organization, the players, the coaching staff, and the new ownership the very best of luck," Belichick read from a statement.

"We all know how Bill is," Belichick said. "Sometimes he reacts emotionally to a loss or a bad season or a series of bad performances. Every time Bill says that, I take it with a grain of salt."

When asked about his contract, Belichick said, "The understanding I had was with Mr. Hess. The situation has changed.... I'm no lawyer, but there are plenty of them and I'll let them deal with that, but I have a lawyer talking to the league."

— —

"I was just watching it on television and wondering what's going on," Steve Belichick, Bill's father, told the press. "We were up there for Christmas and I last talked to him a week ago. My wife talked to him briefly yesterday. He told her Bill Parcells had resigned and he was the Jets' new coach. He told her, 'I'll talk to you later,' but later never came. She never got the idea that things were unsettled."

In Belichick's mind, the Jets situation was cloudy at best. The club did not have a new owner as of yet, and so ownership was still a wild card. Belichick, like Parcells, had been through that before. And as head of football operations, it sounded like Parcells might never leave and Belichick would have to serve several more years of "mental servitude." Belichick would never get to be a head coach again—at least not on his own terms.

Belichick went to court but lost. He then withdrew his suit.

Belichick was an embarrassment not only to the Jets and to Parcells personally, but he was also a sore subject for the NFL. Another border war between New England and the Jets was simply not tolerable.

Kraft and Parcells had not talked since Parcells had left New England. There was bad blood on both sides. But New England was determined. Even though they had secretly met with Miami Hurricanes coach Butch Davis, they were committed to Belichick. Belichick and Kraft had really hit it off in their year together in New England, and after Pete Carroll had driven the program into the ground, Kraft needed a piece of Parcells magic back in New England to buoy his languishing credibility with a grumbling fan base. So both Parcells and Kraft, loathsome of each other as they were, needed one another now.

Kraft knew that after all his histrionics when Parcells left New England that the shoe would now be on the other foot and it would be his turn to hand over draft picks to get what he wanted.

In the meantime, the Jets named Al Groh as their new head coach. Many head coaches were signing on with new teams around the league. Draft scenarios were being prepared. Combines were being evaluated. And still New England did not have a coach, and Bill Belichick did not have a job.

During this whirlwind of press, it was finally announced that Robert Wood "Woody" Johnson IV, the great grandson of Robert Wood Johnson I (co-founder of Johnson & Johnson), had become the owner of the New York Jets. Johnson was born in New Brunswick, New Jersey. His father was Robert Wood Johnson III, president of Johnson & Johnson. He graduated from Millbrook School and the University of Arizona. He bought the Jets for $635 million.

Speculation in the press continued to run rampant about the soap opera between the Jets and Patriots. Some writers accused Parcells of double-dealing Belichick, resigning from the Jets simply to stop Kraft. Others accused Kraft of breaking the NFL rules, having made Belichick, even through back-door channels, an impressive offer. After all, some wondered in the press, why would a man who weighs everything so carefully suddenly dump a $1 million salary for an "opportunity?"

"Belichick did not leave the Jets; he actually left Parcells. He did not think he would ever have the autonomy to run a meeting or make a decision or rule the inbred little bunker as long as Parcells was around," George Vecsey wrote a year later. "He said he was prepared to turn it over to Belichick, but his blustering, dominating ways had created a climate of fear and dependency, with everybody in the Jets' center attuned to Big Bill's moods that range from angry to surly. That Belichick came up with a great deal in New England was mostly extraneous."

"It wasn't easy for me to make that call," Parcells wrote in his book, *The Final Season*. It had been three weeks. While that may have been true, Parcells could have arguably made the call earlier. He had decided to let Belichick and Kraft twist in the proverbial wind a few weeks while so many other signings were going on around the NFL. Parcells called Kraft's office at 7:00 PM. Kraft got on the phone.

"It's Darth Vader," Parcells said to Kraft. "I think that broke the ice."

According to Parcells' memoir, both he and Kraft admitted to each other that they would have done some things differently if given another opportunity.

"Bob, do you want this guy to be your head coach?"

"Yeah," Kraft said.

"Okay, there's going to be some compensation involved," Parcells said. Then the dickering began as they threw draft picks back and forth, but Parcells was adamant, he wanted the Patriots' No. 1 pick this year or no deal. They both agreed to think about it overnight.

The next morning they went around again, coming a little closer.

"I'm going to make a decision here I don't want to make because I want this guy as my head coach," Kraft said, according to Parcells.

Kraft told Parcells to write it up and fax it to him with the final wording. The Jets got a No. 1, No. 4, and a No. 7 for Belichick, and then the Jets would give back No. 5 and a No. 7.

Kraft told Parcells he needed help getting Belichick to sign the contract. Parcells agreed to help. Parcells told Kraft that they needed to put a window on the negotiations so Belichick couldn't hold them both up.

Parcells then called Belichick and told him that he had made a deal with Kraft that would only last 48 hours, and that Belichick would have to make the best deal he could or lose the opportunity. Belichick was in shock but thanked Parcells.

George Vecsey of *The New York Times* summed it all up beautifully, writing, "Let's not nominate Bill Parcells and Robert K. Kraft for the Nobel Peace Prize for speaking to each other on the telephone. They were just playing out the game. Ever since Bill Belichick slugged the Jets' organization in the solar plexus with his resignation this month, it has been a matter of, 'Show me the draft choices.' All the meetings and all the legal briefs were just Xs and Os—dust on a chalkboard."

"Do I want to see Bill Belichick out of coaching? No, but he probably could have been," Parcells said. "I think they got a real good man in Bill Belichick. We both realize this is a business."

Regarding Kraft, Parcells said, "He's a good businessman. Regardless of what went on in the past, if he sees a good deal, he's going to take it."

While Parcells acted as counselor in his first year, he was in fact no longer the head coach. As he looked back, he said he was proud of how he had left the Giants, the Patriots, and the Jets. He'd left all three programs better than when he had found them. And he knew it was time to go.

Parcells did remain very active through the draft, however.

"In one of the most stunning trades in Jets history, Keyshawn Johnson left New York yesterday when he signed an eight-year $56 million contract with the Tampa Bay Buccaneers. In exchange, the Jets received Tampa Bay's two top draft picks, giving New York an unprecedented four first-round selections," sportswriter Judy Battista wrote.

The fact was that Johnson was great trade bait, pure and simple. And the brain trust that ran the draft—Bill Parcells, Woody Johnson, Al Groh, Dick Haley, and Mike Tannenbaum—all felt the same way the head coach felt. Johnson was too valuable on the market. Parcells had always marveled over how Jimmy Johnson had rebuilt the Dallas Cowboys through the Herschel Walker trade, getting seven draft picks for one man. These kinds of machinations were always on Parcells' mind during draft week.

"I wanted to stay in New York as bad as anybody ever. Bill Parcells tried to address the issue. The new people came in and they wanted to go in another direction. He had to play with the team. There were disagreements with him over the situation. He had to let people do their job."

"If we weren't able to get two No. 1 draft choices, I don't think it would have been a consideration," Parcells said. "When that option came up, in addition to the draft choices we got with Bill Belichick, we thought maybe we could revamp our defense, fill a big need at tight end, and then if the quarterback draft pick turns out to be the guy who quarterbacks your team for 10 to 12 years, then I think at the end of the day you have to feel that the trade was worth it."

The War Room atmosphere was tense on draft day.

"[Tannenbaum] remembers listening to Parcells negotiate a trade with 49ers president Bill Walsh, two football legends doing business over the phone. Watching in awe as Parcells challenged a team official in the war room, resulting in a fiery response by the official that left the room in stunned silence. Thinking to himself, after a long day, the Jets had just altered the direction of the franchise," sportswriter Rich Cimini wrote.

The Jets had a historic four first-round picks. Peter King wrote in *Sports Illustrated* after the draft, "The knee-jerkers condemning the Jets for not making Keyshawn the highest-paid receiver in history should remember that it's that sort of live-for-today thinking that got New York into what one NFL capologist calls the worst financial shape of any team entering the next two years. 'They're the 49ers waiting to happen,' said this cap man."

The Jets acquired:

1 12 Shaun Ellis DE Tennessee

1 13 John Abraham OLB South Carolina

1 18 Chad Pennington QB Marshall

1 27 Anthony Becht TE West Virginia

3 78 Laveranues Coles WR Florida St.

5 143 Windrell Hayes WR USC

6 179 Tony Scott S North Carolina St.

7 218 Richard Seals DT Utah

King graded the Jet's draft a C+. Not a great rating given the opportunity. But King was proved wrong. Ellis, Abraham, and Coles were a great draft all by themselves. Throw in Pennington and the value only goes up.

"It really was a remarkable draft," Tannenbaum said, 10 years later. "It's still paying dividends."

CHAPTER 9
The Jersey Cowboy

66 **I** haven't really decided," Parcells said from his home in Sea Bright, New Jersey. "I'll think it over for the next week to 10 days and then decide."

Woody Johnson, the Jets' owner, wanted Parcells to stay on anywhere from one to three years. Alternately, Parcells sneered at the thought of having nothing to do but just sit at one of his two homes in Sea Bright or Jupiter, Florida, at the age of 59.

With the Jets finishing 9–7 and missing the playoffs, Parcells said, "Al has tremendous passion, tremendous dedication. I want to help this guy succeed."

"The average gain or loss of players for each team from the draft or free agency was 20 this season—that's a 40 percent turnover of your roster," he said. "New Orleans had the most, 36, but nobody had less than 15. Fortunately, the league's fiscal year begins March 2; that's when you've got to be under the salary cap."

Soon a soap opera began to play out in the executive office of the New York Jets and then splashed across the sports pages. Would Tuna stay or go? With his contract up on January 31, 2001, Tuna vacillated, one day saying he would like to stay, another speculating on his departure.

On December 30, 2000, Al Groh resigned as head coach of the New York Jets and took a job at the University of Virginia. There was no question he had lost control of his team. The players, especially the veterans, were tired of Groh's long speeches, and many players were going upstairs behind his back to Parcells.

Sportswriter Mike Freeman of *The New York Times* called the Jets, "The most dysfunctional franchise in pro football."

Finally, on January 8, 2001, Bill Parcells informed Woody Johnson he, too, would be leaving. The call of retirement was just too comforting. Parcells tried to be honest with himself and with the media.

"I wasn't the person to make that commitment," he said on a conference call with reporters. "When this season was over and I was faced with hiring a new coach, I don't feel like I want to do all that again. I think it's time for someone else to do it. People do not know how consuming this job is. There's no time off. There's no time away. You can't get away from the job."

— —

In late January, Parcells saw former Giants fullback Ottis "O.J." Anderson at the ceremonial coin-toss at Super Bowl XXXV in Tampa, Florida, where the Giants were playing the Ravens.

"O.J. actually kissed me on the cheek; then we were standing there with Tom Flores. Tom's looking around at the stadium..."

"This is something, isn't it? I wish I could do this just once more," Flores said.

"I know what you mean," Parcells said.

"What you miss are the kids you want to help and that want to be helped," Flores said. "At the Super Bowl, I was hoping the Giants would play well because of my relationship with Wellington Mara, but I couldn't go against the Ravens because they had three of my players: Ben Coates and Sam Gash at the Patriots, Matt Stover at the Giants."

Parcells spent a lot of time relaxing at his home in Sea Girt, New Jersey, near the shore. Sea Girt is one of three towns known as the Irish Riviera. Sea Girt is the smallest and quietest of the three. The others are Spring Lake and Spring Lake Heights. It is also considered one of the best places to live in the Northeast. Bill and Judy Parcells lived there. The late Tim Mara also had a house there. Not too far away is Asbury Park, the childhood home of Leon Hess and the stomping grounds of Bruce Springsteen.

It was time for training camp, and Parcells wasn't feeling the anxiousness of going to training camp.

"I don't feel that now," he said. "I still love the game; it's something I'll always miss. If you're looking for competition, that's where it is, but I don't feel I can't wait to get started."

As a retired coach, it seemed, he was talking to more NFL people around the league than ever before. "I still talk to Al Davis and Ron Wolf. I talk to Bill Walsh more than I ever did before."

But shore life is easy to get used to. "Saturday morning I ran three and a half miles on the boardwalk; Sunday morning I ran three and a half miles on the boardwalk. I was in the ocean swimming, [and] then I was back home by 7:00 and getting ready to go to the golf course."

In August he drove his black Cadillac DeVille up to Saratoga for a few days at the race track. In late December he attended the funeral of George Young, who had died at the age of 71.

Soon after, *Sports Illustrated*'s Peter King paid a visit to Parcells. "Sunday afternoon was still young as Bill Parcells sat in his living room in Sea Girt, New Jersey, four houses west of the Atlantic Ocean, with the whole world in his hands," King wrote.

"Here's what bothers me," he said when Cincinnati tight end Kirk McMullen caught a pass. "I knew [tight end] Marco Battaglia. I knew Tony McGee. But they're both gone. I don't know McMullen. I need to know him."

"Parcells reached into a small bag bearing an NFL logo and pulled out a laminated 8" x 11" card bearing the up-to-date roster of every AFC team. There was McMullen, a first-year man from Pitt. Parcells pulled out a lineup card from the previous day's Giants-Cardinals game, which he had attended, and noted that he had circled the name of Arizona fullback Dennis McKinley, a third-year player out of Mississippi State. He didn't know him either."

"Drove me crazy," Parcells said. According to King, Parcells had a matching deck of information on NFC rosters complete with salary cap data and all.

"What's with all this material?" Peter King asked. It seemed like a lot of information for a guy doing six hours of television a month. "It does seem normal, though, for a man itching to get back into the fray. It also raises the question—will the 60-year-old Parcells, who turned three sub-.500 teams into Super Bowl winners or contenders in the span of 16 years, take one last fling at the NFL?"

"I like football," he said. "Sometimes I miss 1:00 on Sundays. It was my life for a lot of years. But you can't do this forever, and guys like me aren't for everyone. I do feel like this is it for me. If I get through January, I'll be in the clear forever."

"In the clear?" Judy Parcells piped up from the kitchen.

"I mean about being finished with coaching," he said. A few moments later, a visitor asked whether he would coach again.

"Judy," he said, "should I coach?"

"Probably not," she said. "You know, he's a lot less stressed when he's not coaching," she said to King.

In January 2002, the coaching merry-go-round started, and Parcells came up consistently. One of the biggest rumors was that he was taking over the Tampa Bay Buccaneers after their firing of Tony Dungy.

"My status has not changed since January 2000. I've had at least two inquiries and a couple of college inquiries, but nothing is imminent. Nothing is in place. The TV reports are so far ahead of the facts, it's ridiculous," Parcells told the press.

There were rumors that Parcells or his representative, Jimmy Sexton, had reached an informal agreement with the Bucs. Many on the Tampa staff, who thought that Dungy had been treated unfairly, also thought Parcells and his camp had acted unethically. They complained, anonymously of course, that Parcells was plotting to get Dungy's job before Dungy was even fired.

A Tampa Bay press conference got out of hand with the team executives fighting with the press.

"Are you saying you just fired Tony Dungy, who's taken your team to an NFC Championship Game, with no thought of who may replace him?" a reporter asked.

"We haven't started the process, but obviously in the back of your mind you have thoughts. You can look at the college ranks. You can look at the pro ranks. But we haven't started that process going forward. We'll make that decision slowly, and we'll do it properly," Bryan Glazer said.

"We have never talked to Bill Parcells about the job here," brother Joel Glazer said. "We've got a lot of respect for a guy like Bill Parcells. To not think of him would not be exploring all the possible candidates."

But the press felt another way. Several sources confirmed that the Buccaneers were about to announce Parcells' anointing any day.

"Parcells' imminent return is the talk of pro football. Now, what many people in the league want to know is, who will go with him? Parcells is trying to put together a staff of familiar faces. His offensive coordinator is expected to be Dan Henning, the former Jets assistant. Parcells would also like to hire Maurice Carthon, the former Jets and current Detroit Lions running backs coach, and Bill Muir, the Jets' current offensive line coach. Parcells may also keep Monte Kiffin, the current Tampa Bay defensive coordinator," Mike Freeman reported.

According to Freeman, Parcells has persuaded Mike Tannenbaum, the Jets' assistant general manager, to join him in Tampa Bay. "Tannenbaum interviewed for the general manager's job...it was considered a formality."

Reports out of Tampa Bay were that the only reason Parcells' coaching appointment hadn't been announced was that he was trying to scare up a coaching staff. But the NFL Commissioner's office sent out letters formally warning both the Buccaneers and Parcells about rumors of tampering with other teams' staffs.

But on January 18, Parcells jilted the Bucs at the altar again. He had in fact signed a contract with the Buccaneers, but the contract was never filed with the commissioner's office because Parcells backed out.

"At the end of the day, I couldn't make the commitment that I knew it took to do the job the way I know it should be done," Parcells said from his Sea Girt, New Jersey, home. "I couldn't make myself say, 'Let's go.' I didn't want to go there and after eight months say, 'What am I doing here?'"

"After next season I'll be out for three years and I'll be 61, and that's it," Parcells said. "I'm not entertaining any other job—pro or college."

Shortly before Parcells announcement, Tannenbaum told the Jets he would be staying. The Glazers were furious and embarrassed, admitting they were discussing in their offices what time the announcement would be made.

After that, there were some rumors that Parcells would go to the Raiders and work with his old friend, Al Davis, after the departure of Jon Gruden, but nothing ever materialized.

— —

That January, Bill and Judy Parcells divorced. On January 16, the two were granted a divorce in Monmouth County, New Jersey. According to court documents, Judith Parcells complained her husband of nearly 40 years had grown "cold and distant," several sources reported. As part of the settlement, Judy Parcells retained both the house in Sea Girt and the house in Jupiter, Florida.

"My wife and I have an amiable relationship. There's nothing here. It's over and it's done with, and we have a good relationship," Parcells said.

In an unsigned story, *Sports Illustrated* reported "insiders whispered that Bill Parcells would not sign a big deal with Tampa Bay because he was in the midst of divorce proceedings, and did not wish to share this windfall with his outgoing wife, Judith. The rumors were never confirmed."

New Jersey did not allow such quick divorces. Even in settlements that were well orchestrated, New Jersey had a waiting period. If the Parcells' divorce was filed with the Monmouth County courts in January 2002, then the paperwork needed to be set in motion many months before. Parcells was well aware he was in the midst of the divorce long before Peter King came to visit or even before the Buccaneers came calling.

Parcells has since admitted that he was "not proud" of his divorce, and has on numerous occasions taken the blame for not paying enough attention to his marriage, putting career and football before Judy and their three girls.

"I would never blame it on my job. I would blame it on myself and the way I was negligent in a lot of respects," Parcells said.

"I don't resent one minute he spent with football. But there were times when he could have been here when he wasn't working.... We had to grow up together and eventually we grew apart," Judy Parcells said. "I love him still—even though he can be a huge pain."

In the meantime, their daughter, Dallas, had gotten married. She had married of all people, a football man. Scott Pioli was born in Washingtonville, New York, in 1965. Pioli graduated Central Connecticut State University in 1988 with a degree in communications. He had been an Division II All-New England selection as a defensive tackle three years in a row. He earned a master's degree at Syracuse while also serving as a graduate assistant. Pioli then coached for Murray State for two years.

In 1992, Belichick hired Pioli as a pro personnel assistant for the Cleveland Browns. Belichick and Pioli had become friends in the mid-1980s. Pioli's job was to evaluate prospective college players and available free agents. He also worked on contract negotiations. When Belichick was fired and the Browns moved to Baltimore to become the Ravens, Pioli stayed with the team and was promoted. In 1997, Pioli rejoined Belichick and was hired by the New York Jets as the team's director of pro personnel.

Pioli joined Belichick in Foxboro in 2000. He and Belichick split the duties usually held by a general manager on most other NFL teams. Unlike Parcells in Foxboro, Belichick had final say. Unlike Parcells and Belichick, Pioli and Belichick are good friends in and out of the office.

While Pioli was working for Belichick and Parcells at the Jets, he met and married Parcells' daughter, Dallas. To say that it was ironic that Dallas would marry Scott was undeniable.

"We lived together in New England when we first got there," said former New England assistant and former NFL head coach Eric Mangini. "Myself and Jules [Mangini's wife] and him and Dallas, so I've known him for a long time."

That summer, Parcells spent more time with his family.

"He points to a photograph atop a cabinet. It's a portrait of his three daughters as kids, grinning and gussied up in cute dresses and cuter pigtails. The coach smiles sweetly," *Dallas Morning News* scribe Juliet Macur wrote.

"I call them my three little piggies," Parcells said with a smile. Also on the shelf are photos of his grandkids. Kendall, a girl, and Kyle, who was then 13.

"Man, he can hit a golf ball a mile," Parcells said. "He's a good little point guard in basketball, too." He sighs wistfully. "Ah, we had a great time last summer."

Parcells had taken Kyle with him to upstate New York, in Saratoga Springs. "At 6:00 AM the two crawl out of bed and roll to a nearby store, a 'glorified 7–Eleven, but better.' Over the years it has become a morning coffee shop. Kyle has a bagel and orange juice. Parcells has his *Daily Racing Form* and newspaper."

From there, as the sun rises, the two are already walking the backstretch at Saratoga, peeking into the barns, spying some of the world's most famous horses.

"Hiya doin', Hiya doin'," Parcells and his grandson wave.

From there, the twosome races off for an 8:30 tee time at the local golf course. They hack around the course until about 1:00 PM, practicing putting, hitting the driving range, and playing a few holes.

"At about 1:00, they rush home and put on 'our little suits and ties' [to quote Parcells] and return to the racetrack for low-stakes betting," Macur wrote.

"I drive his mother crazy," Parcells said, talking about his oldest daughter, Suzy. "She says, 'You're teaching him your bad habits.' All I can say is, 'Ahh, Suzy.' Yeah, that's Suzy."

After the track Parcells and Kyle raid the local Applebee's or Ruby Tuesday. Upon their arrival at the Parcells home, they take in a ball game on television after dinner. It's a grand, manly life.

"Papa, it doesn't get any better than this," Kyle said. Upon completing this intense schedule, Kyle promptly told his mother he wanted to move in with his grandfather.

In August, Parcells, at the age of 60, joined ESPN. He signed a five-year deal that would pay him $500,000 to $1 million annually to appear on ESPN's *Sunday NFL Countdown*.

"This is the end of it," Parcells said about his future coaching career. "I told you when I retired in January 2000 I coached my last game. I don't have any football plans. I haven't had any for three years."

When asked about his dealings with Tampa Bay, Parcells responded, "My dad used to tell me you never lose anything by listening."

Parcells appeared in the studio each Sunday. He shared the desk with Chris Berman, Tom Jackson, Sterling Sharpe, Steve Young, and Chris Mortensen.

MAMA, DON'T LET YOUR SONS GROW UP TO BE COWBOYS

In 2002, legendary sportscaster Pat Summerall was moved to primarily work Cowboys games. According to Barry Horn of the *Dallas Morning News*, "Flying home on the Cowboys charter after yet another loss last season, Summerall and owner Jerry Jones discussed the team's woes. Among the fixes Summerall suggested was finding a tough coach 'like Bill Parcells.'"

Parcells and Summerall were friends. Summerall had tried to get Parcells to come work the Cowboys games with him, but ESPN had offered more money than FOX.

"Summerall assured Parcells that he would be able to work for Jones. In fact, Summerall thought it a 'very good fit,'" Horn continued.

"I made sure he knew that I liked Jerry, and Jerry wants to win," Summerall said. "Bill said he thought Jerry was a hell of a salesman."

By late December news stories were flying about Parcells. Then on December 18, 2002, Parcells met with Dallas Cowboys owner Jerry Jones. Parcells met Jones for a five-hour conversation (the two first talked for three hours in a private room at the Teterboro Airport, then continued the conversation for another two hours aboard Jones' private plane), in a meeting that both later called a discussion about "pro football, philosophy, and the Cowboys."

They had tried to keep the meeting a secret.

"I don't think anyone saw us together," Parcells said. "But somebody might have seen me and saw his pilot—he wears a Cowboys jersey—and put things together."

"People close to Jerry and Bill talk a lot," said Jay Glazer, the "Insider" reporter for *The NFL Today*, who worked on the story for CBS.

The news went national the next week.

Coupled with a Cowboys loss on December 21 to the Eagles, the Dave Campo–led Cowboys had now sunk to 5–10. The Cowboys had quarterback problems. They had switched from the mercurial Quincy Carter to the lackluster Chad Hutchinson. Their star receiver, Raghib Ismail, was lost for the season early on due to injuries, and the team had also lost two important Pro Bowlers in Larry Allen (offensive tackle) and Darren Woodson (safety). Another liability was that Dallas' defensive backfield was the youngest and least effective in the NFL.

The speculation in the media was that Jones was desperate to bring in a high-profile coach to save his sinking franchise. Jones had been on record saying that it was the most disappointing season in 13 years. Jones had told the press that Campo's evaluation process would begin after the season. But the leak about their meeting put an end to that charade. Campo would be gone.

Parcells immediately offered a statement to ESPN that they released. "Any speculation about the Cowboys' head coaching job would be premature at this time. I have spoken to Jerry Jones several times over the years."

Jones too tried to calm the waters, telling Bloomberg news, "I respect him and I respect his football knowledge. We didn't talk about the job of coaching the Dallas Cowboys. We just had general talks about football and the NFL."

Jones added, "I've also had similar conversations with Bill Walsh and John Madden," Jones told ESPN. "When people like that talk, I want to listen."

Parcells told *The Record*'s Vinny DiTriani, that it would take the "absolute perfect situation" for him to return to coaching. "Tell me what the circumstances are, and I'll let you know. No job offer was made. We didn't talk about those things; we just talked about football in general."

"Last year I had some personal things, but those are kind of behind me now," Parcells said. "I'm not saying I will coach again, but at this time last year I didn't think I would.

"We touched on a number of things like philosophy, the league in general, and the Cowboys. He asked me what I thought about his team, and he told me where he thought their strengths and weaknesses were. This is not the first time I've talked with him. He's been in the league 14 years, and I've talked with him before."

"I love to talk football with Bill Parcells. He gave me some of his thoughts on the Cowboys. I respect not only what he has accomplished as a coach but his thoughts about this business in general," Jones said. "But no, we didn't talk about the job. I am going to wait until the end of the season and evaluate what we will do at this time."

"We really didn't discuss his philosophies," Parcells said. "I don't know if he's going to call me again. We don't have any plans to meet again. But he is going through his third straight losing season and doesn't like it. I don't know if he would include me in any of his plans, but I'll tell you this, the guy wants to win," Parcells added. "I know one thing about the guy—he wants to win, and I wouldn't consider going to an organization that doesn't have that kind of attitude."

"He inquired as to whether I thought I might go back to coaching or not, or would I consider going back to coaching. But he didn't specifically ask me would I coach again or, 'Would you coach the Cowboys?'" Parcells said on ESPN. "And I didn't get the idea that he was sure about what he was going to do."

"My position has been the same for several weeks: I'm going to evaluate this season and take a look at it at the end of the season," Jones said. Jones also told the media that he told Campo about the meeting, the same as he said about the meetings with Walsh and Madden in previous years.

"That's my job, that's what I do—visit with whoever I can to get information and use that to better run the Cowboys," Jones said.

"As a result, ESPN looked awkward in playing catch-up on news about one of its own," media critic Richard Sandomir of *The New York Times* wrote.

"We'd rather have known in advance that he'd met with Jones," said John Walsh, ESPN's executive editor. "We didn't expect this with Bill."

ESPN had Chris Mortensen interview Parcells on *SportsCenter*, then again Sunday for *NFL Countdown*. "Yet when Parcells is evasive and mischievous, which is most of the time, he gets a devilish glint in his eyes. He loves misleading reporters with his verbal misdirection and rendition of Clinton-speak," Sandomir wrote. "He contended in interviews that he and Jones had discussed philosophy [Spinoza on the power sweep?], scouting and assorted opinions, but that Jones never broached the subject of Parcells' coaching the Cowboys.... He offered more 'I don't knows' than an Enron executive."

At one point in the interview, Mortensen asked Parcells if he thought it was fair to be talking with Jones while Campo was still coach. Parcells replied, "This is America. I didn't say we specifically talked about the job."

Fed up with Parcells' game, Mortensen finally shot back at Parcells, "If I don't believe this, why should anyone else?"

Would Parcells take the job?

To friends, Parcells would say, "It's like the [expletive] Yankees!"

"I don't know," he said. "I'd have to understand completely how that was going to be structured, and we didn't discuss that, so at that point, when we have the opportunity to discuss it, then I'll give you the answer to that, but I don't have it now."

According to Sandomir, "The Sunday interview ended, appropriately, with a burst of background laughter from the studio. The commentators probably hadn't heard such gibberish since Cousin Itt prattled in *The Addams Family*."

In time, Mortensen finally received an apology from Parcells for not being forthright.

"It's more embarrassing to Chris than any of us," Walsh said. "I told him, 'You get 90 percent of the stories, but it's a shame the 10 percent you missed happened to be about the guy in the room.'"

By the end of December Parcells was now officially leaning toward signing with Jones. Speculation was rampant on how the two would get along.

— ~

Jerral "Jerry" Wayne Jones was born on October 13, 1942, in Los Angeles, California, but grew up in North Little Rock, Arkansas, from the time he was an infant. Jones was an All-SWC offensive lineman for Hall of Fame college coach Frank Broyles at the University of Arkansas, and was co-captain of the 1964 National Champion Razorbacks. Broyles' coaching tree included such college notables as Hayden Fry, future legendary head coach at the University of Iowa; Johnny Majors, future head coach at the University of Pittsburgh and the University of Tennessee; and most notably Barry Switzer, Hall of Fame coach of the University of Oklahoma.

After graduating, Jones worked at Modern Security Life of Springfield, Missouri, and completed an MBA by 1970. Later, he established Jones Oil, an oil and gas exploration business in Arkansas that attained tremendous success.

In 1989, Jones bought the Cowboys franchise and Texas Stadium for the then-whopping price of $140 million from H.R. "Bum" Bright. The team was at its nadir, suffering three consecutive losing seasons. In successive order, Jones forced out beloved coach Tom Landry and then general manager Tex Schramm. Jones took over Schramm's job, and Jones installed former Arkansas teammate Jimmy Johnson as coach.

Jimmy Johnson came up with the idea of trading the one player Dallas possessed that the rest of the league envied—Herschel Walker—and got seven draft picks for Walker. It was the building block for the nucleus of a sports dynasty. The Cowboys were built on defense with speed and on offense with running and explosive passing. Jimmy Johnson won two Super Bowls, 1992 (XXVII) and 1993 (XXVIII).

Jones and Johnson were a volatile mix. Both wanted the spotlight. Jones was the epitome of the new franchise owner who hung out on the sidelines and insisted on giving interviews and being photographed. Johnson, with his perfectly coiffed hair, was just as big a control freak as Jones, and the relationship between the two (each of whom were both taking credit for the team's success) began to frazzle.

After the 1993 Super Bowl victory, a boozy Jerry Jones declared that given the talent he had acquired, "Any one of 500 coaches could have won those Super Bowls." Not too long later at a cocktail party, again none-the-worse-for-wear with alcohol, Jones stated he intended to replace Johnson with former University of Oklahoma coach Barry Switzer. He later denied the report and then capitulated, "It was the whiskey talking."

"Jimmy orchestrated the thing brilliantly," quarterback Troy Aikman said. "He wanted out, he saw a crack, and he took it. He got a ton of money, and he got everyone to feel sorry for him," Aikman continued, referring to Johnson's huge deal to subsequently coach the Miami Dolphins.

Johnson had been goading Jones since late 1993. "Four days before Dallas played the New York Giants for the NFC East title, Johnson told ESPN that he might consider an offer to coach the expansion Jacksonville Jaguars," *Sports Illustrated*'s Peter King recalled. "Jones, upset at Johnson's ill-timed remark, told the press that Jones and only Jones would decide Johnson's coaching future. This made the strong-willed Johnson furious. On the team's charter flight home after the win over the Giants, Johnson walked up to Jones."

"By the way, I'm the one who's going to decide how long I coach here," Johnson said.

Jones did eventually fire Johnson in 1994 and replaced him with Switzer. Switzer won another Super Bowl for Jones in 1995.

When his teams were successful and popular, Jones was seen as an arrogant newcomer, full of himself and despising of the NFL's old guard. He and New York Giants owner Wellington Mara were fast enemies. Once, after a sizable Giants victory over Jones' Cowboys, the usually quiet Wellington told the press, "It's nice to see arrogance humbled."

How Parcells, the ultimate autocrat, would co-exist with Jones, the press hungry owner, was anyone's guess. All guesses were that the relationship would lead to tremendous pyrotechnics. That and Valley Ranch was in disarray. The team had gone through "salary cap hell," Jones admitted, and the current team didn't fit the Parcells mold at all.

"Parcells is a coach, not a magician, no matter what he did in New England and with the Jets. And times have changed in the few years since he last bailed a floundering franchise out of deep water. No matter how good of a coach you are, or have been, you just can't roll into a new town these days and turn fortunes around with a snap," Kevin B. Blackistone wrote in the *Dallas Morning News*.

Blackistone pointed out that the Cowboys did not have a talented quarterback, veteran or rookie, nor did they seem to have Parcells' prototypical linebackers or defensive linemen or at least one reliable cornerback.

"Not only that, but Parcells would have to find a way to be successful in Dallas without most of the staff he so trusted here and there. That was one of the things that tripped him up as a would-be Tampa Bay coach.... Bill Parcells' mere signing here won't mean Jerry Jones' club is out of the woods, or out of the NFC East cellar, to be more specific. All it means is that the club may have found a road map."

On the 30th a news item from the sports news agency The Sports Network read, "The Buccaneers have verified sending a letter to the agent of Parcells regarding discussions with other NFL teams. The Bucs contend the Cowboys could be in violation of the NFL's tampering rules, claiming Parcells signed a four-year contract with Tampa Bay last year before deciding not to take the job."

"Recent reports that Bill Parcells signed a contract to be head coach of the Tampa Bay Buccaneers after our elimination from the playoffs last season are accurate," Buccaneers general manager Rich McKay said. "We have put Bill Parcells and his representatives on notice that any team that wishes to speak with him must first receive our permission in accordance with the NFL anti-tampering rules and we will require compensation to grant such permission."

"We have to do what is in the best interest of the franchise," Buccaneers head coach Jon Gruden said. "I fully support any action that is necessary, but this really has nothing to do with our play on the field and our pursuit of a championship."

"Anybody who knows anything about the NFL knows that a contract has to be executed by both parties and signed by the commissioner," Parcells said. "If they want to challenge that, if this were a boxing bout, there'd be blood in both corners."

On December 30, 2002, Dave Campo was mercifully released from his coaching responsibilities. He'd been reading about Parcells everywhere. Indeed, in all the news items concerning his exit, every one of them included quotes about or by Parcells and his imminent arrival.

In the meantime, Parcells had talked to Jimmy Johnson. Johnson insisted that things would go well if the two communicated, especially Parcells. Johnson predicted it would work, "for a short time."

"I've talked to Bill about it," Johnson told the *Dallas Morning News.*

"He has to make sure Jerry says the right things publicly."

Parcells and Jones entered into nearly 11 hours of negotiations, including face-to-face meetings and several telephone conversations. On January 2, 2003, Parcells was named the head coach of the Dallas Cowboys. Parcells agreed to a four-year contract worth $17-$18 million. Parcells was among the top-five highest-paid coaches in the NFL. Parcells insisted on being able to hire the coaches, scouts, and personnel people. This was a major concession by Jones.

"I never thought I'd be doing this again—but you never know," Parcells said from his Long Island home. In a nod to NFL scheduling, it was pointed out that the Cowboys were scheduled to play all of Parcells' old franchises in the upcoming season, Dallas played at the Giants, the Jets, New England, and even Tampa Bay.

Many of Parcells' former staffers were otherwise employed, including Belichick, Crennel, Henning, and others were unavailable.

"Get ready for the purge. We'll see what happens when free agency starts. With him, there's never a dull moment. I loved playing for him. He knows how to win and knows how to maintain discipline on a team. A lot of the guys in Dallas are in for a rude awakening," Jets center Kevin Mawae said.

"If football is not the most important thing in your life, he'll weed you out. I've seen it happen with good players like [Pro Bowl defensive end] Hugh Douglas. Bill doesn't care," Jets lineman Jumbo Elliott said.

"That's just what we need," said Dallas safety Darren Woodson, an 11-year veteran who played on the Cowboys' three Super Bowl–winning teams of the 1990s.

On January 2, the Associated Press reported that Commissioner Tagliabue determined the Bucs could not stop the Cowboys from hiring Parcells. He also stated that there was "no basis for ordering Dallas to send draft picks or cash to Tampa Bay." But Parcells personally was on the hook.

The commissioner's office issued a statement saying that it would attempt to determine "whether Coach Parcells as an individual owes money damages to the Buccaneers based on losses suffered as a result of his signing a contract last year and subsequently deciding not to perform under that contract."

"While we are pleased that the commissioner saw the validity of our claim, we did not file this claim to seek monetary damages," Bucs general manager Rich McKay said. "The sole focus of this organization should be the playoffs, and accordingly, we do not intend to pursue this claim any further." The Bucs didn't want the money. They wanted the draft picks. The case was closed.

New York was a buzz. "Bill came back because this is what he does; he's a coach," said Giants co-owner Wellington Mara, a close friend of Parcells. "I believe him when he retires and says he never wants to return to coaching. Then he recharges his battery and he wants to get back into it. He can't stay away from it. It's in his blood."

"I understand when people are infuriated because they think Bill is taking them for a ride year after year," said WFAN Radio host Mike Francesa. "But he's genuine. He's listening to his heart…. If you say he hasn't left cleanly, that's fair."

"He always wants to coach," fellow ESPN analyst Tom Jackson said. "And every Sunday, with us, he coached. Every Sunday morning, we had breakfast, he'd take out a pencil, drew 22 guys, and he said, 'This is what I'm talking about.' He did it all the time."

Dallas was also a buzz. "We sold 177 season tickets yesterday," said Joel Finglass, the director of sales and advertising for the Cowboys the next day, "and interest is as strong today as on Day 1. This is a good football town. The hiring of Bill Parcells has brought a lot of hype that the Cowboys will get back on a winning path."

"I'm looking for big, fast guys who can play football, are aggressive, and have a passion for the game," Parcells said. "I really don't like guys who don't like football…. I know that Bill Parcells is not for everyone in this league."

"It is hard to picture Bill Parcells in a white polo shirt with a blue star on the left breast, working the phones in the office once occupied by Tom Landry. But that's what the new coach of the Dallas Cowboys was doing last Friday. It's shocking to think that he has gone into business with one of the biggest micromanagers in sports," *Sports Illustrated*'s Peter King wrote. "Parcells will immediately make his presence felt in Dallas. He'll work the weight room every morning, bantering with players, getting to know them. He will not prop them up with false encouragement."

In less than a week, Parcells began rearranging the Dallas coaching staff. He named Maurice Carthon as his offensive coordinator and retained Dallas defensive coordinator Mike Zimmer.

"I love this guy," Parcells said of Carthon. "He is the type of guy that I know will work hard. He is the kind of guy you like to have that will cover your backside."

Sean Payton was next on Parcells' shopping list.

"I can remember flying in from Long Island into Dallas and going to the offices and having him explaining to me all the things he wants," Payton said. "He had a big impact on me."

"Energetic, bright, enthusiastic, high energy," were the words Parcells used to describe Payton.

"Bill's influence on me was tremendous," Payton said. "There were so many things I learned from just being around him and observing him, from the structure of the staff to the off-season program, how he wants the training room. You see how he approaches things and really deals with the offense and the defense."

"The way he deals with players, the way he deals with the people in the organization, his expectations are high," Payton said. "He demands accountability."

At 39, Payton had been the offensive coordinator of the New York Giants and had been at the helm when the Giants destroyed the Vikings in the NFC Championship Game on their way to a Super Bowl appearance. But the Giants stripped Payton of his authority on October 29, 2002, when Coach Jim Fassel took over the play-calling for the struggling offense. Fassel doubled Payton's scoring output, which discredited Payton at the time. Payton was still in demand, though, and he turned down an opportunity to go to the Arizona Cardinals before choosing Parcells and Dallas.

"This is a great opportunity that Dallas and Coach Parcells and their organization have presented me," Payton said in a statement released by the Giants. "I'm excited about it, and I'm looking forward to it." Payton went with Giants general manager Ernie Accorsi's blessing.

"I think you would usually refuse permission for him to talk to other teams," Accorsi said. "But we took away what he had been doing, and due to his circumstances, I don't think that would've been fair to keep him here. Certainly you don't want to do anything to give an advantage, especially to an opponent in your division, but there's an air of decency and fairness."

Parcells eventually saddled Payton with the nickname "Dennis" based on Dennis the Menace because "I had hair that spiked a little and stuck up in the back," Payton said.

Parcells hired three more assistants, including George Warhop as offensive line coach, Tony Sparano to coach tight ends, and Mike MacIntyre to be the assistant secondary coach. Warhop had been the offensive line coach with the Arizona Cardinals and the St. Louis Rams, while Sparano had worked tight ends in Jacksonville and Washington and had been an assistant in Cleveland. MacIntyre had been an assistant coach at the University of Mississippi.

Parcells held a press conference to introduce the new coaching staff. He also used the event to send out several distinct and clear messages.

"When there's a coaching change, things change. Players change. Systems change. Philosophies change. Work habits change. The whole place changes," Parcells said.

Parcells made several things quite clear. There were new coaches and a new attitude in the organization. Also, these new coaches were to be seen and not heard from—all postgame remarks from here on in were to come from only once source—Parcells.

Parcells witnessed the same dysfunctional situation in Dallas that he had seen when he first went to New England. All staffers had their own media contacts. Everyone was covering themselves in the press. Nowhere was this more evident than with Coach Joe Avezzano.

Joe Avezzano was the special teams coach of the Dallas Cowboys forever. He was a fan favorite. "Avezzano was perceived as Dave Campo's co-coach," Dallas sportswriter Mike Shropshire wrote. Avezzano went on the Randy Galloway show, a sports radio talk show where the Texas Rangers don't get half the time the Dallas Cowboys do. Avezzano was, "discussing his exclusion from the new staff that Parcells had been assembling. Avezzano seemed to insinuate that the Tuna had been less than upfront with him during the hiring process, that he's strung him along for a couple of weeks before the Tuna cut the strings."

Not long after Avezzano signed off, there was another caller on the line.

"And then there was Bill from Irving. Parcells—the Tuna himself—was on the line and daring to speak with Host Randy," Shropshire wrote. Parcells, unlike his predecessor Jimmy Johnson, dialed the regular number that every local dials, since Galloway had not given him the direct studio dial-in. Parcells directly refuted Avezzano, saying that he had explained to Coach Joe that he had been waiting to see if his first choice of special teams coach could in fact join the team.

"Parcells said that if Avezzano thought that he had been left unfairly dangling during that interim, it was Coach Joe's misunderstanding, not Coach Parcells.'"

In Dallas, it seemed, there was a new sheriff in town.

The final roster of coaches included five Campo holdovers. Parcells let the assistants speak to the media for about a half hour and then abruptly closed the meeting.

"There are three things a coach fights in pro football," Parcells explained. "The division from within is first. The competition is second. The third one is the perception that's created about your team. You have to fight all those elements every day, and there are situations in the perception area where what's being created is counterproductive."

"Parcells wants to exert as much control over the perception business as he can. The encouraging thing is that while conveying his limited perception of the Cowboys on Tuesday, he showed no signs of delusions about where his team stands," sportswriter Tim Cowlishaw wrote.

But inside Parcells was fired up.

"How can you resist this?" Parcells said, slapping his desk with both hands. "Going into this, I knew that this could be it for me. My last stop. You can either do this or pass this by and know that it's over. Then you're going the other way. The rest of your life is going to be comprised of something other than what you're made to do."

The office that Parcells sat in every day was the same office where Landry built the Cowboys into America's team. The place dripped with tradition. Landry hung his fedora there, drew up game plans, and watched game films.

"Behind his metal desk is a framed picture of him with Landry. It's the mid-'80s. Parcells is the New York Giants' coach, Landry still with the Cowboys. They're at Texas Stadium, chatting before a game," Macur wrote. "Now he's walking where Landry walked."

"His few possessions are confined to the tiny space behind his desk," bestselling sports author Michael Lewis wrote. "At his feet rests a single, thick binder in which he has organized every last bit of his personal and financial life: divorce settlement, coaching contracts, book contracts, endorsements, agent agreements. On the desk is his other thick binder, containing practice schedules and other coaching materials."

"This isn't the typical job, and Bill finds that intriguing," said friend Bob Knight, now the Texas Tech basketball coach. "The tradition of the franchise is atypical. The owner is atypical. He finds Jerry Jones intriguing because some guys haven't been able to do it, they haven't been able to work with him. Just the whole idea of being different appeals to him."

"Ultimately, if he's successful, people will say the Cowboys have only had three coaches: Landry, Jimmy [Johnson], and Bill," Pat Summerall said. "The other guys were just passin' time."

"I sure hope we're closer to being a playoff team than we are to going backwards, but I don't know that," Parcells said. "A year from now, I might be saying, 'Hey, fellas, we're starting over.'"

"It's worth the trouble for me. I'm not talking about anybody else. I don't care what the public's impression is. I don't care about the fan. I don't care about the perception. This is my own specific fear of failure. It's about testing myself," Parcells said, trying to answer the question of why he came back to coaching. "I think I'm pretty simple to understand. Very simple. I'll tell you exactly what I'm thinking. I'm afraid. I feel like I'll forget something or do something stupid or do something I know better not to do. I feel like I'm derelict."

On January 9, 2003, one of Parcells closest friends, Will McDonough, died of a heart attack in his home in Hingham, Massachusetts. He was 67 years old. McDonough had been a successful high school pitcher in baseball and quarterback in football. He took a job at the *Boston Globe* as a copy boy in 1965 after graduating from Northeastern University. He became a sportswriter in 1960. In 1979, McDonough gained some measure of fame when he decked Patriots cornerback Raymond Clayborn after Clayborn had poked him in the eye.

In addition to his writings appearing in numerous publications, McDonough was also an accomplished television personality, as well. McDonough was Parcells' co-author on *The Final Season*, Parcells' chronicle of his last year with the Jets.

McDonough's death had further reduced Bill's already very small circle of close friends. In 1999, Parcells had already suffered a severe loss when his agent, Robert Fraley, died in a plane crash. He had been with Fraley since 1983. Although at the time some thought Fraley might have been an instigator in many of Parcells moves and explorations, Fraley was also sometimes a good foil for Parcells' ambitions.

Fraley had a solid roster of sports superstars among his clients, including Bill Cowher, Dan Reeves, Joe Gibbs, Cortez Kennedy, Orel Hershiser, and Payne Stewart. Fraley had been a backup quarterback at Alabama and had started a few games under Paul "Bear" Bryant, which he won.

Fraley died when he was aboard Payne Stewart's Learjet 35 that crashed on October 25, 1999. The passengers had all died of hypoxia when the plane suddenly lost cabin pressure. With all aboard dead, the plane flew well off course on autopilot until it ran out of fuel and crashed in Mina, South Dakota.

According to Parcells himself, you could "count on the fingers of one hand" the number of people who were among his inner circle. All of them were people who understood his drive and his need to be engaged in a competitive situation. They understood his need to go back.

Fraley and McDonough, it had always been assumed, were part of that circle. Mickey Corcoran has always been considered his closest advisor. And it was known that he sometimes counted on his brother, Don. But no one knows for sure. He was always very closed about those personal relationships.

"He never made us part of his inner circle," said daughter Suzy Schwille, his oldest daughter, in reference to Parcells' wife and three daughters.

"The more you try to get to know him," an unidentified friend once told the *Dallas Morning News*, "the more he'll push you away. He has layers to him that some people will never know."

Another friend said, "For sure, we can't understand him. Really, I'm not even sure he understands himself."

In Dallas, Parcells' closest friend was Pat Summerall. He'd known Pat since his first days with the Giants. "He's not what you'd call a social climber," Summerall said. "We go to dinner a lot, but that's about the size of the crowd."

Parcells lived in a rented apartment in Las Colinas during his time in Dallas. With no wife or family near, Parcells' circle of support was small. And with the deaths of his two friends, it was getting smaller.

On July 1, 2003, Scott and Dallas Pioli had a daughter, Mia Costa Pioli. Parcells would not meet the newborn until he traveled north with his team in November. Parcells heard the news on the first day of training camp at the Alamodome in San Antonio, Texas. In the tunnel as the players begin to take the field, fans shouted out congratulations. It was his third grandchild.

"Yeah, I'm a grandpa again," Parcells said with a growl, preoccupied with his team. "Her name is Mia...another girl."

"As he speaks, he slowly but deliberately steps away, as if to separate Grandpa Parcells from Coach Parcells," *Dallas Morning News* journalist Juliet Macur wrote.

"We try not to infringe on each other's territory," Parcells said of his relationship with Pioli. "All I hope is that Scott has been a good husband to my daughter, Dallas, and a good father to my granddaughter. That's all I care about. I don't care about anything else."

It was late January 2002, and Don knew something was wrong. Lately he'd been feeling woozy. He heard a ringing, or even music, in his ears. He would sometimes find a strange metallic taste in his mouth. On January 23, 2002, while driving to meet friends for lunch, Don Parcells experienced a kind of almost fainting spell. He pulled over for a second and rested. Later he felt fine, went to lunch, went home, and forgot all about it.

In the early morning the next day, hours before sunrise, Don woke up with the most painful headache he ever had. Then Don had a seizure in bed. His eyes rolled to the back of head, and he was foaming at the mouth. His body convulsed and shook, rattling the couple's Short Hills bedroom. His attack was so sudden, so violent, and so loud, that it woke up everyone in the house.

Don's wife, Elaine, told her teenage son to call 911. "Oh my God, I think your father just died." Don Parcells didn't die.

Suddenly he was surrounded by the faces of his wife and his two sons, Dan and Chris. He was being carried down the stairs of his new home on a stretcher. At St. Barnabas Medical Center in Livingston, he underwent surgery only a few days later.

"I woke up with the worst headache I've ever had," Parcells said, "and there wasn't enough morphine or codeine to make it go away, either."

"Every time I asked, 'Are we going to beat this?' They would tell me, 'Well, it's hard. We can delay it,'" Don Parcells said. "I said, 'Can we delay it for 20 years? If we can delay it for 20 years, I'll be very happy.'"

Don and Elaine inquired about where the best place for him would be, and so they flew to Duke University in Durham, North Carolina, for a biopsy. A brain tumor biopsy is a scary and painful procedure. The patient's head is placed in a steel cage that is screwed tight to the head—this kind of device renders the patient's head immoble, allowing doctors to drill into the side of the patient's head. That's the only way to get sample tissue.

"Do I have to be awake for this? This is unpleasant. My whole head is vibrating," Parcells asked the doctor.

"Do you have a plate in your head?" the doctor asked.

"You're asking me? You just did the MRI!" Don said. Then came the waiting and then the results.

"This doesn't look good," his doctor told him. "We need to do a second surgery right away."

"That's blood right there," Bill Parcells said. "He is my closest brother, and I love him very much. We're 20 months apart, age-wise. He is one of the closest people I have in this world." The irony of course was that Don was by far the healthier of the two, what with Bill's heart troubles and all.

A very aggressive brain tumor had caused the seizure. It was a grade-IV glioblastoma. Patients diagnosed with this kind of ailment are usually given 12 months to live. Sixty percent of the sufferers die within the first year, and ninety percent usually don't make it past year two. Don underwent surgery, chemotherapy, and radiation treatment.

Don vowed to fight the disease. He assembled a great team of doctors, and he said, "We're going to win."

"All the people I know who had brain tumors, they all died," Don Parcells said. "I'm not afraid of dying. What made me nervous, I was afraid not being there for my family. Not being there for my children as I was growing up. That's what scared me. But I also felt it wasn't going to get me. I just never believed that this was the way it was going to end."

The second surgery seemed a success. Don went through chemotherapy and radiation treatments once again. The pain and exhaustion were unbearable.

Bill called Don and Elaine regularly for updates and to give his little brother pep talks.

"Bill was great. He was very supportive," Elaine Parcells said. "He said to me, 'If you want me to come out there and be with you, I will.' He offered to do anything he could to help us."

After the second round of treatments was completed and Don had gained some strength back, he went back down to Duke University to consult with the surgeons. They did an MRI.

"You see this brown spot right here?" the doctor said. "That's where your tumor used to be."

"What do you mean, used to be?" Parcells replied.

"It's gone."

Don Parcells was a miracle. So much so that the American Cancer Society made him its Man of the Year for 2004. Parcells resumed a healthy life, watching his son's high school football games and visiting with friends. Parcells used the experience he gained and became a counselor to those diagnosed with brain tumors.

"I never felt sorry for myself," Don Parcells said. "I never whined about it. I never asked the question, 'Why me?' It is what it is."

"I decided if this was it, I was going kicking and scratching to the end. Bill liked that attitude. He said, 'I'm with you. I'm with you all the way.'

I really believe you can't lay down. You can't quit. I never figured out how to do that."

Meanwhile, Don's son, Craig Parcells, had been recruited to play football by several colleges. Parcells was a 6'2" 270-pound tight end and defensive end at Millburn High School, in Short Hills, New Jersey. He was a first team All-Northern Hills Conference selection and was chosen to the Super 100 All-Star team in New Jersey. He had been heavily recruited by the University of Maine, the University of Maryland, and the University of South Carolina. He chose Maine.

"He had a lot of people come around early. They were all over him. But when it came time to put up or shut up, Maine put the [scholarship] offer on the table. They really wanted him. And I'm glad he took it," Don Parcells proudly said. Don had retired in 1999 at the age of 55. "Craig visited Maine. He liked it. He liked the coaches. They did a really good job with him," added Don Parcells. "It's a good school, and I think he'll be happy up there. He'll have a shot to contribute right away, which is great."

— —

By mid-March Bill Parcells was operating in full force. Emmitt Smith, the star of the once-vaunted Dallas running attack, was now playing for the Cardinals. Faces were changing by the minute. In the conditioning room, Parcells said to Darren Woodson, "Woodson, you've never met anyone like me. I'm not like Jimmy Johnson or Barry Switzer or those other guys you've played for."

Woodson already knew that.

"The definition of voluntary has changed," Woodson said. "Now it's you-better-get-your-ass-in-there-if-you-want-to-be-on-this-team voluntary."

"I'm gonna be the only fat guy around here," Parcells told the players.

Parcells harangued one lineman, asking him his weight. The lineman offered a number, but he was actually 20 pounds more. "Is it me?" Parcells said. "Am I having trouble reading that scale?"

"The party is definitely over. Players can no longer saunter into the locker room with a Big Mac and fries [Parcells' mandate: no food], and nonplayers can hardly get in at all. The gawking guests who used to amble through Valley Ranch on any given off-season Sunday are now shut out of the locker room and training area by heavy, usually closed double doors," Peter King wrote. "And the players seem to like the crackdown."

Despite Parcells complaining about the small defense, he kept the defensive strategy largely intact, keeping the 4-3 instead of installing his preferred 3-4.

Parcells' most immediate effect on the team was his first draft. It included future Pro Bowl players Terence Newman (cornerback), Jason Witten (tight end), and Bradie James (linebacker). One of the biggest rookie acquisitions came via free agency when the team signed an undrafted rookie named Tony Romo (quarterback).

As he had in the past, Parcells brought along several players from previous stops, including Richie Anderson (fullback) and Terry Glenn (wide receiver). Glenn's signing caused more than a few raised eyebrows.

Parcells gave up an undisclosed sixth-round draft pick in 2004 to bring Glenn to Dallas. Glenn restructured his contract, getting a five-year deal tailored to help the Cowboys' salary cap. Glenn and Parcells had since patched up their relationship, and Parcells was the first person Glenn's agent called when the Packers agreed to see if they could help the wide receiver find a new home.

"I'm still probably the same player that I was my rookie year, but the off-field things have changed," Glenn said. "We really didn't have any issues in New England. It's just something that Coach Parcells does. He demands your attention. He's not afraid to call you out."

"I knew that if I came here and made plays," Glenn said. "Coach Parcells would find a way to get me the ball."

Dallas also resigned offensive lineman Flozell Adams.

The Cowboys training camp was held at the Alamodome in San Antonio, Texas. The players slept on mattresses on the floors and never left the complex for 26 days. It was one of the ugliest lockdowns in NFL history. Everyone was there "voluntarily." The running joke is that the men who made the Alamo famous were trapped there only 13 days. These guys were stuck with Parcells for twice that.

One day during training camp, Parcells was fed up. Practice had gone poorly. He gathered his assistants and walked off the field. The players stood around perplexed. The team finished practice on its own.

"Don't make too much of it," Parcells told the press. "I don't care whether they stand out there [and practice] or not."

"By then, he had delivered his mind-game message: Play that way, I want nothing to do with you, and without me, you're in big trouble," Macur wrote.

"I can honestly tell you that when I first got a look at our training camp this summer, I was extremely encouraged by how quickly and completely our players were buying into Bill's system," Jones later said. "When I would walk into the weight room, I was encouraged by the level of dedication to conditioning and the intensity of the work I was witnessing in some of our younger players."

Parcells was as tough on the assistants as he was on the players

"Parcells' coaches," King wrote, "don't even chafe when he tells them that past disciples, such as defensive guru Bill Belichick, did things better."

"He talks about Belichick all the time," defensive coordinator Mike Zimmer said. "You think that doesn't motivate me?"

After evaluating the light, quick Dallas defensive personnel Jones had assembled, Parcells complained to Zimmer, "Our linebackers look like they could all fit in one of those circus Volkswagens."

— ‿

By August, Parcells found himself embroiled in yet another controversy.

"Let's see how much Parcells wins this year," New York Giants star tight end Jeremy Shockey was quoted as saying. "I'll make him pay when we play them. The homo."

In a *New York Magazine* article by Chris Smith, Shockey was quoted as saying, "The only guy who was hating me was Parcells. I never watch TV. But my buddies were like, 'Why does Bill Parcells hate you so much? He's talking about, "I never seen a player get so much hype off of doing nothing."'"

Shockey added, "Parcells is not my kinda guy. He says he quits then he wants to come back and coach. Do something! Stay in commentary or stay in football or get the hell out of everybody's life."

— —

One day at the Valley Ranch office, a voice on the phone asked for Bill Parcells' office. When Parcells' secretary answered, the person on the other end of the line said, "Tell him Chapter 5 is on the line." It was Jack Giddings from Hastings College.

"How come you didn't cover that play? We went over it six times," said Parcells picking up the phone.

"That's because we probably needed to go over it 18 times," exclaimed Giddings, as the two shared a good laugh and caught up with one another.

Expectations were high going into the 2003 season. They were seemingly dashed in the first game of the season when the Atlanta Falcons beat the Cowboys at Texas Stadium 27–13.

The next game was at the Meadowlands of New Jersey. For a moment it seemed grim when the Giants returned an interception for a touchdown and took an immediate 7–0 lead. But the Cowboys came storming back, put up four unanswered scores, and went into halftime with a 20–7 lead. The Giants took the lead 32–29 on Matt Bryant's 30-yard field goal. The Cowboys rebounded and scored a field goal of their own to send the game into overtime. The game ended on Billy Cundiff's 25-yard field goal, and the Cowboys won 35–32. It was a tremendous win.

After an early bye week, the Cowboys found themselves right back at the Meadowlands to face the New York Jets. Again, the home team scored first, making it 3–0. But in the second quarter, the Cowboys ran for one touchdown, Quincy Carter threw for another, and the Cowboys never trailed again on their way to a 17–6 win.

Parcells had faced a whirlwind of pregame bluster. How could he bring the hated Cowboys into New York? How could he go against his former teams? Fan reaction was mixed.

On October 5, 2003, the Dallas Cowboys beat the Arizona Cardinals 24–7. The team was now 3–1, its best start in a long time. Jerry Jones had assembled a crowd in front of him and regaled them with a story about Parcells. Cigar and wine glass in hand, Jones happily gushed, "Did everyone hear this? Hey everybody! Do you know what Bill Parcells did? Do you know what Parcells did after the game?"

"After his talk," Jones said, "Parcells always points to somebody, and that player leads the team in saying, 'One, two, three, Cowboys!' This time Parcells points to Jason and says, 'Jason, lead us.'"

At that moment Jason Witten, the team's rookie tight end, had dared not remove the towel shoved in his mouth as it was filled with blood. He'd broken his jaw badly during the game.

"So there's poor Jason, standing there all bloody, gauze shoved in his mouth. He can hardly talk.

"'Lead us!' Parcells yells to Witten. And there goes Jason, the tough kid that he is," said Jones mimicking the tough, hobbled player, "He goes, 'Uhn, thew, tree, Cow-hoys!' It was tremendous! The team just loved it! Don't you just love it?"

One of the best examples of coaching in those early days with the Cowboys was the story of Willie Blade. A third-round pick out of Mississippi State, Blade was drafted by the Cowboys in 2001 and cut after his first year. He played for the Houston Texans and was cut there, as well. Parcells brought Blade in as a project. He told Willie that this was his "final chance."

Willie was known for his size and speed, but he didn't have drive or perseverance. He lacked confidence. He was thought of as lazy and as an underachiever by coaches. In two years in football, he had never actually played a down in the NFL.

Parcells called Willie's father, a career Air Force man, who was affable but stern. Parcells told Willie Sr. that his son could be a great player. He just needed to make the right sacrifices.

"Whatever you need, coach," Willie Sr. told Parcells.

"You stay on him, and I'll stay on him," Parcells said.

"I knew Willie was a little lazy. I always told him he couldn't fool those NFL coaches. But Coach Parcells was going to make sure Willie didn't slip up anymore," Willie Sr. said. Willie lied about his weight. Parcells decided to weigh Willie in front of the entire team.

"I won't have any fat guys playing for me. If you're fat, I'm gonna cut you," Parcells told Willie in front of the team. But afterward he told Willie privately, "If you lose the weight, we can start your career."

Willie suffered the indignity of being weighed in front of the team until he reached his goal weight of 315 pounds.

"He knew exactly what to say to get me going, like a psychologist," said Blade, then 24. "He took time and studied me and tried different things on me, and I appreciated that. Nobody in the NFL cared enough to do that before."

Parcells started Willie in the second game of the season. It was Willie's first game. Willie said afterward, "I can do this if Coach Parcells thinks I can. I want nothing else but to play for him because he believed in me."

Parcells even took the time to meet with Willie's mother and sister. Instead of a cursory five minutes, he kept them in his office for more than an hour.

"He had such an aura about him," Willie's sister Toriana said. "By the time I left, I had a crush on him."

Willie didn't go on to become a star, but he would play 15 games that season for Parcells, garnering 11 tackles, five assists, and one sack that season.

The Cowboys won two more games—against the Eagles and the Lions—making them 5–1. Then they lost at Tampa, beat Washington and Buffalo at home, and then played the Patriots in New England. Parcells versus Belichick was all the writers wanted to talk about.

"I have no hard feelings about anything. It's the truth. I wish him well," Parcells told the press.

"That's not what this is about. This is about the Patriots and Cowboys," Belichick said in a conference call.

Of course, the press wouldn't leave it alone that week. In one leak from an unidentified source, Belichick likened his relationship with Parcells to an abusive relationship, reportedly saying, "It was like an abusive relationship in a marriage. After a while, you get frayed."

One of Parcells' unidentified "friends" said of Parcells' thoughts on Belichick, "He has no use for Belichick."

"I'm sure they would like to beat each other," said Jeffrey Kessler, the New York lawyer who represented Belichick against the Jets. "I'm quite certain of that. Both are fiercely competitive people. That was obvious just sitting in the same room with them."

The Patriots won 12–0. The Cowboys did not play well, and Parcells was dejected.

But their next win made up for that. In Week 12, the Cowboys defeated the Carolina Panthers 24–20. It was their eighth win of the season. The Cowboys had been 5–11 for three straight previous seasons. Parcells had tears in his eyes, telling the media, "You can't call them losers anymore."

It was reported that during the training camp, Parcells had confided in a friend that he thought Quincy Carter was a "clown," not a serious leader. Carter had a reputation as a carouser and party boy. Before the season started, Carter promised Jones that he would turn over a new leaf. And Carter was pretty much true to his word, spending countless hours in his hotel room rather than visiting local hot spots and night clubs. He became a film junkie. Under Parcells he was having his best season ever.

In early November, however, Carter was in a slump, and Parcells stood behind him, telling Carter, "Hey, you've led this team to the top of the league and all you gotta do is get this stuff going again."

When the Cowboys beat Carolina and Carter broke his offensive drought, he whooped and smiled. He even threw a towel in the stands. Carter rushed into the locker room and sat down. As Parcells walked into the room, he passed by the rejuvenated Carter, the quarterback he'd stood behind. He stopped and said to Carter, "Hey, don't get full of yourself. You've got to get back out there next week. And you better not screw it up."

Sure enough, the Cowboys lost to Miami and the Eagles before beating the Redskins in Washington. This set up an exciting Week 16 matchup of the New York Giants at Dallas. With a record of 9–5, a win would guarantee Dallas a playoff spot.

The team put up 326 yards of offense, and the defense held the Giants to one field goal for a dramatic 19–3 win. It seemed the result of the game was almost never really in doubt. The Cowboys finished the season 10–6 with a loss to the New Orleans Saints.

Parcells had done it again. He'd taken a franchise with three years of losing behind it and transformed the team into one of the elite teams in the NFL. He'd done it in one year. He was the first coach to bring four different teams to the playoffs. And he'd turned the Dallas defense into the second-best defense in the NFL.

The Cowboys would be playing John Fox's Carolina Panthers in the playoffs at Ericsson Stadium. John Fox was determined that his team would be more aggressive in the payoffs than he had been in the regular season, especially against Parcells. The normally conservative Panthers threw deep on running downs and short-yard passing downs, amassing 380 yards on offense and holding the Dallas offense to 204 yards. Steve Smith had 135 yards on five catches and one touchdown. And the Carolina Panthers went home 29–10 winners.

No matter the loss, Parcells was hailed as a legend. He was the only coach to ever take four different teams to the playoffs. And he had taken a team that had gone 5–11 for three straight seasons and made them one of the top teams of the 2003 season.

"I mean, there's no denying the man's a jerk, but you know, you don't hire pro football coaches because you think they're good guys. There's a couple of reasons why he wins," said Allen Barra, Slate.com contributor and author. "Number one, he's a fierce disciplinarian, but he's also smart, and he's a pragmatist. He doesn't try to impose his football philosophy on the team that he's with. He looks over the material and finds out the best way to win with that material, and he's done this with four distinctly different types of teams in the last two decades."

"The legend of Bill Parcells can mercifully take a breather for an off-season after the Cowboys' revival tent finally folded up last night at Ericsson Stadium," Selena Roberts wrote in *The New York Times*. "One day, Texans will have to pay for these euphoric Tuna times. One day, Parcells will no doubt leave them, having squeezed the last drop out of their 10-gallon team. The pattern of abandonment is well established: whenever Parcells exits a franchise, nothing but the picture hooks remain."

LET'S DO IT AGAIN

There is no denying that 2003 was an incredible season for Dallas. But the 2004 and the 2005 seasons would not be as kind.

In June, the Cowboys announced that they had brought Vinny Testaverde to Dallas. The 40-year-old veteran arrived at Valley Ranch to compete for the starting job and to mentor Carter and the other quarterback backups. After six seasons with the Jets, Testaverde had been released.

"The opportunity to compete to be a starter excites me. I didn't have that opportunity in New York," Testaverde said. "June 1 couldn't get here fast enough for me," he added. "I know good things are ahead for both myself and this organization. Again, I'm very excited to be here."

Parcells told the press that Carter would remain the No. 1 starter for the time being but that, as always, the best player would play.

However, Carter was released by the beginning of August. Rumors swirled about his difficulties with drugs and Parcells' concerns about turning over control of his club to someone who was not focused. In a press release, the Cowboys said a failed drug test, a mediocre training camp, and a poor attitude upon Testaverde's signing all led to the club's decision to release Carter.

Ironically, this scenario positively altered Cowboys history as the fourth quarterback on the depth chart was Tony Romo, who with Carter's release turned out to be a Pro Bowl quarterback for the Cowboys in later years.

Also, Parcells traded Joey Galloway to the Tampa Bay Buccaneers for deactivated wide receiver Keyshawn Johnson. Johnson had come into conflict with Jon Gruden, and the two had come to loggerheads. Johnson was thrilled to be reunited with Parcells.

The draft saw the arrival of running back Julius Jones and cornerbacks Jacques Reeves and Nate Jones.

On June 8, wide receiver Antonio Bryant had a bad day. Bryant was complaining about being the team's third receiver and was unhappy about the number of reps he was getting during a drill. Frustrated, Bryant confronted wide receivers coach Todd Haley. The two fought, then Bryant fought with Keyshawn Johnson.

Bryant took off his pads and jersey and threw them to the ground. He then began to leave the practice field. Parcells told Bryant to stop and reportedly threw the jersey at Bryant, who in return threw it back into Parcells' face. Lots of shouting pushing and shoving ensued, and Bryant was escorted out of the stadium facility by security guards.

"This was my fourth or fifth fight with a player," Parcells laughed, referring to his long coaching career. "All of the other guys I had fights with called me on the phone after it happened."

Bryant later apologized but was eventually traded to the Cleveland Browns for wide receiver Quincy Morgan.

— —

Though the season started off well, with a loss and two wins, the season would prove to be a long one. The defense did not live up to its previous year's promise. Stalwart cornerback Mario Edwards was gone through free agency. Blades was gone, as well. And veteran safety Woodson was felled by an injury.

The defense wasn't stout enough to halt extended drives by opposing teams, and thus played long stretches at a time. The offense was relatively toothless, and that resulted in the defense spending even more time on the field. The result was a tired defense and an offense that was continuously playing from behind.

Testaverde proved solid but could not produce behind a line that was ineffective.

On November 15, Bill Parcells watched as his team got blown off the field 49–21 at Texas Stadium by the Philadelphia Eagles.

One reporter inquired as to whether Parcells would make any changes in personnel. Parcells barked back, "Not right now. I've got to look at the film first. Wouldn't you think that would be advisable?"

At one point Monday, a reporter pushed a point, asking for Parcells feelings on the game. "You're looking for your sound bite now, aren't you?" Parcells said in anger. He then uttered an expletive and left the pressroom.

Subsequently, Drew Henson, who had returned to football after a controversial attempt to catch on with the New York Yankees, started the Thanksgiving Day game. For all their woes, Julius Jones, after sustaining an injury that kept him out of action in the first half of the season, provided highlights for the second half.

Despite these heroics, the Cowboys finished a disappointing 6–10, and finished second in the NFC East. Worse, the defense had slipped from No. 2 to No. 27. The offense was 25th in the NFL. The season had ended with a loss at the Meadowlands to the Giants. They had lost the game in the closing minutes.

"We've been the same since preseason. The team has never changed," Parcells said. "We don't take care of the ball, we're not mentally tough and we're not physically tough enough at certain spots and it transcends to the rest of the team."

Parcells confirmed that he would be back for the next season, saying, "My intention is to continue to coach here."

"Although Parcells knew what had to be fixed six months ago, he couldn't do it," Jaime Aron wrote for the Associated Press. "Tweaks to scheme and personnel weren't enough and coaches were unable to get players to break bad habits, such as false starts on offense."

"A pretty good percentage of the guys fight to do well, then another percentage—that's more than you can tolerate—do not," Parcells said.

The good feeling had started to wear off.

"I'm starting to wonder how badly this will all end for Bill Parcells. His brief tenure with the Cowboys is already taking misguided turns," Jeffri Chadiha wrote on ESPN.com. "The unquestioned faith Parcells inspired in so many other franchises isn't in Dallas right now. Aside from the emergence of Julius Jones and Jason Witten, what has gone right for the man in the last 12 months?"

Chadiha criticized Parcells' acquisitions of Testaverde and Johnson, as neither impacted the team. He was also critical of the possibility of bringing Drew Bledsoe to the Cowboys, "a move owner Jerry Jones reportedly doesn't support."

"I bring all this up because Parcells is running out of time. His current contract expires after the 2006 season," Chadiha concluded. "All the good vibes from that 10–6 season in '03 have vanished, and to be honest, I don't see why Parcells would want to do this job much longer."

— —

On January 5, 2005, Larry Lacewell, who was about to turn 68, announced his retirement from the Dallas Cowboys. He was the director of scouting.

"And it could be another sign of the power base in the organization shifting to coach Bill Parcells," Associated Press reporter Jaime Aron noted. Lacewell had been with the club for 13 seasons.

As a fellow Arkansas native, Lacewell had a close personal relationship with Jones. He was expected to remain an outside advisor to Jones, "but his absence from team headquarters likely means more influence for Parcells," Aron opined.

Parcells pledged to reshape the player roster. Going into 2005 the Cowboys were $20 million under the salary cap, and they had two first-round draft picks.

The biggest problem was still the quarterback position. Carter was gone, Testaverde had not been productive, Drew Henson (Jones' reclamation project) was just not ready for Sunday afternoon, and Tony Romo was their scout team player. There was no one Parcells trusted under center.

Drew Bledsoe, now a 12-year veteran, was available. He was being released by the Buffalo Bills, and Parcells wanted him. Both Parcells and Jones knew that Bledsoe was well past his prime, but in Parcells' eyes he was a veteran with playoff experience. Jones acquiesced because he himself did not have a better idea. No one was giving away playoff-caliber quarterbacks. And Jones himself was determined not to go into the 2006 season with Henson and Tony Romo competing for the starting job. Jones wanted to win now.

"[Parcells] did tell me I was going to be the starting quarterback," Bledsoe said. "He's going to play the best guys on Sunday. I anticipate being the best guy."

Bledsoe got a three-year, $14 million deal that also included incentives should Dallas make the playoffs.

"We all know that if you've got an experienced quarterback with talent and a few other things fall right for you, that you've got a good chance to contend," Jones said.

"I know there's criticism and skepticism about this deal, and I'm not going to sit up here and defend myself," Bledsoe said. "The one thing I will say is that when my time with the Dallas Cowboys is done, the story will be written that will answer all of the questions."

— —

The most important thing on Parcells' mind was improving the Dallas defense. To that extent, the Cowboys helped themselves by drafting Demarcus Ware and Marcus Spears in the first round, and Chris Canty in the fourth round.. Via free agency the Cowboys also picked up some high-priced older veterans like Jason Ferguson (nose tackle), Aaron Glenn and Anthony Henry (cornerbacks), and Scott Fujita (linebacker). On offense they signed free agent Marco Rivera (guard). Ferguson and Glenn both knew Parcells from their Jets days and therefore knew what to expect.

Parcells and Jones had spent $32 million in signing bonuses while on their spree.

Parcells wanted badly to convert to a 3-4 defense from a 4-3 defense, but his down lineman were not happy, and in a May minicamp things got a little heated. La'Roi Glover, who'd been to five consecutive Pro Bowls, who was used to lining up in the gap against a guard would now find himself outweighed by 50 pounds by an offensive tackle. He was not happy.

Parcells begged the team to put aside its individual agendas and goals and trust in the schemes that were being put forward. Parcells knew that the football world was watching and judging. "You're always judged in this business by what you did in the most recent season," Parcells said. "So I certainly feel challenged myself, and I certainly feel that I do have something to prove.... That can be a good thing. I would hope it can."

"Probably as big a reason as any I'm excited is because Bill is here," Jones said. "I have always believed that the biggest measure of working with anyone is how they work in adversity and how they work when things aren't going good and when we're disappointed."

With Cowboy camp opening in Oxnard, California, Parcells showed up in good shape, having slimmed down and having run 15 miles in California alone before camp commenced. "I want to be able to stay on [them] every day," he said. "I did want to make an effort to increase my energy level during the season.... When things don't go well, you evaluate, you scrutinize more closely. We wouldn't stop people and couldn't produce enough offense. We could stay in games, but we couldn't win enough of them."

Parcells brought in some star power during camp. Jim Burt and Carl Banks, both former New York Giants and Super Bowl champions, came to Oxnard to help out during camp. "The thing that you should understand here is there's a long pedigree of teaching. That's why we had so much success as players," Banks told the players.

"Giants doesn't have anything to do with it," Parcells said. "I told the both of them when I asked them, 'Don't feel like you have to say yes. I don't want to interfere with your life.'" But nether could say no to Parcells. Burt was feisty when he arrived, and he and Parcells gave each other big bears hugs and wrestled.

"Like he was as a player, Burt was animated in teaching La'Roi Glover, Jason Ferguson, Leonardo Carson, and Chris Van Hoy," Todd Archer reported for the *Dallas Morning News*. "Coaches do not wear cleats, but Burt did. The helmet never made it in time. Instead, Burt turned his hat backward and jammed his face into Glover's shoulder pads."

During one stretch in practice, Burt hollered to Parcells, "Bill, just so you know, your center is tackling our tackles."

"Are you refereeing or coaching?" Parcells barked back.

As was expected, Banks was somewhat more subdued but no less effective. Having been a linebacker with the Giants and Browns and an assistant with Parcells at the Jets, Parcells had confidence in Banks.

"He knows what he's doing," Parcells said. "He can explain technique pretty well. He knows this defense well. I just thought he'd be a help."

"If he wasn't the coach, we wouldn't have been champions," Burt said. "You only have so many years in this league when you're a player. You get a sense of pride to you when you win a couple of championships, and he's the guy that led us to that because he pushed guys when they didn't want to be pushed.... It brings you to a level normally you wouldn't get to."

Burt and Banks weren't the only experts in camp. Ron Wolf had been coming every year since 2003. Chuck Fairbanks had come in that season, as well. Former New England linebacker Vincent Brown was there in 2005, and so was Lewis Tillman the former New York Giants and Chicago Bears running back.

Bringing famous players into camp, Parcells' "guys," was nothing new. He'd brought in Tom Coughlin during the 2003 camp, as well as Dave

Meggett. Ben Coates and Maurice Hurst worked out with the team in 2004.

The Cowboys won a wild game against the San Diego Chargers in the first week, winning 28–24, and they put up 34 points against the 49ers in Week 3 to start with a 2–1 record. They lost to the Raiders in Oakland before winning two at home, the last one an overtime victory against the New York Giants 16–13. And then they lost on the road to the Seattle Seahawks 13–10 to make their record 4–3.

It was the Monday after the Seahawks loss that the NFL lost Wellington Mara. There was no question that Bill had been Tim Mara's guy. They were closer in age and shared a love of the Jersey shore. But Parcells had liked Wellington, as well. The Giants had been a patriarchal organization, which is why Parcells had fit in so well.

Parcells decided to attend the funeral, held at St. Patrick's Cathedral on Friday, October 28, 2005. The 2,200 seats at St. Patrick's were packed, and more than 1,000 mourners and fans were outside. It was one of the biggest funerals New York City had seen in years.

The pews were packed with the Who's Who of the NFL and New York. New York City Mayor Rudolph Guiliani, former head of the New York Stock Exchange Richard Grasso, NFL commissioner Paul Tagliabue, Art Modell, Tim Rooney, Frank Gifford, Gene Upshaw, John Madden, Pat Summerall, Charlie Weis, Willie Brown, Phil Simms, Phil McConkey, Harry Carson, Mark Bavaro, Dave Brown, Jerry Jones, Jim Irsay, Robert Kraft, Lamar Hunt, Ralph Wilson, Mike Brown, Arthur Blank, Dan Snyder, Tom Benson, Mike McCaskey, John Fox, Romeo Crennel, Bill Belichick, and many, many others.

"This was not merely a funeral for a beloved owner of a beloved New York team. This was a sports state funeral, the state being the National Football League," *The New York Times* reported.

During the course of the funeral, Parcells turned and tapped the shoulder of Pittsburgh Steelers owner Dan Rooney, now the league's most senior owner. Parcells said to Rooney, "The torch has been passed to you."

"He's the one who took a chance, him along with George Young," Parcells said. "They took a chance. Bill Parcells wouldn't have existed if it hadn't been for them. And I know that."

That weekend the Cowboys beat Arizona 34–14 and improved to 5–3. Following an upcoming Bye Week, the Philadelphia Eagles were next.

— —

Then Bill Parcells got the phone call he had dreaded most. His brother, Don, had died at 62 years of age. His brain cancer had come back. Parcells knew, but he never shared it with the media.

Don was a consummate storyteller—reciting and embellishing the same stories over and over again to his personal delight and the delight of others. He was known as an affable man (as was his brother, Doug), with a good sense of humor. He was the proud father of six children: Craig, Chris, Daniel, Matthew, Sean, and Shannon.

Bill told Don's widow, Elaine, "I just lost the person I'm closest to in the world."

Parcells flew into Philadelphia with the team on a Sunday night. The NFL does not stop for personal lives. He did not tell his players that his brother had died.

"If he wanted to fill us in, he would've done that," wide receiver Terry Glenn said. "But he wanted to keep that to himself and handle it with no distractions. You've got to respect a guy like that."

The next morning, Bill woke up and drove 90 minutes up the New Jersey Turnpike for the funeral—to say goodbye to his little brother. They buried Don Parcells on a Monday morning, November 14, 2005, in Short Hills.

"When he gets on the field, he'll do what he has to do, and I'm sure he'll be able to block out everything and do his job," youngest brother Doug said. Doug had been successful in his own right. There was now a sporting complex in Oradell, New Jersey, named for him. It was a large complex with multiple fields and responsibilities. "He's always been able to do that. But I'm sure it was a tremendously difficult day. He and Donnie are less than two years apart in age and they grew up together. So they were very, very close. I know from my conversations with Bill during the week that this has been very troubling and very disturbing, as you would suspect."

"That was hard on me, I have to tell you," Parcells said. "Very hard."

Parcells stayed for a while and then drove back to Philadelphia in the late afternoon. He was on the sideline, coaching the Cowboys in their 21–20 win over Philadelphia.

"I'm at the age now [64] where there are a lot of things that are starting to become more important to me," Parcells said after the game. "I don't say more important than football, but I think about other things a lot more than I used to. The events of this fall have certainly made me cognizant of things." It was clear that Don and Wellington's deaths were very much on his mind.

— —

Coupled with a win over the Detroit Lions the week after the Eagles game, the Cowboys were now 7–3 and seemingly back on top. But the roof was about to cave in. The 2005 Cowboys finished the season 9–7, losing to the Rams 20–10 during the final weekend of the regular season, missing the playoffs. The defense had improved to 12th in the league.

The Cowboys had been contenders through the first two-thirds of the season. But it was obvious that Parcells had them back on a good track, and he had the team in playoff contention up until the last day of the season.

On January 6, 2006, Jerry Jones announced that Parcells had agreed to a new contract that ran through 2007. This ended the speculation over his impending retirement.

The 64-year-old Parcells had shown up at Valley Ranch as he did every morning. "I feel very fortunate to have the opportunity to continue what we have started here," Parcells said in a statement. "The Cowboys organization has been the fairest of fair to me, and hopefully I can repay them with an improved performance."

"This is about continuity and building upon the pieces we have in place as an organization and as a football team," Jerry Jones said. "We aren't where we want to be at this point, but we're definitely moving in the right direction."

That same month, quarterbacks coach and assistant head coach Sean Payton was tapped to be the head coach of the New Orleans Saints.

But the most controversial moment of the season came early when Jerry Jones insisted the Cowboys acquire the rights to Terrell Owens. Owens was a tremendous talent with the 49ers and had helped the Philadelphia Eagles reach the Super Bowl. But in his second season with the Eagles, things had gone incredibly wrong. As with the 49ers, he trashed his quarterback openly in the press, ridiculed the coaching staff, and questioned the ownership. He had been suspended and ultimately deactivated by the Eagles, a ruling he fought and lost.

It was a bold move considering most Cowboys fans loathed the loud-mouthed, fiery, talented young receiver after he had danced on the Dallas star on the 50-yard line of Texas Stadium in 2000 to a cascade of booing when he played with the 49ers. Cowboys safety George Teague had become a local legend after he leveled Owens during the second celebratory dance.

"In general, I am a risk-taker," Jones said. "I probably have a propensity to try and make things work."

In February, Parcells had met with Drew Rosenhaus, Owens' agent, to get the real story on Owens. Parcells and Rosenhaus might not normally seem like the best of intimates, but Parcells appreciated Rosenhaus' self-made story and liked the fact that when you called the office, Drew himself picked up the call. Rosenhaus insisted Owens knew he had made a mistake and was just now trying to get his career back.

But Parcells didn't stop there. Parcells called David Culley, the Eagles' wide receiver coach. Parcells had recruited Culley to Vanderbilt when he was coaching there. Culley confirmed one thing about Owens—despite his off-field antics, at practice and on game day, the man was focused. Parcells asked others and received the same response over and over again—Owens was a competitor.

"Parcells ended up concluding that while he certainly could live without Owens, he wouldn't object strongly enough to keep the deal from happening," wrote Mark Maske, sportswriter at the *Washington Post*.

Jones signed Owens to a three-year contract worth $25 million.

"I'll be a better teammate, a better person, a better man in life," Owens said at the press conference. Turning to Jones later, he said, "Jerry, I know what's expected of me. I won't let you down."

Parcells was on vacation in Florida. How would Parcells and TO get along? Certainly with players like Bryan Cox and Keyshawn Johnson, Parcells had made converts of the NFL's most outrageous outliers. Would he be able to do it again, or would fireworks explode?

"This was not me selling Bill, this was not Bill selling me," Jones said. "This was us taking advantage of getting an outstanding player. Bill has coached a lot of players that, quote-unquote, have the perception that they might not fit in with team chemistry."

On their first meeting, Parcells did not insist that Owens participate in the off-season work out program. Parcells had been assured by others, and knew from reading about him, that Owens was a fitness nut and his coming into camp in shape would not be a problem.

"Hey, this is not going to be like rolling in and getting used to running with what you know," Parcells said to Owens, discussing the differences between Parcells' offense and the west coast offense Owens has been trained in with the 49ers and the Eagles. He got Owens to agree to come in 10 days before the opening of minicamp to start learning the offense with the coaching staff. Owens agreed. Parcells also warned Owens that he would not be catching 100 passes a year.

"You have to be ready for that," Parcells said. Owens shook his head, thinking to himself that Parcells would eventually relent.

— —

Jones also brought in more high-profile players, including Mike Vanderjagt (kicker), Akin Ayodele (linebacker), Jason Fabini (offensive lineman), Kyle Kosier (offensive lineman), and Marcus Coleman (safety).

The Cowboys also lost some veteran talent and leadership that year. Dan Campbell (tight end) went to the Detroit Lions, Keyshawn Johnson (wide receiver) went to the Carolina Panthers, Larry Allen (offensive lineman) went to the San Francisco 49ers, La'Roi Glover (defensive lineman) went to the St. Louis Rams, and Dat Nguyen (linebacker) was lost to a career-ending injury.

Peter King jinxed the Cowboys when he predicted that Dallas would get to the Super Bowl that year and face the New England Patriots.

"All kinds of great angles. Belichick-Parcells. Bledsoe-Belichick. Kraft-Parcells. Brady-Bledsoe. Parcells and his son-in-law, Pats VP of player personnel Scott Pioli, on opposite sides," King wrote mischievously. "Maybe we'd call it the Dallas Pioli Bowl. There are two weeks between the conference championships and the Super Bowl this season. We'd need two months to cover all the angles. That's how many good stories would be connected to this game."

One of the concerns of the season was still the quarterback situation. Bledsoe had been serviceable in 2005. But he'd also been sacked 49 times and hit during the act of throwing 82 times. Those were some of the highest numbers in the league. The question for 2006 was whether Bledsoe would be looking downfield at his receivers or at the oncoming pass rush. The latter would be catastrophic for the team.

"How'd you like to be on ESPN this summer during training camp?" Phil Simms said to Peter King. "There won't be time to get in the sports news of the day when Cowboys camp opens up! Half of *SportsCenter* every night will be Terrell Owens, Bill Parcells, and Jerry Jones. They'll be live from practice. Hey, I'm curious about it. We all are."

But Owens towed the line, and camp went well.

— —

The 2006 season started with a loss at Jacksonville 24–17.

"After the late-night flight home from Jacksonville, he went to his condo to catch a few hours' sleep. He woke up not long after he nodded off, choking on his own bile," bestselling author Michael Lewis reported in *The New York Times Magazine*.

"It only happens to me during the football season," Parcells said. "It happens no other time of the year. And it wasn't something I ate."

Walking around the house in the wee small hours, he happened to find a message from ex-wife Judy on the answering machine, "Please don't let it affect your health," she said. She had seen the game on TV.

Judy had spent many an afternoon watching her husband's teams, either in a club box, in the stands with other players' wives and girlfriends, or at home in front of the television wearing the same hat that had been given to her by a fan club. She was still watching.

The Monday after the game, Parcells watched the tape of the game that had just been played. It pained him to watch it, especially since it was a loss. But it was always a learning tool. On Tuesdays, he always watched tape of the teams they were going to play.

They beat the Washington Redskins 27–10 at Texas Stadium. The following Monday morning, Parcells was in his office by 5:00 AM.

"We had 70 yards in gains negated by 60 yards in penalties," Parcells said. "That's nine points." Lewis asked him if there was any pattern to the penalties. "Yeah," Parcells said, "they were all stupid."

The 2006 season was only two weeks old, and the Cowboys were 1–1 when on September 26, 2006, paramedics raced to Terrell Owens' house. He was found on the floor of his home unconscious.

"Terrell Owens, the flamboyant and often controversial Dallas Cowboys wide receiver, strongly denied Wednesday that he tried to commit suicide and said that his overnight hospital stay was the result of a reaction to prescription painkillers," *The New York Times* reported the next day.

In truth, Owens had broken a bone in his right hand during a game against Washington a week earlier. Doctors had installed a plate in the hand. Owens was prescribed a painkiller, hydrocodone, which is a generic form of Vicodin. Parcells himself had said that the drug was having ill effects on Owens. "I had hydrocodone for my hand, and there were a number of supplements," Owens told more than 100 members of the news media. "The list is too long to tell you exactly everything that I take, but all of them are natural supplements. It was just an allergic reaction. It's just very unfortunate for the reports to go from an allergic reaction to a definite suicide."

Owens apologized to the Cowboys organization for the mistake and for the distraction. Owens denied that his stomach had been pumped or that he was depressed. "No, I'm not depressed by any means," he said. "I'm very happy to be here."

"I know very little about this situation right now," said Parcells, who had not spoken with Owens. "I'm talking with a great deal of ignorance on this subject. When I find out what is going on, you will know. Until then, I'm not getting interrogated for no reason."

Owens' teammates were obviously shaken, but his return to the locker room was reassuring.

"I was concerned when I heard the speculation," quarterback Drew Bledsoe said. "But I just went out and threw him a few balls, and he looks good and seems like he's in good spirits."

"As teammates, we're concerned about his health. And to see him walk through the door and be fine, we were good with that. That's enough for us," Marcus Spears said.

The team went right back to work. They beat Tennessee in the next game and alternated wins until they were 4–4. But in a Week 7 game against the New York Giants, Parcells had seen enough of Bledsoe and put in Tony Romo. Romo's debut was inglorious with two touchdowns and three interceptions. But it was clear that Romo had sparked the offense. He had out-thrown Bledsoe, 227 yards to 111 yards, and thrown two touchdowns to Bledsoe's none.

"I thought he was sick," Burt explained. He'd called up Parcells after the Giants game in which the coach looked listless. "I said to him, 'Bill, what's wrong with you? You're white as a ghost, you're not moving. What are you doing? What's going on?' The team looked like [garbage] and instead of screaming at 'em, kicking them in the [rear], he's in la-la land."

"I knew I needed to come down," Burt said, who planned to come in for the next game, a home game against the Carolina Panthers. "Because he looked lifeless."

"At 5:00 Sunday, I jumped on the plane, got there a little after 7:00, got right to the game," Burt said. "[I] walked right into the stadium...first person I saw was Bill...shook hands...walked into the locker room, got crazy, and pumped it up."

Someone gave Burt a Dallas jacket, and he put it on and became the biggest cheerleader the Dallas fans had ever seen. He was screaming at players, he did a chest bump with Roy Williams after a big play. He was a wild man of enthusiasm that helped to energize the team after it had recovered from a 14-point deficit. He even told Parcells to say something nice to the offensive line for opening up big holes during the game.

"Hey, I'm certainly not going to root for the Cowboys against the Giants, but I'm going to help out Bill when they're not playing. Bill and I, we've got that bond. We did it together," Burt said.

With Romo behind center, the Cowboys went 5–1 and by Week 13, with a 23–20 win at the Meadowlands, the Cowboys were 8–4 and in the thick of the playoff hunt.

"It really was love, that evanescent phenomenon of autumn 2006 known as Romo-mania. From October 29, 2006, the day of his first game as a starter, through December 16, the Cowboys went 6–2, this after a middling 3–3 start under their old QB, the battered vet Drew Bledsoe. Through that stretch, Romo's quarterback rating was 100.1, behind only Pro Bowlers Drew Brees and Carson Palmer. Romo was not merely a factor in the team's change in fortunes but *the* factor," Dave Kamp wrote in *GQ* magazine.

"The same coach has been here," Cowboys owner Jerry Jones observed in December. "What's different? The obvious explanation is we've got some quarterbacking that can make this whole thing jell."

— —

Then the Cowboys' record went to 9–5 with a loss at New Orleans and a win against the Atlanta Falcons. But that was all the team would muster. They were locked in a race for the NFC East title with the Philadelphia Eagles. With two home games to end the season, the Cowboys dropped both—against the Eagles and the Detroit Lions—and finished the season second in the division and secured a wild card birth.

The team had definitely improved. With Romo now at quarterback, the Cowboys had scored 425 points and were the fourth best offense in the NFL. But their defense was ranked 20th.

Their next game would be against the Seattle Seahawks in a wild-card round playoff game. The Cowboys were the fifth seed. The Cowboys took a 10–6 lead into the locker room at the half at Qwest Field in Seattle. In the third quarter, Seahawks quarterback Matt Hasselbeck completed a 15-yard touchdown pass to tight end Jerramy Stevens to retake the lead at 13–10. But the Cowboys regained their lead when rookie Miles

Austin returned a kickoff 93 yards for a touchdown, bringing the score to 17–13.

The fourth quarter saw the Cowboys increase their lead with a 29-yard Martin Gramatica field goal. But the Seahawks stormed back to take the lead with a safety coming off a Terry Glenn fumble, and moments later Hasselbeck completed a 37-yard touchdown pass to Stevens (the two-point conversion failed). The Seahawks were now winning 21–20.

Dallas drove the field, but the offensive drive stalled at the 19-yard line. On the snap for the attempted field goal, Romo botched the hold. He picked up the loose ball and attempted to run with it. He was tackled on Seattle's 2-yard line by Jordan Babineaux. Seattle got the ball back and turned it over, but there was little time. On the game's last play, Romo threw a Hail Mary that fell incomplete. Seattle won. Dallas had ended its season with three straight losses, and Parcells had failed to win a playoff game in four years there.

"Tony Romo's fairy tale ride as the Dallas Cowboys' quarterback took him from forgotten backup to celebrity starter in just over half an NFL season. But his rags-to-riches story ended in ignominy Saturday night in Seattle," sports scribe Nancy Gay wrote in the *San Francisco Chronicle*. "The snap was fine. Romo's grasp was not. The ball squirted loose, and Romo picked it up—momentarily fooling the sellout crowd of 68,058 into thinking that perhaps Dallas was trying some more trickery. Hardly. Romo was simply trying to salvage the season."

"It hurts real bad right now to think about it," a dejected Romo said. "I take responsibility for messing up at the end there, and it's my fault. I cost the Dallas Cowboys a playoff win. That's going to sit with me a long time. I don't know if I've ever felt this low at any point."

"It looked like a pretty good snap. He was the holder all year," Parcells said. "We were in position to win if we could just execute the extra point."

"Wow! Your whole season come down to that!" a shocked John Madden said on NBC.

A few years later Parcells admitted that play helped him make up his mind right there. He knew on his flight coming home he wasn't coming back.

"We'd just lost to Seattle and I'm flying back," Parcells told Andrea Kremer of HBO. "I'm sitting up with the pilots, you know, I have a little fear of flying so I ride up in the cockpit. And I said, 'This is probably going to be my last trip.' And you just know. You don't want to go through the whole process again, to get to right where we were. You know?"

Parcells was still beside himself in disbelief.

"And all you got to do is kick a field goal, the most elementary of plays, and then you just don't do it. And so I don't want to go through that process again. Too much blood."

"Bill Parcells cultivated a couple of hobbies outside of football over the past few years. He loved going to spring training baseball games, particularly Cardinals games with his buddy Ron Wolf, the former Green Bay general manager. He loved the horses, too," Peter King wrote after Parcells announced his retirement.

"Football's year-round now," Parcells, 65, said, a few hours after telling Dallas owner Jerry Jones he was leaving. "Anytime you take a break, you feel guilty."

"Is that all there was? Did the entire Bill Parcells in Dallas era add up to nothing more than a ho-hum 34–32 record including a pair of playoff losses in four years? Talk about much ado about very little. So much hype. So much hoopla. But a bit light on the fulfilled promise," John Biever wrote in *Sports Illustrated*. "He's a Hall of Fame coach to be sure, but he didn't exactly add to his legacy with his final round-up in Dallas.... He leaves Dallas better off than when he arrived—the Cowboys were 5–11 in the three seasons before Parcells—but the team's 9–7, one-and-done playoff appearance this season hardly resembled a dynasty in the making."

"Let's face it, before the Tuna arrived the Cowboys' franchise was... losing, we had a terrible roster and the atmosphere around Valley Ranch was anything but professional. Parcells gutted all that and built a roster that just went 13–3 and sent 13 guys to the Pro Bowl (some deserving, some not)," wrote Dave Halprin, editor of Blogging the Boys, in *The New York Times* in March 2008. "We also have a functioning scouting department and an attitude of expecting to win. All that can be attributed to Parcells' influence." Halprin lamented that Parcells never won a playoff game during his tenure nor did he take them to a Super Bowl, which was the expectation, but he had in fact left the franchise better off than when he started.

PINK FLAMINGOS AND MIAMI

"People point and say that's [Bill] Parcells' house," said the 83-year-old Emil Trapani. "The whole neighborhood knows he's here." Trapani points to a two-story, custom-built, off-yellow home in an affluent residential subdivision named the Lakeside at Riley's in Saratoga County. The 7,500 sq. ft. house sits across the lake from and above Saratoga National's 15th hole. It is Parcells' happy place.

"Absolutely delighted to have him," neighbor Patricia O'Toole said. "He's a gentleman. Talked to him and he's very friendly. He seems to enjoy the neighborhood, and we enjoy having him here."

The neighborhood locals have a welcoming tradition to make newcomers feel more at ease. It was an odd tradition but it broke the ice, and it was called "The Flocking." In February 2007 Bill Parcells was about to be hazed.

"After Parcells moved in, nearly 15 neighbors descended on his property at nightfall and carefully placed 40 pink flamingos on his front yard. The flamingos typically are adorned in attire befitting either the current season or the neighbors' specific interest. In this case, Parcells' flamingos were dressed in horse gear complete with saddles and reins. Some even had football helmets," Bryan Chu wrote in the *Albany Times Union*.

A "Welcome to the Neighborhood" banner was stretched across his front porch.

"He laughed at it," said neighbor Jim Oplinger, the ringleader of the community tradition. "He thought it was funny. What struck me most was he thanked us several times. He was very grateful for the welcoming to the neighborhood."

Parcells enjoyed his new neighborhood and even attended the local community cul-de-sac picnic with his girlfriend, Kelly Mandart.

— —

WELCOME TO RETIREMENT, BILL PARCELLS

By August, Parcells was nearing 66 years of age and was now a local and a regular. He'd been renting a house in Saratoga Springs for five or six years by that point, so he was not new to the area. He could be spotted, tanned and smiling, at Sargo's, which is the fine-dining restaurant at Saratoga National Golf Club. He could also be spotted in the stands at the racetrack or just hitting golf balls.

"I knew when I stopped coaching this time that that was it," said Parcells, who admited, "I felt that way before. I really did. When I left the Jets, I really thought that was it. Quite frankly I know it's it now. My age, I don't want to say it's prohibitive, but it's a young man's game. I recognize that. I don't want to stay too long. I don't want to be propped up out there."

"I don't think so," when asked if he would accept a GM position. It had been rumored the Giants had approached Parcells for an executive position. "That's just as bad [as coaching]. All the GM does is deal with problems: salary cap, injuries, player replacement, and holdouts. That's all life is."

"He's a pleasant enough kid," Parcells said when asked about Terrell Owens. "He's not mean-spirited; he's not vulgar. He's really okay in that respect.... He didn't have anything to do with me [retiring] at the end of the day."

In this fine August idyll, Parcells is at peace...for now. On some mornings he'll go to the racetrack and watch his friends—countless thoroughbred trainers like Shug McGaughey, Nick Zito, and D. Wayne Lukas—work at the Oklahoma barns. He golfs, but not much. He'd rather hit balls from the driving range. He'll bet on a few races, but he's not really a gambler.

"I can't tell you how my life's going to be structured," Parcells said. "All I'm doing is kind of playing it by ear right now. What do the kids say? 'I'm going with the flow.'"

While he lived in Dallas, he only saw his daughters and grandchildren once a year. He saw more of them after his retirement from Dallas. The daughters and their children all came to stay at Papa's new house.

Parcells went golfing with his 17-year-old grandson, and he took his 13-year-old granddaughter riding with Wayne Lukas.

In Parcells' "retirement" that summer, fellow coaches he hadn't spoken to in a while, people whom he used to compete against, called to ask his opinion or pick his brain, including Romeo Crennel, Chris Palmer, and Sean Payton. Several coaches actually invited him to visit their training camps, but he declined.

That fall he worked at ESPN, and the highlight of his broadcasting year was to read in 11 Commandments for a Quarterback that he'd given Tony Romo before leaving the Dallas Cowboys:

1. Press or TV, agents or advisors, family or wives, friends or relatives, fans or hangers-on, ignore them on matters of football; they don't know what's happening here.
2. Don't forget to have fun, but don't be the class clown. Clowns and leaders don't mix. Clowns can't run a huddle.
3. A quarterback throws with his legs more than his arms. Squat and run. Fat quarterbacks can't avoid the rush.
4. Know your job cold. This is not a game without errors. Keep yours to a minimum. Study.
5. Know your own players. Who's fast? Who can catch? Who needs encouragement? Be precise. Know your opponent.
6. Be the same guy every day. In condition, preparing to lead, studying your plan. A coach can't prepare you for every eventuality. Prepare yourself and remember, impulse decisions usually equal mistakes.
7. Throwing the ball away is a good play. Sacks, interceptions, and fumbles are bad plays. Protect against those.
8. You must learn to manage the game. Personnel, play call, motions, ball handling, proper reads, accurate throws, play fakes. Clock, clock, clock, don't you ever lose track of the clock.
9. Passing stats and TD passes are not how you're gonna be judged. Your job is to get your team in the end zone, and that's how you're gonna be judged.
10. When all around you is in chaos, you must be the hand that

steers the ship. If you have a panic button, so will everyone else. Our ship can't have panic buttons.

11. Don't be a celebrity quarterback. We don't need any of those. We need battlefield commanders that are willing to fight it out every day, every week, and every season, and lead their team to win after win after win.

Flamingos and golfing and thoroughbreds. Television. It's a nice vacation. But it's not Bill Parcells—at least not on a full time basis. Where's the "narcotic of winning," as Parcells likes to say? That's why when Arthur Blank of the Atlanta Falcons and Wayne Huizenga of the Miami Dolphins called Parcells in December 2007, he was listening.

Blank and Huizenga weren't asking him to come back to coaching. They were asking him to head up their football operations. Blank had reached out first to Parcells. Blank and Parcells had reached an agreement, in principal, for Parcells to take over as vice president of football operations of the Falcons. However, Blank broke off negotiations after Parcells informed Blank that he was also entertaining an offer from the Dolphins. Rather than compete with Huizenga, Blank balked and backed out.

On December 20, the same day Blank's press release explained that the Falcons and Parcells had broken off their talks, Huizenga issued a press release announcing his four-year deal with Parcells.

"People approach you with certain opportunities, you don't know they're coming your way, you consider all of them, as you would if someone approached you," Parcells told the press.

"He has a proven track record of success everywhere he has been in the National Football League," Huizenga said. "And his football acumen will help put the Miami Dolphins franchise back among the elite of the NFL."

"I'm honored to join such an illustrious franchise as the Miami Dolphins and to work for one of the best owners in the league in Wayne Huizenga," Parcells said. "He shares my same commitment to winning, and I told him I would do everything I can to help turn around the team's fortunes."

— —

"Suzy Schwille laughed when a friend in the dentist office where she works yelled from another room that Schwille's famous father was coming out of retirement. At least, that's what they were saying on TV," Carlos Frias wrote in the *Palm Beach Post*.

"That's got to be wrong," Schwille replied while cleaning a patient's teeth.

Deep down, part of her knew it could be true. So Schwille stepped away from the chair to watch the report herself.

Only after the announcement had been on the news did Bill Parcells call his daughter.

"A little late, aren't you?" she asked her father.

"C'mon, Suzy," Parcells replied. "I already got enough of it from your sisters."

"If you ask Schwille if she is surprised that her 67-year-old father agreed to tackle the task of turning around the 1–15 Dolphins instead of kicking back for good in his homes in Saratoga, New York, and Jupiter, [Florida], the answer is a definite yes," Frias wrote. "If you ask if she's surprised that he didn't talk to a single family member before making the decision, she's just as definitive with a no."

The Dolphins head coach Cam Cameron, whose team had gone 1–15 in 2007, sidestepped as many questions as he could, even refusing to say if he's ever met the coach. "There will potentially be a time to have that discussion," Cameron said. "Today, I don't see it as being that day."

— —

Parcells moved quickly. On January 1, 2008, he fired Dolphins general manager Randy Meuller. On January 2, 2008, former director of player personnel of the Dallas Cowboys, Jeff Ireland, was named the new general manager of the Miami Dolphins.

Parcells used to call Ireland, "Punxsutawney Jeff." Why?

"He'd say, 'You general managers stick your head out of the ground every year in February and, if everything's clear, you come up,'" Ireland said.

On the same day Parcells announced the exit of head coach Cam Cameron. "We just felt in order to move forward and not look back, we needed someone in place who shared the same philosophical compatibilities we shared. We didn't really know the guy that well. We were going to try to get someone that does share those things, and we weren't completely sold that he did," Ireland said.

On January 16, 2008, Tony Sparano was hired as the new head coach of the Miami Dolphins. "Coach Parcells has taught me the most, prepared me the most for this job," Sparano said. "He's taught me a great deal, and I'm going to continue to learn as much as I can." Sparano, then 46 years old, had also interviewed for the head coach openings in Atlanta and Baltimore. Sparano had worked 15 years in the college ranks and 9 years in the professional ranks before attaining this job.

"When Bill and I discussed what we were looking for in a head coach, we talked about one of high character," Ireland said. "We wanted someone who understood how to develop young players, one who could instill a culture that's all about winning. We think we found that guy. We know we found that guy."

"Parcells sat in a corner of the room, smiling occasionally like a proud papa. He declined to meet with reporters, leaving the talk to his protégés," Len Pasquarelli wrote for ESPN.com.

Sparano pursued several Dallas assistant coaches. Assistant David Lee was hired as quarterbacks coach, and Brian Gaine was hired as assistant director of player personnel after three years as assistant director of pro scouting with the Cowboys.

"It does leave a bitter taste in my mouth," Sparano said of the Cowboys having lost a playoff game against the Giants just a week before. "Anybody who knows me knows I'm about finishing. We didn't finish. That left a bad taste in my mouth.... Obviously it has been a real crazy week for me. But I'm glad it ends this way."

By mid-February the bloodletting began, when the Dolphins released quarterback Trent Green, wide receiver Marty Booker, offensive tackle L.J. Shelton, and huge defensive tackle Keith Traylor. Five other players were also released.

In a surprise move, Huizenga sold 50 percent of the Miami Dolphins to Stephen Ross, a New York real estate developer. Ross bought his half of the team for a reported $550 million, with the possibility of becoming the managing general partner. The two sides had been negotiating in April 2007, but with the announcement of Parcells' hiring, many thought the deal would not go through.

Huizenga remained general managing partner, but there was speculation that with him turning 68 years old the time was coming soon when he would have to relinquish his remaining half. "My heart does not want me to do this, but my head tells me it's the right thing to do," Huizenga said. "I will certainly be a part of this team, a partner in this team until I die."

In the meantime, Ireland and Parcells went on a shopping spree in the free agency market. They acquired a quarterback (Josh McCown, Raiders), a guard, a wide receiver, a linebacker (Reggie Torbor, Giants), a tight end and defensive tackles, but none of them were considered marquee players. The Dolphins did trade draft picks to Dallas for defensive lineman Jason Ferguson. While Dallas thought Furgeson was dubious due to season-ending surgery the year before, Ireland and Parcells thought he could anchor a 3-4 defense.

Then the 2008 draft rolled around, and the Dolphins picked mammoth Michigan offensive tackle Jake Long with the first pick. He was the first tackle to be taken No. 1 since Orlando Pace in 1997. Long was 6'7" and 313 pounds, roughly similar to Jumbo Elliott, a fellow Michigan grad.

"Jake was our guy from the beginning," Dolphins general manager Jeff Ireland said. "I don't make it a habit of telling you what's on our board, but Jake Long was on top of our board for a long time. There wasn't a whole lot of debate."

The Dolphins also took two defensive ends in Phillip Merling of Clemson and Kendall Langford of Hampton, as well as a defensive tackle in Lionel Dotson from Arizona. They took Michigan quarterback Chad

Henne, and two offensive guards, Shawn Murphy of Utah State and Donald Thomas of Connecticut. Running backs Jalen Parmele of Toledo and Lex Hilliard of Montana rounded out the draft.

Longtime Dolphins defensive end Jason Taylor took a star turn in early 2008 by participating on *Dancing With the Stars*. But his footwork didn't impress Parcells.

At one point, Taylor took a break from the popular television show and came down to visit the Dolphins. Taylor hit the locker room and visited with his many friends and then went to meet Parcells. Parcells was watching old game tapes, evaluating the team's talent and weaknesses when Taylor walked into the room. Parcells ignored him and went back to work, incensing Taylor.

Taylor was a bona fide superstar, who'd been to six Pro Bowls and who had 11 sacks the previous year. The real problem was that Parcells wanted Taylor to work out at the team's facilities in Davie, Florida. Instead, Taylor became the first active player to join the *Dancing With the Stars* cast. Taylor had also publicly stated he wanted to play for a contending team as he was approaching the final years of his career. By mid-July Taylor was a Washington Redskin—the Dolphins accepted a second-round draft pick in 2009 and a sixth-rounder in 2010 for him.

Zach Thomas, the longtime middle linebacker drafted by Jimmy Johnson and one of the team's best-known players, was also gone. Ironically, he ended up in Dallas. Thomas was one of the first players to be given the heave-ho.

As training camp approached, sportswriter Judy Battista wrote, "Of course they are not going to the playoffs this season. But is anything more fun than watching Bill Parcells do a makeover of a franchise? There has already been a significant uptick in talent over the team that won one game last season, but the Dolphins have to identify, once and for all, their quarterback."

— —

"On this day, Parcells has driven his black Cadillac sedan to a nearby golf course, where he's holding court with three people inside the clubhouse bar. Harness races blare from one television. Another is showing soccer. A third, the one nearest to him, is tuned to a St. Louis Cardinals game, no coincidence since they're managed by Parcells' close friend Tony La Russa. He leans back in his chair, telling a story. Looking tan and relaxed, Parcells is clearly at ease," Tim Reynolds wrote.

"The happiest place I know," Parcells repeats about his new-found nirvana—Saratoga Springs. Parcells has established his favorite haunts, including the West Side Stadium and the Wishing Well. Maybe he'll go for a ride and see Zick Zito or Wayne Lukas. Maybe hit some golf balls.

But training camp awaits. Responsibility beckons.

"It's not my program. It's Jeff Ireland's and Tony Sparano's program," Parcells insisted. "They're the ones that are charged with the day-to-day dealings with the Miami Dolphins. I'm just trying to get the structure in place. That's what I'm charged with doing. That's my job. And it's not the same kind of job I've had before. And people can't separate that."

"But the feeling at the organization has changed. It is unmistakable. Just like his previous stops, the entire organization has been revamped and the roster shaken up to within an inch of its life," Reynolds continued.

Parcells does not stop to smell the roses here like he does in Saratoga. He arrives at 6:15 in the morning, with Ireland already waiting to speak with him. The relationship is more friendly, more teacher-student, than it has ever been for Parcells. He has mellowed. But he is not less demanding.

"It's a whole different attitude," Dolphins linebacker Joey Porter said. "Right now, when you have a coach like Parcells coming in and his coaching staff, it's just a whole different atmosphere with the respect level that you have for Parcells. You know what he's capable of doing. He's got the fire lit up under everybody."

"I would like to think that it would be similar here as it was there," Dolphins offensive coordinator and longtime friend Dan Henning said. "But as Bill would say, they don't sell insurance for this stuff. You've got to get it done. One thing I know about Bill: When he goes someplace and he leaves someplace, the place is better after he left than when he got there. That's a good sign."

"I don't let much of what people say bother me," Parcells said. "When you've been in this business as long as I have, if you don't have a turtle shell, you're in trouble."

On August 8, 2008, the beginning of one of the most interesting story lines in the last decade began to unfold, when the New York Jets signed former Green Bay superstar Brett Favre to be their new quarterback. Lost in the shuffle was Chad Pennington, the Jets starting quarterback, who was simultaneously let go upon Favre's signing.

Even more bizarre was the Dolphins picking up Pennington and making him their No. 1 starter. When he was in New York, Parcells had drafted Pennington and still thought very highly of him. Pennington did not have the big arm of some quarterbacks, but he knew how to manage a game and didn't make many mistakes. He was focused, and he had his own motor. Pennington was named Comeback Player of the Year in 2006 after returning from shoulder surgery to lead the Jets to the playoffs in 2006.

Pennington had a career 65.6 completion percentage with more than 1,900 pass attempts. But more important to Parcells, Pennington was a student of the game. He loved football.

"You spend eight years with an organization and then in the blink of an eye, you're no longer wanted there. That's just the crude part of the business that is hard to accept emotionally," Pennington said. "If something happens with the Miami Dolphins, it will be because I feel good about the situation and good about the opportunity. It won't have anything to do with the New York Jets or me trying to prove a point."

The stage was set.

In the first game of the season, the Dolphins hosted the Jets. The Jets led from the beginning and took a score of 20–7 into the fourth quarter. Favre had thrown two touchdowns. But Pennington and the Dolphins came alive. They scored on an 11-yard touchdown toss from Pennington to David Martin. The Dolphins drove again as time was running down, Chad Pennington threw the ball, but it landed safely in the hands of Darrelle Revis. The Jets had won 20–14. In the minds of Jets fans, Favre had beaten Pennington. This proved that Favre had been the right choice. The Jets were going somewhere.

Following another loss the next week at the Arizona Cardinals, Miami slipped to 0–2. But something out of the ordinary happened when the woeful Miami Dolphins went up to New England and shocked the NFL, handing the vaunted New England Patriots a 38–13 drubbing, one of the most awful beatings they'd received in years.

The Dolphins also won their next game, a home game against the visiting San Diego Chargers, giving them a 2–2 record. Then they lost to the Texans in Houston and came home to another defeat, this time at the hands of the Baltimore Ravens.

The team rallied for a four-game winning streak, beating the Bills, the Broncos, the Seahawks, and the Raiders to run their record to a gaudy 6–4. That was when the embarrassed Patriots came down to Miami and returned the favor to the upstart Dolphins by manhandling them coldly and efficiently for a 48–28 loss.

But the Dolphins rebounded, earning road victories at the Rams and at the Bills, beating the 49ers in Miami, and then beating the Chiefs 38–31 in Kansas City.

The 9–6 Brett Favre–led Jets would now host the 10–5 Dolphins at the Meadowlands. A victory would assure the Dolphins of an AFC East division championship and a playoff berth for the first time since 2001. The Jets were in a more precarious spot. Not only did they need a victory to advance to the playoffs, but they needed a New England or a Baltimore loss, as well.

Before the game Pennington praised Sparano as someone who, "Understands that football goes beyond Xs and Os on the chalkboard, that football is about people.... On the field he really trusts me and my opinions. We're on the same page." This compliment was surely a swipe at Jets head coach Eric Mangini, as well.

Also at stake were bragging rights for Parcells and Belichick. Sporano, it went without saying, was one of Parcells' guys, versus Mangini who had been Belichick's protégé until he decided he wanted a head coaching position. Ironically, Belichick was just as abusive as Parcells. When Mangini wanted to go to the Jets, Belichick immediately tried to forbid Mangini from taking the job. Once Mangini had moved, Belichick cut him off both professionally and personally.

But more than anything, Chad Pennington was playing for personal pride against the hired gun that had booted him out of the organization he had grown up in. Favre and Pennington met at midfield for the coin toss. They had met just like this in 2002, when Pennington led the Jets to a win over the Packers to catapult the Jets into the playoffs. It is ironic to note that Pennington was Mr. December in the 2008 Jets team calendar that year, even as he was here to defeat them. By the time the game started, the Patriots had already won, and by that afternoon, the Ravens were dominating the Jaguars. As several writers pointed out, the Jets had nothing to play for by halftime. Meanwhile, the Dolphins were playing for so much more.

The Jets drew first blood as Pennington fumbled, and the Jets turned it into easy points with a Favre touchdown pass. But Pennington came right back and threw a 27-yard pass to Ted Ginn Jr. for a touchdown. Not too long after that, Favre floated an errant pass right into the hands of the waiting Phillip Merling, who ran it back for a touchdown. A Jay Feely 28-yard field goal closed the gap, and the Miami Dolphins took a 14–9 lead into the half.

In the third quarter, Leon Washington ran 10 yards for a touchdown, and the Jets scored on a two-point conversion, leading 17–14. But the Dolphins responded with a 20-yard touchdown pass from Pennington to Anthony Fasano, and the Dolphins went up 21–17. In the fourth quarter, the Dolphins added another field goal that closed out the scoring at 24–17. The Dolphins were winners.

The Dolphins had gone from 1–15 to 11–5, moving from the worst team in the division to the best, taking the AFC East over even the New England Patriots. Pennington had avenged his slight by the New York Jets, and Bill Parcells had turned around yet another franchise. And the Dolphins had set a new record for fewest turnovers in a season, beating the old record held by Bill Parcells' 1990 New York Giants.

When the game ended, Pennington strutted around the field and threw a hat into the stands. Favre, on the other hand, helmet still on, walked back into the bowels of the stadium with his head down.

"I'm proud of him," said Laveranues Coles, Pennington's best friend. "The people in New York booed him, bashed him, and doubted him when he was here."

Before the Dolphins could even suit up for their next game, a play-off against the Baltimore Ravens, Parcells was in the news again. That week there were rumors Parcells might leave after just one year with the Miami organization.

Parcells had insisted that there be a clause in his contract that allowed him to leave after one season and still receive his full payment if the team was sold. With the announcement of the sale of the majority share to Stephen Ross, Parcells was free to go if he so chose. With the exception of the Dallas Cowboys, every owner Parcells had ever signed a contract with had sold their controlling interest in the club before his tenure was up. Jones was the only one who did not. In order to keep Parcells on, Huizenga and Ross extended Parcells' escape clause. He could now leave at any time and keep his $12 million without any repercussions.

The Ravens-Dolphins playoff was anticlimactic after the incredible atmosphere surrounding the Jets-Dolphins game. The team who had tuned the ball over the least in 2008 turned the ball over five times, and the Baltimore Ravens put the game away in swift and painful fashion by a score of 27–9.

On January 14, 2009, the Dolphins fired offensive line coach Mike Maser and replaced him with Dave DeGuglielmo, who had been the assistant offensive line coach for the New York Giants. The Dolphins hired University of Rhode Island head coach Darren Rizzi as the assistant special teams coach in February to replace kicking coach Steve Hoffman who left for Kansas City.

Four weeks later Brad Van Pelt, the outspoken Pro Bowl linebacker, was found dead in his newly purchased home by his fiancée Deanna. At 57 years old, he had died from an apparent heart attack. Harry Carson was the first person Deanna called. Through all the years, the Crunch Bunch—Lawrence Taylor, captain Harry Carson, Brad Van Pelt, and Brian Kelley—had all still kept in touch. Carson called Brian Kelley. Kelley called Lawrence Taylor. Taylor called Parcells.

"Football was 11 years of our life," Kelley said. "We had 25 other years when we were together, did things together, and still are doing them together, us and LT and Harry Carson."

"I was telling Harry how much something like this hurts when it happens, particularly to a counterpart and a close friend," Parcells said from the Dolphins complex in Miami. "In the last few years, I've had a reasonable amount of contact with him. I've probably seen him three or four times in the last three, four years. We had some conversation about some things.... He was a happy-go-lucky fella, very playful. And he was one of the premier strong-side linebackers in the league. And that 'No. 10' was unique, as well."

"I am just so glad that I got to know the man more so than the athlete," Carson said.

The Dolphins got themselves some help via free agency when they brought in a group of players to shore up their defensive backfield. And through the draft they brought in more defensive backfield help as well as some receivers and a tight end.

The Dolphins went 4–0 in the preseason, but the 2009 season wasn't as kind in the end. They played a tougher schedule, not a last-place schedule as they had the previous year, and their record reflected it with a showing of 7–9 and ending up in third place behind the Patriots and the Jets.

In September 2010 the Tuna cleaned out his Miami office and was gone.

Dan Le Batard of the *Miami Herald* was enraged. How could Parcells leave? How could the fans not be outraged? He accused Parcells of spending lots of money in the free agency market to muddy up the waters, "like a cover-up paper shredding that erases evidence.... So then you can step down with a two-sentence press release a few days before the season. And then, in your first public comments after that, you can announce to the New York media...that you'd be interested in being another team's false prophet soon—thus letting the entire NFL know you are available for the right price while still cashing Dolphin checks," Le Batard wrote. "That Parcells has been able to do this without fan outrage is more amazing than winning a Super Bowl with Jeff Hostetler."

"Once his boss changed, Parcells essentially stopped caring as much but kept cashing the checks," Le Batard added. "I'm not blaming Parcells for exercising a contract clause he negotiated. It is good business. It is excellent work by his agent."

CHAPTER 10
The Tree

Peter King once wrote about a baseball bat that Parcells had given him before he left Dallas. The baseball bat was etched with his favorite Parcells-isms. The funny part of the article was that King interviewed a bunch of coaches asking for their favorite Parcells-isms.

"'One wrong, all wrong' is one that stuck with me," Ireland said. "Use it in meetings. You need to be on the same page in an organization, and when one of us makes a mistake, we all do."

"I like, 'If he doesn't bite as a puppy, he won't bite'—saying if a rookie doesn't do something right away he might not ever," Sparano said.

"'He's like a ball in high grass—lost,'" Belichick said.

"He has a line for every position—'Small corners with great skills can play; small corners with good skills are targets,'" Payton said.

"He uses a couple lines from his dad," Dolphins offensive coordinator Dan Henning said. "'It's darkest just before it goes pitch black.' And, 'Big cigars and motor cars.' That refers to someone whose head's gotten too big. If a player's getting like that, Bill and I just say, 'Big cigars and motor cars.'"

"'He needs a year in Joplin,'" Weis said. "Sometimes I'll say that in a staff meeting and everyone looks at me like, 'What's he talking about?' It was a Mickey Mantle analogy. Bill's a baseball fan, and when Mantle wasn't quite ready for the big leagues he needed a year in Joplin to develop."

"He'll say, 'I want beavers,'" Ireland said. "When you ask what that means, he'll say, 'What's a beaver do?' Chop down trees. 'What else does it do?' Well, nothing. It just chops trees. 'That's why I want beavers.' He wants guys who just think football."

There are countless coaches throughout the NFL who can cite these Parcells-isms. The ones who have worked for him are usually highly regarded and in demand. Everyone hopes a little of the gruff, nasty, critical, magic dust has rubbed off on them so they can transfer it to their team.

Stories about Parcells are traded all the time among coaches. He is the Tuna. He's not "like, a sucker?" any more. He is more the Big Tuna now, a legendary fish, a great untamable specimen.

Parcells won two Super Bowls. Belichick won three Super Bowls. Coughlin and Payton have won one apiece. By NFL standards, that's not just a tree—it's a mighty oak.

New York Giants fans often love to speculate how many more championships he might have delivered if he had stayed in New York. It's a silly question. Whether he liked to admit it or not, Bill Parcells had always been a gypsy. From his college days to his professional days, he was doomed to wander. It wasn't that he didn't like stability. He did, especially in his personal life—he liked routine.

But what he really liked was the lure of the next big challenge. How big of a turn-around could he make? From teams wallowing at 5–11 to teams that had bottomed out at 1–15, the worse the organization, the more intriguing the challenge. Doing it over again after you'd already been to the mountain top was difficult. He'd learned that in New York during the 1988, '89, and '90 seasons. But he'd known that since college.

He became a professional turn-around artist. He is the Rainmaker, and like all rainmakers, he eventually leaves. That's what rainmakers do. And the price a team or franchise might pay could be considerable, but in general, he always left a franchise better situated than it was when he arrived. And no matter if you loathed him or loved him, you had to admit that it was fun watching him do it. It was fun seeing if he might have bitten off more than he could chew. It was always entertaining. It was always a show.

The running joke with owners about George Allen was that "It was more fun to lose without him than it was to win with him." Allen was as maniacal as he was successful on the field. Parcells was the same way. But owners desperate for a winning season were basically willing to give Parcells whatever he wanted to take the reins of their sinking ships. He was always happy to take their money. And he always delivered the goods. After he left the Giants (a sizable enough career in and of itself), he accomplished a Super Bowl berth, an AFC Championship Game, two playoff appearances, and an 11–5 season. Still a great run in anyone's book.

Of course, this gypsy traveling show that Parcells so loves to take on the road has kept him out of the Hall of Fame. Every year his name comes up, but there is also the worry that he will come back. And so he has been shut out.

But somewhere there is a team and a boardroom, and his name is being brought up right now.

ENDNOTES

INTRODUCTION: THE MAKING OF BILL PARCELLS

"Parcells was distracted... Wolff, Craig, "Giants Coach is Harder to Please Now," *The New York Times,* August 14, 1984.

"It is only football... Wolff, Craig, "Giants Try to Forget Losing Past," *The New York Times,* September 2, 1984.

"Tuna is a nickname..., "After that, they called..., N/A, "Man in the News; A Friendly Coach," *The New York Times,* December 16, 1982.

"Players from the..., "The only fault he..., "He knew exactly... Wolff, Craig, "Giants Coach is Harder to Please Now," *The New York Times*, August 14, 1984.

"The New York Giants remind..., "End of parable. Those... Zimmerman, Paul, "NFL Preview, NFC East," *Sports Illustrated*, September 5, 1984.

"I doubt that I'll... Litsky, Frank, "Giants Scatter and Look to Future," *The New York Times,* December 19, 1983.

"Pro football's minicamps... Wallace, William N., "Van Pelt Skeptical on Giants' Future," *The New York Times,* May 25, 1984.

"The years of so many..., "Prior to the draft... Katz, Michael, "Giants Trade Van Pelt," *The New York Times,* July 13, 1984.

"We have no plans... Wallace, William N., "Van Pelt Skeptical on Giants' Future," *The New York Times,* May 25, 1984.

"It wasn't our intention..., "I asked him if..., "The owner of the..., "When the call... Katz, Michael, "Giants Trade Van Pelt," *The New York Times,* July 13, 1984.

"That's between us... N/A, "Simms Quiet on Future," *The New York Times,* March 24, 1984.

"I hope we have peaceful…, "First, starting with me…, "After all our changes… Wolff, Craig, "Cutthroat Time for Giants," *The New York Times,* July 16, 1984.

"My fight never ends…"It's too bad…, "Simms is fighting for… Wolff, Craig, "Another Year of Uncertainty for Simms," *The New York Times,* July 21,1984.

"There is something…, "I was not bitter…, "That's what everyone… Wolff, Craig, "From the Navy to the Giants," *The New York Times,* July 19, 1984.

"The things that have…, "The change has been…, "It's very noticeable… Wolff, Craig, "Giants Coach is Harder to Please Now," *The New York Times,* August 14, 1984.

"He was always coaching…, "He was finding ways…, "For instance, he found… Gutman, Bill. *Parcells: A Biography* (New York: Caroll & Graf, 2000), p. 87.

"Don't make it like…Wolff, Craig, "Giants Coach is Harder to Please Now," *The New York Times,* August 14, 1984.

"Parcells called Carson's…, "I left because of general…, "Everything comes down… Wolff, Craig, "Giants Try to Forget Losing Past," *The New York Times,* September 2, 1984.

"I don't care what… Wolff, Craig, "Giants Embitter; Taylor Lashes Out," *The New York Times,* August 16, 1984.

CHAPTER 1: JERSEY GUYS

"When the Dutch West… N/A, City of Hackensack: History of Hackensack, October 1, 2010, http://www.hackensack.org/content/70/default.aspx

"In 1869 the Hackensack Water… Steuerwald, Linda. *The City of Hackensack* (Englewood, N.J.: L.J. Steuerwald, 1994).

"Parcells and Herron… N/A, "Georgetown on Top 20–0," *The New York Times,* October 6, 1934.

"The ball sailed to…, N/A, "punted from behind… "15,000 See NYU Tie Georgetown," *The New York Times,* October 28, 1934.

"Charles Parcells was a… Gutman, Bill. *Parcells: A Bioghraphy* (New York: Caroll & Graf, 2000), p. 11.

"Parcells thinks it's good…, "If he crosses a black…, "you want to move forward…, "Ida Parcells, Bill's… Arias, Carlos, "Bill Parcells a football man, first and foremost," *Palm Beach Post,* August 28, 2008.

"When I was a little… Anderson, Dave, "All the Christmas mornings," *The New York Times,* December 25, 1984.

"There was the time…, "Bill and Don shared… Arias, Carlos, "Bill Parcells a football man, first and foremost," *Palm Beach Post*, August 28, 2008.

"One afternoon, Bill…, "The family always…, "We used to spend… Politi, Steve, "Bill Parcells' love helps brother Don win battle with cancer," *Newark Star-Ledger*, January 1, 2004.

"We used to go in… Wojanowski, Adrian, "Sad homecoming for Bill Parcells," *The Record* (Bergen, New Jersey), December 1, 2005.

"My father had… Eisenberg, Jerry. *No Medals for Trying* (New York: Macmillan, 1990), p. 30.

"When I was a kid… Eisenberg, Jerry. *No Medals for Trying* (New York: Macmillan, 1990), p. 59.

"When I was a kid…Parcells, Bill, and McDonough, Will. *Parcells, New York Times* (New York: William Morrow, 2000), p. 25.

"You have to… Gutman, Bill. *Parcells: A Biography* (New York: Caroll & Graf, 2000), p. 11.

"Success is never final… Eisenberg, Jerry. *No Medals for Trying* (New York: Macmillan, 1990), p. 30.

"Anything with a ball… Arias, Carlos, "Bill Parcells a football man, first and foremost," *Palm Beach Post*, August 28, 2008.

"That was my first… Parcells, Bill with Lupica, Mike. *Parcells* (Chicago: Bonus Books, 1987), pp. 20-21.

"I could out run… Arias, Carlos, "Bill Parcells a football man, first and foremost," *Palm Beach Post*, August 28, 2008.

"I grew up a Giants…Parcells, Bill, with Lupica, Mike. *Parcells* (Chicago: Bonus Books, 1987), pp. 20-21.

"I went to my first…Parcells, Bill, with Lupica, Mike. *Parcells* (Chicago: Bonus Books, 1987), p. 21.

"By the time Duane…Gutman, Bill. *Parcells: A Biography* (New York: Caroll & Graf, 2000), p. 15.

"He was like a man…, "Myslik hits the ball… Schruers, Fred, "The Not So Gentle Giant," *Sports Illustrated*, December 29, 1985.

"We were a hungry…, "His parents were very… Gutman, Bill. *Parcells: A Biography* (New York: Caroll & Graf, 2000), p. 16.

MICKEY CORCORAN

"I met Mickey Corcoran... Parcells, Bill with Lupica, Mike. *Parcells: The Autobiography of The Biggest Giant of Them All* (New York: Bonus Books, 1987), p. 22.

"Corcoran, loose and cocky... Maraniss, David. *When Pride Still Mattered* (New York: Simon & Schuster, 1999), p. 71.

"He had never coached... Thompson, Jon, "Vince Lombardi Transcended Basketball," Dime, Dec 13, 2010. http://dimemag.com/2010/12/vince-lombardi-transcended-basketball/

"Before practice during...", "All the way out to... Maraniss, David. When Pride Still Mattered (New York: Simon & Schuster, 1999), p. 71.

"He made a point of...", "Rip your butt out...", "That was the method... Maraniss, David. *When Pride Still Mattered* (New York: Simon & Schuster, 1999), p. 72.

"I talk a lot about... Parcells, Bill with Lupica, Mike. *Parcells: The Autobiography of the Biggest Giant of Them All* (New York: Bonus Books, 1987), p. 23.

"Call it youthful exuberance... Gutman, Bill. *Parcells: A Biography* (New York: Caroll & Graf, 2000), p. 17.

"So now I'm playing...", "Mickey Cockhrane was the master...", "See, I was fifteen... Eisenberg, Jerry. *No Medals for Trying* (New York: Macmillan, 1990), pp. 30-31.

"It was always defense... Parcells, Bill with Lupica, Mike. *Parcells: The Autobiography of the Biggest Giant of Them All* (New York: Bonus Books, 1987), p. 27.

"He was a very unusual... Alfano, Peter, "Coach behind the Coach," *The New York Times,* January 19, 1987.

"a bluff Irishman... Parcells, Bill, with Coplon, Jeff. *Finding a Way to Win* (New York, Doubleday, 1995), p. 136.

"He was the kind of...", "I always thought... Parcells, Bill with Lupica, Mike. *Parcells: The Autobiography of the Biggest Giant of Them All* (New York: Bonus Books, 1987), p. 20.

"My father knew... Parcells, Bill, and McDonough, Will. *Parcells, New York Times* (New York: William Morrow, 2000), p. 47.

"There were friends...", "I listened to it on the... Parcells, Bill with Lupica, *Mike. Parcells: The Autobiography of the Biggest Giant of Them All* (New York: Bonus Books, 1987), p. 22.

"I think that was Mickey's... Parcells, Bill with Lupica, Mike. *Parcells: The Autobiography of the Biggest Giant of Them All* (New York: Bonus Books, 1987), p. 29.

"He had quick hands... Gutman, Bill. *Parcells: A Biography* (New York: Caroll & Graf, 2000), p. 22.

"The story goes that... Vacchiano, Ralph, "Memories of Larry Ennis," *Sports Illustrated*, January 21, 2009.

"What are you going... Parcells, Bill with Lupica, Mike. *Parcells: The Autobiography of the Biggest Giant of Them All* (New York: Bonus Books, 1987), p. 30.

"He came to me... Gutman, Bill. *Parcells: A Biography* (New York: Caroll & Graf, 2000), p. 27.

"I got into the car... Parcells, Bill with Lupica, Mike. *Parcells: The Autobiography of the Biggest Giant of Them All* (New York: Bonus Books, 1987), p. 31.

CHAPTER 2: TRAVELING MAN
WICHITA LINEMAN

"It was a brand of... Gutman, Bill. *Parcells: A Biography* (New York: Caroll & Graf, 2000), p. 30.

"When we saw another... Gutman, Bill. *Parcells: A Biography* (New York: Caroll & Graf, 2000), p. 29.

"The tone of the game...", "Villanova led 7-0 throughout...", "The story of the game... Bolding, Mark, My Favorite Bowls, Sun Bowl 1961, as retrieved on September 1, 2010, http://www.mmbolding.com/bowls/Sun_1961.htm

"My roommate was Gene... Gutman, Bill. *Parcells: A Biography* (New York: Caroll & Graf, 2000), p. 35.

"Chelo Huerta was a born...", "The son of Ybor City...", "After retiring from... Canning, Michael, "Calling Plays and Changing Lives," *St. Petersburg Times*, July 2, 2004.

"Bill always had a...", "Bill wasn't the easiest... Gutman, Bill. *Parcells: A Biography* (New York: Caroll & Graf, 2000), p. 35.

"Bill punished Tulsa... Gutman, Bill. *Parcells: A Biography* (New York: Caroll & Graf, 2000), p. 30.

"Four other guys on... Parcells, Bill with Lupica, Mike. *Parcells: The Autobiography of the Biggest Giant of Them All* (New York: Bonus Books, 1987), p. 33.

"I was just an in between... Verigan, Bill, "Dedication has paid off for Parcells," *Sports Illustrated*, July 24, 1983.

"I went to the Lions... Parcells, Bill with Lupica, Mike. *Parcells: The Autobiography of the Biggest Giant of Them All* (New York: Bonus Books, 1987), p. 33.

"I thought I did real... Parcells, Bill, and McDonough, Will. *Parcells*, *New York Times* (New York: William Morrow, 2000), pp. x-xi.

"He was a pretty darn...," "I knew it's what... Gutman, Bill. *Parcells: A Biography* (New York: Caroll & Graf, 2000), pp. 33-34.

"He didn't want... Izenberg, Jerry. *No Medals for Trying* (New York: Macmillan, 1990), p. 42.

"He told me he couldn't... Parcells, Bill with Lupica, Mike. *Parcells: The Autobiography of the Biggest Giant of Them All* (New York: Bonus Books, 1987), pp. 34-35.

"We lived in a basement... Izenberg, Jerry. *No Medals for Trying* (New York: Macmillan, 1990), pp. 42-43.

"I was coaching... Parcells, Bill with Lupica, Mike. *Parcells: The Autobiography of the Biggest Giant of Them All* (New York: Bonus Books, 1987), p. 33.

"I loved it right away... Parcells, Bill, and McDonough, Will. *Parcells*, *New York Times* (New York: William Morrow, 2000), p. xi.

"Lesson? You always... Parcells, Bill with Lupica, Mike. *Parcells: The Autobiography of the Biggest Giant of Them All* (New York: Bonus Books, 1987), p. 40.

"That year the team... Verigan, Bill, "Another Big One for Bill," *Sports Illustrated*, December 21, 1984.

"At the end of the season...," "We packed everything... Izenberg, Jerry. *No Medals for Trying* (New York: Macmillan, 1990), p. 43.

"The best running...," "I am honestly impressed... N/A, "Cadets Impress, As Drills Close," *The New York Times*, May 13, 1962.

"The 2,400 cadets in the... Danzig, Allison, "Late Drive Fails," *The New York Times*, December 8, 1963.

"The [North's] second touchdown... Danzig, Allison, "Hayes, Stauback, Excel in Defeat," *The New York Times*, December 26, 1964.

"One night, during an... Politi, Steve, "Bill Parcells' love helps brother Don win battle with cancer," *Newark Star Ledger*, January 1, 2004.

"Bill was going crazy... Carlos, Frias, "Bill Parcells is Back in the Game," *Palm Beach Post*, August 28, 2008.

"Don spent four months..., "You know, I lived... Politi, Steve, "Bill Parcells' love helps brother Don win battle with cancer," *Newark Star Ledger*, January 1, 2004.

CHAPTER 3: YOU'RE IN THE ARMY NOW
"When he was an... Izenberg, Jerry. *No Medals for Trying* (New York: Macmillan, 1990), p. 43.

"See what I mean... Parcells, Bill with Lupica, Mike. *Parcells: The Autobiography of the Biggest Giant of Them All* (New York: Bonus Books, 1987), p. 40.

"Until the children really... Izenberg, Jerry. *No Medals for Trying* (New York: Macmillan, 1990), p. 43.

"Volatile. No, not just..., "What wasn't good..., "He was an impossible... Davis, Rece, A conversation with Bob Knight and Bill Parcells, ESPN.com, March 31, 2008. http://sports.epsn.go.com/espn/news/story?id=3316528

"We were the same age... Parcells, Bill with Lupica, Mike. *Parcells: The Autobiography of the Biggest Giant of Them All* (New York: Bonus Books, 1987), p. 43.

"The thing people find..., "During the basketball... Parcells, Bill with Lupica, Mike. *Parcells: The Autobiography of the Biggest Giant of Them All* (New York: Bonus Books, 1987), p. 45.

"He's winning twenty... Parcells, Bill with Lupica, Mike. *Parcells: The Autobiography of the Biggest Giant of Them All* (New York: Bonus Books, 1987), p. 46.

"You know, I used..., "As we were leaving..., "I gotta talk to... Delson, Steve, and Heisler, Mark. *Bob Knight: The Unauthorized Biography* (New York: Pocket Books, 2006), pp. 58-59.

"Well the thing I..., "Well, you know, I..., "Hey, let me tell you... Davis, Rece, A conversation with Bob Knight and Bill Parcells, ESPN.com, March 31, 2008. http://sports.epsn.go.com/espn/news/story?id=3316528

"The circle of coaching friends... Delson, Steve, and Heisler, Mark. *Bob Knight: The Unauthorized Biography* (New York: Pocket Books, 2006), p. 154.

"I guess it was April..., "We both have a lot..., "That's when I tapped... Izenberg, Jerry. *No Medals for Trying* (New York: Macmillan, 1990), p. 185.

"I was like everybody..., "I liked Peterson..., "Suzy would get the worst..., "It's hard to intimidate... Parcells, Bill with Lupica, Mike. *Parcells: The Autobiography of the Biggest Giant of Them All* (New York: Bonus Books, 1987), pp. 54-56.

"I was thirty-four years... Parcells, Bill with Lupica, Mike. *Parcells: The Autobiography of the Biggest Giant of Them All* (New York: Bonus Books, 1987), p. 59.

"The next thing I knew... Parcells, Bill with Lupica, Mike. *Parcells: The Autobiography of the Biggest Giant of Them All* (New York: Bonus Books, 1987), p. 55.

"We had 20 spring..., "No, a little further..., "He asked, 'Why you... Rhoden, William C, "Parcells Old Texas Inspiration," *The New York Times*, August 2, 1997.

"his ever-sharpening tongue..., "We didn't understand..., "His first year he hated..., "You guys make me sick..., "I think he's ready coach..., "Part of the problem... Gutman, Bill. *Parcells: A Biography* (New York: Caroll & Graf, 2000), pp. 43-44.

"You can't make the club... Gutman, Bill. *Parcells: A Biography* (New York: Caroll & Graf, 2000), p. 48.

"We nicknamed him 'Pretty... Gutman, Bill. *Parcells: A Biography* (New York: Caroll & Graf, 2000), p. 50.

"Ben Martin was the coach... Parcells, Bill with Lupica, Mike. *Parcells: The Autobiography of the Biggest Giant of Them All* (New York: Bonus Books, 1987), p. 61.

"Bill had a fine... Gutman, Bill. *Parcells: A Biography* (New York: Caroll & Graf, 2000), p. 53.

"I was told they wanted... Parcells, Bill with Lupica, Mike. *Parcells: The Autobiography of the Biggest Giant of Them All* (New York: Bonus Books, 1987), p. 61.

"It was a great staff..., "At that point, I think..., "It was an amazing year..., "His goal was to get... Holtz, Randy, "Parcells Made Mark in Short Stay," *Rocky Mountain News* (Denver, Colorado), January 13, 1999.

"That was a very fun..., "I think that it tied in... Parrish, Paula, "Al Groh remembers days in the Rockies," *The Gazette* (Colorado Springs, Colorado), November 3, 2000.

"He loves to win... Holtz, Randy, "Parcells Made Mark in Short Stay," *Rocky Mountain News* (Denver, Colorado), January 13, 1999.

"In 1978, the Yellow Jackets...", "Neither snow, nor a... Featherspoon, Winfield, "Georgia Tech vs. Air Force: Re-visiting the 1978 Game," December 16, 2010.

"He transferred to UCLA... "I looked down the... Parcells, Bill with Lupica, Mike. *Parcells: The Autobiography of the Biggest Giant of Them All* (New York: Bonus Books, 1987), pp. 62-63.

"I just felt like it... Ramsey, David, "Good Ol' College Try," *The Gazette* (Colorado Springs, Colorado), November 24, 2005.

"That summer Perkins... Halberstam, David. *The Education of a Coach* (New York: Random House, 2006), p. 141.

"We were in Colorado and... Izenberg, Jerry. *No Medals for Trying* (New York: Macmillan, 1990), p. 43.

"It wasn't sitting well... Ramsey, David, "Good Ol' College Try," *The Gazette* (Colorado Springs, Colorado), November 24, 2005.

"One day, Parcells asked... Halberstam, David. *The Education of a Coach* (New York: Random House, 2006), p. 141.

"That irritated a lot of...", "Parcells' complaints about...", "Parcells didn't turn... Holtz, Randy, "Parcells Made Mark in Short Stay," *Rocky Mountain News* (Denver, Colorado), January 13, 1999.

"the tone of the household...", "For most of my life...", "I don't think he knew..., "When I was young... Frias, Carlos, "Bill Parcells, A Football Man," *Palm Beach Post*, August 28, 2008.

"So that was the only... Izenberg, Jerry. *No Medals for Trying* (New York: Macmillan, 1990), p. 43.

"So, the football coach... Verigan, Bill, "Dedication has paid off for Parcells," *Sports Illustrated*, July 24, 1983.

"At the beginning... Gutman, Bill. *Parcells: A Biography* (New York: Caroll & Graf, 2000), p. 60.

"I was Julie from 'the...", "When I told the Giants... Verigan, Bill, "Dedication has paid off for Parcells," *Sports Illustrated*, July 24, 1983.

"I frankly think it took...", "I was leaving for work... Lupica, Mike, "Lost Horizon," *Sports Illustrated*, January 25, 1987.

"Bill was an effective... Gutman, Bill. *Parcells: A Biography* (New York: Caroll & Graf, 2000), p. 60.

"One Friday night, Parcells... Ramsey, David, "Good Ol' College Try," *The Gazette* (Colorado Springs, Colorado), November 24, 2005.

"Bill was all right in the..., "we both knew he ought..., "I always believed he... Izenberg, Jerry. *No Medals for Trying* (New York: Macmillan, 1990), p. 185.

"They had a great team... Cimini, Rich, "Tuna's Rocky Mountain Low," *Sports Illustrated*, January 13, 1999.

CHAPTER 4: SEARCHING FOR A BAND OF GOLD

"I thought you would..., "I've got this offer..., "Give 'em hell. You've... Lupica, Mike, "Lost Horizon," *Sports Illustrated*, January 25, 1987.

"Looking back, all the... Izenberg, Jerry. *No Medals for Trying* (New York: Macmillan, 1990) p. 44.

"Jeter I was never too... Parcells, Bill with Lupica, Mike. *Parcells: The Autobiography of the Biggest Giant of Them All* (New York: Bonus Books, 1987), p. 93.

"We had a group of veteran... Gutman, Bill. *Parcells: A Biography* (New York: Caroll & Graf, 2000), p. 69.

"Well, the first year... Izenberg, Jerry. *No Medals for Trying* (New York: Macmillan, 1990), p. 185.

"Unless any of you fuckin... Izenberg, Jerry. *No Medals for Trying* (New York: Macmillan, 1990), pp. 186-187.

"When he got here... N/A, "Man in the news, A friendly coach," *The New York Times*, December 16, 1982.

"He was making major... Gutman, Bill. *Parcells: A Biography* (New York: Caroll & Graf, 2000), p. 70.

"He would always tell you..., "For 14 years George Martin... Izenberg, Jerry, "Giants Legend George Martin Taking a Stand for Retired NFL Players," *Newark Star Ledger*, February 4, 2008.

"Bill was great at what... Gutman, Bill. *Parcells: A Biography* (New York: Caroll & Graf, 2000), p. 71.

"A coach can't be in..., "There's no one I've met... Parcells, Bill with Lupica, Mike. *Parcells: The Autobiography of the Biggest Giant of Them All* (New York: Bonus Books, 1987), p. 94.

"He had a real good... Gutman, Bill. *Parcells: A Biography* (New York: Caroll & Graf, 2000), p. 71.

"Talented. Extremely goddamn... Parcells, Bill with Lupica, Mike. *Parcells: The Autobiography of the Biggest Giant of Them All* (New York: Bonus Books, 1987), p. 89.

"On the first day of minicamp..., "You try to find out... Taylor, Lawrence, and Serby, Steve. *LT: Over the Edge* (New York: Harper Collins, 2003), p. 33.

"I came to camp... Parcells, Bill with Lupica, Mike. *Parcells: The Autobiography of the Biggest Giant of Them All* (New York: Bonus Books, 1987), p. 89.

"No human being should... Lewis, Michael. *The Blind Side* (New York: W.W. Norton, 2008), p. 16.

"he was arrogant as hell... Parcells, Bill with Lupica, Mike. *Parcells: The Autobiography of the Biggest Giant of Them All* (New York: Bonus Books, 1987), p. 91.

"They all liked the kid... Parcells, Bill with Lupica, Mike. *Parcells: The Autobiography of the Biggest Giant of Them All* (New York: Bonus Books, 1987), p. 90.

"By November 18, 1985... Lewis, Michael. *The Blind Side* (New York: W.W. Norton, 2008), p. 17.

"The game of football evolved... Lewis, Michael. *The Blind Side* (New York: W.W. Norton, 2008), p. 15.

"He had to walk down... N/A, "Parcells, Belichick highlight tribute to ex-Giant Carson," Associated Press, July 18, 2008.

"I'm just Irish enough..., "The three characteristics... Furman, Andy, "George Young Speaks," UltimateNYG.com, October 11, 2008 http://ultimatenyg.com/2008-articles/october/george-young-speaks.html

"Bill Parcells walked by my... Pepe, Phil, "Young Kept the Flame Burning," *Sports Illustrated*, December 16, 1982.

"George told me that... DeVito, Carlo. *Wellington* (Chicago: Triumph Books, 2006), p. 238.

"With Ray leaving..., "When the man offers... Parcells, Bill with Lupica, Mike. *Parcells: The Autobiography of the Biggest Giant of Them All* (New York: Bonus Books, 1987), pp. 101-2.

"Parcells was never Young's... Verigan, Bill, "It's Time for Giants Young to Take Noose off Parcells," *Sports Illustrated*, December 22, 1983.

"It wasn't the first time... Politi, Steve, "Bill Parcells' love helps brother Don win battle with cancer," *Newark Star-Ledger*, January 1, 2004.

"My main objective was…, "The one thing I asked… Pepe, Phil, "Young Kept the Flame Burning," *Sports Illustrated*, December 16, 1982.

"Very few people in…, "He has a good relationship… N/A, "Man in the news, a friendly coach," *The New York Times*, December 16, 1982.

"I hope success doesn't…, Kellner, Jenny, "Giants Players Sad but Wish Perk Luck," *Sports Illustrated*, December 16, 1982.

"All right Tuna!… "He can get on you… Amdur, Neil, "Perkins Shift Surprises Team," *The New York Times*, December 16, 1982.

THE LOST SEASON

"There was never any… Madden, Bill, "Parcells Rehires Former Boss Erhardt," *Sports Illustrated*, January 14, 1983.

"Don't worry what's… Gutman, Bill. *Parcells: A Biography* (New York: Caroll & Graf, 2000), p. 79.

"It was kind of an…, "Belichick called the player… Holley, Michael. *Patriot Reign* (New York: Harper Collins, 2004), p. 15.

"They nicknamed him… Battista, Judy, "Belichick Left the Giants, But They Haven't Left Him," *The New York Times*, January 28, 2008.

"We were skeptics…, "In the beginning… "There were times we… N/A, "Parcells, Belichick highlight tribute to ex-Giant Carson," Associated Press, July 18, 2008.

"When I first became…, "You're not on scholarship…, "The things I told… Rogers, Thomas, "Scouting, The Parcells Way," *The New York Times*, April 30, 1983.

"The linebacker Harry Carson… N/A, "Kotar Visited by Giants," UPI, August 11, 1983.

"Parcells took over a…, "More than a dozen… Verigan, Bill, "Pal: LT Relapsed at End of '87," *Sports Illustrated*, September 11, 1988.

"I think it was my second… Parcells, Bill, and McDonough, Will. *Parcells, New York Times* (New York: William Morrow, 2000), p. 43.

"I think Bill related… Gutman, Bill. *Parcells: A Biography* (New York: Caroll & Graf, 2000), p. 80.

"He joined the Giants… Litsky, Frank, "Bob Ledbetter, 49, coached backfield for Giant's offense," *The New York Times*, October 9, 1983.

"I knew the ownership... Parcells, Bill with Lupica, Mike. *Parcells: The Autobiography of the Biggest Giant of Them All* (New York: Bonus Books, 1987), p. 120.

"It was the talk everywhere... Baker, Jim and Corbett, Bernard M. *The Most Memorable Games in Giants History* (New York: Bloomsbury, 2010), p. 209.

"had fought an inoperable... Litsky, Frank, "Doug Kotar of Giants Dies," *The New York Times*, December 17, 1983.

"By keeping the pressure... Verigan, Bill, "It's Time for Giants Young to Take Noose off Parcells," *Sports Illustrated*, December 22, 1983.

"It was a big mess... Schruers, Fred, "The Not So Gentle Giant," *Sports Illustrated*, September 29, 1985.

"It took the threat... DeVito, Carlo. *Wellington* (Chicago: Triumph Books, 2006), p. 239.

"MY GUYS." HIS WAY.

"He came away scarred... Schruers, Fred, "The Not So Gentle Giant," *Sports Illustrated* December 29, 1985.

"My father worked for... Izenberg, Jerry. *No Medals for Trying* (New York: Macmillan, 1990), p. 30.

"Simms was great... Parcells, Bill with Lupica, Mike. *Parcells: The Autobiography of the Biggest Giant of Them All* (New York: Bonus Books, 1987), p. 134.

"After only the third..., "This is not a game... Alfano, Peter, "Burt has memories of good times and bad," *The New York Times*, January 23, 1987.

"Fucking Parcells... Baker, Jim, and Corbett, Bernard M. *The Most Memorable Games in Giants History* (New York: Bloomsbury, 2010), p. 209.

"Honestly, there are times..., "I never use the media... Parcells, Bill, and McDonough, Will. *Parcells, New York Times* (New York: William Morrow, 2000), p. 55.

"He didn't give a shit... Gutman, Bill. *Parcells: A Biography* (New York: Caroll & Graf, 2000), p. 134.

"Unless he knew an..., "A long weekend of... Janofsky, Michael, "Dolphins win 28–21, put Giants in playoffs," *The New York Times*, December 18, 1984.

"The Giants are in the... Verigan, Bill, "Parcells Playoffs," *Sports Illustrated*, December 19, 1984.

"The Giants' final regular...", "They have climbed from... Litsky, Frank, "Inconsistent Giants showing progress," *The New York Times*, December 17, 1984.

"We're not in this for... Verigan, Bill, "Another Big One for Bill," *Sports Illustrated*, December 21, 1984.

The Giants woke up... Litsky, Frank, "Giants are adopted by Raisin capital," *The New York Times*, December 25, 1984.

"'We had our chances... Anderson, Dave, "5 opportunities, 3 points," *The New York Times*, December 30, 1984.

"Neither Parcells nor the... Litsky, Frank, "New Parcells Pact," *The New York Times*, April 30, 1985.

"I was a hold out when..., "How close are you?... Schaap, Dick. *Simms to McConkey* (New York: Crown, 1987), p. 107.

"The toughest cut I've..., "We were very close... Parcells, Bill with Lupica, Mike. *Parcells: The Autobiography of the Biggest Giant of Them All* (New York: Bonus Books, 1987), p. 144.

"Parcells came into the..., "He would make little..., "So Carson and Burt both... Gutman, Bill. *Parcells: A Biography* (New York: Caroll & Graf, 2000).

"If you looked at our... Lewis, Michael. *The Blind Side* (New York: W.W. Norton, 2008), p. 18.

"I think the main thing..., "The scouts and the... Media Q& A With Bill Parcells

Eric from BBI : 9/30/2010 5:32 pm http://corner.bigblueinteractive.com/index.php?mode=2&thread=386243

"I've always felt this..., "I don't have anything... Schruers, Fred, "The Not So Gentle Giant," *Sports Illustrated*, December 29, 1985.

"The Giants played a... Litsky, Frank, "Giants stop 49ers in wild card playoff," *The New York Times*, December 30, 1985.

"The wind just blew..., "You what?" Parcells... Anderson, Dave, "But they can't kick," *The New York Times*, January 6, 1986.

"You wouldn't know a..., "He must have been..., "Wild-card games and..., Izenberg, Jerry. *No Medals for Trying* (New York: Macmillan, 1990), p. 35.

"He came here to have..., "Parcells used to go to... Macur, Juliet, "Sentiment split in Parcells old haunts," *Dallas Morning News*, Dallas, TX, 2003 http://apse.dallasnews.com/contest/2003/writing/over250/over250project.fifth1-3.html

"They talk some about…, "If the Giants win…, Izenberg, Jerry. *No Medals for Trying* (New York: Macmillan, 1990), pp. 154-55.

"You guys have got…, "What the hell are…, "I think I should… Schaap, Dick. Simms to McConkey (New York: Crown, 1987), p. 134-35.

"They were believing…, "When they lost, I… Litsky, Frank, "Parcells Recalls Early Doubts," *The New York Times*, January 13, 1987.

"When you get back here…, "We had to give up a…, Schaap, Dick. *Simms to McConkey* (New York: Crown, 1987), p. 148.

"The first thing I found…Parcells, Bill with Lupica, Mike. *Parcells: The Autobiography of the Biggest Giant of Them All* (New York: Bonus Books, 1987), p. 20.

"I don't know what you're… Schaap, Dick. *Simms to McConkey* (New York: Crown, 1987), p. 158.

"Ron, I don't give a… Baker, Jim and Corbett, Bernard M. *The Most Memorable Games in Giants History* (New York: Bloomsbury, 2010), p. 217.

"Parcells began abusing… Schaap, Dick. *Simms to McConkey* (New York: Crown, 1987), p. 181.

"We don't have any… Pooley, Eric, "True Blue," *New York Magazine*, January 26, 1987.

"Bill tended to get real…, "I need a ball, Oates… Friend, Tom, "My Passer, My Friend, My Prey," *The New York Times*, January 11, 1995.

"He was always telling us… Schaap, Dick. *Simms to McConkey* (New York: Crown, 1987), p. 182.

"There must have been 9… Schaap, Dick. *Simms to McConkey* (New York: Crown, 1987), pp. 194-95.

"Aside from his very…, "That's okay," Parcells… Sell, Dave, "Parcells prefers own profile," *Chicago Sun-Times*, January 11, 1987.

"Parcells had me find the…, "This is coach Parcells… Baker, Jim and Corbett, Bernard M. *The Most Memorable Games in Giants History* (New York: Bloomsbury, 2010), pp. 218-19.

"Parcells, a player's coach…, "They know where the line… Pooley, Eric, "True Blue," *New York Magazine*, January 26, 1987.

"When the Giants left…, "We talk every week and… Alfano, Peter, "Coach Behind the Coach," *The New York Times*, January 19, 1987.

"After the national anthem… Baker, Jim and Corbett, Bernard M. *The Most Memorable Games in Giants History* (New York: Bloomsbury, 2010), p. 221.

"I don't mind losing the...", "I just don't think we... Parcells, Bill with Lupica, Mike. *Parcells: The Autobiography of the Biggest Giant of Them All* (New York: Bonus Books, 1987), p. 230.

"Everything is working... Baker, Jim and Corbett, Bernard M. *The Most Memorable Games in Giants History* (New York: Bloomsbury, 2010), p. 227.

"Don't you guys start the... Parcells, Bill with Lupica, Mike. *Parcells: The Autobiography of the Biggest Giant of Them All* (New York: Bonus Books, 1987), p. 234.

"This one going home from... Schaap, Dick. *Simms to McConkey* (New York: Crown, 1987), p. 238.

"It's pretty difficult...", "With a minute to go... Janofsky, Michael, "Parcells and Simms Bask in Glow," *The New York Times*, January 27, 1987.

"It was such an emotion...", "When it ended... Izenberg, Jerry. *No Medals for Trying* (New York: Macmillan, 1990), p. 184.

"If it wasn't for you... Anderson, Dave, "Parcells Always Has a Plan," *The New York Times*, January 28, 1991.

"The Giants denied Atlanta... N/A, "Wooing Parcells," *The New York Times*, January 30, 1987.

"Atlanta was reportedly...", "It seems it was a case... N/A, "Rozelle Closes Door," *The New York Times*, January 31, 1987.

CHAPTER 5: DO IT AGAIN

"Don't get me wrong it...", "In the season opener... Litsky, Frank, "It's time to retire, Doctor," *The New York Times*, December 29, 1987.

"I think the strike put Bill...", "Bill felt as if we did... Gutman, Bill. *Parcells: A Biography* (New York: Caroll & Graf, 2000), p. 123.

"I don't think we ever... Litsky, Frank, "It's time to retire, Doctor," *The New York Times*, December 29, 1987.

"Losing is frustrating to... Verigan, Bill, "Parcells: I'll Accept the Blame," *Sports Illustrated*, December 23, 1987.

"I don't think our team... Litsky, Frank, "It's time to retire, Doctor," *The New York Times*, December 29, 1987.

TAYLOR AND DRUGS

"I prepared this week...," "and that he had been...," "I assume he's working out... Litsky, Frank, "Taylor Confirms Substance Abuse," *The New York Times*, March 21, 1986.

"Bill has taken so much... Litsky, Frank, "Taylor Provides many faceted interview," *The New York Times*, January 4, 1987.

"was to try to help me...," "he stayed in a Houston... Litsky, Frank, "One Giants Angry And 3 Hold Out," *The New York Times*, August 1, 1987.

"When you find a player... Parcells, Bill with Lupica, Mike. *Parcells: The Autobiography of the Biggest Giant of Them All* (New York: Bonus Books, 1987).

"spent nearly $60,000 trying to help... Anderson, Dave, "Parcells Drug Vigilance," *The New York Times*, July 28, 1987.

BELICHICK

"When Belichick came in...," "Bill [Parcells] wasn't a people... Baker, Jim and Corbett, Bernard M. *The Most Memorable Games in Giants History* (New York: Bloomsbury, 2010), p. 213.

"In his job, you can't be... Parcells, Bill with Lupica, Mike. *Parcells: The Autobiography of the Biggest Giant of Them All* (New York: Bonus Books, 1987), pp. 186-87.

"What the hell is this?"...," "Don't you think we need... Halberstam, David. *The Education of a Coach* (New York: Random House, 2006), p. 153.

"One of the things I... Battista, Judy, "Belichick Cool on Parcells," *The New York Times*, February 2, 2002.

"All the film guys in the...," "I just wanted to give...," "If you're getting away... Izenberg, Jerry. *No Medals for Trying* (New York: Macmillan, 1990), p. 127.

"I'm so fucking tired... Taylor, Lawrence, and Serby, Steve. *LT: Over the Edge* (New York: Harper Collins, 2003), p. 86.

MOVING FORWARD

"Shortly after the aborted talks...," "Ever since Parcells had...," "A few months ago I...," "Twenty-two," was all... Anderson, Dave, "Huge rookies and huge appetites," *The New York Times*, July 19, 1988.

"I didn't like my '88 Giants... Parcells, Bill, and McDonough, Will. *Parcells*, *New York Times* (New York: William Morrow, 2000), p. 102.

"I sometimes think about... Izenberg, Jerry. *No Medals for Trying* (New York:

Macmillan, 1990), p. 30.

"One day at practice…, "You %$@#&^$ linemen…, "I think Bill's full of it… King, Peter, "A Matter of Style," *Sports Illustrated*, September 4, 1995.

"I want these guys…, "I've seen them so often…, "Buddy Ryan is a Neanderthal…, "Personally I like him… Izenberg, Jerry. *No Medals for Trying* (New York: Macmillan, 1990), pp. 2-29.

"What [tees] me off is… N/A, "The Book on Giants-Eagles," *The New York Times*, September 9, 1990.

"Judy Parcells wasn't on the…, "It's so vivid, even now… Powers, John, "The lure of the game," *Boston Globe*, September 5, 1993.

"The game was lost in…, "One of the toughest losses… Pepe, Phil, "Parcells Live, Can't Sleep, With It," *Sports Illustrated*, January 9, 1990.

"The thing that hit me…, "I want my players… Meyers, Gary, "Giants Make Up Has Familiar Ring," *Sports Illustrated*, September 10, 1990.

"It's not just veterans…, "You think this team has… Madden, Bill, "Parcells' Team Super?," *Sports Illustrated*, October 30, 1990.

"After practice he came…, "Parcells was very good…, "Parcells had an unusual… Baker, Jim and Corbett, Bernard M. *The Most Memorable Games in Giants History* (New York: Bloomsbury, 2010), p. 253.

"Everson, did you revolve…, "I have nothing but great… McCallum, Jack, "Hard Man, Hard Job," *Sports Illustrated*, December 14, 1998.

"His team has won only two…, "Hard not to like Parcells… Ziegel, Vic, "Bill Parcells: One in a Million," *Sports Illustrated*, December 28, 1990.

"They are so over confident…, "But he didn't tell them… Baker, Jim and Corbett, Bernard M. *The Most Memorable Games in Giants History* (New York: Bloomsbury, 2010), p. 267.

"the happiest days I ever…, "Everybody was congratulating…, "Then of course the trip… Eric at Big Blue, Media Q&A With Bill Parcells, Big Blue Interactive, September 30, 2010 5:32pm as retrieved on December 21, 2010 http://corner. bigblueinteractive.com/index.php?mode=2&thread=386243

THE GAME PLAN

"It allowed us to jump… Bendetson, William, and Marshall, Leonard. *When the Cheering Stops* (Chicago: Triumph Books, 2010), p. 145.

"Parcells couldn't have designed...," "Two drives, that's all it...," "The defense that Parcells...," "There comes a time when...," "Belichick used all these... Zimmerman, Paul, "High and Mighty," *Sports Illustrated*, New York, NY, February 4, 1991.

"He told them that Thurman...," "The thing about Thomas was... Bendetson, William, and Marshall, Leonard. *When the Cheering Stops* (Chicago: Triumph Books, 2010), p. 150.

"You guys get me to the...," "Well, we got you here...," "I always hold up my...," "Off the field, Jumbo... Taylor, Lawrence, and Serby, Steve. *LT: Over the Edge* (New York: Harper Collins, 2003), p. 133.

"The thing about Jumbo was... Bendetson, William, and Marshall, Leonard. *When the Cheering Stops* (Chicago: Triumph Books, 2010), pp. 146-47.

"I started talking a little... Taylor, Lawrence, and Serby, Steve. *LT: Over the Edge* (New York: Harper Collins, 2003), p. 133.

"LT's relationship with Bill...," "Are you gonna play today?... Taylor, Lawrence, and Serby, Steve. *LT: Over the Edge* (New York: Harper Collins, 2003), p. 142.

"Bill was my number one... Taylor, Lawrence, and Serby, Steve. *LT: Over the Edge* (New York: Harper Collins, 2003), p. 136.

"The year isn't over yet...," "They haven't talked to us...," "He's under contract to...," "The last time we won... N/A, "First 4-Team Super Bowl," *The New York Times*, January 27, 1991.

"I hate waiting," Parcells... "As a creature of habit and...," "Mickey's like my second father... Anderson, Dave, "Parcells Always Has a Plan," *The New York Times*, January 28, 1991.

"I was at a Super Bowl five... Litsky, Frank, "The Game: Giants Win," *The New York Times*, January 28, 1991.

"Power football wins games...," "I'll see you next year...," "Everything written about... Anderson, Dave, "Giants Not a Dynasty, Just Champs," *The New York Times*, January 29, 1991.

"And what a picture it made...," "I'd like a copy of that... Pennington, Bill, "Portrait of the coach as a truly wise man," *The Record* (Bergen, NJ), January 29, 1991.

CHAPTER 6: MOVIN' OUT

"Bill left the Giants four... Taylor, Lawrence, and Serby, Steve. *LT: Over the Edge* (New York: Harper Collins, 2003), p. 136.

"The silence at Giants Stadium..., "I don't really know what..., "Bill is at the age..., "I expect Bill to be back... Anderson, Dave, "Will Parcells Quit Giants," *The New York Times*, March 31, 1991.

"Is that what I did?"..., "I'm being most frank... Sandomir, Richard, "Parcells Auditions for Future in TV," *The New York Times*, May 8, 1991.

"Ron will always be with... Anderson, Dave, "Will Parcells Quit Giants," *The New York Times*, March 31, 1991.

"Any of us in this business... Anderson, Dave, "For Parcells, It's more than a money matter," *The New York Times*, May 15, 1991.

"I feel like it's time..., "There's a big difference..., "Players come and go... Eskenazi, Gerald, "A Giant Among Giants, Parcells Says Goodbye," *The New York Times*, May 16, 1991.

"Yeah, I think they ought..., "That's a good question... Anderson, Dave, "Parcells to Tampa in 1992," *The New York Times*, May 16, 1992.

"We kinda got this feeling..., "I heard 'em from time to time... Meisel, Barry, "Giant Memories," *Sports Illustrated*, May 19, 1991.

"I always thought if Bill... Bendetson, William, and Marshall, Leonard. *When the Cheering Stops* (Chicago: Triumph Books, 2010), p. 185.

TALKING HEADS

"This is a chance to stay..., "Parcells said one of the... Sandomir, Richard, "Parcells Lands an NBC Studio Job," *The New York Times*, June 19, 1991.

"Over time, we'd talked... Sandomir, Richard, "Baseball Broadcasts and the Bottom Line," *The New York Times*, May 17, 1991.

"a two-day conclave of..., "They had put together a..., "I'm learning about the... Sandomir, Richard, "Parcells Staying Cool at NBC Training Camp," *The New York Times*, July 19, 1991.

"The Parcells humor—very... Raissman, Bob, "Parcells Winning In Debut," *Sports Illustrated*, September 12, 1991.

"He defined mediocrity... Sandomir, Richard, "It's Only Words," *The New York Times*, March 14, 2000.

"Parcells: "I'll bury you..., "This is a crisis?..., "Parcells is the dominating..., "I don't think Mike will... Sandomir, Richard, "Parcells on Airwaves: Coach in Him Lingers," *The New York Times*, August 30, 1991.

"My dad was interested...", "The best was a little filly...", "Shug is one of my best...", "I go to the barns in the... Heller, Bill, "A Passion for Thoroughbreds," *Thoroughbred Style*, November 2007.

TOTAL ECLIPSE OF THE HEART

"He used to smoke...", "We were having problems... Powers, John, "The lure of the game," *Boston Globe*, September 5, 1993.

"It was tough to admit... Bendetson, William, and Marshall, Leonard. *When the Cheering Stops* (Chicago: Triumph Books, 2010), p. 185.

"Mr. Parcells tolerated... Litsky, Frank, "Parcells Undergoes Procedure on Artery," *The New York Times*, December 17, 1991.

"No matter what you...", "If he were 20 years old... N/A, "Second Medical Procedure Is Performed on Parcells," *The New York Times*, February 11, 1992.

"In this procedure, the plaque...", "I feel fine," Parcells told... Madden, Bill, "Parcells Faces Toughest Fight," *Sports Illustrated*, June 1, 1992.

"I went to Temple University...", "He said to me, 'Coach... Jeung, Rebecca, "The Coach," Associated Press, August 31, 2003.

"This could have been... N/A, "Parcells Has Surgery," *The New York Times*, June 3, 1992.

OF PIRATES AND MEATPACKERS

"Hugh Culverhouse, the owner...", "He's gone off in the hope... N/A, "Culverhouse Is Seeking 'Big Trophy,'" Associated Press, December 25, 1991.

"Most of the key points... Werder, Ed, "Parcells, Bucs Near Agreement," *Orlando Sentinel*, December 27, 1991.

"Before his next round... Sandomir, Richard, "Another Parcells Smoke Screen," *The New York Times*, December 24, 2002.

"There's no truth to...", "I won't touch that...", "Bill likes the idea that the... Litsky, Frank, "Parcells Coy Amid Talk of Coaching," *The New York Times*, December 27, 1991.

"In the end, I thought...", "I was to hear from him...", "He said we were all set...", "Your contract will not...", "In the end," said the... Litsky, Frank, "After Further Review, Parcells Says No to Bucs," *The New York Times*, December 30, 1991.

"Bill Parcells pulled off... Stellino, Vito, "Parcells leaves shocked Tampa Bay at the altar," *Baltimore Sun*, December 30, 1991.

"I met with him. No… N/A, "Parcells Not Done Talking," *The New York Times*, January 3, 1992.

"I had spoken to Ron Wolf… Sandomire, Richard, "Parcells Snubs Chance To Join the Packers," *The New York Times*, January 5, 1992.

"Mr. Culverhouse stated that…, "Bill was disappointed… Litsky, Frank, "Finally, the Bucs Rule Out Parcells as No. 1 Man," *The New York Times*, January 9, 1992.

"Explain why you continue…, "I told her she didn't… Izenberg, Jerry. *No Medals for Trying* (New York: Macmillan, 1990), p. 189.

"Standing in the Super Bowl… Anderson, Dave, "Can Parcells Ignore 'Big Game Thrill,'" *The New York Times*, October 26, 1991.

"I'm not into nostalgia… Meyers, Gary, "Bill Won't Fan Flames," *Sports Illustrated* October 26, 1992.

"If the Giants wanted me…, "By waiting instead of… De Vito, Carlo. *Wellington* (Chicago: Triumph Books, 2006), p. 277.

"I think Bill felt it was…, "He also liked the… Gutman, Bill. *Parcells: A Biography* (New York: Caroll & Graf, 2000), p. 173.

"This is the first day I've…, "I could get the same… Powers, John, "The lure of the game," *Boston Globe*, September 5, 1993.

"I told him I wasn't interested…, "It's something I've missed… Needell, Paul, "Patriot Gains," *Sports Illustrated*, January 22, 1993.

"The Maras are the two…, "Did George Young think…, "Bill had a great career… Anderson, Dave, "What Parcells Didn't Say," *The New York Times*, January 22, 1993.

CHAPTER 7: PLEASE COME TO BOSTON

"In 1990 my brother Don…, "The bank is on a death… Parcells, Bill, with Coplon, Jeff. *Finding a Way to Win* (New York, Doubleday, 1995), pp. 13-14.

"One day in 1993, Don…, "I was the P.E. major… Politi, Steve, "Bill Parcells' love helps brother Don win battle with cancer," *Newark Star-Ledger*, January 1, 2004.

"Good afternoon. You've… McCabe, Jim, "Brother had found his calling," *Boston Globe*, November 11, 1994.

"In 1996, he was appointed...", "Don made about $5 million... Politi, Steve, "Bill Parcells' love helps brother Don win battle with cancer," *Newark Star-Ledger*, January 1, 2004.

"Very intense guy," recalled... White, Jeff, "Parcells' influence on Groh obvious," *Times-Dispatch*, December 24, 2002.

"One of the most important...", "Every kid who grew up... McGovern, Robert. *All American: Why I Believe in Football, God, and the War in Iraq* (New York: Harper Collins, 2007), p. 58.

"last round-up...", "He knows the downside...", "You really want to do... Powers, John, "The Lure of the Game," *Boston Globe*, September 5, 1993.

"I've been eating twice...", "This job is like being... Madden, Bill, "Man at Work," *Sports Illustrated*, February 21, 1993.

"Coach Bill Parcells emerged...", "The offers could be a...", "I don't know if the Patriots...", "We're trying to get things... Eskenazi, Gerald, "Parcells Isn't telling the Number 1 Secret," *The New York Times*, April 22, 1992.

"I 'detest' the word... Myers, Gary, "Parcels Picks Bledsoe in Effort to Arm Patriots," *Sports Illustrated*, 1993.

"Parcells would not name...", "Everyone thinks it is...", "I don't know what...", "I promise you that we... N/A, "Parcells Practices in New York Style," *Boston Globe*, July 17, 1993.

"Judy Parcells over the...", "If they can block for the...", "We will look and see... Price, Terry, "Patriots' House Still Not In Order," *Hartford Courant* (Hartford, CT), August 31, 1993.

"When he wakes up... Macur, Juliet, *Dallas Morning News*, 2003.

"You guys high-five... Powers, John, "The Lure of the Game," *Boston Globe*, September 5, 1993.

"A lot of people are...", "He helped his chances... N/A, "Bledsoe a star as starter for Patriots," *The New York Times*, August 21, 1993.

"When you're happy...", "You can't compare him... Litsky, Frank, "For Starters it's Bledsoe and Mirer," *The New York Times*, August 31, 1993.

"Bill Parcells returned to...", "Quite obviously," Parcells..., "At least the old sarcasm... Litsky, Frank, "Lesson for Parcells: They're the Patriots, Remember?," *The New York Times*, September 6, 1993.

"A stadium is just a... Myers, Gary, "No Place Like Parcells," *Sports Illustrated*, September 21, 1993.

"There was no strange…, "I didn't think he played… Bunn, Curtis, "Pats, Past Haunt Parcells," *Sports Illustrated*, September 27, 1993.

"My team is hanging…, "I think it does create…, "Like I tell 'em, I'm not…, "I feel sorry for my… Serby, Steve, "Tuna Learns to Take Bad with the Bad," *Sports Illustrated*, November 25, 1993.

"How do you like…, "How did they do?"… Eskenazi, Gerald, "Dolphin Disappearance Leaves Shula Hurting," *The New York Times,* January 3, 1994.

NO REST FOR THE WEARY

"I made the best bid…Meyers, Gary,

"I'm not going to be the…Meyers, Gary,

"Bill Parcells has created…Meyers, Gary,

"My expectations are…Meyers, Gary

"I guess some of the…George, Thomas, "These Patriots Think They're Contenders," *The New York Times*, July 22, 1994.

"Sometimes I'll sting the…Gutman, Bill. *Parcells: A Biography* (New York: Caroll & Graf, 2000).

"McGinest assured me…Gutman, Bill. *Parcells: A Biography* (New York: Caroll & Graf, 2000).

"We've been through so…, "I looked around the…, "I try to get the team… George, Thomas, "These Patriots Think They're Contenders," *The New York Times*, July 22, 1994.

"I'm even watching… Borges, Ron, "Parcells Expands Horizons," *Boston Globe*, May 27, 1994.

"The process is going…, "Just remember one thing… King, Peter, "A Matter of Style," *Sports Illustrated*, September 4, 1995.

"It only takes a minute… George, Thomas, "These Patriots think they're contenders," *The New York Times*, July 22, 1994.

"Bill was a power football… Gutman, Bill. *Parcells: A Biography* (New York: Caroll & Graf, 2000), p. 179.

"Has he talked to you…, "The more experienced… Anderson, Dave, "Parcells's Family Portrait," *The New York Times*, October 16, 1994.

"He turned Drew Bledsoe… Gutman, Bill. *Parcells: A Biography* (New York: Caroll & Graf, 2000), p. 179.

"Ten years from now, you...", "No matter where I...", "The same day, Bledsoe...", "I'm quite sure people... Holley, Michael, "Patriots business booming Popularity explosion felt far beyond New England," *Boston Globe*, December 23, 1994.

"They're like Dracula... Silver, Michael, "About Face," *Sports Illustrated*, December 26, 1994.

"I didn't want to play Bill...", "I think our team made... Myers, Gary, "Hungry Pats Will Fill Bill-Tuna or Later," *Sports Illustrated*, January 2, 1995.

"My wife said, 'You paid...", "When Dave Meggett... Smith, Timothy W., "To Patriots, Meggett is worth every cent," *The New York Times*, March 4, 1995.

"The joke going around... Freeman, Mike, "Slow Ride on the Meggett Merry-Go-Round," *The New York Times*, March 5, 1995.

"Some people fall by the...", "I am just saying when... Smith, Timothy W., "NFL '95: Patriots might be the team to lead AFC to the Promised land," *The New York Times*, September 3, 1995.

"Look, we're going to...", "I had become aware... McDonough, Will. "An inside look at Krafts-Parcells," *Boston Globe*, February 16, 1997.

"Soon after the 1995...", "The next-to-last game... Eskenazi, Gerald, "Health May Be Parcells Concern," *The New York Times*, May 5, 1998.

"In Parcells, we had a... Felger, Michael. *Tales from the Patriots Sidelines* (Champaign, IL: Sports Publishing LLC, 2006), p. 150.

"In addition, a marketing...", "Parcells thought he was...", "I told Kraft he could... McDonough, Will, "An inside look at Krafts-Parcells," *Boston Globe*, February 16, 1997.

"Robert is careful and...", "He is someone who... Holley, Michael. *Patriot Reign* (New York: Harper Collins, 2004), p. 20.

"We've had some success...", "The Browns got off to a... Smith, Timothy W. "Belichick isn't moving to Baltimore," *The New York Times*, February 15, 1996.

"He did so with certain... Halberstam, David. *The Education of a Coach* (New York: Random House, 2006), p. 200.

"Obviously a lot of things... Holley, Michael. *Patriot Reign* (New York: Harper Collins, 2004), pp. 20-21.

"The scales of power...", "Parcells's record of... Felger, Michael. *Tales from the Patriots Sidelines* (Champaign, IL: Sports Publishing LLC, 2006), p. 150.

"Any time before the... George, Thomas, "With Parcells Gone, the Patriots' Grier calls the shots," *The New York Times*, April 17, 1997.

"Well, it all depends on...," "Within 30 minutes of that...," "We're not taking a receiver... McDonough, Will, "An inside look at Krafts-Parcells," *Boston Globe*, February 16, 1997.

"Just before the selection...," "Okay, Bill, who do you... George, Thomas, "With Parcells Gone, the Patriots' Grier calls the shots," *The New York Times*, April 17, 1997.

"I didn't know what... "I almost fired him right... McDonough, Will, "An inside look at Krafts-Parcells," *Boston Globe*, February 16, 1997.

"My father—I think people... Holley, Michael. *Patriot Reign* (New York: Harper Collins, 2004), p. 24.

"When the draft was...," "That was the beginning...," "For about 24 hours I... Felger, Michael. *Tales from the Patriots Sidelines* (Champaign, IL: Sports Publishing LLC, 2006), p. 151.

"I coach year to year...," "He has missed an awful... N/A, "Training Camp Report," *The New York Times*, August 15, 1996.

"She's making progress...," "That's not the standard... "Patriots Owner Scolds Parcells," Associated Press, August 28, 1996.

"McGinest," Parcells said...," "Parcells has taken the...," "From week to week...," "If you beat a guy... Madden, Michael, "Going on-line after three seasons at linebacker," *Boston Globe*, August 30, 1996.

"Your boy wants to coach...," "He was talking to me... McDonough, Will, "An inside look at Krafts-Parcells," *Boston Globe*, February 16, 1997.

"That was twice he...," "We've been showing... O'Connor, Ian, "Parcells Sells Bill of Goods," *Sports Illustrated*, November 11, 1996.

"Everybody knows how I... Myers, Gary, "For Parcells, a Pat Answer," *Sports Illustrated* December 22, 1996.

"Even with a chai... Eskenazi, Gerald, "Parcells and the Patriots go deep," *The New York Times*, January 6, 1997.

"I was choking a little...," "I don't enjoy it," Parcells... Gutman, Bill. *Parcells: A Biography* (New York: Caroll & Graf, 2000), p. 205.

"On Christmas Day Parcells...," "He's someone who I have... Freeman, Mike, "In Coughlin vs. Parcells, it's Student vs. Mentor," *The New York Times*, January 5, 1999.

"That's it. Just a pair...," "I smile when I get them... Hyde, Dave, "Parcells coaching tree has many branches," *Sports Illustrated*, October 14, 2009.

"Parcells was ripping mad...", "Listen, I'll grab Kraft...", "Bob, this is what I'm...", "Kraft withdrew his hand...", "I want to talk with Bob... McDonough, Will, "An inside look at Krafts-Parcells," *Boston Globe*, February 16, 1997.

"Talk about his deteriorating...", "Fellas, whenever we see... Myers, Gary, "Tuna and Kraft Like Best Fins," *Sports Illustrated*, January 22, 1997.

"This should be a great... Eskenazi, Gerald, "Patriots And Jets Negotiating For Parcells," *The New York Times*, January 31, 1997.

"Next week divorce is... Myers, Gary, "Tuna and Kraft Like Best Fins," *Sports Illustrated*, January 22, 1997.

"Yeah, I'd say it was a... Holley, Michael. *Patriot Reign* (New York: Harper Collins, 2004), p. 29.

"We were still new to... Holley, Michael. *Patriot Reign* (New York: Harper Collins, 2004), p. 30.

"I have a greater appreciation... Smith, Timothy J, "Parcells Charmed this time around," *The New York Times*, January 20, 1997.

"Bill Parcells went over to... Myers, Gary, "Worst of Times for Tuna," *Sports Illustrated*, January 27, 1997.

"Anytime you get to this...", "I talked to my players...", "In winning two Super...", "I'll know more very... Anderson, Dave, "The Many Questions Are Written on Bill Parcells Back," *The New York Times*, January 27, 1997.

"Not flying back after... Holley, Michael. *Patriot Reign* (New York: Harper Collins, 2004), p. 30.

CHAPTER 8: ONCE YOU'RE A JET

"'In Boston, three things...", "As an oil baron, Hess once... Anderson, Dave, "Tagliabue Does the Right Thing," *The New York Times*, February 11, 1997.

"In what has escalated... Eskenazi, Gerald, "Tagliabue to Rule on Parcells Dispute," *The New York Times*, January 28, 1997.

"You tell me what... Eskenazi, Gerald, "After examinations by Tagliabue," *The New York Times*, January 30, 1997.

"I've been through hell...", "It's just like a friend... Vecsey, George, "Parcells Seeking New Kitchen," *The New York Times*, February 1, 1997.

"Give me your phone... Cimini, Rich, "Jets Weighing Price of Tuna," *Sports Illustrated*, January 31, 1997.

"We're in a tough... Eskenazi, Gerald, "Patriots and Jets Negotiating For Parcells," *The New York Times*, January 31, 1997.

"When I became the Jets'... Cimini, Rich and Myers, Gary, "Jets Hire Belichick," *Sports Illustrated*, February 4, 1997.

"I was the head coach... Eskenazi, Gerald, "Belichick Helps build Jets Future and His own," *The New York Times*, July 27, 1998.

"They haven't made a... Cimini, Rich and Myers, Gary, "Jets Hire Belichick," *Sports Illustrated*, February 4, 1997.

"A penthouse conference..., "They broke for lunch..., "Kraft showed some give... Anderson, Dave, "How Hess 'Wouldn't Give Up'", *The New York Times*, February 16, 1997.

"We're very happy... Cimini, Rich, "Tags Orders Tuna Today," *Sports Illustrated*, February 11, 1997.

"When I told him the price... Parcells, Bill, and McDonough, Will. *Parcells*, *New York Times* (New York: William Morrow, 2000), p. 29.

"Personally, I don't much... Lipsyte, Robert, "Parcells Is the Bully that New York Needs," *The New York Times*, February 16, 1997.

"Leon Hess was greeted..., "Bill talked about going... DiTriani, Vinny, "One Owner Feels Like a Winner," *The Record* (Bergen, NJ), February 12, 1997.

"look it, I don't have a..., "I'll tell them what we... Eskenazi, Gerald, "Parcells Arrives With a Plan, And Very Early," *The New York Times*, February 12, 1997.

"What's the highest rating... DiTriani, Vinny, "One Owner Feels Like a Winner," *The Record* (Bergen, NJ), February 12, 1997.

"I think he likes it here... "Here's the relationship... Eskenazi, Gerald, "Belichick helps build Jets Future, and His," *The New York Times*, July 27, 1998.

"Today's deal gives us... Eskenazi, Gerald, "Parcells and Jets Deal Quality for Quantity in Draft," *The New York Times*, April 18, 1997.

"We improved the size... Eskenazi, Gerald, "Parcells Focuses Heavily On Defense," *The New York Times*, April 21, 1997.

"my kind of guy..., "It's time for me to win... Eskenazi, Gerald, "Parcells Joins Action as Jets Start Minicamp," *The New York Times*, May 20, 1997.

"It was one of the most... McCallum, Jack, "Hard Man, Hard Job," *Sports Illustrated*, December 14, 1998.

"Everybody knows it's... Eskenazi, Gerald, "Under Parcells, a Sense of Renewal," *The New York Times*, July 18, 1997.

"Even the coaches were...", "Brady, get off the field... Macur, Juliet, "Sentiment split in Parcells old haunts," *Dallas Morning News*, 2003. http://apse. dallasnews.com/contest/2003/writing/over250/over250.project.fifth1-3.html

"He had a few choice words...", "When the coach screams... Eskenazi, Gerald, "Players Get to Hear Parcells at Full Roar As Jets Open Camp," *The New York Times*, July 19, 1997.

"If I didn't have Bill...", "He'd show up, smiled... Cimini, Rich, "Keyshawn Catches on with Tuna," *Sports Illustrated*, July 30, 1998.

"Parcells loves boxing...", "When the fighters went back...", "Every time he hit me... Lewis, Michael, "What Keeps Bill Parcells Awake," *New York Times* Magazine, October 29, 2006.

"It's tough. He kinda...", "If Parcells were named... Leung, Rebecca, "The Coach," Associated Press, August 31, 2003.

"Before the game, there...", "I can't get rid of you...", "As the Jets went through...", "I told them good teams... Eskenazi, Gerald, "Parcells Wins Game of Nerves and Nostalgia," *The New York Times*, August 17, 1997.

"Ninety percent of it here...", "We both like football... Eskenazi, Gerald, "A Coaching Partnership Reshapes the Jets," *The New York Times*, August 30, 1997.

"Bill Belichick stole my heart...", "We get written tests... "They really comple-ment... Anderson, Dave, "Don't Forget Parcells's Coaching Staff.," *The New York Times*, September 1, 1997.

"I'm disappointed because... Eskenazi, Gerald, "Patriots 27, Parcells 24," *The New York Times*, September 15, 1997.

"I always identified...", "When I met Bill Parcells... Eskenazi, Gerald, "Mawae is eager to work," *The New York Times*, March 9, 1998.

"This was an opportunity... Pennington, Bill, "Jets Make an Offer for Patriots' Martin," *The New York Times*, March 21, 1998.

"Parcells told me he believed... Allen, Eric, "Ring of Honor: Martin Was Committed to Excel," New York Jets.com, August 14, 2010 http://www. newyorkjets.com/news/article-1/Ring-of-Honor-Martin-Was-Committed-to-Excel/7627a7ed-8b87-47a4-97d9-9f5233d674e2

"Bill Parcells is a great... Freeman, Mike, "Signs and Portents," *The New York Times*, March 25, 1998.

"Certainly if I had a...", "I played well when I... Eskenazi, Gerald, "O'Donnell is Out," *The New York Times*, June 24, 1998.

"I've been lucky with...," "I used to see him in... Eskenazi, Gerald, "Swift, if flammable, Solution: Jets Get Cox," *The New York Times*, August 2, 1998.

"I feel good about what... Cimini, Rich, "Bill Gives Foley a Ribbing," *Sports Illustrated*, September 22, 1998.

"We've shortened the season...," "With his team facing a crucial... Cimini, Rich, "Parcells Stuns Jets by Leaving Practice," *Sports Illustrated*, October 18, 1998.

"You've been riding on...," "No, we don't, Simms... McCallum, Jack, "Hard Man, Hard Job," *Sports Illustrated*, December 14, 1998.

"I'm going to keep that...," "You here same old Jets... Bondy, Filip, "Tuna's Tears for a Crown," *Sports Illustrated*, December 20, 1998.

"He ran for one touchdown...," "This wasn't baby steps... Eskenazi, Gerald, "The Jets Move One Step Closer to 1969," *The New York Times*, January 11, 1999.

"We buried Mr. Hess, and...," "a couple of times a week... Parcells, Bill, and McDonough, Will. *Parcells*, *New York Times* (New York: William Morrow, 2000), p. 25.

"The most eagerly awaited...," "God is playing sometimes... Cimini, Rich, "Vinny, Jets, Down and Out," *Sports Illustrated*, September 13, 1999.

"The reason [Parcells] is... Gutman, Bill. *Parcells: A Biography* (New York: Caroll & Graf, 2000), p. 280.

"During that last season... Parcells, Bill, and McDonough, Will. *Parcells*, *New York Times* (New York: William Morrow, 2000), p. 209.

"I don't know what my...," "I took Bill's words to heart...," "Due to various uncertainties... N/A, "Quotation of the Day," *The New York Times*, January 5, 2000.

"We all know how Bill is... Gutman, Bill. *Parcells: A Biography* (New York: Caroll & Graf, 2000), p. 286.

"The understanding I had...," "I was just watching it on... N/A, "Belichick Shocks His Father," *The New York Times*, January 5, 2000.

"Belichick did not leave the... Vecsey, George, "Success/Turmoil/Parcells," *The New York Times*, January 10, 2001.

"It wasn't easy for me to... "It's Darth Vader...," "Okay, there's going to be... Parcells, Bill, and McDonough, Will. *Parcells*, *New York Times* (New York: William Morrow, 2000), p. 218.

"Let's not nominate Bill...," "Do I want to see Bill... Vecsey, George, "Sports of the Times," *The New York Times*, January 28, 2000.

"In one of the most stunning...", "I wanted to stay in New York... Battista, Judy, "Johnson Gets His Raise and a New Team," *The New York Times*, April 13, 2000.

"If we weren't able to... Battista, Judy, "The Jets' Thomas and Young, Side by Side on the Field and Off," *The New York Times*, July 27, 2000.

"[Tannenbaum] remembers...", "It really was a remarkable... Cimini, Rich, "New York Jets Drafted Big in 2000," *Sports Illustrated*, April 11, 2010.

CHAPTER 9: THE JERSEY COWBOY

"I haven't really decided...", "The average gain or loss... Anderson, Dave, "Parcells Leaning Toward Remaining With Jets," *The New York Times*, December 26, 2000.

"the most dysfunctional...", "I wasn't the person to... Freeman, Mike, "Groh Loses His Players' Respect," *The New York Times*, December 31, 2000.

"O. J. actually kissed me... Anderson, Dave, "Parcells Hopes to Stay Retired," *The New York Times*, July 23, 2001.

"Sunday afternoon was still...", "Parcells reached into...", "What's with all this material?... King, Peter, "Coach in Waiting," *Sports Illustrated*, December 24, 2001.

"Are you saying you just...", "We have never talked... Nobles, Charlie, "Buccaneers Make Move in Parcells Direction," *The New York Times*, January 16, 2001.

"Parcells's imminent return... Freeman, Mike, "Parcells May Be Bending the Rules," *The New York Times*, January 17, 2002.

"At the end of the day...", "After next season I'll be... Battista, Judy, "Parcells Latest Twist: Parcells Jilts Buccaneers Again," *The New York Times*, January 19, 2002.

"My wife and I have an... N/A, "Parcells, wife divorce after 40 years," Associated Press, January 30, 2002.

"insiders whispered that... N/A, "Athlete divorce is still an ugly sport," *Sports Illustrated*, January 14, 2007.

"I don't resent one... Frias, Carlos, "Bill Parcells a football man, first and foremost," *Palm Beach Post*, August 28, 2008.

"He points to a photograph...", "Man, he can hit a...", "At 6:00 am, the two crawl... Macur, Juliet, "Bill's world: Chasing NFL immortality," *Dallas Morning News*, 2003.

"This is the end of it... Eskenazi, Gerald, "Parcells to Join ESPN's NFL Team," *The New York Times,* August 1, 2002.

MAMA, DON'T LET YOUR SONS GROW UP TO BE COWBOYS

"Flying home on the Cowboys..., "Summerall assured Parcells... Horn, Barry, "Parcells has a fan, friend in Fox booth," *Dallas Morning News,* January 5, 2003.

"I don't think anyone... DiTriani, Vinny, "Parcells hints at return as coach," *The Record* (Bergen, NJ), December 22, 2002.

"People close to Jerry... Sandomir, Richard, "Another Parcells Smoke Screen," *The New York Times,* December 24, 2002.

"I respect him and I... George, Thomas, "Parcells Meets Jones And Speculation Begins," *The New York Times,* December 22, 2002.

"I've also had similar..., "Last year I had some..., "We touched on a number..., "We really didn't discuss..., "He inquired as to... DiTriani, Vinny, "Parcells hints at return as coach," *The Record* (Bergen, NJ), December 22, 2002.

"As a result, ESPN..., "Yet when Parcells is..., "This is America. I didn't... Sandomir, Richard, "Another Parcells Smoke Screen," *The New York Times,* December 24, 2002.

"It's like the [expletive]... Macur, Juliet, "Bill's world: Chasing NFL immortality," *Dallas Morning News,* 2003.

"I don't know," he said..., "It's more embarrassing... Sandomir, Richard, "Another Parcells Smoke Screen," *The New York Times,* December 24, 2002.

"Jimmy orchestrated the..., "Four days before Dallas..., "By the way, I'm the one... King, Peter, "Bad Blood," *Sports Illustrated,* April 11, 1994.

"Parcells is a coach, not..., "Not only that, but... Blackistone, Kevin B., "A real mess awaits Bill Parcells," *Dallas Morning News,* December 31, 2002.

"The Buccaneers have..., "We have to do what is... N/A, "Parcells and Cowboys nearing deal; Bucs want compensation," *The Sports Network* (Landover, MD), December 30, 2002.

"Anybody who knows..., "I've talked to Bill about... LaPointe, Joe, "An Old Foe, Parcells, Has Dallas Buzzing," *The New York Times,* January 4, 2003.

"I never thought I'd..., "Get ready for the purge... George Thomas, "Parcells Will Take Reins of America's Team," *The New York Times,* January 2, 2003.

"If football is not the..., "That's just what we... King, Peter, "Are You Kidding Me?," *Sports Illustrated,* January 13, 2003.

"While we are pleased... N/A, "Bucs won't seek financial compensation from Parcells," Associated Press, Tampa Florida, January 2, 2003.

"Bill came back because..., "I understand when people... Sandomir, Richard, and Freeman, Mike, "Parcells Brings Bag of Fixes to a New NFL," *The New York Times*, January 5, 2003.

"He always wants to..., "I'm looking for big... LaPointe, Joe, "An Old Foe, Parcells, Has Dallas Buzzing," *The New York Times*, January 4, 2003.

"It is hard to picture Bill... King, Peter, "Are You Kidding me?," *Sports Illustrated*, January 13, 2003.

"I love this guy... N/A, "Parcells Building His Staff," *The New York Times*, January 7, 2003.

"I can remember flying..., "Bill's influence on me..., "The way he deals with... Archer, Todd, "Saints' Payton mimics his mentor—Parcells," *Dallas Morning News*, August 21, 2006.

"This is a great opportunity..., "I think you would usually... Olney, Buster, "Cowboys Hire Giants' Payton As the Quarterbacks Coach," *The New York Times*, January 11, 2003.

"discussing his exclusion..., "And then there was Bill..., "Parcells wants to exert... Shropshire, Mike. *When the Tuna Went Down to Texas*, (New York: Harper Collins, 2005).

"How can you resist..., "Behind his metal desk..., "His few possessions are... Lewis, Michael, "What Keeps Bill Parcells Wake at Night?," *New York Times Magazine*, October 29, 2006.

"This isn't the typical job..., "Ultimately, if he's successful... Macur, Juliet, "Bill's world: Chasing NFL immortality," *Dallas Morning News*, 2003.

"I sure hope we're closer... Cowlishaw, Tim, "Bill Parcells fits his assistants for muzzles," *Dallas Morning News*, January 28, 2003.

"It's worth the trouble... Macur, Juliet, "Bill's world: Chasing NFL immortality," *Dallas Morning News*, 2003.

"He never made us part... Frias, Carlos, "Bill Parcells a football man, first and foremost," *Palm Beach Post*, August 28, 2008.

"The more you try to..., "He's not what you'd call..., "Yeah, I'm a grandpa... Macur, Juliet, "Bill's world: Chasing NFL immortality," *Dallas Morning News*, 2003.

"We try not to infringe... Stellino, Vito, *Florida Times Union*, November 16, 2003.

"Oh my God, I think…, "I woke up with the…, "That's blood right there…, "All the people I know…, "Bill was great. He was…, "I never felt sorry for… Politi, Steve, "Bill Parcells' love helps brother Don win battle with cancer," *Newark Star-Ledger*, January 1, 2004.

"He had a lot of people… Mahoney, Larry, "Maine lands Parcells Coach's nephew to play football," *Bangor Daily News* (Bangor, ME), February 6, 2003.

"Woodson, you've never…, "The party is definitely…, "I'm still probably the…, "Don't make too much of… Fitzpatrick, Frank, "Question and answer with Cowboys' Jerry Jones," *Philadelphia Inquirer* (Philadelphia, PA), December 4, 2003.

"Parcells's coaches," wrote…, "He talks about Belichick… King, Peter, "Ride them Cowboys," *Sports Illustrated*, March 31, 2003.

"Let's see how much…, "Parcells is not my kinda…, Parry, Wayne, "Shockey Insults Parcells in magazine," Associated Press, August 8, 2003.

"After his talk," Jones…, "And there goes Jason… Macur, Juliet, "Jerry's running a reverse," *Dallas Morning News*, 2003.

"Whatever you need…, "I won't have any fat… Macur, Juliet, "Parcells: The method to his madness," *Dallas Morning News*, 2003.

"I have no hard feelings…, "That's not what this…, "I'm sure they would like… Steelino, Vito, *Florida Times Union*, November 16, 2003.

"Hey, you've led this…Macur, Juliet, "Parcells: The method to his madness," *Dallas Morning News*, 2003.

"I mean, there's no denying… Barra, Allen, interview with Madeine Brand, "Analysis: Impact of coach Bill Parcells on the Dallas Cowboys," NPR, November 10, 2003.

"The legend of Bill Parcells… Roberts, Selena, "The Parcells Legend Retold, In the Voice of the Panthers," *The New York Times*, January 4, 2004.

LET'S DO IT AGAIN

"The opportunity to compete… Hawkins, Stephen, "Testaverde, Parcells Reunited in Dallas," Associated Press, June 3, 2004.

"This was my fourth or… Tafur, Vittorio, "Parcells Enjoys a Few Laughs Before Getting to Business," *The New York Times*, July 31, 2004.

Bryant later apologized… N/A, "Cowboys Receiver Fights With Parcells," *The New York Times*, June 9, 2004.

"Not right now. I've...", "You're looking for your... Hack, Damon, "Losing Puts Frustrated Parcells in Foul Mood," *The New York Times*, November 17, 2004.

"We've been the same since...", "Although Parcells knew... Aron, Jaime, "Cowboys Frustrate Parcells to Bitter End," Associated Press, January 3, 2005.

"I'm starting to wonder...", "I bring all this up... Chadih, Jeffri, "The magic is fading," espn.com, February 22, 2005.

"(Parcells) did tell me...", "I know there's criticism... Taylor, Jean-Jacques, "Bledsoe at news conference: Parcells says I'm starting," *Dallas Morning News*, February 23, 2005.

"You're always judged... "Probably as big a... Hawkins, Stephen, "Parcells Feels He Has Something to Prove," Associated Press, July 30, 2005.

"The thing that you...", "Like he was as a player...", "Are you refereeing... Archer, Todd, "Parcells' former players happy to lend a hand during training camp," *Dallas Morning News*, August 9, 2005.

"He's the one who took... Wojnarowski, Adrian, "Sad homecoming for Bill Parcells—Deaths of brother and Mara are on his mind," *The Record* (Bergen County, NJ), December 1, 2005.

"If he wanted to fill us... Daley, Ken, "For Parcells, Little Time for Grieving," *The New York Times*, November 24, 2005.

"When he gets on the...", "I'm at the age now [64]... Wojnarowski, Adrian, "Sad homecoming for Bill Parcells—Deaths of brother and Mara are on his mind," *The Record* (Bergen County, NJ), December 1, 2005.

"I feel very fortunate...", "This is about continuity... Jenkins, Lee, "Retirement Can Wait: Parcells Has New Deal in Dallas," *The New York Times*, January 7, 2006.

"In general, I am a risk-taker... Maske, Mark. War Without Death (New York: The Penguin Press, 2007), p. 87.

"I'll be a better teammate...", "This was not me selling... Anderson, Dave, "It's Jones's Bet, but Parcells Holds Cards," *The New York Times*, March 20, 2006.

"All kinds of great... King, Peter, "Pats-Cowboys matchup awaits in Super Bowl XLI," *Sports Illustrated*, May 29, 2006

"How'd you like to be ESPN... King, Peter, "Don't worry, Dallas," *Sports Illustrated*, March 20, 2006.

"After the late-night...", "Please don't let it...", "We had 70 yards in... Lewis, Michael, "What keeps Bill Parcells Awake," *New York Times Magazine*, October 29, 2006.

"Terrell Owens, the...," "I had hydrocodone for...," "I know very little about... Daley, Ken, "Owens Denies Suicide Attempt and Cites Reaction to Painkillers," *The New York Times*, September 27, 2006.

"I thought he was...," "At 5:00 Sunday... Gola, Hank, "Burt With Boys as Tuna Helper," *Sports Illustrated*, November 1, 2006.

"...it really was love...," "The same coach has... Kamp, David, "Tony Romo Gets Back in the Saddle," *GQ*, September 2007.

"Tony Romo's fairy tale...," "It hurts real bad right... Gay, Nancy, "Hold on— Romo drops it!," *San Francisco Chronicle*, January 07, 2007.

"We'd just lost to Seattle...," "Bill Parcells cultivated a... King, Peter, "The Pugilist at Rest," *Sports Illustrated*, January 29, 2007.

"Is that all there was?...Beiver, John, "Is this it?," *Sports Illustrated*, January 22, 2007.

"Let's face it, before... Monikovic, Toni, ed. Halprin, David, "Blogging the Boys," *The New York Times*, March 16, 2008.

PINK FLAMINGOS AND MIAMI

"People point and say...," "Absolutely delighted to... Chu, Bryan, "A new place to bunk," *Albany Times-Union* (Albany, NY), February 1, 2007.

"I knew when I stopped...," "He's a pleasant enough... Ettkin, Brian, "Parcells Says Retirement Fits," *Albany Times Union* (Albany, NY), August 12, 2007.

"People approach you with... Ettkin, Brian, "Head Games," *Albany Times Union* (Albany, NY), December 20, 2007.

"He has a proven track...," "I'm honored to join such... N/A, "Bill Parcells signs 4-year deal to lead Dolphins' football operations," Associated Press, December 20, 2007.

"Coach Parcells has taught...," "When Bill and I discussed...," "It does leave a bitter taste in... Pasquarelli, Len, "Dolphins hire Sparano as head coach, replacing Cameron," ESPN.com, January 16, 2008.

"My heart does not... N/A, "Huizenga Sells Half of Dolphins," Associated Press, February 23, 2008.

"Jake was our guy from... Battista, Judy, "Stopping Clock, Dolphins Sign Tackle as Top Pick," *The New York Times*, April 23, 2008.

Long time Dolphins defensive... Monikovic, Toni, "Jason Taylor Dances," *The New York Times*, May 10, 2008.

"Of course they are not... Battista, Judy, "In the N.F.L., It's Time to Get Back to Work," *The New York Times*, July 20, 2008.

"On this day, Parcells has...," "The happiest place I know...," "It's not my program...," "It's a whole different...," "I don't let much of... Reynolds, Tim, "With retirement house waiting, Dolphins czar Bill Parcells still hearing football's siren song," Associated Press, July 12, 2008.

"I'm proud of him... Bishop, Greg, "Dolphins 24, Jets 17; The Bitter End: Pennington Does What Favre Cannot," *The New York Times*, December 29, 2008.

"Football was 11 years of... Vrentas, Jenny, "Former Giant Brad Van Pelt dies of apparent heart attack; Bill Parcells among those remembering him," *Newark Star-Ledger*, February 18, 2009.

"So then you can step... LeBatard, Dan, "Bill Parcells avoids the wrath of Miami Dolphins fans," *Miami Herald*, October 9, 2010.

CHAPTER 10: THE TREE

"'One wrong, all wrong...," "He needs a year in Joplin...," "He'll say, 'I want beavers...," Hyde, Dave, "Parcells Coaching Tree has many branches all over football," *Sports Illustrated*.com, October 14, 2009.

SELECTED BIBLIOGRAPHY

BOOKS

Baker, Jim, and Bernard M. Corbett. *The Most Memorable Games in Giants History*. New York: Bloomsbury, 2010.

Bendetson, William, and Leonard Marshall. *When the Cheering Stops*. Chicago: Triumph Books, 2010.

Carson, Harry, and James E. Smith. *Point of Attack: The Defense Strikes Back*. New York: McGraw-Hill Books, 1987.

Delson, Steve, and Mark Heisler. *Bob Knight: The Unauthorized Biography*. New York: Pocket Books, 2006.

Eisen, Michael. *Stadium Stories: New York Giants Insider's Guide*. Guilford, CT, 2005.

Felger, Michael. *Tales from the Patriots Sidelines*. Champaign, IL: Sports Publishing LLC, 2006.

Freedman, Lew, and Pat Summerall. *New York Giants: The Complete Illustrated History*. Minneapolis, MN: MVP Books, 2009.

Freeman, Mike. *Bloody Sundays*. New York: William Morrow, 2003.

Gutman, Bill. *Parcells: A Biography*. New York: Caroll & Graf, 2000.

Halberstam, David. *The Education of a Coach*. New York: Random House, 2006.

Holley, Michael. *Patriot Reign*. New York: Haprer Collins, 2004.

Izenberg, Jerry. *No Medals for Trying*. New York: Macmillan, 1990.

Lewis, Michael. *The Blind Side*. New York: W.W. Norton, 2008.

Magee, David. *Playing to Win, Jerry Jones and the Dallas Cowboys*. Chicago: Triumph Books, 2008.

Maraniss, David. *When Pride Still Mattered*. New York: Simon & Schuster, 1999.

Marshall, Leonard, and Dave Klein. *Leonard Marshall End*. New York: Signet, 1988.

Maske, Mark. *War Without Death*. New York: The Penguin Press, 2007.

Maxymuk, John. *The 50 Greatest Plays in New York Giants Football History*. Chicago: Triumph Books, 2008.

McCullough, Bob. *My Greatest Day in Football*. New York: Thomas Dunne Books, 2001.

Miller, Stuart. *Where Have All Our Giants Gone?* Lanham, NY: Taylor Trade, 2005.

Parcells, Bill, with Mike Lupica. *Parcells: The Autobiography of the Biggest Giant of Them All*. New York: Bonus Books, 1987.

Parcells, Bill, with Jeff Coplon. *Finding a Way to Win*. New York: Doubleday, 1995.

Parcells, Bill, and Will McDonough. Parcells: *The Final Season*. New York: William Morrow, 2000.

Price, Christopher. *The Blueprint*. New York: Thomas Dunne Books, 2007.

Schaap, Dick. *Sims to McConkey*. New York: Crown, 1987.

Schwartz, Paul. *Tales From the New York Giants Sideline*. Champaign, IL: Sports Publishing, 2007.

Shropshire, Mike. *The Tuna Went Down to Texas*. New York: Harper Collins, 2005.

Simms, Phil, and Vic Carlucci. *Sunday Morning Quarterback: Going Deep on the Strategies, Myths, and Mayhem of Football*. New York: Harper Collins, 2004.

Taylor, Lawrence, and Steve Serby. *LT: Over the Edge*. New York: Harper Collins, 2003.

Weis, Charlie, and Vic Carlucci. *No Excuses*. New York: Harper Entertainment, 2006.

Whittingham, Richard. *Giants in their Own Words*. New York: Contemporary Books, 1992.

Whittingham, Richard. *Illustrated History Of The New York Giants*. Chicago: Triumph Books, 2005.

Zipay, Steve. *Then Bavaro Said to Simms: The Best New York Giants Stories Ever Told*. Chicago: Triumph Books, 2009.

MAGAZINE ARTICLES

Beiver, John. "Is this it?" *Sports Illustrated* (January 22, 2007).

Chadih, Jeffri. "The Magic is Fading." ESPN.com (February 22, 2005).

Davis, Rece. "A Conversation with Bob Knight and Bill Parcells." ESPN.com (March 31, 2008).

Heller, Bill. "A Passion for Thoroughbreds." *Thoroughbred Style* (November 2007).

Hyde, Dave. "Parcells Coaching Tree Has Many Branches." *Sports Illustrated* (October 14, 2009).

Kamp, David. "Tony Romo Gets Back in the Saddle." *GQ* (September 2007).

King, Peter. "Bad Blood." *Sports Illustrated* (April 11, 1994).

King, Peter. "A Matter of Style." *Sports Illustrated* (September 4, 1995).

King, Peter. "Coach In Waiting." *Sports Illustrated* (December 24, 2001).

King, Peter. "Ride Them Cowboys." *Sports Illustrated* (March 31, 2003).

King, Peter. "Don't Worry, Dallas." *Sports Illustrated* (March 20, 2006).

King, Peter. "Pats-Cowboys Matchup Awaits in Super Bowl XLI." *Sports Illustrated* (May 29, 2006).

King, Peter. "The Pugilist at Rest." *Sports Illustrated* (January 29, 2007).

Lewis, Michael. "What Keeps Bill Parcells Wake at Night?" *New York Times Magazine* (October 29, 2006).

McCallum, Jack. "Hard Man, Hard Job." *Sports Illustrated* (December 14, 1998).

Pasquarelli, Len. "Dolphins Hire Sparano as Head Coach, Replacing Cameron." ESPN.com (January 16, 2008).

Pooley, Eric. "True Blue." *New York Magazine* (January 26, 1987).

Silver, Michael. "About Face." *Sports Illustrated* (December 26, 1994).

Zimmerman, Paul. "NFL Preview, NFC East." *Sports Illustrated* (September 5, 1984).

Zimmerman, Paul. "High and Mighty." *Sports Illustrated* (February 4, 1991).

NEWSPAPER ARTICLES

Alfano, Peter. "Coach Behind the Coach." *The New York Times* (January 19, 1987).

Anderson, Dave. "But They Can't Kick." *The New York Times* (January 6, 1986).

Anderson, Dave. "Huge Rookies and Huge Appetites." *The New York Times* (July 19, 1988).

Anderson, Dave. "Parcells Always Has a Plan." *The New York Times* (January 28, 1991).

Anderson, Dave. "The Many Questions Are Written on Bill Parcells' Back." *The New York Times* (January 27, 1997).

Anderson, Dave. "What Parcells Didn't Say." *The New York Times* (January 22, 1993).

Archer, Todd. "Saints' Payton Mimics his Mentor—Parcells." *Dallas Morning News* (August 21, 2006).

Arias, Carlos. "Bill Parcells a Football Man, First and Foremost." *Palm Beach Post* (Palm Beach, FL) (August 28, 2008).

Battista, Judy. "Belichick Cool on Parcells." *The New York Times* (February 2, 2002).

Canning, Michael. "Calling Plays and Changing Lives." *St. Petersburg Times* (St. Petersburg, FL) (July 2, 2004).

Chu, Bryan. "A New Place to Bunk." *Albany Times-Union* (Albany, NY) (February 1, 2007).

Cimini, Rich, "Vinny, Jets, Down and Out." *Sports Illustrated* (September 13, 1999).

DiTriani, Vinny. "One Owner Feel Like a Winner." *The Record* (Bergen, NJ) (February 12, 1997).

DiTriani, Vinny. "Parcells hints at return as coach." *The Record* (Bergen, NJ), (December 22, 2002).

Fitzpatrick, Frank. "Question and Answer with Cowboys' Jerry Jones." *Philadelphia Inquirer* (December 4, 2003).

Frias, Carlos. "Bill Parcells, A Football Man." *Palm Beach Post* (August 28, 2008).

Gay, Nancy. "Hold on—Romo Drops It!" *San Francisco Chronicle* (January 07, 2007).

George, Thomas. "These Patriots Think They're Contenders." *The New York Times* (July 22, 1994).

Holley, Michael. "Patriots Business Booming Popularity Explosion Felt Far Beyond New England." *Boston Globe* (December 23, 1994).

Holtz, Randy. "Parcells Made Mark in Short Stay." *Rocky Mountain News* (Denver, CO) (January 13, 1999).

Horn, Barry. "Parcells has a fan, friend in FOX booth." *Dallas Morning News* (January 5, 2003).

Jenkins, Lee. "Retirement Can Wait: Parcells Has New Deal in Dallas." *The New York Times* (January 7, 2006).

Jeung, Rebecca. "The Coach." Associated Press (August 31, 2003).

Katz, Michael. "Giants Trade Van Pelt." *The New York Times* (July 13, 1984).

LaPointe, Joe. "An Old Foe, Parcells, Has Dallas Buzzing." *The New York Times* (January 4, 2003).

LeBatard, Dan. "Bill Parcells Avoids the Wrath of Miami Dolphins Fans." *Miami Herald* (October 9, 2010).

Litsky, Frank. "It's Time to Retire, Doctor." *The New York Times* (December 29, 1987).

Litsky, Frank. "Parcells Undergoes Procedure on Artery." *The New York Times* (December 17, 1991).

Lupica, Mike. "Lost Horizon." *Sports Illustrated* (January 25, 1987).

Macur, Juliet. "Bill's World: Chasing NFL Immortality." *Dallas Morning News* (2003).

Macur, Juliet. "Jerry's Running a Reverse." *Dallas Morning News* (2003).

Macur, Juliet. "Parcells: The Method to His Madness." *Dallas Morning News* (2003).

Macur, Juliet. "Sentiment Split in Parcells Old Haunts." *Dallas Morning News* (2003).

Madden, Bill. "Man at Work." *Sports Illustrated* (February 21, 1993).

Madden, Bill. "Parcells Faces Toughest Fight." *Sports Illustrated* (June 1, 1992).

Madden, Michael. "Going On-line After Three Seasons at Linebacker." *Boston Globe* (August 30, 1996).

McDonough, Will. "An Inside Look at Krafts-Parcells." *Boston Globe* (February 16, 1997).

Meisel, Barry. "Giant Memories." *Sports Illustrated* (May 19, 1991).

Meyers, Gary. "Bill Won't Fan Flames." *Sports Illustrated* (October 26, 1992).

N/A. "Parcells Practices in New York Style." *Boston Globe* (July 17, 1993).

Needell, Paul. "Patriot Gains." *Sports Illustrated* (January 22, 1993).

O'Connor, Ian. "Parcells Sells Bill of Goods." *Sports Illustrated* (November 11, 1996).

Parrish, Paula. "Al Groh Remembers Days in the Rockies." *The Gazette* (Colorado Springs, CO) (November 3, 2000).

Pasquarelli, Len. "Dolphins Hire Sparano as Head Coach, Replacing Cameron." ESPN.com (January 16, 2008).

Pennington, Bill. "Portrait of the Coach as a Truly Wise Man." *The Record* (Bergen, NJ) (January 29, 1991).

Politi, Steve. "Bill Parcells' Love Helps Brother Don Win Battle with Cancer." *Newark Star-Ledger* (Newark, NJ) (January 1, 2004).

Powers, John. "The Lure of the Game." *Boston Globe* (September 5, 1993).

Price, Terry. "Patriots' House Still Not In Order." *Hartford Courant* (Hartford, CT) (August 31, 1993).

Raissman, Bob. "Parcells Winning in Debut." *Sports Illustrated* (September 12, 1991).

Ramsey, David. "Good Ol' College Try." *The Gazette* (Colorado Springs, CO) (November 24, 2005).

Reynolds, Tim. "With Retirement House Waiting, Dolphins Czar Bill Parcells Still Hearing Football's Siren Song." Associated Press (July 12, 2008).

Rhoden, William C. "Parcells Old Texas Inspiration." *The New York Times* (August 2, 1997).

Sandomir, Richard. "Another Parcells Smoke Screen." *The New York Times* (December 24, 2002).

Sandomir, Richard. "Parcells Staying Cool At NBC Training Camp." *The New York Times* (July 19, 1991).

Schruers, Fred. "The Not So Gentle Giant." *Sports Illustrated* (December 29, 1985).

Serby, Steve. "Tuna Learns to Take Bad with the Bad." *Sports Illustrated* (November 25, 1993).

Stellino, Vito. "Parcells Leaves Shocked Tampa Bay at the Altar." *Baltimore Sun* (December 30, 1991).

Wojnarowski, Adrian. "Sad Homecoming for Bill Parcells—Deaths of Brother and Mara are on His Mind." *The Record* (Bergen County, NJ) (December 1, 2005).

Wolff, Craig. "From the Navy to the Giants." *The New York Times* (July 19, 1984).

Wolff, Craig. "Giants Try to Forget Losing Past." *The New York Times* (September 2, 1984).

Wolff, Craig. "Giants Coach is Harder to Please Now." *The New York Times* (August 14, 1984).

Vecsey, George. "Parcells Seeking New Kitchen." *The New York Times* (February 1, 1997).

Verigan, Bill. "Dedication Has Paid Off for Parcells." *Sports Illustrated* (July 24, 1983).

Ziegel, Vic. "Bill Parcells: One in a Million." *Sports Illustrated* (December 28, 1990).

INDEX